The Eve of Spain

The Eve of Spain

*Myths of Origins
in the History of Christian, Muslim,
and Jewish Conflict*

PATRICIA E. GRIEVE

The Johns Hopkins University Press
Baltimore

© 2009 The Johns Hopkins University Press
All rights reserved. Published 2009
Printed in the United States of America on acid-free paper

2   4   6   8   9   7   5   3   1

The Johns Hopkins University Press
2715 North Charles Street
Baltimore, Maryland 21218-4363
www.press.jhu.edu

Library of Congress Cataloging-in-Publication Data

Grieve, Patricia E.
The eve of Spain : myths of origins in the history of Christian,
Muslim, and Jewish conflict / Patricia E. Grieve.
p. cm.
Includes bibliographical references and index.
ISBN-13: 978-0-8018-9036-9 (hardcover : alk. paper)
ISBN-10: 0-8018-9036-5 (hardcover : alk. paper)
1. Spain—History—711–1516.   2. Spain—History—House of Austria, 1516–1700.
3. Legends—Spain.   4. Spain—Ethnic relations—History.   5. Christians—Spain—
History.   6. Muslims—Spain—History.   7. Jews—Spain—History.   I. Title.
DP99.G75 2009
946'.02—dc22   2008024724

A catalog record for this book is available from the British Library.

Frontispiece: The Mediterranean Sea and Atlantic. Manuscript on parchment.
Signed and dated. Messina, 1582. Courtesy Hispanic Society of America.
Map by Joan Martines.

*Special discounts are available for bulk purchases of this book. For more information, please
contact Special Sales at 410-516-6936 or specialsales@press.jhu.edu.*

The Johns Hopkins University Press uses environmentally friendly book materials,
including recycled text paper that is composed of at least 30 percent post-consumer
waste, whenever possible. All of our book papers are acid-free, and our jackets
and covers are printed on paper with recycled content.

For Emily,
and for the members of my family, the Smiths,
from whom I learned the power of stories

CONTENTS

List of Illustrations   ix
Acknowledgments   xi

Prologue   1

ACT ONE: FALL AND REDEMPTION
(711–1492)

1   Setting the Stage   21
Of Women, Kings, and Nation   31
Origins of a National Myth   38

2   Granada Is the Bride   46
Using History to Shape a National Past   50
La Cava and the King . . . and Pelayo and His Sister   53
"She Came to Him in His Prison Cell"   58
The Jewess of Toledo and Rising Anti-Semitism   60

3   Blood Will Out   65
The Return of the Goths   72
Corral Casts Spain's Founding Myth   80
Training Isabel, the Princess of Asturias   83
Isabel, the Warrior Queen   90
Bad Women and Good in the Late Fifteenth Century   96
The Inquisition and the Holy Child of La Guardia   98
The Fallen and the Promise   104

ACT TWO: PROMISE AND FULFILLMENT
(1492–1700)

Interlude   109

4   Desiring the Nation   122
The Influence of Pedro de Corral's Chronicle of King Rodrigo
in the Sixteenth Century   122
The Woman's Body and the Fate of the Nation   125
The Loss of Spain in the Oral Ballad Tradition   129

Philip II's Chronicler, Ambrosio de Morales, and the
Development of the Heroic Pelayo   139
Philip II and the Power of Prophecy   148

5   Here Was Troy, Farewell Spain!   158
A Tale of Tales   158
Miguel de Luna and Spain's Prophetic History   166
Father Juan de Mariana and Early Modern Nationalism   175
Spain's Second Helen   180
Lope de Vega and the Stage of King and Nation   186
The Legend of the Fall of Spain after the Expulsion   191
Either Rise or Fall   197

ACT THREE: IMAGINING SPAIN
(The Enlightenment to the Present)

6   Ancestral Ghosts and New Beginnings   205
The Challenge of Foundational Myths in the Age of Enlightenment   207
Fallen Women Take the Stage   210
Orientalism, Romanticism, and Visigothic Spain   213
The Search for Spanish National Identity in Medieval Spain   223
Pelayo, the Role of Women, and Contemporary Spain   231
The Founding Myth and the New Millennium   235

Epilogue: Cultural Dialogues   241

Notes   245
Bibliography   281
Index   303

"La Alhambra. Vista general desde Albaicín," 1863   3

Santiago Matamoros (St. James the Moorslayer), 1610   5

Title page of *Crónica del rey don Rodrigo,* 1499   7

Title page of *Crónica del rey don Rodrigo y de la destruyción de
España y como los moros la ganaron,* 1527   22

Witiza, 1684   42

View of Toledo, 1572–1593   48

"La Alhambra. Puerta en la Sala de Justicia," 1863   71

50 excelentes, Seville, 1497–1504   95

Hebrew Bible folio, Spain, 1490–1500   103

Charles V, ca. 1600   112

The Apotheosis of the Spanish Monarchy   116

Philip II, 1597   118

The Battle between Christians and Moors at El Sotillo, ca. 1637–1639   147

View of El Escorial, 1572–1593   151

Battle of Lepanto illustration in *Felicissima victoria concedida del
cielo al señor don Juan de Austria,* 1578   160

Philip III, 1687   162

Title page of *El fénix católico don Pelayo el restaurador,* 1648   177

Pelayo illustration in *El fénix católico don Pelayo el restaurador,*
1648   181

Juan José de Austria as Atlas Supporting the Spanish Monarchy, 1678   200

"La Alhambra. Patio de los Leones," 1863   214

Florinda, 1853   216

Commemorative stamps on the early history of Spain, 2000   239

My sincerest thanks to all who have helped me in this project. I am fully cognizant that my personal revels in the discovery of yet another version of the stories of Pelayo, La Cava, Raquel, and others were matched by an obliviousness to what I undoubtedly inflicted on my family, friends, and colleagues as I recounted hundreds of details and tried to sort out thorny issues of dates, transmission of sources, and frequently contradictory versions of the legend. Teodolinda Barolini, Robin Bower, and Michele Moeller Chandler are the dear friends who most encouraged me to start this project in earnest, and who continued to provide support at various stages of the project—and always when it was most needed.

I especially thank Robin Bower, Marcia Welles, Josiah Blackmore, and George Greenia for reading the entire manuscript. For the many tips, hints, obscure references, and acts of kindness and encouragement through what must have seemed to them, as well as to me, a project without end, I am grateful to Gonzalo Sobejano, Kathryn Yatrakis, Austin Quigley, Julio C. Rivas, Patrick McMorrow, Carmela Franklin, Michael Agnew, Mary Elizabeth Perry, Diana Sorensen, Alan Deyermond, Constance Wilkins, Martha Howell, David Freedberg, Jeffrey Hildner, Elizabeth Amann, Bryan Scoular, Robert Baldwin, Steven Wagschal, Jerrilyn Dodds, Edward Sullivan, Patricia Chiono, Susan Rieger, Eileen Gillooly, Partha Chatterjee, Deborah Martinsen, Alicia Zuese, Chela Bodden, Akeel Bilgrami, Diane Wolfthal, Joseph Connors, Keith Moxey, Alban Forcione, and James Shapiro for their advice and support of many different kinds. My thanks to the research assistance over the years of Emily Francomano, Jorge Coronado, Emily Beck (now faculty colleagues), Michal Friedman, Maria Gerbi, and Kosmas Pissakos. I am indebted to the following libraries: Butler Library of Columbia University; the Hispanic Society of America, especially the library's director, John O'Neill, and Patrick Lenaghan for their generous help with the illustrations; Chapin Library of Williams College (Bob Volz and Wayne Hammond); the library of the Sterling and Francine Clark Art Institute, Williamstown, Massachusetts; the British Library; Biblioteca Nacional de Madrid; and Biblioteca del Museo de Lázaro Galdiano, also in Madrid. I am grateful for the support of Columbia University for various research funds, five semesters' leave, and the much-needed and always appreciated support of various university administrators and colleagues, Nick Dirks, Margaret Edsall, Alan Brinkley, David Cohen, Roxie Smith, and especially Lee Bollinger, for the unexpected question that helped give the book its final framework. For the last seven years, it has been my privilege to hold the Nancy and Jeffrey Marcus Chair in the Humanities, and I am grateful to the Marcuses for their devotion to Columbia.

Parts of this book were presented as lectures and conference papers, including talks at the Humanities Center of Harvard University, Indiana University, the University of Kansas, the Modern Language Association, various branches of the Columbia University Alumni Association and Columbia College Alumni Association, Rutgers University, the University of Virginia, Queen Mary and Westfield College–London, the CUNY Graduate Center, and over the years, Columbia University's Medieval Guild, the annual Department of Spanish and Portuguese Graduate Student Conference, the University Seminar on Medieval Studies, and the Heyman Center for the Humanities. I am grateful for the audience support and questions raised in those venues that helped me hone my arguments. Many people have helped me during the writing of this book, but errors and other shortcomings remain mine alone.

I am especially grateful to my editor, Michael Lonegro, for his unwavering support for my project, and his wise guidance throughout this process, and to Josh Tong, Robin Rennison, Juliana McCarthy, and Claire McCabe Tamberino for their help in bringing the book to fruition. I am especially grateful, too, for Melanie Mallon's painstaking editing of the text. I have adopted her suggestions—logical, precise, insightful, and often elegant—readily and with great appreciation for her efforts. Thanks go to Courtney Bond at the Johns Hopkins University Press, Tom Broughton-Willett for the index, and Bill Nelson for the map of Spain.

Finally, I thank my daughter, Emily, for a love of life that helps to infuse mine with joy.

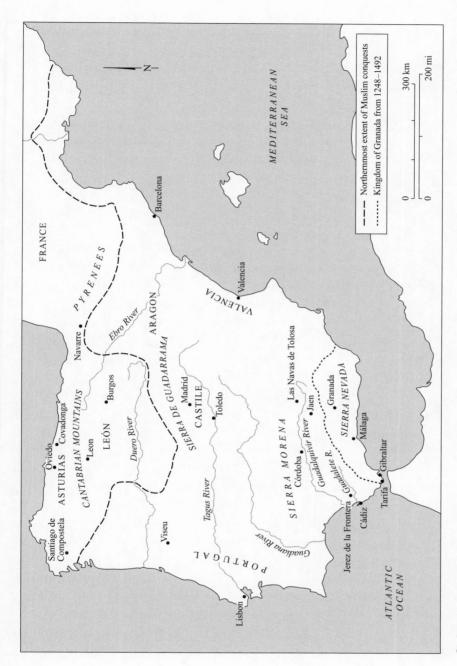

FRANCE

MEDITERRANEAN SEA

Barcelona

PYRENEES

Navarre

ARAGON

Ebro River

VALENCIA

Valencia

SIERRA DE GUADARRAMA

Madrid

CASTILE

Toledo

Burgos

León

LEÓN

Duero River

CANTABRIAN MOUNTAINS

ASTURIAS

Oviedo
Covadonga

Santiago de Compostela

Tagus River

Viseu

PORTUGAL

Lisbon

Guadiana River

SIERRA MORENA

Las Navas de Tolosa

Córdoba

Guadalquivir River

Jaén

Granada

SIERRA NEVADA

Málaga

Guadalete R.

Jerez de la Frontera

Cádiz

Tarifa

Gibraltar

ATLANTIC OCEAN

— N —

Northernmost extent of Muslim conquests

Kingdom of Granada from 1248–1492

300 km

200 mi

0

0

Spain, 711–1492

The Eve of Spain

Prologue

Consider the first of all women, Eve, and what she brought upon
the world, consider La Cava, through whom all Spain was lost,
next consider Helen, through whom Troy was destroyed, and
although there be not many examples of such great matters, still
many other cases occur of which women are the cause.

Pedro Ximénez de Urrea, *Penitencia de amor*
(Penitence of love, 1516)

Fourteen hundred ninety-two. Is any date more iconic? The Genoese navigator
Christopher Columbus, sailing under the flag of Spain, embarked from the port city
of Palos on Spain's Atlantic coast, not far from Portugal, in search of the Far East.
Though the facts are straightforward enough, the very quest assumed mythic proportions. To find the East by heading west, Columbus's epic journey began on the
other side—the western side—of the Strait of Gibraltar. This area was known as the
Pillars of Hercules, which referred to two promontories on either side of the strait,
in the south of the Iberian Peninsula and on the northern coast of Africa.

More important than location is the symbolic significance: the strait, legendarily
created by Hercules, linked the eastern, Mediterranean side, or known world, to the
western, Atlantic side and the unknown—and unknowable—world. Columbus's
three ships sailed west, away from the coasts of Spain and France, in the same waters
of fatal danger and irresistible allure into which the arrogant, overly curious, and
reckless Ulysses, according to Dante, had ordered his men to sail, knowing that they
faced certain death. Defying the odds, and the weight of superstitious legend that
prophesied defeat, Columbus charted his discovery for others to follow, and returned, victorious, to Spain. To this day, Spain's and Columbus's ambitious quest
finds visual representation on the national coat of arms, which, from the sixteenth
century to the present, depicts the Pillars of Hercules, signifying Spain's quest for
empire and its prowess as a nation of explorers.

But the fact is, in Spain, 1492 triggers associations with other events, just as mythic—events of no less significance to the development of world history and of great relevance to world affairs today.

On January 2, 1492, three months before authorizing Columbus's epic voyage, Queen Isabel and King Ferdinand (Fernando) of Spain entered the city of Granada in splendor and triumph. After ten years of war, their powerful Christian army, aided in no small measure by divisions among the ruling-class Muslims, had defeated King Boabdil, monarch of the last Muslim kingdom on the Iberian Peninsula. Boabdil's home, the Alhambra, a stunning and sumptuous palace with equally breathtaking gardens, constructed in the thirteenth and fourteenth centuries, was the architectural jewel in the crown of the Emirate of Al-Andalus (medieval Muslims' name for Spain). Córdoba, the former capital city of the caliphate and, famously in the words of the tenth-century Saxonian nun Hrosvitha of Gandersheim, "the ornament of the world," fell to the Christians in 1236. The Alhambra's symbolic importance had come to replace the now Christian-dominated Córdoba. Spanish art through the centuries depicts this pivotal historical moment of Granada's conquest—though the formal military surrender had occurred in the fall of 1491—as King Boabdil literally handing the Alhambra's keys to Queen Isabel and King Ferdinand. In exchange for Boabdil's and Granada's surrender and continued cooperation, the signed agreement, known as the Capitulations of the Holy Faith, promised to protect the rights of the Muslims to practice their faith openly and to maintain their Arabic customs. Only a few short years later, with promises torn asunder in the name of Christianity and national unity, Spain's Muslims faced the choice of forced baptism or exile.

But why, in 1492, did the victory of Isabel and Ferdinand matter so much? For almost eight hundred years prior to 1492, since the fall of the Visigothic (or western Gothic) kingdom to Muslims from North Africa in 711, the Islamic world had claimed Spain as part of its empire, and many would say a most precious part. Early legend had it that the Visigothic King Rodrigo raped Florinda La Cava, daughter of his friend Count Julian, and that Julian, seeking revenge, plotted with the Muslims to overthrow the kingdom. Later, as the epigraph to this prologue indicates, La Cava became Spain's own Eve, "through whom all Spain was lost." Whatever the truth of the matter for much of the legend remains historically dubious today, in 711, the invading North African Berber army swarmed into Spain, led by Tarik, in whose honor Gibraltar is named. Jabal Ṭāriq comes from the Arabic for Tarik's Mountain. The North African Muslims defeated King Rodrigo in battle and took over most of the Iberian Peninsula, with the exception of the northwest part that today consists of the Spanish provinces of Asturias and Galicia.

Sometime between 718 and 722, a man named Pelayo, who lived in the moun-

"La Alhambra. Vista general desde Albaicín," 1863, by Charles Clifford (1819–1863). Albumen photograph, 31.7 × 41.9 cm. From *Album de Andalucía y Murcia*, 1863. Courtesy of The Hispanic Society of America, New York.

tainous region of Asturias, near the French border, mobilized a small group of Christians to fight the Muslims and drive them back. His victory, the Battle of Covadonga, named for a cave in the Cantabrian Mountains, legendarily initiates what medieval and early modern histories called the Restoration, later named by modern historians the Reconquest—that is, the Christian enterprise to win back the land lost in 711. Covadonga became a shrine to the Virgin Mary, who had aided the Christians in the battle. And because the Asturians elected Pelayo as their ruler, that battle also marks the birth of the Spanish monarchy, which even today traces its origins to Asturias, the region they call the "cradle of Spain" and the "cradle of the Reconquest." Since 1369, Spain's heir apparent to the throne bears the title prince of Asturias. To this day, Asturians claim pride of place in Spanish national history as the only territory that was never subjected to Muslim rule and that remained under Christian control. The pilgrimage route through the area to the tomb of the apostle St. James of Compostela (Santiago de Compostela) in today's province of Galicia led to that site's fame as the third most important city in Christendom after Jerusalem and Rome. The sacred and the secular fuse in the legends of Santiago and

Pelayo. The legend of St. James the Moorslayer (Santiago Matamoros) claims that he appeared in battle on a white steed and spurred the Christian soldiers to victory against the Muslims. In *The Spaniards,* Américo Castro outlines brilliantly how the legend and the cult of the saint became a symbol of Christian military might for centuries, and a principal galvanizing force to rally the people in the continuing military drive against the Muslims. He explains that while Santiago remains the patron saint of Spain and greatly beloved, his political importance declined by the fifteenth century once the Christian kingdoms had gained control over all but the kingdom of Granada.

And so, when the wars against Granada, which had spanned the 1480s, ended in victory for the Christian rulers, Isabel and Ferdinand enjoyed multiple gains. In addition to more territory and rule over the Muslims of Granada, the Spanish rulers now controlled the Mediterranean coastline that faced Africa, important for their own navigations, but more important for the protection of the realm from invaders by sea or across the strait of Gibraltar, as had happened centuries earlier.

From their new stronghold in Granada, three months after their victory over that city, Isabel and Ferdinand signed the Edict of Expulsion on March 31, 1492, which ordered the Jews in all their realms to convert to Christianity or pack up what belongings they would be allowed to take and leave their homeland forever by the end of July. Long despised in Spain, which had a history of anti-Semitic legislation from the sixth century on, the Jews suffered from more than discriminatory laws when violent anti-Semitism engulfed Spanish society with a series of massacres of Jews in 1391. Before 1391 many Jews had converted to Christianity, and after that date, a significant number converted or emigrated to other countries. Conversion had long been the goal of the Spanish Church. But assimilation and full integration into Spanish Christian society eluded the converts. By the last quarter of the fifteenth century, the *conversos,* or New Christians, encountered as much prejudice as they had faced as practicing Jews. The Inquisition, instituted in Spain in 1478 to root out heretics, devolved into a witch hunt for Jews who pretended to be Christian. As long as a family had any known Jewish blood in its ancestry, that family remained New Christian, with all the social and cultural limitations that implied. Although the Church and Spanish society treated New Christians quite poorly, they nonetheless pursued the path of converting the Jews, embarking on a final solution of forced conversion or expulsion that, in theory, would leave Spain with only two faiths, Christianity and Islam. Numbers vary, but historians estimate that perhaps forty thousand Jews chose to leave, while some fifty to sixty thousand accepted baptism. Whatever the numbers, when the last Jew chose expulsion over forced conversion in the summer of 1492, Sepharad (or Sefarad), the Hebrew name for their Spanish

Santiago Matamoros, by anonymous Andalusian artist.
Tempera on parchment. From *Carta ejecutoria for Gaspar
Guerra del Cañamal,* issued by Philip III. Granada, 1610.
Images of St. James the Moorslayer were often used for let-
ters that confirmed or awarded noble status to the recipi-
ent, especially in the sixteenth and seventeenth centuries.
Courtesy of The Hispanic Society of America, New York.

homeland, ceased to exist. Their longing for it endured, as abundant testimonies
from as close as Portugal and Morocco to as far away as the New World make pain-
fully clear.

After 1492, Spain embarked on its national and imperial mission to Christianize
the world, but they soon found themselves wrestling with issues of homeland security. The Church and Crown of Christian Spain pondered what to do about a potential threat, the Muslim Turks, who battled the Spanish on the high seas and who
threatened the shores of the nation. As Christian Spain saw it, these "barbarians"

could be aided and abetted by the enemy within, Moriscos (Muslims who had converted to Christianity) and crypto-Muslims, whose allegiance to Islam would outweigh any fidelity to Christianity or spirit of Spanish nationalism they might possess.

A historical romance had circulated in Spain during the second half of the fifteenth century, in multiple unsigned and untitled manuscripts, though known to some of the elite readers as *Crónica sarracina* (Saracen chronicle). In 1499, the romance was printed for the first time as *Crónica del Rey don Rodrigo, postrimero rey de los godos* (Chronicle of King Rodrigo, the last king of the Goths) and attributed to Pedro de Corral. This popular work enabled the widespread dissemination of the myth of how the Muslims had conquered Spain, and the miraculous beginning of when Pelayo and Spain fought back. Significantly, but unsurprisingly, the tale inspired many oral ballads—a popular form of cultural expression known to kings and peasants alike—that shaped the way Spaniards thought about their history and origins. Because Corral combined grand myth and domestic historical narrative, people easily understood and gravitated to the story of the fate of the Visigothic kingdom cast in familiar terms of love, lust, and family honor. That same year, 1499, the confessor to Queen Isabel, Francisco Jiménez de Cisneros, the archbishop of Toledo, and later Cardinal Cisneros, pondered how best to assimilate the Muslims of Granada into the larger fabric of Christian Spain. Though his counterpart in Granada, Bishop Hernando de Talavera, had initiated a sensitive process of introducing Christianity to the Muslim inhabitants of Granada after 1492 (by insisting that his clergy learn Arabic, for one thing), Cisneros convinced Ferdinand and Isabel of the need for much more rigorous and speedy tactics, including, first and foremost, forced mass baptisms. And so, after chipping away at the promises made to Boabdil in 1492, the Church and Crown reneged completely. Sometime between 1499 and 1501, Cisneros ordered thousands of Arabic manuscripts burned in Granada. Ostensibly an offensive move to rid the city of the Koran, thought to be a dangerous book to Christianity, the burning destroyed many other works, signaling the beginning of the widespread and relentless destruction of Arabic culture in Spain.

The first wave of expulsion of the Muslim citizens of Castile, who refused to convert to Christianity, began in 1500 and was completed in 1502, after which there were no more openly practicing adherents of Islam in Castile, though they were tolerated in the territories of Aragon and Valencia until 1526 (Kamen, *Empire* 22). And after 1502, the Inquisition, of which Cisneros became the inquisitor general, encouraged the effacement of Arabic culture and customs, including the writing of books in Arabic. The Moriscos of Granada were relocated to other provinces in order to decrease their collective power. The Church and Crown feared covert and open resistance to new laws that regulated the behavior and rights of the Moriscos. Life became

Title page of the first printed edition (Seville 1499) of
Pedro de Corral's *Crónica del rey don Rodrigo*. [Seville?:
Meynardo Ungut and Stanislao polono?], 1499. Courtesy
of The Hispanic Society of America, New York.

even more arduous for the Moriscos in Spanish society, in a hostile climate that
feared Islam and continued to view them as false converts and enemies not unlike
the Jewish conversos, who also continued to face discrimination and inquisitorial
scrutiny throughout the sixteenth century. At this time, Christians believed that the
Muslims were a violent people, and biologically enslaved by an uncontrollable lust,
especially the men. Therefore, they were incapable of eliminating their highly sexualized drive to conquer.

A series of increasingly restrictive and discriminatory regulations against the
Moriscos caused various uprisings and rebellions throughout sixteenth-century
Spain. Threats of a final solution, expulsion of the Moriscos, marked the last decade

of the sixteenth century, becoming more pronounced as a national desideratum in the first decade of the seventeenth century, after the death of King Philip (Felipe) II in 1598. King Philip III's council likened the current danger of the king's position vis-à-vis the Moriscos to that of King Rodrigo, alleging that now, as in the eighth century, the invasion plans were well known in advance, but the current situation was even more dire. According to an undated court document, but from some early year of his reign, King Philip III had fewer skilled warriors than Rodrigo did, and more importantly, Philip counted many more enemies than his Visigothic predecessor had (Janer 275). In a letter dated September 11, 1609, King Philip III, caving in to the relentless pressure of his councilors, ordered the expulsion of the Moriscos from Valencia and offered as justification the security of the homeland and the need to heal Spanish Christendom of the wounds inflicted by false converts. Later that month, town criers announced to the people of Valencia that they would have to leave the country. The expulsions of the descendants of Spain's Muslim community began in Valencia one month later, in October 1609, and spread throughout the kingdom until 1614, although many exceptions were made to allow some Moriscos to remain, such as children under the age of twelve (Harvey, *Muslims in Spain;* Perry, *Handless Maiden*). Legend has it that King Boabdil lamented Islam's loss as he moved from lord of the realm to exile from it and, looking back in anguish and longing at the Alhambra, heaved "the Moor's last sigh." Who could have guessed in 1492—though the fate of the Jews in that same year might have been a predictor of continued intolerance in Spain—that just over one hundred years later, one Moor's sigh would become the cry of all his descendants in Spain? When this history is told from the point of view of the conquerors, 1492 stands for new beginnings, with the defeat of Granada, the expulsion of the Jews, and the start of an overseas empire, but for the Jews of Spain and the Muslim communities inside and outside of Spain, that year meant anything but victory. For both Judaism and Islam, 1492 marks a time of great tragedy.

Centuries later, in 2001—more than five hundred years after the expulsion of the Jews and the fall of Granada, and almost thirteen hundred years after the fall of Spain in 711—Spain commemorated its national shrine at the Cave of Covadonga, site of Pelayo's victory over the Muslims; the exposition was a time of regional and national pride, and the prince of Asturias, Crown Prince Philip, visited on September 9, the feast day of the Virgin of Covadonga. During the time I have worked on this book—more than a decade—sad and horrifying world events brought renewed focus to Spain's historical conflict between Islam and Christianity, showing that Spain is not alone in its insistent return to the years between 711 and 1492 as defining moments that resonate even today. The first event occurred on U.S. soil on September 11, 2001, two days after the commemorative visit of the prince to Covadonga.

After the destruction of the World Trade Center in New York, Osama bin Laden appeared in a videotape that was widely aired on October 7, 2001, and for days following. Bin Laden began with the following warning and challenge: "Let the whole world know that we shall never accept that the tragedy of Andalusia be repeated in Palestine." He is referring to the official end of the Christian Reconquest of Al-Andalus, the conquest of the Andalusian city of Granada by Ferdinand and Isabel, in 1492, and the beginning of what became the official erasure of Islam in Spain, however much the daily reality of the people differed. His dramatic declaration underscores the grip that these two dates—711 and 1492—have on Islamic and Christian histories and memory alike, though of course with the dates of victory and defeat reversed. Bin Laden demonstrates, in chilling fashion, that the fall of Spain in 711, and its centuries-long aftermath of bloodshed, exile, and expulsion in the name of religious fervor, are far from over, far from being merely ancient history. The history is relevant now.

Shortly after the attacks of 9/11, televised footage of cave-dwelling Muslims recounting dreams and prophecies of conquest collapsed for me the difference between the present and sixteenth- and seventeenth-century Spain, a time with endless prophecies of war, by Christian and Muslim alike, each foretelling about the other's impending victories and defeats. Then, the tragic bombing in Madrid on March 11, 2004, opened old wounds on Iberian soil, which were the making of centuries of conflict among Christians, Muslims, and Jews. After the Madrid attack, synagogues suffered defacement, and the Spanish Muslim community expressed understandable fears about cultural backlash and new anti-Islamic sentiment in their country. This particular brand of terrorism highlights the fact that the intersections of politics, religion, and identity, and their capacity to inspire violence, not only remain as powerful as ever, but are now geopolitical tensions, extending well beyond geographic boundaries.

Former Spanish prime minister José María Aznar brought the past and the present into sharp focus when he asserted in a lecture at Georgetown University in September 2004 that the attack in Madrid had nothing to do with foreign policy that supported a war in Iraq; rather, in his view, the attackers sought revenge for the Christian Reconquest of Muslim Spain. Aznar's point, shared by many people, removes the focus from any specific political reason for the attacks. To say that future terrorism on Spanish soil might be averted if the country avoids a particular domestic or international policy implies a reasonable debate between two opposing groups.

Instead, as leaders of the Muslim world remind us, the Islamic radicals who perpetrate such crimes against humanity do so in violation of Islam's teachings, which opposes hatred and violence. The radicals have stated openly that they want Western military bases out of the Holy Land, if not also the complete annihilation of the West, and they claim the side of right through their declaration of jihad, or holy war. Aznar did not invent the argument of a relationship between terrorism and the battles of the Reconquest. Bin Laden himself brought up "the tragedy of Andalusia," but instead of confining the jihad to Spain alone, he targeted the West.

The current reality of geopolitical tensions, with its emphasis on the "global," requires more forcefully than ever that we not neglect the study and understanding of individual cultures. The notion of community, however imperfectly it captures each individual's multiple identities, remains central to how we see ourselves. Our best hope for the future lies in our ability to understand the world's communities. My late colleague Edward Said put this very well. Said received Spain's Prince of Asturias Concord Award in 2002, which he shared with the acclaimed musician Daniel Barenboim, for their efforts to promote new communities through a shared love of music. The Prince of Asturias Award, instituted in 1980 and broadly conceived as a humanitarian award to honor individuals and groups throughout the world, of all ethnicities, races, and religions, who exemplify the best of the human spirit and a dedication to the betterment of the world, is in and of itself a beautiful sign of hope for peace and understanding, and for an ever-widening circle of community. It is also a very obvious political gesture toward transforming the symbolism of Asturias from representing modern Spain as an ancient Christian kingdom to representing, more generally, new beginnings.

In his acceptance speech, Said stated,

> The world today is full of battling identities and nationalisms . . . In every case, though, both sides of the battle over identity consider that they have justice on their side. But where is the justice? . . . The underlying problem with all this is that it is impossible to be neutral or to look at such tensions from on high. No matter how detached we try to be, these are life and death matters for every human being in one way or another. Each of us belongs to a community with its own national narrative, its own traditions, language, history, foundational ideas, heroic figures.

His comments touch on themes that are the subject of my book. History matters, because history is used to define the present and predict the future. Historiography matters, because the way history is written shapes perceptions of where we come from and who we are. And finally, stories and symbols matter, and the national narratives of communities, the identity battles that accompany them, and the foundational ideas and heroic figures that structure these narratives matter today. It is crucial that we not dismiss national stories as old tales, ancient history best laid to rest, but understand that the long historical arm of these narratives are keys to present understanding now that we have learned how important cultural patrimony and literary pillars are in forming national identity.

What do national narratives, foundational ideas, and heroic figures provide for a people? First of all, stories are not supplemental to life but are central to life's meaning, as is the inspiration to tell stories. Narratives are not neutral. Stories articulate the ideas, feelings, sentiments, and deep-seated beliefs that, for better or worse, people recognize as their own. Communities are good "readers" of story, good interpreters of meaning; they understand when and how a story stands for something larger. They understand when a story helps explain their struggles, including who they are and where they came from. Communities are about membership—who is in, who is out, what rights and liberties membership brings, what rights might be denied or withheld from those who fall into another category, perhaps a less favored, minority group. These questions vexed the peoples of medieval and early modern Spain. They are no less pressing as modern questions. In Spain, in the fifteenth, sixteenth, and seventeenth centuries, Church and Crown operated on the principle of fixed identities and separable communities—Christian, Muslim, Jew—and of a secondary, suspect class of citizens, the hybrid, problematic New Christian, that is, the Muslim or Jewish convert to Christianity. But, with generation after generation of intermarriage and sexual intermingling, and of long periods of *convivencia,* or "peaceful coexistence," in different parts of the Iberian Peninsula at differing times, was it really possible to declare purity of blood in any group of people living there at the time? Was it really possible not to see hybridity everywhere? Logic, reason, and the testimony of one kind of history say no. But the official history—or what we might call the official myths—which later gave rise to national identity and nationalism, and which evolved from the ninth through the seventeenth centuries, prove otherwise. The power of myth led to real-life and grave consequences for those who were exiled, for those whose lives were turned upside down as rights were restricted, goods and property confiscated, and relocation to other realms forced upon them, and for those who suffered torture and death at the hands of the Inquisition.

It is one of the ironies and triumphs of Spain's official histories and grand literary production that they crafted an idea of "Spain" as early as the thirteenth century, when in fact people spoke different dialects and identified themselves regionally and religiously. It is one way we can account for the conflicting double narrative of convivencia and violent conquest. Church and Crown—and, in the Middle Ages, that meant principally the kings of León-Castile, later the kingdom of Castile, and its capital city of Toledo, and the Crown of Aragon—had vested interests in acquiring more territory. The histories reveled in relating these conquests as an overturning of the fall of Spain in 711. At the same time, daily life in the peninsula often went on as before, though religious and other kinds of conflicts did assail groups of people at different times. Unsurprisingly, people of different religions often belonged to and derived identity from the same community. And just as we identify ourselves in multiple ways—through professions, towns, clubs, race, ethnicity, gender, hobbies, religion, political affiliations, and social, educational, and cultural organizations— the medievals and early moderns identified themselves in different ways.

Not until the marriage of Ferdinand of Aragon and Isabel of Castile joined the kingdoms of Aragon and Castile in 1469 did anything even close to a politically unified "Spain" exist. At that point, the Jews spoke Ladino, a Hispanized Hebrew, the Muslims spoke Arabic, and they and the Christians spoke their particular regional dialects, and many of them could communicate in multiple dialects. Poets often wrote in Galician-Portuguese, and Castilian Spanish replaced Latin as the language of choice for history, other forms of nonfiction, and fiction. The symbolic importance of Antonio de Nebrija presenting a Castilian grammar to Queen Isabel in that iconic year—1492—cannot be overstated. In an anecdote much recounted by historians, Isabel found the gift somewhat baffling. The archbishop of Talavera intervened in the conversation to assure her with relish that this book contained the "instrument of empire," the language that would make possible Spain's imperial dreams and unite the world through a single tongue, a state of the world unheard of since before the Biblical Tower of Babel, when the world splintered into chaos and confusion through the multiplicity of languages. While Nebrija's gift implied a tool for overseas empire, the lesson struck even closer to home. To make the world homogeneous, he was asserting the primacy of Castilian over the languages of the world, and over all other dialects in Spain, just as Christianity was to be the religion of Spain and the world. As with other aspects of the medieval experience that resonate even today, this competition between the regional and the national in Spain speaks to an urgent contemporary issue. After the death of Francisco Franco in 1975, Spain's regional cultures reacted against long years of repression, giving rise to actions that range from the reestablishment of languages in schools, such as the teaching of Catalan (and the return of street signs and menus in that language), to calls for secession from the larger state demonstrated by violent uprisings, as in the decades-long efforts of ETA, the Basque group.

The Eve of Spain is a book about stories. It is about how Spain created itself through fiction and narrative history. Although not a conventional history, it is a history of the nation through the examination of its literary and historical texts, of how the country crafted its own story, and of how that story became the official history of Spain. Most of the stories I tell came into being between the ninth and fifteenth centuries. In Golden Age Spain—the sixteenth and seventeenth centuries—they were retold, retooled, and reworked, becoming official history and the subject of influential literary works. When, in the nineteenth century, all of Europe became obsessed with their national origins, Spain was no less so. And to determine those origins and bolster their claims to an ancient and Christian national lineage, the Spanish turned, like good scholars, to the historical and literary production of the medieval and early modern periods. The tales and legends I include in this book are essential to understanding what led to the expulsion of the Jews from Spain in the fifteenth century and the Moriscos in the seventeenth century. They are essential for understanding how and why Jews and Muslims needed to be excluded, even expunged, from the national narrative of history. In my account of the tellings of Spain's foundational myths and popular legends, we see the struggles for identity, for this dynamically evolving thing called national identity, with its dramatic life-and-death underpinnings. Historians, moralists, theologians, politicians, poets, dramatists, and writers of prose fiction battled each other with the pen rather than the sword, some to define themselves and their countrymen through a politics of exclusion, others to fight against the fixed definitions of identity, in pleas for inclusion, which I intend *The Eve of Spain* to bring to life for the reader.

One of Spain's most important stories springs from the eighth-century Muslim defeat of King Rodrigo, "last of the Goths," and the Christians' subsequent symbolic victory. In the chapters that follow, readers will recognize familiar literary, folkloric, and mythic patterns from centuries of making and remaking the legend, as blame and praise of the story's characters switch places over and over, depending on the teller and the time. But the legend does more than surface through the centuries as an entertaining tale well told. Rather, it is inextricably linked to the history and culture of Spain, to its conflicted and contested notions of national identity, and to the political climate that led to the expulsion of the Jews from Spain in 1492, the mass baptism of Muslims in the early sixteenth century, and the expulsion from Spain of the descendants of these Muslim converts through the systematic expulsions from 1609 to 1614. This multi-episodic story permeates and shapes the fiction and historiography of Spain in all centuries since the fall of Spain in 711, and these works have in turn shaped the nation itself. This foundational myth, forged to identify the Spain of the Visigoths as the original unified Christian nation and counter the powerful reality of Al-Andalus, has had an enormous impact on Spanish national identity, nation building, and empire building, through the eroticization of myth and political language, and through the fear of women, Jews, and Muslims. How this is so, and how the legend intersects and reflects the cultural, social, political, and historical events of Spain from the eighth century to the present, is the main subject of this book.

The title, *The Eve of Spain,* suggests that the fall of the Visigothic kingdom to the Muslim invaders signaled a significant moment just prior to the birth of the real Spain, at least in the way medieval, early modern, and modern historians recount the fall and position their own historical moment in relation to it, and in relation to the subsequent deeds of Pelayo the Goth. Many times over the course of the almost thirteen centuries since the fall of Spain in 711, authors, historians, philosophers, and politicians have raised what were often referred to as neo-Gothicist ideals. Neo-Gothicism is a myth of national origins and identity that defines a Spaniard as a Christian whose roots extend back to the eighth century, specifically to those western Goths who survived the invasion of the Muslims in 711. Those Christians, who had fled to Asturias in the north, and were led by Pelayo, nourished the tiny seeds of Christianity that remained after the beginning of Muslim rule in Spain. In short, neo-Gothicism alludes to Spain's sociopolitical arguments from the fifteenth century to the present, which look back nostalgically and shrewdly to the myth of a politically unified, and ethnically and racially pure, land of Spanish Goths. Neo-Gothicism flourished in varying degrees of intensity, renewed, and reinvigorated time and again. However, the arguments over what made an "authentic Spaniard," and whether the authentic Spaniard must have descended from the Visigoths, reached fever pitch in the nineteenth century and in the twentieth century, before, during, and after the Spanish Civil War.

Second, this volume explains, among other things, how neo-Gothicist ideals intersect with national myths about women as symbols of the fall of nations and the building of them. The second meaning of this book's title, then, is in the evolution of Florinda La Cava, the Eve figure in the legend, who came to be blamed for the fall of Spain. At the same time, it examines sociocultural, political, and other historical events that produce the contexts in which this Eve figure grows and develops. Alongside both these figures, Pelayo and La Cava, the book traces the patterns of prejudice against those deemed Other—the women, Muslims, and Jews of Spain— within the telling of this myth and within the larger drive to create a collective Spanish national identity. In short, a theme throughout the book is the gendering and demonizing of the enemy Other, which resulted in legends of Jewish blood libel and rampaging Muslims. Woven throughout the book are the emblematic, nationalistic stories of women: treacherous Christian women, stalwart Gothic wives, sexually available Muslim princesses who always convert to Christianity, and powerfully seductive Jewish women, all of whose tales become metaphors for political and religious conquest.

I became interested in the foundation myth of the fall of Spain while conducting research for my 1997 book on the medieval story of the fictional mid-eighth-century lovers Flores and Blancaflor. It became clear to me that a little-known thirteenth-century Spanish chronicle version of *Flores and Blancaflor* had been written as a redemption narrative—that is, as a counterpoint or reversal—of the story of the fall of Spain in 711. In it, the Saracen prince Flores marries the Christian captive Blancaflor, after rescuing her from sexual peril in an emir's harem, and is converted to Christianity by Benedictine monks. Subsequently, the newly crowned Flores insists on the conversion of the entire peninsula to Christianity from Islam, thereby restoring Christianity to its rightful place as the "national" religion and reversing the fall that had occurred in the earlier part of the century. The chronicle tells us, however, that this happy state lasted for only a few years beyond the reign of Flores, after which Spain fell again; in a fictional flight of fancy, this fall of Spain must wait to be reversed by Flores's grandson, the Holy Roman Emperor Charlemagne! But the story of Flores and Blancaflor functions, among other things, as an analogue of the bad woman and good woman: if the kingdom fell to Islam in 711 because of fornication between an unmarried woman—La Cava—and a lustful ruler—King Rodrigo—this time the kingdom becomes Christian because of the fortunate marriage between Blancaflor and Flores.

Interested in the legend, I dug deeper into the history of Spain's fall. Like most people who think she or he knows this story, I expected to find in the earliest extant chronicles an elaboration of the role of Florinda La Cava in this foundational chapter of Spanish history. But I was surprised to see how small a role, if any, this young woman played, even to the point of being unmentioned in some chronicles, unnamed in many other chronicles, and given one or two lines of story in others. After all, as a student of early modern Spanish literature and history, I was familiar with the sentiment expressed in the epigraph to this chapter: La Cava, like Eve, played an active role, one often characterized negatively. But when, I wondered, did the blame of Florinda La Cava come about? And why is it that historians have reinforced as the central event of the collective national myth of the fall of Spain—often called, plaintively and with great longing for an irrecoverable past, the "loss of Spain" or the "destruction of Spain"—the sexual scandal between King Rodrigo and a young girl from North Africa, entrusted to his court in Toledo? The search for the answers led to this book, intended for both general readers and specialists, which quickly moved beyond La Cava to much more encompassing questions. Instead, my book posits, quite simply, that to understand the story of the fall of Spain, you must understand the legend of its Restoration, and to understand Spain today, you must understand both parts of the national narrative and its multiple perspectives on gender, religion, ethnicity, and race.

As so frequently happens in life, a remark made casually, tucked away in one's memory, bounds back to the forefront of thought, imbued with new meaning. Early in my junior year abroad in Seville, shortly before the end of Franco's oppressive dictatorship, a Spaniard wryly said to me, "Oh, in Spain, we're all Catholic, even those who aren't; and make sure you tell people you're Catholic, even if you aren't." When pressed, she declined to elaborate. At the time I found it a somewhat mystifying statement. But the remark came back to me as I pored over centuries of tales and historical documents about prejudice, intolerance, persecution, and expulsion. It has been said that in the medieval and early modern periods in Western Europe, especially in Spain, religion was politics. Twentieth-century Spain embodied something similar. The advice to hide one's true identity, if one were not Catholic, referred on the one hand to the fact that the Franco regime identified itself completely with a National Catholic ideology; on the other hand, it alludes to the idea that people employ strategies—masking of real identity—to conform to a society that might otherwise prove hostile. Medieval Jews and early modern Moriscos employed numerous strategies of resistance as people sought to hold on to their place in a community that increasingly defined itself as Old Christian, in which one claimed "purity of blood" by having neither Jewish nor Muslim ancestors, even if they had been converts to Christianity. Jews and Moriscos tried, unsuccessfully, to belong to the dominant society, to conform to its ever-evolving and restrictive customs and laws, and to stave off what became the inevitable: exile from the homeland. *The Eve of Spain* deals with some of these strategies. Over and over, the history of Spain asks the questions, "Who is Spanish?" and "Who may live in Spain?" Most of the stories in this book tell how the myths and legends that attempted to answer those questions justified repression and expulsion and were sustained as national history to the present.

Why should we care about these stories of Spain's past? They're not even about the heroes and saints one might actually know of, like the national hero El Cid or the patron saint Santiago of Compostela. Who has even heard of Pelayo, Rodrigo, and La Cava? Though little known outside of Spain, at least today, however much English and American writers of the nineteenth and twentieth centuries seemed to be aware of them, these stories are far from trivial. I believe these underexplored stories of medieval and early modern Spain, stories of uncommonly rich topics, offer lessons for our day.

As early as the thirteenth century, one historian, the archbishop Rodrigo Ximénez de Rada, attributes Pelayo's stand against the Muslims as one for "the liberation of the homeland," the "patria." Medieval and early modern materials themselves often call the Visigothic kingdom a nation or empire. While I in no way suggest a bald transference of medieval meanings into modern ones—"España" in thirteenth-century Spain is not the España of the nineteenth century—it is nonetheless the case that the medieval chroniclers did conceive of a larger entity than the regional kingdoms, and they conceived of it abstractly as "Spain." Such narratives were indeed designed to instill a kind of national pride. Moreover, they exploited the idea of Spain in order to cast the events of the peninsula as one grand historical narrative in the service of specific religious and political goals. While not nationalism and national identity in the way we see them in the twenty-first century, there is nonetheless some resemblance to them, if not as a conscious belief among the people, then at least present among the medieval elite who wrote about these beliefs and sentiments. I suggest, too, that the advantages and problems of medieval and early modern multicultural societies, while not a mirror of our own communities, nonetheless are seedlings of, and bear some relationship to, today's globalized world and geopolitical issues.

A book like this runs many risks; minefields are everywhere. Medieval and early modern historical accounts frequently contradict each other, particularly as the mythic and fictional elements accrued to the legends over time. To offset one of the most obvious risks, the huge sweep of time the book covers, I have included a bibliography that offers the interested reader many avenues of pursuit. I have tried to maintain sensitivity to the materials I examined, and the people behind them, centuries of recountings of so many contradictory and paradoxical feelings. Telling the stories of the dominant culture in Spain, the myths, legends, and tales that became the official history, reveals some of the less noble impulses of human beings, carried out in the name of religion and "homeland security." And in writing about the Inquisition, the expulsions and violence against humanity, about the calculating political appropriations of religious faith to justify such cruelty, which often went hand-in-hand with the creation of national myths, and this foundational myth in particular, one might appear to dismiss or even disparage religious beliefs in general. In fact, the opposite obtains. I am keenly aware that behind the national myths lie the personal tragedies of thousands of people—those forced to leave their homeland to remain true to their religion, those who died rather than give up their faith, those who were true Christian converts who died or who were imprisoned, falsely accused of heresy, witchcraft, and sundry crimes, or those who did pretend to be Christian to survive in their homeland and were turned over to the Inquisition. In their hour of need, these people clung to their religion—Judaism, Christianity, or Islam—from which, as some testimonies tell us, they derived strength, comfort, and hope, if not for this life, then for the hereafter. I am also keenly aware that any polarization of the larger historical narrative into good and evil, victims and oppressors, fails to take into account how many good people there were in all three of Spain's castes, as Américo Castro called them, the Christians, Muslims, and Jews. Every history has its villains, and this history is no exception. The tragedy, not unfamiliar to us today, is that so much of Spain's painful history came about because otherwise good people acted in the belief that they were right and that God was on their side.

The great playwright Lope de Vega, a pillar of Spain's unparalleled national dramas of the Golden Age, plumbed Spain's early stories for material of contemporary relevance. One of the foremost American Hispanists of the twentieth century, Stephen Gilman, described Lope's view of history itself as a three-act play, in which Spain's origins and founding myths, including those discussed in my book, formed the first act, followed by the second act of the Middle Ages (approximately 1000–1492), and then the third act of contemporary, post-1492 events. Resting on the principle that in life, stories matter, and following in the footsteps of a writer who saw life as a play, it seems fitting to structure my own nonfiction book in a fictive container, as a drama in three acts. The first act, Fall and Redemption, begins with the defeat of the Visigothic kingdom in 711 and ends in the watershed year 1492. The second act, Promise and Fulfillment, takes us through the sixteenth and seventeenth centuries, as Spain sought to define itself through its myth of origins as a nation restored in territory and importance to the grandeur of its eighth-century original Christian state, which could only reach its fullest potential with the expulsion of the Moriscos between 1609 and 1614. The third act, Imagining Spain, moves from the Enlightenment to the present.

But before we enter the world of court chronicles and popular fiction, hear tales of Muslim princesses, Jewish temptresses, and besieged Christian maidens, stand alongside failed kings and valiant Christian warrior-rulers, and trace the legends of victorious enemies and persecuted minorities, we must first set the stage with the founding myth itself and a bit more introduction to its relevance to contemporary Spain.

FALL AND REDEMPTION

(711–1492)

CHAPTER ONE

Setting the Stage

Power, friendship, trust, religion, beauty, betrayal, rape, honor, revenge, war, devastation. In Spain, these themes and narrative elements form the most enduring founding myth of the nation, and to many it remains not Myth but History. What follows is the story of the fall of Rodrigo's Spain in 711 to the Muslims of North Africa and of the resistance to Muslim domination by a tiny band of eighth-century Christian freedom fighters as you might have heard it in fifteenth-century Spain.

The friendship of three men, King Rodrigo, Count Julian, and the Archbishop Oppas, the three most powerful men in the Iberian Peninsula, seemed unassailable in early eighth-century Toledo, the seat of the Visigothic kingdom. Individually, they held the keys to the three institutions of the land: the government, the military, and the nascent Christian Church. Together, their imperial dreams for Spain and the growth of Christianity seemed not an impossible quest, but achievable.

One day, though, against the counsel of his senior advisers, Rodrigo defied the injunction against entering an enchanted edifice, known as the House of Hercules (after the first ruler of the peninsula), to which each of the previous twenty-four Visigothic kings had added an iron lock, as custom dictated. Rather than add his lock, Rodrigo broke into the house—a sin of hubris and greed, because he thought there might be treasures within—and discovered an ark, containing a parchment with sketchings of men with beards and turbans as well as a prophecy, which stated that he who broke the covenant by entering the house would lose his kingdom to people who looked like the figures on the parchment. Rodrigo sealed the house and forbade his advisers to speak of it.

Count Julian entrusted his only daughter to Rodrigo's court, as was the custom with the Visigothic nobles, removing her from the North African Berber community where his job required the family to live. Toledo provided her instead with the protection of the king and the rich comforts of court life. Who better to look after her safety than his friend the king? The sumptuous gardens of the palace enclave became a favorite retreat for the queen and the maidens of her entourage. But they were not alone in the garden sanctuary: the king also took his leisure along the ramparts of the palace, which gazed down upon the garden and the carefree maidens in it. The beauty of La Cava, as Count Julian's daughter was called, enchanted the king,

Title page of *Crónica del rey don Rodrigo y de la destruyción de España y como los moros la ganaron.* Valladolid: Nicolás Tierry, 1527. The top of the woodcut states, "This is the tower that Hercules built in Toledo." In the woodcut, Rodrigo orders the breaking of the locks, while his counselors try to dissuade him. Courtesy of The Hispanic Society of America, New York.

even bewitched him, until he could restrain his lust for her no longer. One day, he summoned her to his private rooms. At first, she laughingly dismissed his entreaties, reminding him that the queen was in the palace. Then she pleaded, she fought, she cried, but to no avail. He raped her and threatened her with harm if she spoke of it to anyone. Perhaps, though, perhaps she could have done more to stop him, or she even led him on—who's to say? Dishonored and disgraced without the flower of her maidenhood, she confided in her father, and that she should not have done.

Women, it is said, talk too much and never know when silence should be the order of the day.

Outraged, with a murderous desire for revenge, Count Julian conspired with the Muslim groups of North Africa, who longed to conquer fair Spain, particularly the Berber ruler Tarik and his military leader Muza. Though Rodrigo thought he could stem the tide of fate by ensuring the silence of his advisers and of La Cava, it was too late. Between July 19 and 23 in the year 711, approximately twelve thousand warriors of Islam swarmed into southern Spain. When Rodrigo learned of the enemy's presence, he moved his army south, but the ensuing battle left the king's entire army slaughtered on the banks of the Guadalete River, and in the middle of the peninsula, the capital—Toledo—unguarded and vulnerable to invasion. Some say the king died that day, but others say he borrowed a shepherd's humble garb—leaving his own scepter and ermine-trimmed cloak at the river's edge—made his escape from the devastation wrought by the invading Muslims, and lived out his remaining days in grueling penitence. Meanwhile, in Toledo, the Jews, never soldiers in the king's army, determined to aid the Muslims in the defeat of the Visigothic kingdom, and— it must be said—in the defeat of Christianity, by opening the gates of the city. Thus, the proud, Christian, Gothic nation fell to the unthinkable: the yoke of Islam.

But one hope remained. In the unforgivingly rugged terrain of the Cantabrian Mountains of Asturias, in a northwestern portion of the Iberian Peninsula, sometime between 718 and 722, refugees from the crushed Visigothic kingdom decided to fight back. A Gothic nobleman named Pelayo (possibly a relative of the defeated King Rodrigo) and a small band of followers, with the help of miracles attributed to God and the Virgin Mary, drew a line at the cave of Covadonga, beyond which the Muslims, for all their numbers and sheer military strength, could not advance. Launched from this tiny stronghold, the Christian Restoration, or Reconquest, would inspire valiant Christian kings and soldiers to strive to recover the lost kingdom and drive out the enemy infidel.

The author of this fifteenth-century version of the legend, Pedro de Corral, never signed any manuscript of the historical romance attributed to him, which circulated among elite readers for decades and was referred to as *Crónica sarracina*. Corral did not live to see the first printing of his book in 1499, under the title *Crónica del Rey don Rodrigo, postrimero rey de los godos,* nor even to see the date that changed history, 1492.

But before the post-1492, triumphant days of empire, the ignominy of national defeat. The story of the fall of Spain to the Muslims in 711, Spain's enthralling foundational myth, shatters the illusion that wars are fought for the glory and honor of great principles, showcasing instead, in grand narrative fashion, lust and anger, two of the seven deadly sins. These personal acts—the sexual desire of King Rodrigo and the rage of his former friend, Count Julian—had changed the course of history. However, the legend of the fall of Spain, like the story of the fall from the Garden of Eden, came to be identified not by the acts of men, but by its Eve: Florinda La Cava, the cause of Spain's perdition. And the legend of the origins of the new Spain, the real Spain, the restored Christian Spain, celebrated even today in Spain's post-Franco coat of arms and reinvigorated principality of Asturias, came to be identified by its redemptive figure, Pelayo, a David-like refugee from the fallen kingdom of Rodrigo, who battled the Goliath-like Arabs in Asturias, the cradle of the tiny, barely surviving Christian nation. The story of Spain's Restoration, through the centuries, recalled the dangers of a king's weakness, at the same time it invoked the unshakable courage, bravery, and success of Pelayo as proof that God and the Virgin Mary favored the growth not only of a Spanish Christian kingdom, but of an empire.

Though La Cava is often cited as the woman who caused Spain's perdition, there is blame enough to go around: Rodrigo is the very embodiment of the reason why self-control and self-discipline, however tempting the sexual partner may be, were so highly valued in a ruler. Control over one's sexual appetite was commonly considered an outward measure of one's strength in other arenas. Even Plutarch, in his *Life of Antony,* disparages how Antony was in thrall to the seductive Cleopatra, pointing out the dangers—indeed, disasters—that had come from his failing to put the well-being of the state before his personal pleasure.[1] La Cava's father, Julian, allowed his need for revenge to outweigh his love of country and loyalty to Christianity, for which he burns in the hellfire of national revilement. Or at least he did until Juan Goytisolo's late twentieth-century trilogy of modern revisionist novels subjected the legend of Spain's origins to a scathing critique, proposing Julian as a hero whose "treachery" instead permitted the influx of Arab blood that gave Spanish society a passion, character, and intellectual dimension it otherwise lacked and would have continued to lack. More pervasive, intense, and ultimately destructive to medieval Spain, however, than the blame heaped on Rodrigo and Julian, was the hatred and prejudice that attached to the Muslims and Jews within the larger Spanish society, which the evolving and mutating legend of the fall of Spain dramatically captures and illustrates. While the ancient traditions that cast women as harlots or saints can thrive anywhere and anytime, in Spain they are linked, legendarily and historically through this founding legend, to the virulent anti-Semitism that characterized Spanish society, and the treatment of Jews and Muslims through the centuries. In other words, sometimes a woman is more than a woman. For that reason, the story of how the figure of La Cava developed over the centuries from victim to villain, as well as the stories of virtuous Christian women, beautiful Jewesses, and

Muslim princesses, are emblematic and central to an understanding of the national narratives that sought to define Spanish national identity.

In the early sixteenth century, the writer Pedro Ximénez de Urrea equated Eve and Helen of Troy with La Cava, accusing all three of leaving ruin in their wake. The other two names are iconic, but who was Florinda La Cava? And how did the legend evolve from the bonds of male friendship, betrayed and broken, to the legend of the national harlot, the Eve of Spain? If one asks a Spaniard even today, it seems that everyone knows La Cava caused the fall of Spain in 711, although the king is not held blameless. It has become as clichéd as knowing that Eve gave Adam the apple in the Garden of Eden, for which Eve holds special blame as the woman whose first step set in motion their collective disgrace. Astonishingly, however, in the earliest chronicle from the eighth century, there is no mention of a woman in connection with the fall of Rodrigo's government, a defeat ascribed to his own failings. Other early Christian chronicles attribute the downfall variously to the sins of the previous ruler, Witiza, or to his envious sons, Rodrigo's rivals to the throne, or to Rodrigo's and his kingdom's general iniquity, or even to his great pride, another deadly sin. Instead, early Arab chroniclers first mention the Christian king's rape of his army commander's completely blameless daughter as a way of explaining why Julian sought revenge for the family dishonor by conspiring with the Muslim forces to overrun the Iberian Peninsula.

Christian histories of the thirteenth and fourteenth centuries began to include the episode of Rodrigo and La Cava, maintaining as simple fact that he raped La Cava. In the story's later, more misogynistic manifestations, beginning in the sixteenth century, she used her sexuality shamelessly, tempting the man who was powerless against such a seduction, as men have been since the time of Eve. Although there is ample testimony to defend La Cava and squarely blame Rodrigo—centuries of versions, in fact—the legend evolved over time so that the name most associated with the fall is La Cava. For all intents and purposes, she is the Eve of Spain, a Helen of Troy with a Christian moral dimension added to her.[2]

Florinda La Cava. Where does the name come from? The earliest histories leave her unnamed, simply the daughter of the count; in the thirteenth century, they begin to use something akin to an Arabic name, Alataba or Alacaba. By the time Spanish chroniclers told the story in the fourteenth century, she became la Caba, which comes from their assumption that "Al," Arabic for "the," should be removed from the rest of the name Taba or Caba. Logic tells us they were right. The name for Eve in Arabic is a word that means an archetypal, seductive bad woman in Arabic literature, rendered in histories of literature as Hubba, and the word continues today to mean "prostitute." In the case of a fifteenth-century reworking of an earlier history, a Jewish convert to Christianity drops the article and calls her simply Caba. The Hebrew for Eve is Chava, and it seems crystal clear that writers—Christian, Muslim, and Jewish—have long connected her to Eve, even if, to our modern eyes, La Cava appears quite removed from the name Eve. In the sixteenth century, popular oral song most often called her Cava or La Cava, and in 1592, a Morisco named Miguel de Luna christened her Florinda La Cava, changing forever the way she would be known.

Ancient wisdom warns that a king's sexual sins do not simply represent his individual failing. Rather, these acts of vice, weakness, or recklessness have powerfully destructive consequences, which far exceed the sexual act and any effect it may have on the individuals themselves, instead often culminating in the loss of a nation. In these legends of lusts of the flesh, the blame for the destruction of a kingdom may fall on a man or a woman, be shared by both, or may change over time, as in the case of Helen of Troy. As told and retold throughout the centuries, Helen is alternately cast as victim or whore, resistant or wanton and complicit, and Paris as either bold and decisive, or weak and reckless, or the entire story resurrected to be political allegory for a current political dispute. In works whose provenance is not Christian, there may be moral issues in a general sense, but far more important is the political havoc wrought by the decadence of the ruler.

When a ruler of Christian Spain commits a sexual sin, much more is at stake than merely the blot on the soul of the two fornicators, however dangerous that may be for their chances of attaining eternal life in Heaven. In medieval chronicles and histories with a strong Christian foundation, both the body politic and the Christian soul of the nation perish, and if the ruler's moral comportment is not beyond reproach, he can—and in the case of Rodrigo, did—bring down the kingdom. In the history of Christian Spain, the ruler's sexual sins cause a downward spiral into events of political and spiritual decline, resulting in the perdition of the Christian nation, of both the land and its inhabitants. If the head of the body politic—the king—is morally corrupt, his citizens will follow suit, casting a blight on the nation and its collective soul. This is the argument of St. Boniface, which later resurfaces in medieval Spanish chronicles.

The legend of the fall of Spain as a king's sexual scandal began with the briefest of mentions in ninth-century chronicles and ended fully developed as the single cause of Rodrigo's defeat as king, becoming the story of the woman who brought a nation—Spain—to political and spiritual ruin. As I see it, at the heart of this significant shift—at the heart of the fully developed La Cava myth—is the idea of the body. If Covadonga and the start of the "Reconquest" signal the birth of a new, revitalized and restored Christian Spain, as histories have long argued, then the rape of Florinda La Cava can be seen not only as an act by a single lustful individual, King Rodrigo, but as an event on a monumental scale, that takes place, we might say, on the eve of Spain. Indeed, in the legend of the fall—and restoration—of Spain, every conceivable metaphor for the word "body" is at play. In its earliest manifestations, we find the sinning body of the king, head of the body politic, and the victimized body of the young woman in his court's care, the iniquitous body of the nation, and in the king's refusal to heed either precedent or prophecy, bodies of knowledge and bodies of evidence. Later, after the fifteenth century, much more prominent in the legend is the body of the harlot and the paradoxical traits of the sinning yet victimized, and then penitent, body of the king, upon which the Christian nation is destroyed. In restoration tales, subsequent leaders and bodies of government— Pelayo, Alfonso III of Asturias, Alfonso VIII of Castile-León, Alfonso the Learned, Isabel and Ferdinand, Philip II—employ their own unique metaphors of the body to reverse the earlier fall of Spain and create both nation and empire, particularly by creating additional eroticized stories intended to stand for troubled relationships with Spain's Jews and Muslims. Two important features of Pelayo's story, as it developed over the centuries, emphasize the body. Early modern histories elaborated on Pelayo's purity and chastity, as opposed to his lustful predecessor Rodrigo, and both medieval and early modern histories embellished the origins of his rebellion against the Muslims as the desire to rescue his sister from the clutches of Munuza, a Muslim who had abducted her.

There is a longstanding tradition in Europe of the historicization, fictionalization, and allegorization of female chastity and political order, with a particular emphasis on the negative example, that is, the dangers of a lack of female chastity to Christianity and Christian nations. Medieval Spanish history found ample opportunity to exploit the connections of the bad, sexual Christian woman and the seductive Jewess, who were dangerous to men, as well as their surprising opposite, the sexually available Muslim woman, who serves as an instrument to further the growth of Christianity and the recovery of Christian lands in Spain. In the sixteenth century, the political agenda to create a centralized, unified, and above all Christianized Spanish national history dominated historiography. The recognition of this fact helps to explain why La Cava increasingly came to be seen as Eve in the sixteenth century: historiographical and poetic efforts joined forces to insist on the fall of Spain in 711 as a reenactment of the Fall from Paradise. In Spain's case, though, the result was not simply humankind's inheritance of original sin. Rather, the dominant and official histories told of the overrunning and domination of God's most pleasing earthly paradise—the Iberian Peninsula—by unworthy and non-Christian occupants. Christian chroniclers invented historical events designed to trace their lineage back to the roots of Christianity in the Iberian Peninsula, beginning in the Visigothic kingdom of the sixth century. Morisco historians did the same kind of historical invention but to prove their right to live in Spain and argue for their role as participants in the earliest stirrings of the creation of the nation.[3] No match for the combined forces of the Spanish Crown and the Catholic Church, the Moriscos' attempts to include themselves in the definition of authentic Spaniards failed, and Spanish historiography forged a relentlessly linear view of the nation as Christian through and through from the time of the Visigoths to the present rulers.

As is well known, Spain's imperial dreams and realities declined in the seventeenth and eighteenth centuries, and the final blow was struck in the late nineteenth century. In 1898, Spain lost the last colony—Cuba—of what was once arguably the greatest empire on earth. Accounts of national origins, searches to define national identity and the essence of one's selfhood in an individual country fascinated Western Europe in the second half of the nineteenth century. Spain participated in the same kind of national soul searching that England, France, and other countries experienced, but because of the pervasive atmosphere of despair that set in with the loss of Cuba, Spanish soul searching acquired an acute sense of urgency in the twentieth century. Discussions of dynastic chains of Christian leaders were joined by the search for "the essence of Spain" and "true" Spanish art and literature, following a linear Christian development. The need to celebrate the eleventh-century warrior El Cid as the national Muslim-slaying hero, to locate the birth of Spanish literature in the thirteenth-century, hagiographic writings of a humble, pious monk from the Riojan region, named Gonzalo de Berceo, as well as the drive to prove that the origins of the nation were rooted in Rodrigo's Visigothic Christian kingdom obsessed the greatest philosophers, historians, literary critics, and politicians of the nineteenth century. As with sixteenth-century historiography, nineteenth-century historiography was a double-pronged obsession. Not only was it fundamental to define nationhood and national identity in order to go forward in the face of defeat and humiliation, but it was crucial to trace the Spain of the nineteenth century as a direct descendant of the Visigothic kingdom, specifically the Visigoths who had converted to Roman Catholicism in 589 C.E. By casting true "Spanishness" as an unbroken link since the sixth century, the theorists of national identity in the nineteenth century, from Modesto Lafuente in 1850 to Marcelino Menéndez y Pelayo in the 1880s, could claim that Jews and Muslims had always been rightly excluded from the "real Spain." Although such a claim found favor among many people, many other strong, articulate voices excoriated the mission they found to be both anti-Semitic and demonstrative of centuries-long fear of Islam, indeed a fear founded in the defeat of Spain in 711.[4]

Most nineteenth- and early twentieth-century Spanish historians and many literary historians did not question the overall historical authenticity of the fall of Spain legend and its principal players—Rodrigo; La Cava; Julian; Bishop Oppas; Egilona, Rodrigo's wife; Pelayo and his sister Ermesinda—but started from the point of view that the core legend was historical. They committed themselves passionately to a search for the truth of the proper details of the legend, not to discredit it, but to flesh out the facts of what they believed to be the historical truth. For sources, they returned to the earliest extant medieval chronicles and relied heavily on the histories and literature of the early modern period, especially of the sixteenth and seventeenth centuries.

A significant figure in the literary excavations surrounding the Visigothic kingdom was the phenomenally prolific Ramón Menéndez Pidal, who died in 1968 at the age of ninety-nine. Along with his elder fellow Spaniard Marcelino Menéndez y Pelayo, Menéndez Pidal was responsible for shaping—more exactly, creating—Spain's literary canon, a fact that has provoked both joy and woe.[5] While rescuing and editing countless medieval manuscripts and fragments of texts, Menéndez Pidal heavily contributed to the national mission of a linear Christian history of Spain, alongside a similarly Christian literary canon, of which Spain could be proud. Central to those efforts, and most pertinent to the present study, was Menéndez Pidal's monumental three-volume study, *Rodrigo, el último godo* (Rodrigo, the last Goth). It would be impossible to overestimate the value of his work for anyone interested in reading about the founding myth. Nevertheless, two points need to be made. One, in his zeal to establish the purely Christian origins of the legend of the fall of Spain, Menéndez Pidal was capable of some rather remarkable blind spots, for it is clear that the rape of Julian's daughter, as well as the prophecy of the fall because of the king's pride, are both Arabic contributions. That Christianity could so easily accommodate the integration and expansion of the daughter's role to an Eve figure is testimony only to the misogyny embraced by Christian mythmakers, not evidence of Christian origins of the legend. Second, Menéndez Pidal's focus—and hero—was King Rodrigo. There is no full and systematic study of either Pelayo's or La Cava's evolution through the centuries, and certainly no feminist study that examines the shifts in how La Cava is portrayed and how those shifts accompany other kinds of Spanish national stories. This book addresses those gaps, always with an eye to the larger social, political, religious, and cultural contexts in which these changes take place.

The twentieth century brought no respite from the bitter debates about national origins and the essence of a Spaniard, nor from the anti-Semitism and anti-Islamic sentiment that had characterized earlier centuries.[6] The 1947 protest by the eminent

Hispanist Américo Castro in his brief essay "Los visigodos no eran aún españoles" (The Visigoths were not yet Spaniards), came after continuing decades of polemic. Ultimately, and in large part aided by the Franco regime's insistence on a connection to Spain's Christian origins in the mountains of Asturias, as well as by the publications of such historians as Claudio Sánchez Albornoz, Castro's body of work initially had little effect on the national imaginary in its conviction that the myth of the fall of Spain was history, and the Visigoths their kin. For Sánchez Albornoz, the "real Spain" began in the eighth century after Florinda La Cava caused the fall of the nation on the eve of Spain. And if the Visigoths were kin—what were referred to as "authentic Spaniards"—then conveniently left out of the Spanish national identity and the origins of the nation were Muslims and Jews.

Sánchez Albornoz's *El reino de Asturias: Orígenes de la nación española* (The kingdom of Asturias: Origins of the Spanish nation), published in 1972, resulted from decades of research that began in 1921. Convinced that the truth of Spain's beginnings, as well as the history of Spanish "blood," began in the mountains of Asturias, Sánchez Albornoz represented the last of a generation of scholars, but it is a powerful representation. The legend of Pelayo—who may or may not have existed—developed over centuries of time. Nevertheless, Sánchez Albornoz believes firmly not only in his existence, but in the serendipitous, indeed, providential fortune that plucked an unsuspecting minor nobleman "out of nowhere" (unsuspecting in terms of the greatness that would soon be thrust upon him), turning him into "el caudillo de un pueblo, el fundador de una monarquía, el restaurador de la cristiandad, el paladín de la civilidad europea frente a la religión y a la cultura islamitas y africanas" (the leader of his people, the founder of a monarchy, the restorer of Christianity, the paladin of European civility in the face of the Islamic and African religion and culture; 121). Américo Castro, for his part, pursued his theories of the Spanish people as a cultural mix of the three "castes," as he called them, the Jews, Muslims, and Christians, which gained wide acceptance in the last decades of the twentieth century. His works remain highly influential today. In short, while Castro argued that contemporary Spain resulted from the fortuitous mixture of the three castes, Sánchez Albornoz and others preferred the view that an essential "Spanishness" preceded the fall of Spain in 711, was little affected by the presence of the Jews and Muslims in Spain for hundreds of years, and emerged vital, healthy, and victorious after the expulsions of the Jews and Moriscos in 1492 and 1609, respectively.

The twentieth-century Spanish novelist and essayist Juan Goytisolo borrowed the original title of Corral's work, *Crónica sarracina,* and called his collection, *Cronicas sarracinas* (*Saracen Chronicles*). In his essay, "From *Count Julian* to *Makbara*," he writes, "The greatest historic tragedy of the peninsula—the Saracen invasion and

the consequent 'destruction of sacred Spain'—was blamed *ab initio* by our chroniclers and poets on a sexual crime: the illicit love of the last Visigothic King for the
daughter of his vassal, Count Julian" (217). But this has resulted, he tells us, in a "sexual terror" that manifests itself in images of the vile Moor, "a pitiless rapist" of the
wounded country, and countless representations—literary, political, and historical—
of "the Moor as ferocious and lustful" (216–20). And, he continues, the legend and
the fear of Islam pervaded the political discourses during the Spanish Civil War
(1936–1939) of both the Right and the Left (220–22).[7] By way of example, Goytisolo
cites a particularly hate-filled speech by Dolores Ibárruri, the former president of the
Spanish Communist Party, known as La Pasionaria (the Passionate One): "Savage
Moorish hordes, drunk with sensuality, who pour forth to wreak horrendous viola-
tions of our daughters and our wives; Moors brought from the backward encamp-
ments of Morocco, from the most uncivilized mountain villages" (221).

Historians of the late twentieth century were open to searching for less mythic
and fanciful explanations of the fall of Spain in 711. These range from recent reassess-
ments of the earliest historical documents, leading to the conclusion that the Goths
were simply unsophisticated and readily vulnerable to defeat, to psychoanalytical
explanations, mostly involving the fear of strangers and of "strangeness." The fear of
Islam continues today, as the contemporary essays by Goytisolo demonstrate, and
the fear reaches far beyond the boundaries of Spain. But within Spain, the legend
of the fall and restoration of Spain remains highly significant, kept alive by tradition and political design. This attests to the power of myth to enthrall long after
the specific elements of the myth have any actuality, and to endure because it re-
sponds to conditions, beliefs, and prejudices that continue to hold sway over human
emotions.

But before turning to Spain's stories of medieval Spain and beyond, let's move
backwards one more time, first to look at some of the associations of women and
the nation, and then for some background on the earliest Muslim and Christian accounts of the fall of Spain.

Of Women, Kings, and Nation

Perhaps the most striking literary example of the successful regulation of a king's
inappropriate lust before great harm befalls the kingdom is from a Near Eastern
text, and one that does not insist on the customary Christian dichotomy of good
woman / virgin, bad woman / nonvirgin: the *Alf Layla wa-Layla,* popularly known as
the *Arabian Nights* or *Thousand and One Nights.* The king's custom is to have sexual
intercourse with a virgin each night and order her beheading the next day before

choosing a new virgin for the coming night. The beautiful Shahrazad staves off her execution by weaving nightly tales of bewitching fantasy. However, I would argue, it is no accident that Shahrazad's name means "savior of the city."[8]

But how does she save the city? By preventing the king's normal routine and "healing" him through storytelling, she is training and reeducating the king to renounce his lustful practices and take a wife, to live and love monogamously, and to pay more attention to the matters of the kingdom. Shahrazad simultaneously regulates the king's sexual desire until he marries her at the end of the collection, not only making her queen, but ending the barbaric practice of ritual sex and murder.[9] Shahrazad is a model of the woman who is able to influence the course of government through what can only be called the domestication or sexual regulation of the ruler, earning the meaning of her name, "savior of the city."

That Shahrazad is not a virgin after her first night with the king has no relevance at all to her value in the tale. Her ability to change the king's behavior for the better is completely independent of her status as nonvirgin. In the Western tradition, the association of female sexuality and government brings nothing good with it, and a woman's active sexuality usually carries with it the label of harlot. When women are associated with the positive values of government, as symbols or characters in a narrative, their virginity and chastity matter a great deal, and there are far fewer of them than of sinners. An interesting exception is the case of the sexually available Muslim or Saracen princess, neither virgin nor harlot, a positive figure who aids the Christian nobleman and helps foster and protect Christianity. Her Christian and Jewish sisters fare much worse.

Marbod of Rennes, bishop of Rennes in Brittany (c. 1035–1123), writes in his *Liber Decem Capitulorum* (Book with ten chapters) a section on the whore, in which he rails against the female sex:

> Countless are the traps which the scheming enemy has set throughout the world's paths and plains: but among them the greatest—and the one scarcely anybody can evade—is woman. Woman the unhappy source, the evil root, and corrupt offshoot, who brings to birth every sort of outrage throughout the world. For she instigates quarrels, conflicts, dire dissensions: she provokes fighting between old friends, divides affections, shatters families. But these are trivia I speak of: she dislodges kings and princes from the throne, makes nations clash, convulses towns, destroys cities, multiplies slaughters, brews deadly poisons. (Blamires, *Woman Defamed* 100)

Of the many slings and arrows hurled toward woman, contained within the almost relentless misogyny of centuries of writings, one of the most interesting and titillating is the accusation that a single woman's sexuality can topple a nation. Clearly, Marbod of Rennes believed it not only to be so, but to be woman's most devastating of evil achievements. Centuries earlier, St. Jerome's treatise on the inferiority of marriage, *Against Jovinian,* stated, "In all the bombast of tragedy and the overthrow of houses, cities and kingdoms, it is the wives and mistresses who stir up trouble" (Blamires 74). And further, in his *Letter 22, to Eustochium,* the daughter of his friend Paula, both of whom had dedicated themselves to a life of chastity, Paula as a chaste widow, her daughter as a virgin, Jerome connects the defeat of Samson by Delilah, David's lust for Bathsheba, Solomon's lust for women in general, and Amnon's "illicit passion" for his own sister, Tamar, to the sins of Eve. Even the male gaze was thought to be victimized, rather than the other way around, the male gazer as appropriator of the female gazed-upon: "David was a man after God's own heart, and his lips had often sung of the holy one, the future Christ, yet as he walked upon the roof of his house he was fascinated by Bathsheba's naked beauty, and added murder to adultery. Notice here how, even in his own house, a man cannot use his eyes without danger" (Blamires 75).

Bathsheba is violated by the king, made a widow by his judgment to send her husband to certain death in battle, and yet, in Christian Patristic writings, she bears the blame for inciting the passion of the king. As we can see, then, man was not safe anywhere, not even in his own home; if not assailed by the evils of his wife, other temptations abounded. Removing oneself from society to the wilds of nature provided little relief from the torments of the flesh, as Jerome himself, in recounting his travails in the desert, paints a vivid picture of how much more dangerous woman was to his soul than the most deadly of creatures in his ascetic outpost: "When I was living in the desert, that vast solitude which is parched by the burning sun and affords a savage home for hermits, how often I fantasized that I was among the pleasures of Rome! . . . Now, although in my fear of hell I had consigned myself to this prison, where I had no companions but scorpions and wild beasts, I often found myself surrounded by dancing girls! . . . [T]he fires of lust kept boiling up within me when my flesh (before its tenant) was as good as dead" (Blamires 74–75).

Christian belief in Mary's perpetual virginity ushered in a new law and a new era of female virginity, with an emphasis on female chastity if not virginity for all, and Christ's sacrifice on the cross made possible each individual's eternal salvation. Unfortunately for mankind, however, the daughters of Eve did not disappear with the overturning of the old law and the start of the new. And unfortunately for womankind, an unattainable ideal—the Virgin Mary—captivated the imaginations of sacred and secular writers alike. This resulted in the dichotomy known as Ave-Eva, from the Latin Ave Maria (Hail Mary) in Gabriel's greeting to Mary, and her fallen counterpart, Eve, reinforcing the categories of virgin-harlot and angel-whore, which haunt women to this day. Men born after the time of Jesus Christ continued to have to negotiate the dangerous seas of a world filled with sirens—the female sex—whose only purpose in life appeared to be the spiritual destruction of men through design or even unintentionally, simply through their inherently evil nature. The writings of the Church Fathers and the low opinions of male writers about the ability of women to control their own sexuality, coupled with the Augustinian view of man's own now-frail self-discipline, allowed relentless attacks on woman, sometimes tedious and condescending, sometimes lively and humorous, often dichotomized into catalogs and categories of good women (extremely rare) and bad women (the vast majority).

Certainly, Augustine contributed much to the dichotomous view of women, the implicit, if not explicit, view of the Garden of Eden as the first loss of "nation" through a woman's temptation and man's ongoing vulnerability to female sexuality, establishing a link between sexual activity and the health or sickness of society. Legitimate procreation, sanctioned by the Church, led to civic and national construction of an orderly society. Illicit sexual activity threatened order, and order was always under attack by the inherent evil of woman and the insatiable, often uncontrollable, lustful female sexuality. One of his conclusions about the fall of Adam and Eve, and the fallen state of humanity, is that men lost their original ability to govern themselves. This loss, according to Augustine, ranges from men's inability to prevent involuntary physical reactions to women or thoughts about women, to a penchant for social disorder.[10] As Elaine Pagels tells us, "The war within us [the passions] drives us to war with one another—and no one, pagan or Christian, remains exempt" (113). Another of Augustine's beliefs, shared by other early Christian writers, was the link between the domestic and the public, home and government: "The union of male and female is the seed-bed, so to speak, from which the city must grow . . . Since, then, a man's home [hominis domus] ought to be the beginning or elementary constituent of the city, and every beginning serves some end of its own, and every part serves the integrity of the whole of which it is a part, it follows clearly enough that domestic peace serves civic peace, that is, that the ordered agreement of command and obedience among those who live together in a household serves the ordered agreement of command and obedience among citizens" (*De civitate Dei* [*The City of God*] 15, 16: 19, 13). As with many of Augustine's premises, the loss of self-government—the loss of control over one's own body—lent itself to lavish narrative elaboration and extensive allegorical treatment throughout the Middle Ages and beyond. Extensive writings that predate Christianity expounded on the necessity for a ruler to hold lust in abeyance for the good of the country. Once Augustine promoted the view that the sin in the Garden of Eden was a sexual one initiated by Eve, causing the loss of the first nation that sent us all east of Eden, Christian writers of late antiquity and the Middle Ages accepted this view with unbridled enthusiasm. It was not long before the misogynistic expression expanded the representations of women not just as the physical and political downfall of individual men, and of entire nations, but as the spiritual downfall of both as well, leading to the perdition of the national soul. And from this, it was almost inevitable that such a story as the fall of the Spanish Visigothic kingdom in 711 to the Muslims, with its references to a paradisiac peninsula and the hint of a scandal with a woman, would develop into the legend of the national harlot.

In fifteenth-century Spain, the general consensus on woman's devastating power over monarchs still intact, as well as the view that the overall moral turpitude of a people could destroy a society, Clemente Sánchez de Vercial, archdeacon of Valderás in León, began one of the five hundred brief stories in his *Libro de los enxemplos por a.b.c.* (a book of anecdotes arranged according to the alphabet, translated as *A Book of Tales by A.B.C.*) with the aphorism, "Lewd women make kingdoms fall, for chastity has failed them all."[11] Lest anyone fear that the lewd woman might escape unpunished, Sánchez de Vercial follows this with an anecdote involving the impaling of a lustful queen through her genitalia. Centuries later, the Mexican diplomat Ignacio Ramírez stated in a speech on September 16, 1861, to celebrate that country's independence, "It is one of the mysteries of fate that all nations owe their fall and ignominy to one woman, and to another its salvation and glory; everywhere is repeated the myth of Eve and Mary" (Franco xviii).

The quotation from Sánchez de Vercial's *exemplum* collection reflects a view held about women that predates Christianity, while the second, by Ramírez, ties into at least two strains of the collective popular imagination, as well as that of learned historians, theologians, and fiction writers throughout the centuries. The histories of nations have often been recounted through the mythic pattern of falling and rising again, and more specifically as rehearsals of the Fall of humankind in the Garden of Eden. In stories about a reversal of a fall, the ruler whose tale is being told becomes a kind of Christ figure, whose divinely ordained role on earth is to restore his Christian kingdom or create a Christian empire. In these stories, nations become paradise on earth, and the ruler, God's chosen earthly leader. Such stories look forward and backward: when told by contemporary historians (of any age), they inspire those who must wage war in order for the ruler to achieve his imperial or nationalistic goals; at the same time, the pattern of a rise and fall (and rise again) salves the wounded pride of those citizens whose histories recount bloody and bitter defeats at the hands of their enemies.[12] In Spanish histories and fiction, writers often glorified the reign of a current ruler by portraying contemporary events as a reversal of the fall of Spain in 711, especially up to the conquest of Granada in 1492, after which they tended to portray the rulers as links in the Christian continuum begun by Pelayo. By casting the rise and fall of nations as the handiwork of latter-day Marys and Eves, Ramírez signaled a particular strain of the fall of nations pattern: the woman whose sin—usually a sexual encounter with the ruler—results in the downfall of the individual leader, of his soul and his rule, and extends to the downfall of the nation, civically and spiritually. When a nation's history is told as a manifestation of divine providence, the blame for defeat does not have to be shared by the citizens. In some cases, a decline is the will of God for any number of reasons, or it is a punishment for the transgressive action of the leader himself. Nations have fallen because of women, or so legends claim: Troy had its Helen, and Cleopatra famously used her beauty and seductive powers for her political aims. But what happens when a woman not only "dislodges the king," in the words of Marbod of Rennes, causing the fall of the nation, but at the same time causes the loss of the nation's Christian soul? The evolution of La Cava's story through the centuries reinforces the staying power and the pervasiveness of the myth that a single woman can bring down an entire nation—in the case of eighth-century Spain, using her body to destroy its very soul.

In Alexander Krappe's study, inspired in part by a desire to prove that the source of the story of Rodrigo and La Cava could be other than Arabic, and preferably Christian, he recounts precedents in which the ruler falls because of his inappropriate lust.[13] These examples are human representations of something that had been anthropomorphized centuries earlier, the city as the virgin or the harlot. Indeed, the Bible, myth, and folklore employ this metaphor for the city, and Jung includes it in his catalog of female symbolic fields and exploration of maternal, feminine imagery: "The city is a maternal symbol, a woman who harbours the inhabitants in herself like children . . . Strong unconquered cities are Virgins . . . Cities are also harlots" (208).[14]

Sixteenth-century Europe witnessed an explosion in the use of the dichotomized figure of the woman, angel-whore and Ave-Eva, as the most general categories.[15] This view applied to the lowliest of women and to the most exalted. The ancient attributions of the city as virgin or harlot—stepped up to become nation and empire—enjoyed an extraordinary reincarnation in political discourse, literature, and art. In her book *Chaste Thinking: The Rape of Lucretia and the Birth of Humanism*, Stephanie Jed examines the story of the tyrant Tarquin, his rape of the chaste matron Lucretia, and her subsequent suicide as emblematic of the birth of the nation, and as a symbol used over and over, particularly from the fifteenth century on. Because Lucretia's male relatives were then galvanized to overthrow the tyrant, Lucretia's rape "constituted a founding myth of liberty in the aftermath of sexual violence" (5). The image of the female chaste nation abounded in the sixteenth and seventeenth centuries, particularly the vulnerable chaste nation who needed male protection, for she faced the constant threat of rape, invasion by enemies. This view was aided in no small part in Spain by the memory of Queen Isabel the Catholic and in England by the reign of Queen Elizabeth I.[16] Paintings of chaste Lucretia were popular, and even King Philip II of Spain, who reigned in the second half of the sixteenth century, received a gift of Titian's spectacular rendering of *The Rape of Lucretia*.

While the publicly declared virginity of Elizabeth I of England (however feigned that virginity seems to have been) functioned as empowerment, allowing her access to the world of men, as in the days of earliest Christianity, when public virgins were accorded protection, respect, and above all, mobility, this was not the case for the typical woman of the sixteenth century.[17] For the chaste woman is a powerless one: although she signals no invitation, the mere sight of her and knowledge of her inaccessibility incites the lust of men. Only silence and enclosure can protect the third and most precious aspect of woman, her chastity. Shakespeare alludes to the paradoxical sexual provocativeness of the chaste woman, and the link between sexual possession and the city or nation, not coincidentally, in his work *The Rape of Lucrece:* "This moves in him more rage and lesser pity / to make the breach and enter this sweet city" (vv. 468–69). In other words, Shakespeare's tyrant is excited by Lucrece's chastity, which incites this ruler and military leader to penetrate the "sweet city" of her body.

For all the visual and literary representations of a chaste icon such as Lucretia, Renaissance Europe saw no dearth of harlots. The sixteenth century provided extremely sensual paintings and woodcuts of Eve in seductive poses, Mary Magdalene as the penitent harlot, Jezebel, Delilah, and other women whose dangerous sexuality defined them. The dates of four of Titian's paintings nicely demonstrate the tension of the dichotomized woman in this period, and how they shared the same cultural landscape, if not the same canvas: *The Rape of Lucretia* (1568–1571 and 1570–1576), *The Rape of Europa* (1559–1562; here, rape means "abduction," not sexual violation), and *The Penitent Magdalen* (c. 1560). In this world of heightened depictions of Ave-Eva, the story of La Cava and the king enjoyed renewed interest, and the sexuality of the woman became the focal point of the tale. Consequently, La Cava found herself in this period—post-fifteenth century—in two undesirable locations: (1) she is raped but guilty because she is woman, inherently seductive, even though chaste in personal behavior and modesty, or (2) she is not raped, because

she herself was Eve, who tempted Adam to fall. We will see a few attempts to rehabilitate the reputation of La Cava after the sixteenth century during Romanticism,
though most rehabilitative efforts were exerted on behalf of Rodrigo, as a result of
the Romantic tendency to see tragic heroes everywhere, and because the renewed
efforts to connect modern Spain to the Visigothic kingdom desired a heroic ancestor rather than a scoundrel.

Origins of a National Myth

The peoples of Spain and Provence and Burgundy . . . turned away
from God and lived in harlotry until the Almighty Judge let the
penalty for such crimes fall upon them through ignorance of the
law of God and the coming of the Saracens.

St. Boniface, mid-eighth century

Many a worthy scholar has stumbled trying to sort out the complicated history of
manuscripts and their dates in order to track the evolution of the Muslim conquest
legend. Manuscript transmission, never an easy feat in classical and medieval studies, is particularly difficult here because of the competing versions and the fact that
almost no surviving manuscripts are close in time to the actual historical events.[18]
For our purposes, five puzzle pieces tell us what we need to know: the remarks of
St. Boniface, and two Christian and two Arabic chronicles. Together they laid the
groundwork for Castilian historians of the thirteenth and fourteenth centuries to
begin crafting in earnest a national narrative of the past.

When Boniface, in his missionary letters of the mid-eighth century, refers to "the
harlotry of Spain," he addresses the events that led to the destruction of the Visigothic kingdom in 711. In 746–747, he sent a "Letter of Admonition to King Aethel-
bald of Mercia," on the findings of his travels, that iniquity abounds. He chastises
the king for refusing to marry, preferring instead a debauched life, which included
adulterous lust, and for his encouragement of the clergy and the nobility to embrace
the same behavior: "these crimes are committed in convents with holy nuns and virgins consecrated to God, and this, beyond all doubt, doubles the offense . . . Peter,
prince of the apostles, in his prohibitions against lust says: . . . 'The price of a
harlot is scarcely that of one piece of bread, but a woman steals the precious soul of
a man' . . . [F]ornication is worse than almost any other sin and may truly be described as a snare of death, an abyss of hell, and a whirlpool of perdition" (126–27).
After railing against harlots of all kinds—nuns, married women, disgraced virgins—

Boniface warms to his theme, calling upon the rhetorical tools of fire and brimstone, and the lessons of travel and history:

> If the English people, as is reported here and as is charged against us in France and Italy and even by the heathen themselves, are scorning lawful marriage and living in wanton adultery like the people of Sodom, then we must expect that a degenerate and degraded people with unbridled desires will be produced. At last the whole race will become debased and finally will be neither strong in war nor steadfast in faith, neither honored among men nor pleasing in the sight of God. So it has been with the peoples of Spain and Provence and Burgundy. They turned away from God and lived in harlotry until the Almighty Judge let the penalty for such crimes fall upon them through ignorance of the law of God and the coming of the Saracens. (128)

Many historians refer to this moralizing view of a country's decline as a Decadence Tradition, a national debasement that could assail pagan and Christian kingdoms alike.[19] Boniface's sermonizing tirade asserts the absolute necessity of the ruler's chaste behavior to ensure the continued success of a Christian nation and the general moral well-being of that nation's populace.

The earliest surviving account of the fall of Spain in 711, from either the Christian or Muslim point of view, is the anonymous *Crónica mozárabe de 754* (*Mozarabic Chronicle of 754*), probably written by an ecclesiastic in Toledo, a Mozarab—a Christian living under Muslim rule—slightly after Boniface's epistolary sermons.[20] This chronicle strongly promotes a Decadence Tradition, depicting the invasion as God's scourge to punish the Goths for transgressions of divine law. According to this anonymous chronicler, Rodrigo had usurped the kingdom of the Visigoths, to which he had no entitlement. When the Muslim leader Muza crossed into the Iberian Peninsula, Rodrigo "wretchedly lost not only his rule but his homeland, his rivals also being killed."[21] Muza returned to Spain a second time, forging on to the royal city of Toledo, where he decapitated the nobility, with the help of the treacherous nobleman Oppas.[22] He "condemned lords and powerful men to the cross; and butchered youths and infants with the sword," after which they set up "their savage kingdom . . . in Córdoba." Muza returns to North Africa, leaving his son, Abd al-Aziz (in later accounts, Abdelasis), to govern in Seville. His son marries Egilona, Rodrigo's widow. His men kill him, purportedly because Egilona encouraged him to rebel against the Arab caliphate and keep Spain for himself (Constable 29–32).[23] Many centuries later, historians suggest that good Christian Egilona's advice to her husband was a stratagem to turn the lands back over to the Christians.

The mid-ninth-century Arab historian Ibn 'Abd al-Hakam recounts the events of the fall of Spain from the Muslim perspective in *Futūh Misr'* (*The History of the Conquest of Egypt*) and introduces the storyline of a raped daughter as reason for Julian's willingness to help the Muslims.[24] His history reflects the influence of his likely source material, oral storytelling, which had developed in this period for the purposes of religious devotion, instruction, and entertainment (Constable 32). Ibn 'Abd al-Hakam's *History* retains an authoritative place in Arabic writings. He was the first Arab historian of Egypt, and his seven-volume work (of which book 5 described the Arab conquest of North Africa and Spain) was a source for many subsequent histories. According to Ibn 'Abd al-Hakam, Julian entrusted his daughter to the care of the king for her instruction and education, but the king impregnated her.[25] In general, Arabic chronicles from the ninth century and beyond tended to inflate the prophetic quality of the legend to showcase the providential nature of their victory over the Christians, one that Allah had willed. We saw, in the fifteenth-century version of the legend that opened this chapter, how Rodrigo forced his way into the House of Hercules. That episode originates in Ibn 'Abd al-Hakam's account: Rodrigo refused to honor the ancestry of Toledo by placing a lock on the enchanted edifice, a tradition that endowed the new ruler with authority over his people. Ibn 'Abd al-Hakam includes the prophecy that was to appear repeatedly, that the locked building, rashly and imprudently penetrated by Rodrigo, housed the parchment with drawn pictures of Arabs and the prediction of Muslim triumph over, and domination of, the Iberian Peninsula: "When this door is opened, these people will conquer this country."

Tarik and Muza storm into Toledo, hoping to acquire a valuable jewel-encrusted table that Rodrigo reputedly had, and which had legendarily belonged to King Solomon.[26] Later in the narrative, instead of Rodrigo's widow marrying Muza's son, Abd al-Aziz (or Abdelasis), it is Rodrigo's daughter who does so.[27] She brings him a fortune in worldly goods, but misfortune in life: "When she came to him she said, 'Why do I not see the people of your kingdom glorifying you? They do not prostrate themselves before you as the people of my father's kingdom glorified him and prostrated themselves before him'" (Constable 32–36).[28] Abd al-Aziz constructs such a small door in his palace that all who enter must bow down to him. The people are angry at this show of pride, and further, they suspect that his wife has convinced him to become a Christian. They ambush him in a garden one night, where he cowers under a bush. In spite of his pleas for mercy, they cut off his head.

Our second important Christian history after the *Crónica mozárabe de 754* is the Asturian *Crónica de Alfonso III* (Chronicle of Alfonso III), which invents the story of the hero Pelayo. From the late ninth century, *Crónica de Alfonso III* is modeled on

Bishop Isidore of Seville's seventh-century *Historia Gothorum* (*History of the Goths*).[29] Isidore traces the rise of the Goths, while the Asturian chronicler shows how they fell from grace, lost their kingdom, and had to rebuild it.[30] *Crónica de Alfonso III* was a self-congratulatory history, designed to demonstrate that "Alfonso was not to be just another conqueror of Spain, but the heir to a past regime, fighting to restore his birthright" (Wolf 48).[31] Alfonso, who reigned from 866 to 910, ordered the composition of the chronicle, in which the theory was first presented that the Asturian king was the legitimate heir to the defeated Visigothic king.

Crónica de Alfonso III depicts this king's crucial role as the driving force to initiate reconquest of the peninsula. Instead of attributing all blame to Rodrigo's governance, *Crónica de Alfonso III* finds that iniquity pervaded the kingdom, and stemmed from the debasement of King Witiza, King Rodrigo's predecessor. Among Witiza's sins, he took many concubines and wives, and ordered the clergy to do the same, a sin that Alfonso III would repress in his rule. Contradicting the earlier Christian chronicle of 754, this chronicle insists on Rodrigo's right to the Visigothic throne, indeed that his entitlement to the throne came from his family legacy, and that his grandfather had been a Visigothic king. The idea that Witiza had already weakened the kingdom, making repair impossible for Rodrigo, and thereby justifying why the Muslims defeated the peninsula so handily, became an important theme much later, gaining great currency in the sixteenth century, such that it was repeated as fact in the nineteenth century and even in Sánchez Albornoz's 1972 history of the Asturian kingdom.

By far, the longest part of the *Crónica de Alfonso III* invents the history of Pelayo at Covadonga. Pelayo, the sword-bearer of the kings Witiza and Rodrigo, fled to the region of Asturias, in the north of Spain, where the Muslims and Christians lived in an uneasy relationship, although the Muslims clearly dominated. The local Muslim ruler, Munuza, fancied Pelayo's sister, so he sent Pelayo away to Córdoba on a mission of sorts and married the sister.[32] He then instructed his men to return Pelayo to Asturias bound in chains. Pelayo escaped the trap and sought refuge in a cave dedicated to the Virgin Mary, Covadonga. The men to whom Pelayo had given the slip reported to Munuza that Pelayo's goal was to stir up a rebellion. Sending both an enormous army and the treacherous Bishop Oppas to negotiate with Pelayo, Munuza determined to quash the rebels one way or another. Pelayo's defiant speech to Oppas, repeated in the legend for centuries thereafter, places his trust in God and Christianity.

Convinced by the failure of Oppas' conversation that only the sword could deter Pelayo, Munuza's army prepared for battle, setting up catapults, drawing their flashing swords, brandishing spears, and preparing slings. But when the Muslims launched

Witiza, by Arnold van Westherhout (Flemish, 1651–1725).
Engraving, 17 × 13 cm. From Agustinus Niphus, *Effigies et
series regum Hispaniae, primum ex gothis christianorum dein
ex iisdem castellanis et austriacis catholicorum.* Rome, 1684.
Courtesy of The Hispanic Society of America, New York.

the stones and shot the arrows toward the Christians, and very near Mary's cave, the
Lord, who tolerates no disrespect or sacrilege to his mother, miraculously intervened,
causing the weapons to turn around in midair and fall upon the "Chaldeans," as the
chronicle calls the Muslims, killing some 124,000 warriors. The survivors, 63,000 of
them, scaled a mountain in the hope of escaping with their lives. But upon reaching the summit, the Lord cracked open the mountain at its base, hurling the enemy
into the river below, and crushing them under the falling rock and soil. Pelayo's victory sets the Christians on the road to restore what had been lost, which they—and
Pelayo's own words—attributed to God's divine plan.

Pelayo lived as king for nineteen years (718–737), and his son Favila succeeded
him: but Favila had ruled for only two years (737–739) when he was mauled by a

bear. Alfonso, the son of the duke of Cantabria, a region of Asturias, and a member of the royal line, had married Pelayo's daughter Ermesinda.[33] The coronation of Alfonso I formally initiated the Asturian line of kings, but it was the rule of Alfonso III that forged a number of significant convergences, which brought together the religious, the political, and the military. Under Alfonso III, late ninth-century Christians "considerably extended the boundaries of the Asturian-Leonese kingdom. Alfonso's sons and subjects speak of him as 'magnus imperator.' No longer did the Christians feel themselves humbled in the face of the Moors: their monarchs, once simply *principes* or *reges,* they now called *imperatores*" (Castro, *The Spaniards* 383).

At the beginning of the ninth century, Christians in northwest Spain began to venerate a sepulcher in the city of Compostela, reputed to be the resting place of James the Apostle. Castro tells us that the cult of St. James developed precisely as a means of furthering Christian military zeal:

> If Spain had not been submerged by Islam, the cult of Santiago of Galicia would not have prospered; but the anxiety of the eighth and ninth centuries fortified the faith in a Santiago the brother of Christ, who, like a new manifestation of Castor, would achieve magnificent victories, riding his shining white charger. Similar miracles had occurred elsewhere occasionally, but without taking on transcendent importance; . . . The cult of Santiago was not a simple manifestation of piety eventually useful in the struggle against the Moor. The truth is, on the contrary, that the belief emerged out of the humble plane of folklore and assumed immeasurable dimensions as an answer to what was happening on the Muslim side: a type of war sustained and won by religious faith was to be opposed (not rationally, of course) by another fighting faith, grandly spectacular, strong enough in turn to sustain the Christian and carry him to victory. (382)

Alfonso III supported the view that Santiago, the place, rivaled Rome as a center for Catholicism, and he "is precisely the one who had the first proper church built in honor of the Apostle: 'And he caused the church of St. James to be built, all of carved stone, with pillars of marble; *for the one before this had been made of earth*'" (Castro, *The Spaniards* 386, quoting from Alfonso the Learned's *Estoria de España* [History of Spain]). In sum, Alfonso III increased the size of the kingdom, which greatly increased the morale of his subjects; ordered the composition of the chronicle that documented an origin for that kingdom in the legend of Pelayo, as well as providing an exemplary tale of the victory of the outnumbered but valiant and ultimately successful Asturians against the Muslims; and by ordering the construction of the church in honor of Santiago, he recognized the significance or potential significance of the Moor-slaying saint for a people launched on a religious, military mission.

Historians believe that Muslim, not Christian, writers further contributed to the development of the legend of the daughter, especially in specifying the sexual act as a rape. Not until the thirteenth and fourteenth centuries did Christian chroniclers begin, first of all, to include this episode and then showcase it as the central event of the legend. The Arab historian credited with developing this aspect of the legend is the most important historian of Al-Andalus, Ahmad al-Razi, typically referred to in Christian writings as Rasis the Moor (c. 950–970). His popularity helped diffuse the legend, and many historians believe he enlarged the role of the daughter and gave the name House of Hercules to the locked edifice. The specific nature of Rasis' contributions remain greatly debated since all manuscripts are lost. What we think we know about Rasis and the legend of the fall comes from references to him in other Arab histories; from later manuscripts that purport to be translations of his history, specifically a thirteenth-century Portuguese translation; and from various attempts to reconstruct the lost work, which depends on a tremendous amount of luck and guesswork. Although historians can find no direct evidence of Rasis' contributions, indirect, though possibly incorrect, historical testimonies abound, even in the sixteenth and seventeenth centuries, in which authors cite Rasis and then reveal that they did not see Rasis' work firsthand but are borrowing from others who claim Rasis as one of their sources.[34]

Most Arab historians portrayed the aggrieved father, Count Julian, with great sympathy. As the loving father whose cherished daughter had been deflowered by the very king who should have protected her, the Count Julian of Muslim legend behaves in an understandably human fashion. The exception comes from the historiographer Ibn al-Kittaya, who lived in the late tenth century and claimed descent from Witiza.[35] Interested in redeeming the reputation of his forefather Witiza, so bitterly denounced in the *Crónica de Alfonso III,* Ibn al-Kittaya deviates from the Muslim historical line of argument in his notably hostile portrayal of Julian.

One small piece of the storyline—often absent in the earliest versions of the tale—will prove to be of utmost importance for the increasingly gendered, antifeminist versions of La Cava's seduction and rape, especially in the oral ballad tradition. How did her father find out what the king had done? Two earlier Arabic examples, from the second half of the twelfth century, propose a clever and unusual way for the daughter to get word to her father.

Both the anonymous *Kitab-al-Ictifa* and the *Fatho-l-Andaluci* concur that Rodrigo's greed for treasure led him to break the locks of the seemingly impenetrable palace in Toledo, despite the petitions and warnings of the counts and bishops who counseled him. They pleaded with him that if it were diamonds, pearls, gold, and silver that he wanted, they would get him all he needed. These historians go beyond the earlier, somewhat succinct, prophecy to say that the parchment contained "drawings of men wearing turbans, astride noble steeds, and carrying scimitars, lances and a banner that read: 'These men are Arabs. They will conquer the land when the locks of this palace have been forced open, and the violator will repent his deed'" (Menéndez Pidal, *Floresta* 1: 40–41). Repentance was in short supply until this version, but again, Christian chronicles picked up this detail, which engendered Pedro de Corral's historical romance and an entire ballad cycle on the topic of Rodrigo's remorse. The king draws no parallel between the forcing of the locks and the forcing of the girl, the prophecy and the sexual act, though every self-respecting reader does.

He does, however, regret the rape out of fear of her father's vengeance. The king keeps Alacaba under lock and key, forbidding her to speak alone with anyone, or to write to her father. However, he grants her permission to gather some precious objects to send to her father as a gift, into which she is able to slip a rotten egg. The count, perplexed at first to find this broken, unsavory object among the rich and luxurious offerings, pensively considers it until the light dawns: his daughter, like the rotten egg, is no longer intact, but broken and corrupted.[36]

To recap, then, the earliest chronicle, a mozarabic history from around the mid-eighth century, crafts the details of the fall of Spain in 711 as a story of moral decadence. The chronicler carefully avoids any language that casts the invasion as a holy war. The way he tells it, God witnessed his people's iniquity and punished them. Any plunderer could have succeeded because it was God's will. He always refers to the Arabs by regional names, for good reason, to avoid any mention of Islam and Allah, and to insist on a vanquished people but not a defeat of Christianity. At roughly the same time, the mid- and late ninth century, two competing narratives develop, one Muslim, one Christian. The Muslim chronicle, which does claim that Allah willed an Islamic victory over Christianity, introduces the features of the king's pride, the prophecy of Arab victory in the Toledan edifice, and the sexual dishonor of Julian's daughter as the event that impelled the conquest. The Asturian Christian chronicle continues the theory of the iniquitous kingdom and God's justified punishment of it, makes no mention of Julian or a specific sexual act by the king, but, most significantly, invents the history of Pelayo, conqueror of the conquerors. At the same time, the cult of St. James the Moorslayer begins to serve as a focal point for the growing belief that Christian military expansion in the peninsula enjoys divine support.

CHAPTER TWO

Granada Is the Bride

Granada is the bride whose headdress is the Alhambra, and whose jewels and adornments are its flowers.

Ibn Zamrak, poet (1333–1393)

In ancient times the Goths agreed among themselves that the empire of Spain should never be divided but that all of it should always be under one lord.

Spoken by Prince Sancho to his father,
King Fernando I (1035–1065), from Alfonso the Learned's
Estoria de España (History of Spain)

The Christians' thirst for al-Andalus became quite evident.

Memoirs of 'Abd Allah, King of Granada (1073–1090)

A story circulated in the Middle Ages about the parents of the English saint Thomas Becket, archbishop of Canterbury (1118–1170). During his father's travels to the East—he was a pilgrim or a crusader—Zulima, the daughter of the emir of Acre in Jerusalem, fell deeply in love with him. Held captive by her father, Gilbert Becket saw no escape. But the princess helped him deceive her father, and Becket fled from Jerusalem. The princess, unable and unwilling to live without him, journeyed across the continents to find him. Aside from the dangers and difficulties of such travels, Zulima had no knowledge of the countries or of geography. She wandered through Europe, repeating the only two English words she knew, "London" and "Becket," until at last she found him. It was just in the nick of time, for Gilbert was about to marry another woman. Zulima converted to Christianity, married her beloved, and fostered in her son Thomas a devotion to Our Lady and Christianity in general.[1]

Becket was not the only famous medieval with putative Muslim roots. Spanish and French stories of Floire and Blancheflor, or Flores and Blancaflor, claimed Charlemagne as a grandson of the Muslim King Floire, who converted to Christianity.

Much more popular than that storyline was one about Charlemagne's first wife being a Muslim princess, daughter of Galafre, a Muslim king of Toledo:

The young, brash prince Mainete (Charlemagne) traveled with his valet and tutor Morante to Saracen country in the Iberian Peninsula, after a falling out with his father, King Pepin. Mainete's prowess so impressed King Galafre of Toledo that the young French prince participated in military service for the Muslim ruler. Then news riveted the kingdom, of the imminent arrival of Bramante, the Muslim suitor of the king's daughter, Galiana, who intended to win her against the wishes of her father. While Bramante and his men cut a swath across Galafre's army, Morante attempted to awaken the sleeping French prince, who was missing all the action. The French had joined the Muslims in the fight, leaving the castle empty. Upon awakening, Mainete complained aloud that he was all alone in the castle. Galiana heard him, and after extracting from him a promise that he would take her to France, make her a Christian, and marry her, she gave him the sword Joyosa, a gift to her from Bramante. Galiana dressed him in armor, prepared him for battle, and provided him with a horse, also a gift from Bramante. Mainete rode into battle, and with one fierce stroke cut off Bramante's arm, gaining the famous sword Durandarte in the bargain. Bramante sped away on his horse, but Mainete followed him, cut off his head, and took his horse. The victorious Mainete returned to Toledo but feared that the king would never allow such a valuable vassal to leave, even to return home. On the pretext that he was going hunting, Mainete and his men stole away to France. Morante returned for Galiana, and after a breakneck escape in which Galafre's soldiers pursued the French, Galiana arrived in France, converted to Christianity, and wed her prince.

This is the legend of the exploits of the young Charlemagne as told in the monumental thirteenth-century *Estoria de España,* or *Primera crónica general* (First general chronicle), compiled during the reign of King Alfonso X, el Sabio or the Learned, of Castile and León (1252–1284); according to Alfonso, a castle in Toledo became known as the "palaces of Galiana," the ruins of which still appears today in guidebooks to Toledo.[2] Although Charlemagne's historically verifiable campaigns against the Saracens south of the Pyrenees in the late 770s grew to be the stuff of epic and legend, we have no historical evidence to support the legend of a Toledan apprenticeship, let alone that he married a Muslim princess. To form a cohesive narrative, the tale combines various well-known folk motifs. The backbone of the story, a motif known as "the ogre's daughter," derives from tales in which the daughter of the enemy Other betrays her father (and often, by extension, her religion, homeland, or both) by aiding the hero, usually in return for marriage.[3] Even though

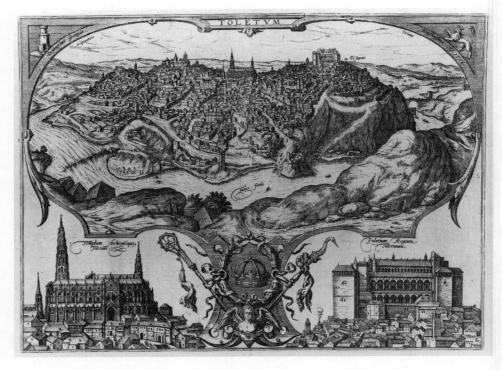

View of Toledo, 1572–1593, Joris Hoefnagle (Flemish, 1542–1600). Engraving, 37.8 × 49 cm. From Georgius Bruin and Franz Hohenberg, *Theatre des cites du monde* (Civitates Orbis Terrarum), Trans. unknown [Brussels: ca. 1572–1593]. Courtesy of The Hispanic Society of America, New York.

Mainete is not a prisoner—though that element enters once Mainete fears he will be kept in Toledo against his wishes—the narrative sets up the initial conflict as one of religious and cultural difference between the Christian hero and the Muslim heroine. The hero must show his prowess far from home, which Mainete does, before a triumphant homecoming. The protagonist is often a "reluctant hero," which this narrative renders by Mainete's inability to wake up in time for the fight, delaying his entry to battle. The hero often kills the villain with the villain's own weapon, usually a sword or knife, metaphorically casting the battle in phallic terms, which Mainete does here using the sword Joyosa, while riding Bramante's own horse, another folk image of sexual power and domination.

Generally, in this strain of medieval tales of love, of which many existed, the Christian nobleman stands for Christianity itself. Love, marriage, and Christianity become inextricably linked. It is a hallmark of the medieval Saracen or Muslim princess that nothing obstructs her determination to become a Christian, just as nothing stands in the way of her marriage to the prince or nobleman. That is certainly the moral of the story of Becket's mother, and one of the morals in the case of Galiana and Charlemagne. But, as Louise Mirrer demonstrated in her fascinating study on women, Jews, and Muslims in medieval texts, medieval Spain offers abundant variations of this story, including the formula that the Christian hero stood not only for Christianity, but for Christian dominance in the form of territory control, while the Muslim woman stood for Islam and Muslim-controlled lands: if you dominate the woman, you dominate the enemy and take his property.

This chapter has two goals: first, to consider how the thirteenth and fourteenth centuries, a formative time for the growth of the Christian kingdoms, developed the legend of the loss of the Visigothic kingdom in 711 and the beginning of Spain's "restoration"; and second, to suggest, by way of examining stories of the "helpful Muslim princess" and the "seductive Jewess," that gendered narratives form an essential part of the national legends of Spain. The first two topics—what happened in eighth-century Spain and tales of "Muslim princesses"—develop as part of the evolving narratives of Christian conquest of Muslim-controlled lands. In both cases, stories about women become metaphors for the broader conflict between Christianity and Islam. Unlike the Salomes and the Helens, who specialize in the death of men, the Saracen princess is a type in narrative that represents sex in the service of life, love, and land. The archetypal "seductive Jewess" finds Iberian representation in the story of the concubine of Alfonso VIII, the beautiful Jewess of Toledo, in later accounts named Fermosa or Raquel. In its historical context, the tale is a metaphor for the concern of the Christian nobility about the strong connections between the Jews and the monarchy, and for the growing and more openly demonstrated hostility toward Jews, which ended the fourteenth century with massive slaughters of Iberian Jews. All the narratives discussed in this chapter contribute to an increasing tendency to expand the role of women, albeit in extremely different ways, in the creation and evolution of Spain's national legends.

The three most informative histories for the legends discussed in this chapter are by the erudite and powerful archbishop of Toledo, Rodrigo Ximénez de Rada, known as El Toledano, King Alfonso the Learned, and the anonymous *Crónica de 1344* (Chronicle of 1344).[4] In very broad terms, we can say that El Toledano legitimized in 1243 the telling of the fall of Spain as a rape narrative. Before his Latin history, the rape could have been dismissed simply as a fictional Arabic invention and ignored in favor of the Decadence Tradition, the argument of the iniquity of the general populace of Spain. In addition, El Toledano elaborated the legend of Pelayo, creating a narrative diptych that the fall of Spain began with the dishonor associated with a woman, and that the restoration began the same way.[5] King Alfonso's history, written in Castilian and widely diffused, contributed a tonal or attitudinal difference to the telling of the legend by focusing on the failure of kingship and the grave responsibility held by kings—and by his inclusion of nationalist legends that highlighted the role of women. The author of the anonymous *Crónica de 1344*, like El Toledano, utilizes Arabic and Latin sources but elaborates the material about La Cava in particular.

Using History to Shape a National Past

The Spanish quest for military expansion and a Christian empire, encouraged by the Church and the powerful nobility of the Iberian Peninsula, consumed the rulers of thirteenth-century Spain. The encyclopedic histories compiled during the thirteenth century, a time that witnessed the continuation of the great Hispano-Latin tradition of historical writings and the birth of vernacular historiography, celebrated Spain's past in order to foster nationalistic impulses and patriotic sentiments. Spain enjoyed a period of self-confidence. By mid-century, major Muslim cities had fallen to Christian forces, leaving only the still-powerful Granada.

El Toledano completed his *Historia de los hechos de España* or *De Rebus Hispaniae* (History of the deeds of Spain) in 1243, in which his formidable erudition allowed him to draw on a wide range of historical testimony, including manuscripts of Arabic histories. Regarded without exception as the pinnacle of the Hispano-Latin historiographical tradition, El Toledano's ambitious and lengthy chronicle is the immediate forerunner of the vernacular high point in Castilian historiography, King Alfonso X's *Estoria de España*.[6] Probably born in 1170 in Puente la Reina, Navarre, of Navarrese and Castilian nobility, Rodrigo Ximénez de Rada became one of the most influential bishops of his time, indeed of the Hispano-medieval period. Diplomat and confessor to kings, El Toledano played a formative role in the 1212 Battle of Las Navas de Tolosa, of which his history offers a firsthand account. He was also instrumental in the founding of universities and other centers of learning. His power and influence were such that he was often an emissary to Rome on behalf of the kings of Spain and was used as a diplomat by the pope himself. He died in 1247, and his body, reputed to be incorrupt, in the state of sanctity reserved for the holiest of human beings, to this day lies in the monastery of Santa María de Huerta.[7]

King Alfonso X's role as the constructor of Castilian culture cannot be overestimated. As a poet, defender of the use of the vernacular as the dignified expression of a nation's history, compiler, collaborator, and patron of the encyclopedic gathering of knowledge in thirteenth-century Spain, Alfonso X stands as a monument to learning. He yearned to be the Holy Roman Emperor and extend Christian territory as his father had done. His great-grandfather, Alfonso VIII, along with a coalition of Christian princes from Iberia and foreign kingdoms, won the Battle of Las Navas de Tolosa on July 16, 1212, widely considered the military triumph that turned the tide of ongoing conquest in favor of the Christians. Alfonso X's father, Fernando III, later called the Saint and formally canonized in 1671, permanently united the kingdoms of Castile and León and captured the important cities of Córdoba in 1236, Jaén in 1246, and Seville in 1248. Alfonso was poised to extend his kingdom inside the peninsula and beyond, as long as the Muslims could be contained and the French could be controlled politically. And, as had happened in the earlier chronicles and would continue to happen for centuries, the legend of the fall of Spain served as an authentic touchstone for commentary on the contemporary period.

For the most part, the stylistic differences between El Toledano and the Castilian king are of degree and tone rather than of content. El Toledano emphasizes the deeds and counsels of wise and virtuous bishops throughout his history, while Alfonso's work tends to locate itself temporally through references to which king was governing when, or how long into a particular monarch's reign certain events took place. At times, and not surprisingly, El Toledano's chapters read like church history punctuated by references to the world outside the ecclesiastical concerns, such as the leader's cruel treatment of the people, or the bubonic plague that assailed the populace, all calling for yet another council of church hierarchy, usually held in Toledo. As Averil Cameron demonstrated for the early centuries of Christianity, the bishops and their councils—from the papal-sanctioned grand councils to the smaller, regional and partial ones—forged a Christian discourse that was often characterized by their views on political theory, in particular on the nature of monarchy. El Toledano contributes to the ongoing narrative of Christian history and appropriates as well the view of the past as a way to shape the present and the future. In fact, Américo Castro points out that El Toledano's history initiates the descriptions of the military conflicts between the North African Arabs and the Christians of the Iberian Peninsula as one of continuous holy war between Islam and Christianity (*The Spaniards* 12). In that sense, although we tend to reject the idea that the Iberian medievals writ large thought in terms of "reconquest," a term that is a modern invention, it is the case that even early official historians, such as El Toledano, did cast the conflicts as a series of Christian falls and redemptions in a large, providential design of returning the peninsula to Christian domination.[8]

Like El Toledano, Alfonso masked a political agenda in his history, and both of them moved Castile to the center of their narratives. Charles Fraker demonstrates in *The Scope of History* how Alfonso develops two parallel lines of argument about the lineage of kings. On the one hand, he traces an unbroken line of Visigothic kings, locating himself as the current holder of that throne and heir to that line of descent, not an easy task given the history of the Visigoths and the realities of the medieval Spanish kingdoms.[9] On the other hand, Alfonso relentlessly pursued the notion of empire and himself as the heir to the imperial crown, which manifests itself in the linkages he creates between himself and political and historical roads to Rome. He was determined to be crowned Holy Roman Emperor, which he believed was his right as a grandson of Frederick of Barbarossa, king of Sicily and Holy Roman Emperor, and which Alfonso did achieve in 1257.

Both El Toledano and Alfonso the Learned promote the view, found earlier in St. Boniface, that the morally corrupt body politic, as embodied by the king, adversely affects the already morally corrupt inhabitants of the kingdom. All three writers employ the concept of *flagellum Dei,* in which such national debauchery is punished by God, resulting in a spiritual fall from grace, as well as death and destruction. But it is toward the reign of Witiza, the king so roundly denounced in the Asturian Christian chronicles we saw earlier, that El Toledano truly releases the fire and brimstone—Witiza may have hidden his lustful appetites until assuming the throne, but having achieved this goal, he gave full rein to his desires: "Y si bien antes su libidinosidad quedaba a escondidas, ahora ya saca por completo a la luz la desvergüenza de su pasión y, a rienda suelta, no se abstuvo de ningún pecado" (And if earlier he kept his libidity hidden, now the shame of his passion was completely out in the light, and, unbridled, he did not abstain from any sin whatsoever; *Historia de los hechos,* bk. 3, chap. 15: 140). Not content with his own debauchery, he sets a terrible example, imitated subsequently by the nobility and the lower classes, Ximénez de Rada tells us. Most shockingly, Witiza forces the clergy to take as many wives and lovers as they want, completely disregarding the prohibitions issued by the Church in Rome. The language El Toledano employs to convey the moral decay is heavy with sermonizing drama, the people "drowning in the depths of their sins," the customary resilience of the Visigoths overcome by the accumulation and weight of their iniquity. One of his most eloquent lamentations mirrors earlier sources in extolling the physical amplitude of the Visigothic kingdom and its bounty, and the beauty of Spain, but he adds his own personal elegy for the wisdom of its many bishops, naming ten of them, all of whose struggles to further the Church would now appear to have been for nought.[10] In describing the debased Witiza, and particularly in stating that Witiza forced the priests into sexual debauchery, El Toledano shows his debt to the earlier Asturian chronicles, specifically *Crónica de Alfonso III.*[11]

Interestingly, in spite of the pervasive sins of the people, with their emphasis on sexual licentiousness, from which the Visigothic kings are not exempt, El Toledano most blames Count Julian, beginning his criticism with a powerful phrase from Genesis: "Maldita sea la obcecación de la ímpia locura de Julián y la crueldad de su rabia, maniático por su ceguera, empujado por su rabia, arrojado por su locura, olvidado de la lealtad, descuidado de la religión, desdeñador de la divinidad, cruel contra sí mismo, asesino de su señor, enemigo de los suyos, aniquilador de su patria, culpable contra todos. Que su recuerdo amargue cualquier boca y que su nombre se pudra para siempre." (Accursed be the obsession of Julian's impious madness, and the cruelty of his rage, maniacal in his blindness, impelled by his rage, driven by his madness, forgetful of loyalty, disregarding of religion, disdainer of Divinity, cruel against himself, assassin of his lord, enemy of his own people, annihilator of his country, guilty against everyone. May his memory be bitter on every tongue and his name rot forever; *Historia de los hechos*, bk. 3, chap. 20: 148).[12] The influence of El Toledano and his history through the centuries was enormous, and the cursing of Julian, which El Toledano claimed could be found engraved on the very tomb, lasted for many centuries in the subsequent historical and literary reportings of the tomb in Viseu, Portugal, and the epitaph. In the sixteenth century, Ambrosio de Morales declared it to be apocryphal, but this specific invention of El Toledano had endured without serious challenge until then, and historians and poets continued to include it, disregarding the criticism by Morales.

The arguments in these histories of the thirteenth century were religious and political, but they were not racial. What is not in El Toledano's account, according to Castro—and he is correct—is the belief in or emphasis on bloodlines, that the inhabitants of thirteenth-century Castile, which El Toledano calls variously Hispani or Christiani, were direct descendants of the Visigoths, whom he refers to as Gothi (*The Spaniards* 10–14). This distinguishes the kind of Gothic theories that were advanced in thirteenth-century Spain from their manifestations in the fifteenth century, with its sociopolitical conflicts based on so-called "purity of blood." Only then did it become significant for society's members to trace their roots back to the Visigoths themselves.

La Cava and the King . . . and Pelayo and His Sister

Arabic chronicles included references to Julian's violated daughter, which the early Christian chronicles did not. Christian chronicles crafted their narratives as an Iberian fall from paradise, while the ninth- or tenth-century chronicles invented a story of redemption in the legend of Pelayo, initiating what later chronicles and kings would celebrate recurrently, their own "redemptive acts" of regaining lost Christian land. None of these Arabic or Christian chronicles initially perceived this as the story of a woman and her dangerous sexuality, nor did the thirteenth- and fourteenth-century histories that included the falling out between the king and the count over Julian's daughter.

Hispano-medieval works of various genres positively revel in scenes of illicit sex and adultery, and the association of sex and bloodletting, when they suit the purpose of the narrative. One can find accounts, as early as the twelfth century, of female sexual carnivores, women who made the lives of the counts of Castile hell when they did not wreck those lives completely.[13] It was not reticence and restraint that stayed the hand of the chroniclers who recounted the fall of 711. Nor was it a lack of imagination; we saw in chapter 1 of this study how inventive writers could be on the topic of woman as threat to king and throne, and Hispano-medieval writers and audiences were no strangers to invective against woman. It was, quite simply, that the story possessed far and away enough richness in the exploration of the broken bonds of male friendship, the threat to Church and State of corrupt and treacherous clergy, the elements of dynastic struggles, and the idea of God's divine punishment to an iniquitous though still-favored people. When circumstances changed that welcomed an antifeminist treatment of La Cava and other women, the malleability of the legend allowed for room to rail against women.

La Cava becomes a much more prominent character thanks to El Toledano's inclusion of the rape in his history, and the *Crónica de 1344*'s elaboration of her as a character. Alfonso X's version of the legend follows almost exactly El Toledano's treatment of it. None of the three works blames La Cava directly for the fall of Spain. There is a distinction to be made, however, between blame and cause. In all three histories, the sexual sin precipitates—causes—the chain of events that leads to the invasion and defeat, but the blame lies with the king and, even more in this particular period, with Julian. The distinction between being a cause but not to blame begins to blur in the fifteenth and sixteenth centuries, as authors warmed generally to the theme of "dangerous woman, the downfall of men," and saw the potential for just such a headline—"Woman topples throne"—in the story of Rodrigo and La Cava. In that sense, the works I am about to discuss serve as transitions by making accessible the material previously found only in Arabic histories, and by expanding the role of La Cava in the narrative. But we can easily see how little medieval writers had associated La Cava with blame by considering briefly a work written during the reign of Sancho IV, the son of Alfonso the Learned, that includes La Cava in anecdotes about both wretched and exemplary behavior of men and women.

Castigos e documentos para bien vivir ordenados por el Rey don Sancho IV (Correctives and advice for proper living, a compilation ordered by King Sancho IV) was a manual designed to give rulers sound moral, ethical, and political advice by example, anecdote, maxim, and historical experience. Composed in the late thirteenth or very early fourteenth century, the work offers strong evidence that La Cava bore no blame until Pedro de Corral's depiction of her in the fifteenth century. The prologue of *Castigos e documentos* attributes the fall to "la maldad e trayçión abominable delo malo conde don Julián" (the evil and abominable treachery of bad Count Julián; 33), and references to the Visigothic kingdom occur twice, in chapters that warn of the dangers of the flesh and the iniquity of the traitor. The ruler must be on his guard against both. Failure in the realm of the flesh brings God's wrath and wreaks havoc on a kingdom. Kings who give in to their appetites are like pigs who roll in their own filth and see no shame in it. While the majority of the anecdotes on the dangers of the flesh focus, sometimes in a humorous manner, on the corruption and lasciviousness of woman, whose garrulousness, along with her unbridled sexuality, will surely result in the publicity of any secret sin, the reference to La Cava follows directly on the few anecdotes of good women the author provides and places the blame squarely and solely on Rodrigo, a sinner: "Para mientes quánto mal vino en Espanna por lo que fizo el rey don Rodrigo con la Caba, fija del conde don Julián" (Note how much evil was visited upon Spain because of what King Rodrigo did with la Caba, the daughter of Count Julián; 60).

The wise ruler looks for loyalty and truth from his councilors. The dangerous traitor gives bad counsel and even conspires to kill the ruler. In this chapter, all the traitors are men: Aeneas lost Troy and then betrayed the noble Dido; Judas betrayed Jesus; traitors sold out Alexander; and even the counts of Castile were betrayed by their friends and vassals. Reiterating the prologue, the last example states that Count Julián caused Rodrigo to lose all of Spain.

For his part, El Toledano makes an important contribution in his history to how the story was later told. The ninth-century Asturian chronicles had invented the story of how Pelayo stopped the Muslim marauders advancing north, and they included brief mention of a sister abducted by the Muslim leader Munuza. But these old Christian chronicles did not include any reference to Julian's daughter, while El Toledano does. He creates a narrative "diptych of dishonor," in which Julian's loss of honor leads him to betrayal of the homeland, allowing the Muslims in, while Pelayo's dishonor awakens in him the conviction that, in his nascent homeland, it is up to him to get the Muslims out. He refused to accept the stain of dishonor that Munuza's abduction of his sister placed on him, El Toledano tells us, and retires to the Cave of Covadonga, where he contemplates a plan for "the liberation of his homeland" (la liberación de la patria; *Historia de los hechos de España*, bk. 4, chap. 1: 161), with the successful outcome, helped along by miraculous aid, that the earlier Christian chronicles relate. In this narrative creativity, El Toledano avails himself of symbols that medieval society easily recognized. As Peggy McCracken showed in her work on medieval queenship and sexual transgressions, any sexual acts performed by women, such as adultery, or in the case of rape, acts done to women, always reflected on the honor of the husband or male relative and remained a challenge for him to take up.[14]

The *Crónica de 1344* is a crucial link between the early Muslim chronicles and fifteenth-century versions that make La Cava and the rape central to the legend. This accompanied a narrative development that focused on the historical event as cautionary tale: "Greater emplotment favored fictionalization of data, and the protagonists began to live personal lives outside their office. Once-marginalized characters— commoners, women, children, Jews—now occupied the stage of history formerly dominated by male monarchs" (Dyer 148). In this chronicle, Julian's daughter, Alataba, goes to the court at the suggestion of the king, who wants to use the position and power of the court to find her the best husband possible. The text makes a point of the virtue of the daughter: "Avía nonbre don Jullano, e avía huna hija muy fermosa e muy buena donzella e que avía muy gran sabor de seer muy buena muger" (His name was don Julian, and he had a most beautiful and virtuous daughter, who greatly desired to become a very good wife; chap. 56: 97). New to this version is the information that the daughter was out walking with other maidens, and the king, passing by, caught a glimpse of her lovely leg, which sent him reeling. He gets her alone, pleads with her to sleep with him, flattering her and promising ecstasy, then resorting to force when she won't agree. This starts a trend, for in the fifteenth century and beyond, Rodrigo's lust and act of rape will be cast as the natural and understandable impulses of a man in love. Ballads will be created that speak of Rodrigo's amorous feelings, attempts at seduction, and forcing himself upon her as the result of passionate love. The verb *esforçar*, "to force," which would be a logical one for rape, was widely and popularly used in its adjectival form *esforçado*, often to define the valiant and courageous acts of knights. Manly force, so necessary in a leader or any warrior, can also be expected in sexual activity: the knight who forces himself on a lady is simply behaving characteristically of a man who knows what he wants and obtains it.[15]

New also in the *Crónica de 1344* is Alataba's reaction to the loss of virginity by force. She confines herself to her room, and as the weight of what has happened descends on her, she considers the consequences of her deflowering, her beauty begins to wane, and she becomes more ill by the day. Finally, confiding in her friend Alquifa, she tells her that she fears informing her father because men in general "juzgan las más de las mugeres por malas" (adjudge most women to be bad; chap. 58: 100), and she cannot risk being disbelieved in her claim of rape. Convinced by Alquifa to write to her father, Alataba composes a letter in which she threatens to kill herself if she cannot come home. She announces her dishonor, but unlike versions we will see later in which she hints of her misfortune to her father, here she simply blames the king outright—quite rightly, according to the chronicle's description of the event—and tells her father that she has been dishonored, "perdida" (lost), which will be the later fate of Spain itself.

Essential to the development of the story is that the rape is framed by Rodrigo's two visits to the locked house. Upon being named king, he visits the edifice that all his predecessors had been to before him, but immediately after the rape, he goes to the House of Hercules and breaks into it. Indeed, the chronicler sophisticatedly evokes the simultaneity of events by writing that while a messenger carries Alataba's letter, traveling province by province across the peninsula to bring the explosive document to the count, the king penetrates the house room by room, section by section. Finding the ark and the painted cloth with figures of Arabs, as described in earlier chronicles, the king refuses to believe there is danger ahead but nevertheless forbids his wise men and councilors to speak of what was found. The *Crónica de 1344* heightens dramatically the linking of the two actions, the penetration of the girl and the penetration of the house, and makes them one grand event of impending doom and destruction.

The topic of counsel—when to take it, whose counsel to trust and then follow, when to distrust the advice given—fascinated medieval writers. In the Christian tradition, this topic is amplified by such issues as dreams, prophecies, miracles, augurs, visions, and how to assess if they are divinely inspired or the work of the devil. A secondary but very popular topic is that of the false or misguided counsel given by women to men. In the *Crónica de 1344,* Count Julian's wife fits the critical portrayal of women in the Middle Ages as false councilors. Although she appeared indirectly in earlier chronicles as part of Julian's excuse to remove his daughter from the king's household in order to be with her sick mother, in *Crónica de 1344,* the wife, rather than Julian, is shown to be the direct cause of the fall of Spain. She incites Julian and his men to avenge the dishonor of their daughter, and by extension, that of the whole family. Without her counsel, it is not at all certain that Julian would have marshaled forces against the king. Several chapters follow in which the pros and cons are discussed of taking action against the king, and the theme is always advice and counsel. The countess implores the men to act, telling them that she would act if she could, and that she cannot believe that her lifelong devotion to the Virgin Mary would leave her in such straits, with her daughter dishonored and unavenged.[16] The countess represents the bad Christian woman, unfaithful to Christianity, and willing to lose Christian territory in pursuit of a personal act of vengeance.

"She Came to Him in His Prison Cell"

If the sexual submission of Muslim women to Christian men symbolized conquest and the superiority of Christianity over Islam, then Spanish legendary material found this to be a successful formula, employed repeatedly. The young, archetypal, virginal Muslim women, often referred to in French and English tales as Saracen princesses, are beautiful and sexually ripe.[17] One metaphorically conquers the Other, the enemy, by conquering their women sexually, even if, as happens in many of these medieval stories, two young people fall in love. The story of Mainete, or Charlemagne, and Galiana is one such tale; other Spanish works highlight similar relationships. For example, Gonzalo Gustioz, one of the counts of Castile, depicted in learned chronicles and popular oral ballads, lost his seven sons to murder in a plot that arose out of sexual dishonor and a Christian woman's bloodlust. While he languished in a prison in al-Andalus, after the heartbreaking identification of seven heads that he recognized as his sons, a noble Muslim princess—the sister of powerful King Almanzor—"came to him in his prison cell," as one balladeer sings. She conceived a son, who grew up to be the avenger of the count and his seven sons.[18] In a work considered by many to be one of Spain's important national epics, *Poema de Fernán González*, this count, too, is saved by a Muslim woman from enslavement or death, and the episode is a device to signal the birth of Spain.

There is an interesting hybridity in how the same story gets told. In the case of the ballad cited above, the king, out of pity for the tragedy Gonzalo Gustioz suffers, sends his sister to him, in essence making a gift of his sister to the noble Christian captive (Mirrer 17–18). While the Muslim woman's sexual submission, as the gift from the king, retains symbolic value as domination over woman, this is a different case from the stories in which the Muslim male is deceived or betrayed into losing the woman, which stands generally for the loss of property, and sometimes concretely for the loss of Muslim-controlled lands. Instead, in the ballad, there is a moment that speaks to shared humanity, at least on male terms, and even in the reality of imprisonment in a Christian-Muslim struggle, supports the notion that convivencia and mutual understanding could and did exist.

Finally, in another legend, found in a number of twelfth- and thirteenth-century chronicles, including Alfonso the Learned's *Estoria de España,* Alfonso VI (best known as the king who conquered Muslim-held Toledo in 1085 and who wrongfully exiled El Cid from the kingdom) fell in love with a Muslim woman, Zaida, who bore him his only son. Alfonso's military incursions into southern Spain raised the fears of Muslim kings, who called for reinforcements from the Almoravids of North Africa, led by the formidable Yusuf Ibn Tasufin. Yusuf defeated Alfonso in a battle at Zallaca in 1086, and then proceeded to conquer the lands of his fellow Muslim leaders. Before he captured the southern cities, however, while Seville was still in the hands of al-Mutamid, Alfonso married Zaida or had her as his concubine. Muslim chroniclers state over and over that she was al-Mutamid's daughter-in-law; Christian histories claim that she was his daughter. Rather than a known fact, this detail of who she was developed over time, and not surprisingly, it makes her the stock literary figure of the sexually available Muslim princess, who chooses to love the Christian man and leave her own people.

Stories circulated in the thirteenth and fourteenth centuries, well after the facts, that Alfonso VI and al-Mutamid played a chess game together; at stake was the fate of Seville. If the Muslim king won, Alfonso would retreat and would also help keep out other Christian warriors who might try to capture Seville; if Alfonso won, Seville was his. In one version, Alfonso lost the match to the superior skill of the Muslim king, which spared Seville, but gave him Zaida. Another version of the story claimed that Zaida was the prize: al-Mutamid chose to give away the woman instead of the land, which still argues for an equivalency of the two. Some chronicles claimed that Alfonso won some land concessions from al-Mutamid, along with Zaida.

The story of Alfonso VI's love for Zaida may have developed as a way to explain away his inability to win back Seville, the Christian conquest of which did not happen until Alfonso the Learned's father, Fernando III, conquered it in 1248. We know that Alfonso did not try to defeat al-Mutamid in battle, and that he did afford him some protection from Christian forces who would have tried to conquer Seville, although Yusuf did eventually cause al-Mutamid to surrender Seville to him. Little wonder that writers found the story of true love more pleasing than the chess game, and even less wonder that Zaida's renunciation of Islam and dowry of at least ten fortresses made a more attractive history than one of Yusuf's military superiority and Alfonso's failure to dominate Andalusia.

How Zaida came to be in Alfonso's life is legendary, but that she was indeed a historical figure seems indisputable. Some chronicles recount the details of their love affair almost exactly as the Charlemagne and Galiana story. As a way of justifying the prominence of a Muslim woman in the Christian king's life, and mother of the heir to the throne, it helped to cast Alfonso's story as a mirror of the Charlemagne legend, which insisted on the tricking of the Muslim king to take the woman away from him, and on the conversion to Christianity of the Muslim princess. Twelfth-century Christian chronicles claimed that Zaida was a concubine, but thirteenth-century chronicles turned her into his legitimate, Christian-convert wife. As with almost everything associated with the story of Zaida and Alfonso VI, historians continue to disagree about her status in the kingdom of León-Castile.[19]

The Jewess of Toledo and Rising Anti-Semitism

Writers often juxtaposed the "helpful Muslim princess" to the power-hungry, sexu-ally voracious, and totally treacherous bad Christian woman, who struck terror in the hearts of men. "Beautiful Jewesses," dark, seductive, and very available, abounded in literature.[20] Hatred of Jews, fear of women's sexuality, and the stock image of the fallen woman, that quintessential outsider, melded together in the story of the Jew-ess of Toledo, which most modern historians discount as fiction. Great-grandfather of Alfonso the Learned, Alfonso VIII, the "child-king" who reigned from 1158 to 1214, gained lasting fame as the king who had won the battle of Las Navas de Tolosa in July 1212, earning him the epithet "the Good." But before he became the Good, by turning to the full-time occupation of winning lands back from the Muslims, Al-fonso was very, very bad, spending seven years in an affair with a woman known as the Jewess of Toledo. First written as marginalia in two early manuscripts of Alfonso the Learned's *Estoria de España,* this account provides only the barest essentials of the legend, that Alfonso VIII committed adultery with a Jewess for seven years, and that God had punished him by allowing Alfonso's defeat at the Battle of Alarcos in July 1195.[21] Alfonso learned the reason for the defeat two years later, when a man, bathed in light, appeared in the palace to tell Alfonso of God's mandated punishment for adultery, which would include the death of any son born to Alfonso. The repentant king ordered the construction of a monastery, Huelgas in Burgos, along with a hos-pital to be tended to by nuns. By the next century, the *Crónica de 1344,* which elab-orated and embellished material about La Cava, also gives a fuller account of Fer-mosa and Alfonso than previous histories had done, including an accusation that the Jewess was an evil sorceress.

A good example of the legend as it was told in the late fourteenth and fifteenth centuries comes from Lope García de Salazar, a nobleman and chronicler hailed today by the Basques as one of their most important ancestral heroes. For colorful-ness, García de Salazar's own life story rivals any legend. He claimed to be the great-great-grandson of the first Lope García de Salazar, known as "brazos de hierro" (arms of iron), and who reputedly had 120 illegitimate children. Our chronicler Lope, himself quite a swordsman, belonged to the still-illustrious Basque family, and in his early years, participated in politics and dangerous disputes, for which his bravery was renowned. He built the Tower of Muñatones, and when his wife died in 1469, he continued to live there with a bevy of young servant girls. Father and sons had a falling out when one son, Juan, attempted to seduce not one, but two of Lope's fa-vorite mistresses. Lope exiled his son, who refused to stay exiled, returning and im-prisoning his father in the tower; indeed, assuming the servant girls were still there, this could not have been a particularly harsh incarceration. Happily for us, for his chronicle is quite well written, this imprisonment afforded Lope the time to write, between 1471 and 1476, the twenty-five books of his *Bienandanzas e fortunas* (Happiness and fortunes). Lope escaped from the tower to a church, where he sought sanctuary, convincing the townspeople to intercede for him with his sons. The sons agreed not to lock him up, but—their word clearly not their bond—when he left the church edifice, they returned him to the tower. On November 9, 1476, in what was an apparent suicide, Lope poisoned himself and his daughter.

García de Salazar rejects the rape of La Cava as insufficient cause for God's wrath toward an entire kingdom.[22] But the story of a woman's seductive power that he recounts with relish is the Jewess's hold over Alfonso VIII, whose neglect of his queen and country dismayed his councilors and court. The councilors fear that Jewish political leaders manipulate the king through the Jewess, and that the king is drawing closer to them and ignoring his own court councilors. Rather than being a man in love, the king is bewitched, almost by sorcery. The only solution that occurs to the courtiers is to murder the Jewess and the Jewish political councilors. But unlike the earliest and more succinct recountings, in which she is taken away and strangled, or the method of her death unspecified, the late fourteenth- and fifteenth-century chronicles include details of violent beheading. Once the murderous deed is done, the threat abates that a Jewish political cohort could insinuate itself into the highest part of government, but killing the woman and the Jews fails to resolve the court's dilemma. The Jewess's death only further entrenches the king's devotion to her, while he continues as before, leaving his kingdom to languish. But God has a plan: "E aquella noche, yoguiendo él pensando en aquella maldita judía, aparecióle un ángel" (and that night, while the king was lying awake thinking about that accursed Jewess, an angel appeared to him; bk. 16: 275v). When the angel makes clear to him that he has sinned, and that the country needs him and his full dedication, he pledges himself to God, country, and charities. Dyer calls this the "awakening motif," since the king is now awake both literally and figuratively, having recognized the error of his ways (149). His punishment will be the lack of a male heir, though his line will continue through his daughter. The angel departs, leaving the room bathed in light and smelling of a sweet strong odor. Shortly afterwards, his first victory against the Muslims sets him on the path to greatness. What is significant is the anti-Semitism directed at the Jewess herself—"accursed Jewess"—absent in the earliest tellings of the story.[23]

According to Dyer, late fourteenth- and early fifteenth-century versions began to insist on the link between the woman's murder and the country's subsequent success, rather than the earlier, more narrow focus on the sin of adultery and God's punishment of it. Story was important in these developing nationalist narratives, and Alfonso's failings became a moralistic tale of the dangers of woman to a kingdom. And while the story focused on woman, only faintly removed from view was the real message, as recently argued by David Nirenberg, the need to remove Jewish men from any position of power because Judaism and Jewish members of society threatened Christian political theology ("Deviant Politics").

This intensified virulence against the Jewess is connected to the use of the story as a specific counterpoint to La Cava and the king in chronicles that recount both legends. Rodrigo lost Spain because of his rape of La Cava, but in the narrative pattern of "reversing the fall" employed by chroniclers, Alfonso's agreement to reject the Jewess, and violently so, sets him on the direct path to a decisive victory, the Battle of Las Navas de Tolosa, an overturning of the fall of 711. By bringing together the demise of woman and the defeat of Muslims as one grand story, this tale becomes a microcosm of Spanish Christianity's struggle against the Jews and Muslims.

García de Salazar's choice to include the story of Alfonso VIII and the Jewess in his voluminous history stands for a significant preoccupation of the period regarding Jews, women, and the threat they pose. According to St. Paul, and sermonized by St. Vincent Ferrer below, the concubine posed a threat to the entire community: "If even just one man should have a concubine, 'it is something very dangerous for the community.' Had not St. Paul explained that, on account of one concubine alone, an entire 'city was corrupted, and suffered great plagues'? 'Do you not know that a little leaven corrupts the entire dough?'" (cited in Nirenberg, "Conversion, Sex, and Segregation" 11).

In an article on the political significance of Alfonso VIII's love for the Jewess, Nirenberg traces medieval Spain's fear of Jewish councilors or ministers to kings from the late thirteenth century well into the fifteenth century ("Deviant Politics"). He suggests that the Christian king's adulterous love for the Jewess of Toledo finds an equivalency in his dependence on the Jewish ministers rather than on the Christian noblemen: "[S]exual access and political influence are mapped onto each other, with deviant love producing corrupt governance" (31). For Nirenberg, this particular confluence between the sexual and the political continued: "[W]e might almost say that, over time, *privados* (councillors) became 'Jewish concubines'" (31).

As the story of the fall of Spain in 711 demonstrated, how much more devastating is the fate of the "community" when the fornicator is the king, and the community is the entire kingdom? In the case of both King Rodrigo and King Alfonso VIII, the fate of the nation and of Christianity rests on their ability—or inability—to resist illicit relations with women. Rather than visiting a plague or a famine on Spain, the sexual sin impels the "plague" of Islam to overtake the country. Rodrigo's sin with the "bad Christian woman" with the Hebraized name, Cava, invites the religious plague, while Alfonso's sin with the Jewish woman weakens the central government both by allowing Jewish councilors to exert negative influence on the king, and by distracting him from the religious and military imperative to conquer Islam in Iberia. Unlike the unlucky Rodrigo, whose sin brought collective punishment, in Alfonso's case, the elimination of the threat—the murder of the woman and the Jewish men—permits him to return to the path that will spare collective punishment and ensure Christian victory in the future. Prominent in García de Salazar's work is a general anti-Semitism, the belief in the connection between Jews and black magic, and the bewitching seductiveness of Jewish women, all of which related to the threat of Jewish power in fifteenth-century Spain.

During the last third of the fourteenth century, the region of Asturias and the throne of Castile became linked beyond the purely mythic connections celebrated in El Toledano and Alfonso the Learned's grand national histories. The illegitimate son of Alfonso XI, Enrique of Trastámara from the Asturias, challenged his half-brother Pedro I (also known as the Cruel) for the throne. Enrique used anti-Semitism as a political tool, accusing Pedro of favoring the Jews, by which Enrique fomented an already weighty envy and fear of the Jews among the nobility. Enrique invaded Castile in 1360 and ordered a massacre of the Jews in Nájera, which a chronicler at the time asserted had been done to gain some popularity for Enrique. The encouragement of the Church, and Enrique's increasing success in stirring up generally antagonistic, anti-Semitic behavior among the people, set the stage for both the change in dynasty and the violent destruction of Jewish communities at the end of the fourteenth century.

Enrique murdered his half-brother Pedro in 1369, taking over the throne as Enrique II of Castile. His own son, Juan I, inherited both the throne in 1379 and continuing struggles over dynastic claims. Challenged on two fronts simultaneously—by his cousin Catherine, the daughter of Pedro I of Castile, and by another Enrique, his half-brother, an illegitimate son of Enrique II, to whom had been willed the region of the Asturias—Juan I created a solution. First, he defeated his half-brother and claimed the Asturias for the kingdom of Castile, and then brokered the marriage of his son, yet another Enrique, to the daughter of Catherine and her husband, John of Lancaster. He created a visible and linguistic link between Pelayo's ancient Asturian kingdom and the Trastamaran dynasty now ruling Castile: in 1388, he bestowed the titles of prince and princess of Asturias on his son and daughter-in-law, and the prince of Asturias became the official title of the heir apparent to the throne of Castile.

During the early years of the Trastamaran dynasty, Spain witnessed inflamed popular agitation against the Jews. Ferrand Martínez, prominent as the archbishop of Ecija and holder of other important ecclesiastical offices in the late 1370s and throughout the 1380s, harangued relentlessly against the Jews from the pulpit.[24] Martínez encountered some resistance to his quest to destroy the Jews—for example, royal letters that threatened him to cease and desist—but his message of hate found many people willing to take up the challenge of ridding Spanish Christendom of this blight upon its cities and towns, as they came to regard the Jews. After the death of Juan I in 1390, the ascension to the throne of the eleven-year-old Enrique III, and the combined fanaticism of Martínez and the preacher who became a saint, Vincent Ferrer, the bloodshed that began with the sacking of Seville and massacre of the Jews in June 1391 rapidly spread to many cities, including Toledo, Burgos, and Córdoba. Ostensibly a campaign to convert the Jews, mob activity instead turned one city after another into a fiery furnace and a slaughterhouse for Jews. Although hatred attached to the Muslim communities as well, they were largely spared, historians believe, because the presence on Iberian soil of the caliphate in Granada afforded all Muslim communities some protection. As to the Jews, any who survived the massacres submitted to baptism. On July 9, the massacre of Valencia claimed thousands and thousands of lives, at the same time that, reportedly, Vincent Ferrer welcomed some eleven thousand converts to Christianity, including the chief rabbis of the synagogues. Between July 9 and October of that year, 1391, pogroms took place in Barcelona, Zaragoza, Palma, and many other places in Spain. The zealous fanaticism abated in the 1390s but never came close to disappearing. Jews converted by the thousands, and Jewish communities became much smaller. Fifteenth-century Spain found paralyzing conflict with a new enemy, the converso, or New Christian— socially despised, always suspected of being a false convert, a crypto-Jew, and a conspirator against Church and Crown, although historians believe that the real fear was the swelling numbers of conversos, and their growing wealth and political importance (Haliczer, "The Jew as Witch" 148). The renewed ties of the throne to Asturias encouraged the inventive emphasis on Spain's mythic Gothic roots. And with that return to origins came a profound sense that the Jews—and those deemed crypto-Jews, which included most conversos—should have no place in the inheritance of national identity.

CHAPTER THREE

Blood Will Out

The Goths were unaware of the now popular Spanish saying: *There is no such thing as a little enemy.* Many large nations have failed to heed that truth. Moreover, the Jews have never been little enemies.

Claudio Sánchez Albornoz, *El reino de Asturias: Orígenes de la nación española* (The kingdom of Asturias: Origins of the Spanish nation), 1972

The scattered fragments of the ancient Visigothic empire were now again, with the exception of the little state of Navarre, *combined into one great monarchy as originally destined by nature;* and Christian Spain gradually rose, by means of her new acquisitions, from a subordinate situation to the level of a first-rate European power.

William H. Prescott, *History of the Reign of Ferdinand and Isabella, the Catholic* (italics mine)

In the year 1250, a little acolyte in Zaragoza, a boy with the voice of an angel, used to sing on his way to church. As he passed by the Jewish quarter each day, his songs in honor of Jesus angered the residents. A group of evil men decided to kidnap him, and in a particularly gruesome travesty of Holy Friday, try him in a simulation of Pilate's tribunal of Christ, then crucify him and cut out his heart. Their ultimate plan was the widespread killing of Christians, by mixing the child's heart with a ground-up consecrated Host, which sorcery had taught them could poison the waters of the river, causing the immediate death of any Christian who drank from it. The first time they tried the plan, it failed because the Jews charged with snatching the boy did not want to kill him; they substituted a pig's heart for the boy's, but this backfired when all the pigs in town died after drinking the water from the river. The next time, they succeeded in killing the boy, but the plan was foiled by a miracle. When one of the Jews pretended to be a devout Christian, entering a church to steal a Host, a book he was holding gave off sparks of miraculous light. Others thought he must be a very holy man, but upon inspection, they recognized him for what he was, a malevolent Jew who was up to no good in the church. The scheme unraveled, and too late for the little boy, who became known as Little Saint Dominic of the Valley (Santo Dominguito del Val), the men were punished. Finding this to be such a barbarous, but not isolated, outrage upon the bodies of little children, Alfonso the Learned included the outline of the story in his book of laws, *Siete Partidas:* "oyemos que en algunos lugares los judíos ficieron et facen el día del Viernes Santo remembranza de la pasión de Nuestro Señor Jesucristo en manera de escarnio, furtando los niños et poniéndolos en la cruz, or faciendo imágenes de cera et crucificándolas cuando los niños non pueden haber" (we have heard that in some places the Jews reenact the passion of Our Lord Jesus Christ as a mockery of it, by stealing children and crucifying them, or by making wax images and crucifying them if no children are to be had). If such an act occurs in any part of his kingdom, he writes, the perpetrators must be taken prisoner, brought before the king, and if the charges are proven, the prisoners must be killed (7: 24, law 2).

Other such preposterous tales achieved widespread acceptance in Spain within fifty years of this example and continued to be believed for centuries, even to be repeated as fact by twentieth-century historians.[1] And in fifteenth-century Spain, they were not tales, but fact, serving as inspiration and justification for the Edict of Expulsion that would forever end Sepharad, Jewish Spain.

The events of fifteenth-century Spain changed the world. The joining of two of the four major power blocks of the Iberian Peninsula, the kingdoms of Aragon and Castile, through the marriage of Prince Ferdinand of Aragon and Princess Isabel of Castile in 1469, gave hope for a politically unified government that would, among other things, strengthen the idea of "Spain." Despite having been glorified in national chronicles, especially in works intended to invent a history (a narrative continuum of a centuries-long, sweeping, providentially designed Christian conquest), or to inspire kings' and citizens' continued efforts to win land for Christian crowns, Spain—as country and united citizenry—nevertheless had been far from a reality. In the thirteenth century, King Fernando III, the Saint, captured Córdoba (1236), Murcia (1243), Jaén (1246), and Seville (1248), but the dearth of military victories over the remaining kingdom of Granada between then and the end of the fifteenth century frustrated those in power for almost 150 years. In the fifteenth century, the abstract concept of Spain remained stronger than the reality, so chroniclers continued to promote by allegory, implication, or direct statement their collective view that the monarchy needed to sustain the spirit of Reconquest. The monarchs' relentless quest to bring the minorities into line through conversion or expulsion resulted in a facade of social and political unity that masked a harsh judgment of those deemed threatening to Spanish society, the Jews and the Muslims, even though they had inhabited the Iberian Peninsula for centuries. Christian Spain increasingly chose to believe in the dangerous power of the Jews to subvert every norm and custom, from the pinnacle of the monarchy to the basest legal brothel.

Following the 1391 massacre of Spanish Jews, the fifteenth-century Church and monarchy heightened society's fears about sexual intermingling. They taught that such relationships brought the inevitable corruption of society as a whole, invited God's wrath to be visited upon the entire country in a collective punishment—not the first time Spain would experience such punishment—and threatened the promise of eternal life for every Christian citizen. And, as David Nirenberg explains, fourteenth- and fifteenth-century Spain represented "a society in which complaints about disorder [often involving widespread famine, disease, or violent threats to the monarchy], the subversion of hierarchy, or the erosion of privilege were often written in the shorthand of interfaith sex" ("Conversion, Sex, and Segregation" 26). The creative hypotheses about the pervasive danger of the "Jewish threat" resulted in laws and practices designed to separate and segregate the Jews from Christian society.

Social anxieties extended into the economic market. In 1449, the city of Toledo enacted the first *limpieza de sangre* (blood purity) statute, which forbade Jews and Jewish converts to Christianity from holding certain jobs and offices. But even this seemingly commercial prohibition against Jews could not be divorced from the realm of sex, as the Church argued that "blood purity" protected the future Spain from the threat of contaminated lineage. In the second half of the fifteenth century, society's focus shifted from the threat of sexual intermingling with the Jews, with its invitation to Old Testament–style divine retribution, to a fear of corrupted bloodlines. Spanish society began to consider the children of Old Christians as naturally superior to the progeny of a converso and a Christian, two conversos, or even descendants of conversos.[2] Fifteenth-century Spain increasingly cemented a belief in its Gothic origins for reasons that ranged from putative rights to the Castilian throne to social mobility, a belief that by definition excluded the Jews and the Muslims, as well as their descendants. The Inquisition, established in 1478 by Isabel and Ferdinand as a state-controlled arm of the Church, designed to root out heresy, quickly developed into a litmus test of blood purity, in which Spaniards attempted to prove that they were Old Christians, with no Jewish ancestry. The inquisitors, zealous in extracting confessions and proving that conversos continued their "Judaizing" in secret, often sought to mask their own ancestry by proving their devotion to Christianity. The most famous participant of all, the Grand Inquisitor Torquemada, denied his Jewish heritage—his mother was most likely a convert to Christianity—and it was much whispered about even during his lifetime.[3]

When humanist Antonio de Nebrija presented his Castilian grammar, a Latin-Spanish dictionary, it forged a foundation between language and empire. This grammar, rather than being an isolated incident of pride in things Castilian, reflected a growing trend in humanistic inquiry in the service of nationalistic goals.[4] And the idea of imparting "language" to people, as Kamen reminds us, "was not limited to vocabulary and grammar. It implied, rather, the imposition of culture, customs and above all religion on subjected peoples" (*Empire* 4). In this regard, then, the New World enterprise would parallel the efforts within Spain to eliminate Judaism and Islam, and to eradicate traces of their cultures. Spanish historiography had evolved dramatically in the fifteenth century, and the soul-searching quest to uncover and codify national origins and identify the essence of the Castilian nobleman resulted in a return to, and wholehearted embracing of, the peninsula's early Visigothic kingdom, which modern historians have termed neo-Gothicism.[5] Although we have already seen chroniclers' frequent return to the myths of the fall of Spain and Pelayo's resistance to the Muslims, most often the point had been to claim monarchical, religious, and territorial links to the eighth century. The emphasis of fifteenth-century Spain on determining how long one's family had been Christian went hand-in-hand with tracing one's own bloodlines back to the eighth-century Goths.

R.B. Tate tells us that Spain was not alone in its quest to reconstruct—or reinvent—a national past, and that France and Italy were engaged in something similar: "Era como si toda la Europa occidental, estimulada por la erudición humanista, se hubiese sentido simultáneamente presa de un ansia por descubrir los secretos de su nacimiento, de la misma manera que los estudiosos bíblicos de aquellos días volvían a reconstruir los textos originales del Nuevo Testamento por medio del estudio de los antiguos manuscritos." (It was as if all of Western Europe, stimulated by humanist erudition, simultaneously fell captive to an anxiety to discover the secret of their birth, in the same way that Biblical scholars in those days sought to reconstruct original texts of the New Testament by means of the study of ancient manuscripts; *Ensayos* 26). The reference to Biblical studies is particularly apt here. Spain, more than any other country, had long cast its history in providential terms and as Biblical narrative, as early as the seventh-century writings of Isidore of Seville. In addition to the importance of such writings to fifteenth-century and early modern Spain, this Iberian tradition inspired—indeed, drove—the New World evangelism of the sixteenth and seventeenth centuries.

This chapter will examine three interrelated topics within the larger context of the century's heightened anti-Semitism, its attempts to claim Gothic roots for its Christian inhabitants and, increasingly, to cast historical events in gendered terms. First, we will look at some examples of the deeds and lineages of notable men and how Pedro de Corral's historical romance of King Rodrigo and Pelayo fits into that enterprise. Late fourteenth- and fifteenth-century biographies of the moral and ethical deeds of notable men functioned not only as the story of a life, but as an analysis of political attitudes and individual men's comportment in political arenas, that is, their lives as a sign of the times. Fifteenth-century chronicles and biographies enable us to understand the context in which Pedro de Corral produced his "biographical" historical romance of Rodrigo, last king of the Goths. The fifteenth-century development of the legend of the fall ties in with how these biographies of notable men negotiated between personal claims of ancient illustrious lineage, which returned repeatedly to Visigothic ancestry, and the political realities of a growing national anti-Semitism. Pedro de Corral's heroic narrative, sometimes called *Crónica sarracina* (Saracen chronicle), but printed as *Crónica del Rey don Rodrigo* (Chronicle of King Rodrigo), changed the way Spain viewed its national origins, as well as its view of the Jews.

Heroic narratives need heroes at their center, and the legend of the fall of Spain provided the opportunity for a tragic hero and a victorious one. The emerging hero of the Gothic revival was Pelayo, and Corral's hefty prose work supplied the stuff of legend in this regard. Corral's work, from which I drew the legend's summary at the start of chapter 1, carefully and compellingly crafts the story of Rodrigo's sin and defeat, and Pelayo's dogged struggle to victory for Asturias—the cradle of Spain—to represent an encyclopedic touchstone for all of fifteenth-century Spain's most salient anxieties, about the Jews, the Muslims, national origins, and religious concerns, which he shapes within the sexualized framework of anxieties about women.

In fifteenth-century histories and poetry written by the nobility and upwardly mobile, what we find especially is the importance of identifying with those who resisted the Muslims. It was a mark of honor to trace one's lineage back to soldiers who fought under Rodrigo unto the death for the survival of Christendom, or even better, those who carried the torch of Christianity to Asturias and stood side by side with Pelayo, as he staved off the Muslim wave that surged north. Many chronicles, poems, and very minor histories opined on the legend of the fall—who to blame, whether it happened at all, whether this detail or that was correct. Even though late medieval writers disagreed about the facts, the tendency of the century was to intensify the belief in the historical truth of the legend, and to embrace it as the key to both Spanish national identity and the enduring legitimacy of the Castilian throne. This intensification came about for different reasons. In the examples given above, gentlemen and would-be gentlemen engaged in highlighting or even inventing an illustrious lineage. For such endeavors, the longevity of one's ancestry mattered a great deal. But for political writers, who engaged in defending the legitimacy of the

Trastamaran dynasty, begun by Enrique II through political strife and an act of fratricide, and continued by Juan I, Enrique III, Juan II, Enrique IV and Queen Isabel, these invented familial links to the earliest Iberian Christian kingdom legitimated the claim of the fifteenth-century Castilian rulers to the throne and to be the inheritors of the religious and cultural mantle of the noble Goths.

The second part of the chapter will consider how poets and historians responded to the reality of a Castilian queen, Isabel, by portraying her along centuries-old gendered cultural lines about women that found new expression in the fifteenth century. Isabel of Castile, who reigned from 1474 to 1504, captured the imagination of her countrymen, who exalted her in historical accounts, poetry, and painting, as the triumphant figure both of the fall of the last Muslim stronghold in Spain in 1492, thereby restoring the land to Christian sovereignty, and of the birth of the Spanish empire. The transition from the tradition of male monarchs to a queen of Castile was not an easy one for Spanish politicians and chroniclers. It provoked a crisis of male anxieties, as Barbara Weissberger has demonstrated in *Isabel Rules,* her analysis of chroniclers' gendered construction of that monarch, and their support for, or criticism of, her rule.[6] But reactions to Isabel's gender, however significant, were only part of the story. The final part of the fifteenth century saw an almost monolithic attempt to justify the ascension of Isabel to the throne, and the legitimation of that monarchy, which was accomplished more often than not by positing the new rule of "light, peace, and prosperity" (luz, paz y prosperidad) as emergent concepts of government that interrupted in timely fashion the egotism, brutality, and corruption of the preceding reigns of Isabel's father, Juan II, and her half-brother, Enrique IV (Tate, *Ensayos* 288). Obviously, this had nothing to do with being a woman given that her rival for the throne was her niece Princess Juana of Castile, Enrique's daughter, slanderously known as la Beltraneja. Politicians who hoped to see Isabel crowned asserted that Juana (b. 1462) was the illegitimate product of an adulterous relationship between Enrique's second wife, Juana of Portugal, and the king's favorite courtier, Beltrán de la Cueva.[7] Bowing to pressure from his powerful councilors, in 1468 Enrique signed the pact of Toros de Guisando, naming Isabel the princess of Asturias, which made her heir to the throne, and formally labeled his own daughter Juana illegitimate. When Isabel married Ferdinand of Aragon without her brother's approval, he took away her title and reinstated Juana as princess of Asturias in 1470, but to no avail: Isabel was crowned queen of Castile in 1474. Isabel was the formal successor to King or Prince Pelayo of Asturias, and Tate tells us that Alonso de Cartagena's 1470 history of Spain "se cuida de dejar perfectamente claro que Rodrigo, aún siendo el último rey de los godos, no fue el último miembro de la línea. El mismo día que Rodrigo fue asesinado, alega, Pelayo le sucedió por *dispensación*

"La Alhambra. Puerta en la Sala de Justicia," by Charles
Clifford (1819–1863). Albumen photograph, 38.6 × 39.9
cm. From *Album de Andalucía y Murcia*, 1863. Courtesy of
The Hispanic Society of America, New York.

divina" (is careful to make perfectly clear that Rodrigo, although he was the last
king of the Visigoths, was not the last member of the dynasty. The same day that
Rodrigo was assassinated . . . Pelayo succeeded him by divine dispensation; *Ensayos*
69). What this means is that Spain wanted to tap into its Gothic, Asturian, roots
when it was useful for social, political, and religious arguments, but also wanted to
distance itself from King Rodrigo, his personal disgrace, and his kingdom that became, after his defeat, a land of Jews, Christians, and Muslims.

And so the narrative wheel of fortune had turned. As part of the moral continuum of Spanish narrative, the Castilian rulers as overturners of Rodrigo's sins, Juan
de Mena's influential 1430 *Laberinto de Fortuna* (Labyrinth of fortune) had prophesied Juan II as the defender of Christianity, sure to emerge in mid-century as a world
leader. The fashionable political propaganda of the last part of the century aban-

doned that line, asserted a moral condemnation of his and Enrique's reigns, and justified pushing aside Princess Juana. Several historians used Biblical citations to explain, in retrospect, the crowning of Isabel as the result of divine or providential intervention (Tate, *Ensayos* 288). Even converso writers participated in this sense of enthusiastic expectation, the result of a latent messianic tendency among this group (288). If the Isabelline faction justified itself by means of fulfillment of Biblical prophecy, it is not at all surprising that the biographical impulses of the century, and the popular manifestations of those impulses, tended toward sanctifying and exalting Isabel as beyond mere woman.[8] An essential belief in the national imaginary about the Isabelline monarchy and the Goths links Isabel to Pelayo himself, both pious devotees of the Virgin Mary, and both builders of a nation. Writers who favored a man as the true ruler of Spain linked Isabel not with Pelayo directly, but with his daughter, Princess Ermesinda, whose marriage to the nobleman Alfonso had made him the first of the official line of Asturian kings.

The final part of this chapter examines the anti-Semitic story of the Holy Child of La Guardia, which encapsulates the anxieties of Christian Spain about Jews and conversos, and which contributed to the decision to expel the Jews from Spain in 1492. The 1490 legal case of the Jewish and converso men accused of the ritual murder of a small boy continues and contemporizes the centuries-long belief that the Jews killed Christian children for their blood, and in this instance, that it was part of a plot to exterminate an entire town of Christians. The hatred of the Jews near the time of the expulsion mixed religion and politics, as it always had done, but now embraced the view that Jews and conversos, as crypto-Jews who had never truly converted to Christianity, worked in concert to destroy Christianity. In a country whose historical events would underscore, and whose historiographical bent would return to, the notion of the Visigothic origins of its citizenry, the perceived threat of the Jews would not be ignored.

The Return of the Goths

With its emphasis on humanism, the recovery of Greek and Latin classics, and their application to the contemporary period, the century was characterized by a profound interest in the particular and the universal. Knowledge was gathered in volumes great and small, encyclopedic enterprises that sought to capture Spain's national history and place it in larger world contexts. At the same time, lives were portrayed through biographies, within chronicles and in catalogs that often cast those named in moral or ethical terms and categories. Early Christians, particularly in the fourth century C.E., crafted numerous biographies, which served what Averil Cameron has called the "rhetoric of empire" in the building of Christianity. These popular stories linked the telling of a life with the subject's interest in public service; often, these were tales of kings in the service of Christian truth. But in addition to these particular kinds of biography, there was, at the same time, simply an increase in interest in the biographic form in general. This is the epoch of the *Life of Anthony of the Desert*, and the *Confessions* of St. Augustine, among others, of the pious and saintly, of martyrs, healers, ascetics, contemplatives, and of those in public service, as Augustine was. There is a similar development in fifteenth-century Spain. People wrote saints' lives, biographies of political figures—Christian knights and noblemen—and most popularly, compiled catalogs of the virtuous as well as the morally and ethically wanting. The interest in literary biography contributed to the development of fiction, as evidenced by the abundance of chivalric and pastoral romances, which were often crafted as the pseudo-biography of a single figure.[9]

The progressive trends in fifteenth-century historiography increasingly examined national origins. Through this national self-scrutiny, the casting of fifteenth-century Spain as the land of the Goths, and its Christian peoples—rulers, aristocracy, and peasants alike—as their descendants, became the historiographical narrative that most defined the century, and subsequent centuries of Spanish history to the present.[10] How to relate fifteenth-century Spain to the classical world, what to do with the failed kingship of Rodrigo, and how to showcase Pelayo and his Asturian connections preoccupied *letrado* chroniclers (that is, learned writers who drew from Latin ecclesiastical chronicles, among other elite texts), who responded to the challenges in different ways.

In terms of classical figures, earlier medieval historiographers, such as Lucas de Tuy (El Tudense) and Rodrigo Ximénez de Rada (El Toledano), treated Hercules in different ways. For El Tudense, he was not significant. But for El Toledano, Hercules proved to be the link between the classical world and the Spanish line of kings. Hercules is often postulated as the first king of "Spain" in a dynastic line that ended with Rodrigo's defeat. Hercules also was reputed to have formulated an interior map of Spain by constructing temples in important locations and erecting columns—the Pillars of Hercules—in the south of the peninsula.[11] In Spanish historiography, between the encyclopedic works of Alfonso the Learned and the reign of Isabel's father, Juan II of Castile, chroniclers tended to lack the drive to inscribe the nation within a universal and learned circle. This begins to change in the early part of the fifteenth century, when historians broadened their interest in uncovering Spain's most remote origins and changed their focus from linking Hispania to a remote past to emphasizing Castile and the ancient world. According to Helen Nader, Pablo de Santa María (1350–1435), a Jewish convert to Christianity who had been the chief rabbi of Burgos, articulated the theory of Castilian history between 1412 and 1418, when he was bishop of Burgos, which found favor with the legists, highly educated men of letters (letrados) who followed in his footsteps. In his *Siete edades del mundo* (Seven ages of the world),

> don Pablo adapted early Spanish history to Old Testament names and chronology. He retained the tradition that Hercules was the first Spanish king, but he changed the name . . . to Gideon, claimed that Gideon had ruled the Castilian nation rather than a province that later formed part of the Roman Empire, and treated the Carthaginian and Roman periods very briefly in order to devote more attention to the Goths and the Reconquest. This shift of emphases from the classical myth to Old Testament history, from the Romans to the Goths, and from Roman province to Castilian nation became one of the distinguishing characteristics of the letrado treatment of Spanish history. (Nader 22–23)[12]

The letrado Alfonso de Cartagena (1384–1456), building on the arguments of his father, Pablo de Santa María, cemented the historical rationale for the centrality of the Castilian throne to the global defense of Christianity, opposing England's claims with riveting oratory, in a speech he entitled "Anacephaleosis," delivered to the Council of Basle in 1434. By using a theological term that means "summary" or "recapitulation," Cartagena cleverly underscored both the indisputable nature of his arguments, rather than the proposition of a theory, and the theological links to his statements that the Castilian monarchy drew its divinely ordained legitimacy from God.

From the middle of the century to the end, the interest in defining the early kingdoms intensified, and some historians both decried the lack of material about Spain's origins and criticized those chronicles that started with Hercules's entry into the peninsula. For example, the intellectual heir to Alfonso de Cartagena, Rodrigo Sánchez de Arévalo (1404–1470) in his *Compendiosa Historia Hispánica* (Concise history of Spain) wrote with the goal not only of defending the besieged Enrique IV, but of demonstrating the centrality of the monarchy in Castile, by suggesting that there had been "una Castilla nominal como corazón espiritual de *Hispania* mucho antes de la destrucción de Troya, y que hubo allí reyes mucho antes de Gerión" (a nominal Castile as the spiritual heart of Hispania that greatly precedes the destruction of Troy, and that had kings much earlier than Geryon [Hercules]; Tate, *Ensayos* 22). This fifteenth-century historian ignores the feats of Hercules as the first Spanish king, preferring instead to suggest that some form of Spanish culture predated Greek culture by a significant number of centuries, and then moves to link Spain and Rome as the culturally superior empire to the Greek one from which Hercules had come, and to integrate Spain into the broader canvas of European history. Sánchez de Arévalo's writings exhibit both nationalistic and worldly goals, whose main aim of foregrounding Castile's Gothic heritage influenced the path taken by Spanish politics and its chroniclers in the rest of the fifteenth century, and first half of the sixteenth century, with enduring influence.[13] Even English Romanticism subscribed to the notion of a pre-Visigothic Spaniard.

Near the end of the fifteenth century, open attacks on Hercules replace the generally negative or dismissive attitude towards him, including one by the little known Fray Gauberto Fabricio de Vagad, author of *Corónica de Aragón* (Chronicle of Aragon), first printed in Zaragoza in 1499. Fray Gauberto, directly rejecting the Hercules story, asserts that historians should avoid opening their histories of Spain with that legend, since it gives a false impression of Spain's earliest origins. In fact, the good cleric tells us, Homer would turn over in his grave were he to know how many great deeds the truly ancient Spaniards performed that eclipsed anything the Argives and Trojans accomplished in the *Iliad* (cited in Tate, *Ensayos* 24).[14] In a 1498 history of Spain by Giovanni Nanni, Hercules survives the complete purge he suffered in other chronicles of the time, but for Nanni, he is nothing but a pirate, who is the last of the line of primitive monarchs, rather than the start of the line that ended with Rodrigo.

For those fifteenth-century writers less concerned with tracing Iberia's origins and more concerned with the sensational aspect of early Spain's history, the legend of the fall offered great opportunities for commentary. An excellent example of the literary spirit of the first half of the fifteenth century is *El Victorial* (The victorious one), Gutierre Díaz de Games's biography of a valiant nobleman, don Pero Niño, count of Buena (1378–1453). The proem to the lengthy story of Pero Niño begins with a 210-page recounting of important world events that preceded his life and times. Included in this prefatory material is the author's balanced account of three possibilities for the fall: Rodrigo's penetration of the House of Hercules, the sin with "la fija del conde Julián" (the daughter of Count Julian), and the Decadence Tradition, the explanation from late antiquity and the Middle Ages that the iniquity of the king and the entire population caused the fall.

Written in the first decade of the fifteenth century and then revised in the 1430s (the same decade Corral wrote in), and quite probably the work of Gutierre Díaz de Games in both the original writing and the revision, it is the history of the knight Pero Niño, the Victorious One, whose courageous fighting during the early decades of the fifteenth century contributes to ongoing quest to reverse the consequences for Christianity of the 711 defeat. Drawing from Corral's embellishment of the legend, Díaz de Games describes the House of Hercules, the elaborately contrived locks and inner rooms, and the prophecy that Hercules had made about Spain's future destruction. According to Díaz de Games's description, greedy King Rodrigo discounts the cautionary legend because he believes instead that Hercules had counted on a return to life in another's body, and that he therefore had left great treasures in the house for his return (194). Interestingly, the author offers an opinionated commentary that he, for one, finds the House of Hercules episode unbelievable: "Esto creedlo vos si quisieredes, mas yo non lo quiero creer, porque estas tales cosas no las sufre la ley, la razon no las consiente" (You can believe this if you want to, but I do not want to because the law does not suffer such things, and reason does not consent to them; 194–95). More palatable to him, historically speaking, is the Decadence Tradition: "Otrosi, el pasar de la mucha gente e el destruymiento de España non lo fizo por el abrir de las puertas, mas la justicia de Dios por los pecados de los honbres, como fue en el gran diluvio de Thesalia, e quando vinieron las plagas sobre Egito, la submersion de las siete çivdades, e de Ninive, e de la çivdad de Jerusalem. Todas estas cosas avinieron por justicia de Dios e por pecados de la gente." (Now, the arrival of so many people and the destruction of Spain was not done by the opening of the gates, but by the justice of God on account of men's sins, as happened with the great flood of Thesalia, and when plagues came to Egypt, the submersion of the seven cities, and of Nineveh, and of the city of Jerusalem. All these things came to pass through God's justice and because of the sins of men; 195). Therefore, the author is not persuaded by those who suggest that Spain was lost through the sin of the king with Julian's daughter: "No fue aqueste tan gravisimo pecado, en tomar el rey una moça de su reyno, como las gentes lo notan, nin casada nin desposada. E aun, que podia ser que el rey no hera conjugado, ansi que el pecado hera en mucho menor grado" (And that was not such a grave sin, enjoying a maiden of his kingdom, who, as people have noted, was not married or even engaged. Furthermore, given that possibly the king himself was not married, it is a very minor sin; 195). The historian suggests that a king's enjoyment of a female subject is hardly news, and even less a punishable offense, and then he discredits the story completely. First of all, he reasons that God does not inflict a universal punishment for the sin of a single individual. This kind of wrath of God is, of course, precisely the view of many societies, to say nothing of the view of the most fundamental of all collective punishments, the expulsion from Paradise and the stain of original sin for all humankind because of the sin of Adam and Eve. Second, he argues in a most inventive way that the story of the violation of the daughter was created by supporters of Count Julian to vitiate the guilt of the count's conspiracy, whose behavior Díaz de Games finds to be much more reprehensible than anything the king might have done.

Lope García de Salazar's encyclopedic *Bienandanzas e fortunas* (Happiness and fortunes) demonstrates that competing legends circulated in the same period. García de Salazar blames both Witiza, Rodrigo's predecessor, for the impious state of the nation, and Count Julian, for the downfall of the nation. Rodrigo is the legitimate ruler of the Goths, in this version, not a usurper as in some cases, and a character named Perca de la santa vida (Perca of the Holy Life) extracts many vows from the king in order to uphold state and church. Failure to do so, he warns, will cause "perdición de cuerpos e ánimas e vienes" (loss of bodies, souls, and goods; bk. 13). According to García de Salazar's recounting, Rodrigo died in battle, was buried in Portugal in Viseu, and Julian, the more culpable of the two, was of the line of Caesars of Rome. By making the traitor of Roman descent and the betrayed Rodrigo a Goth, García de Salazar offers a good example of how creatively and subtly writers moved away from things Roman and towards the valorization of the Gothic heritage in fifteenth-century Spain and beyond.

Fifteenth-century historians overtly compared current events to the eighth century. For example, Aureliano Sánchez Martín, in his recent edition of Diego Enríquez del Castillo's *Crónica de Enrique IV* (Chronicle of Enrique IV), the history of the king who reigned just prior to his half-sister Isabel, reminds us that the fifteenth-century historians who preceded the reign of Isabel and Ferdinand tended to write highly partisan biographies and chronicles that promoted one faction of the nobility over the other, without the humanistic erudition we see in later historiography. Of interest for the present study is the chapter in Enríquez del Castillo's highly favorable chronicle of Enrique IV's reign, written in the 1460s and early 1470s, in which a current event is compared to the fall of Spain in 711. Around the time that Enrique IV's opposition was actively seeking his deposal and the crowning of Isabel's brother Alfonso as king, his fortress in Simancas, near Valladolid, was under siege. Enrique asked his own troops to defend the fortress no matter what the cost, and this they did with courage and vigor. The archbishop of Toledo, Alonso Carrillo, a supporter of the opposition and later a most important advisor to Isabel, was imprisoned and burned in effigy. Enríquez del Castillo's chronicle states that those handing down the sentence of death by burning ordered that punishment because Archbishop Carrillo had followed in the footsteps of the eighth-century traitor Bishop Oppas. Therefore, he should be dragged through the streets of Simancas, with a sign labeling him Oppas, that most ignoble of betrayers of kings. The chronicle ascribes as much guilt to the eighth-century Visigothic bishop, Oppas "destruidor de las Españas" (destroyer of the Spains), as he does to Julian or Rodrigo (chap. 77: 242–43).

The chronicler then tells us that the people invented an insulting little ditty that included calling Alonso Carrillo "don Opas traydor" (don Oppas, traitor), a song that remained popular for quite some time. Aside from the obvious point that the chronicler and, more importantly, the nobility themselves cast their treacherous contemporary archbishop of Toledo as the reincarnation of his eighth-century counterpart, Archbishop Oppas, we see how the legend of Rodrigo, Julian, and Oppas remains palpably alive in fifteenth-century Spain. As in Corral's work, written some thirty years earlier, in which Rodrigo is characterized as a just and noble, but personally flawed, ruler, betrayed by those men he should have been able to trust the most, Enrique IV is flatteringly depicted as a judicious and noble king who battles the opposition and is betrayed even by the archbishop of Toledo. What is at stake, Enríquez del Castillo implies, is the fate of Spain itself: the use of the words "pérdida de España" (loss of Spain) and "destruidor de las Españas" (destroyer of the Spains) suggests that the nation is once again imperiled should Enrique be overthrown, and Spain would once again be lost.

If some of the historiography produced in fifteenth-century Spain was merely a straightforward, chronological outline of the facts as the chronicler saw them, without humanistic learning to enhance the exemplarity of the events, the most famous exception was Juan de Mena's *Laberinto de Fortuna* (Labyrinth of fortune), finished in February 1444. As Florence Street and others have shown, Mena's work was considered by many of his contemporaries to be the pinnacle of learned historiographical and poetic production in the fifteenth century, and it enjoyed highly favorable assessments throughout the sixteenth century as well. A three-hundred-stanza poem, *Laberinto de Fortuna* celebrates King Juan II of Castile and praises his virtuous qualities, his abilities as king and leader, and his judiciousness—indeed, all the qualities another chronicler, in contrast, Fernán Pérez de Guzmán, found so sorely lacking in both the king and his favorite and extremely powerful advisor, don Alvaro de Luna.[15] Mena's poem exhibits classical learning in a stylized way that accomplishes for Juan II what the anonymous *Poema de Fernán González* or Alfonso the Learned's *Estoria de España* (History of Spain) did for those rulers by presenting their actions as reversals of the earlier fall of Spain and advancements of the noble and divine mission of Reconquest. But it goes beyond earlier works in positing a shake-up of world order in which Spain will emerge as the supreme world power, with Juan II as the universal ruler.

Except for a few references to chaste queens, who were in short supply according to Mena, *Laberinto de Fortuna* is truly a male master narrative. Gender plays no role: disorder enters mostly from the failings of men through the ages, and while women are not blamed, neither is there a place for them in the triumphs of society. References—and sometimes fairly oblique ones—to classical figures and myths intermingle with past events in Spanish history and current political players and contemporary events. Mena makes a few references to Rodrigo's reign. Like Enríquez del Castillo, he cites Count Julian and Bishop Oppas as the significant villains of that sad period of Spanish history, and makes no reference whatsoever to any sexual scandal.[16] Mena claims that similar misdeeds are being perpetrated in his own circle of society, but his fear of retribution forbids the naming of names. What appears to be most important in this period's mixture of church and state politics is the alternating all-powerful support or betrayal of Castilian nobility and leaders by members of the Church hierarchy, themselves often members of powerful Castilian families.

Another stanza mentions Rodrigo near the end of the work in which Mena creates a list of Spain's kings and predicts that Juan II's deeds will eclipse the others' and cause them to be forgotten: "Será olvidado lo más de lo antigo, / veyendo su fama cresçer atan rica; . . . / e ante los suyos serán como sueño / los fechos mayores del godo Rodrigo" (the most venerable will be forgotten, seeing your fame climb so high; and before your deeds, the greatest deeds of Rodrigo the Goth will be like a dream; st. 273, p. 177). There is some continuation here of the suggestion we saw in the previous chapter in which the author of the *Poema de Fernán González* calls Rodrigo "enemigo mortal de los moros" (mortal enemy of the Moors), when there is nothing in the earlier histories to support this view of Rodrigo as a heroic warrior scourge against the Saracens. But Mena's characterization of Rodrigo's deeds as great ones does fit with the ecclesiastical histories that strove to portray the Visigothic reign as strong and vigorous such that its vanquishing, while painful, did not have to be regarded as an ignominious defeat.

Both the puzzled tone of Díaz de Games, when he speculated that the taking by force of one of the king's subjects was surely not a "pecado grave" (grave sin) meriting such widespread and devastating punishment by God, and his subsequent firm denunciation of the traitor, Count Julian, reflect the general view of fifteenth-century historiographers. As cavalier a dismissal of violence against women as this may appear to our modern-day perspective, the story focuses almost exclusively on the social and chivalric contract between king and nobleman and the rupturing of that contract by the king's lust and Julian's retaliatory actions. In the historiography through most of the fifteenth century, the legend remains a tale of male bonding and the destructive national and spiritual consequences that emerged from broken trust.

In addition to his chronicle, Fray Gauberto Fabricio de Vagad wrote a poem he calls a "conpendio, que es una breve memoria de los reyes hasta oy" (compendium, which is a brief history of the kings to the present time; st. 207) that begins with Count Julian's uncontrollable urge for vengeance. Fray Gauberto includes some familiar details, but he also puts an interesting spin on his version in recounting the heroic efforts of the Christians against "Caudillos moros valientes" (valiant Moorish generals; st. 11), returning to some extent to the early Iberian chronicles such as the *Crónica mozárabe de 754* and John of Biclaro's work, in which the Moors are shown to be worthy opponents, lest the chronicle underscore the weakness of the Visigothic kingdom. Fray Gauberto tells us that the Christians fight with tremendous energy, force, and unwavering commitment. One knight named Torres is singled out for his valor and bravery, and his descendants, "muy claros varones" (truly exemplary men), have inherited his fortitude, making them "valientes como leones" (valiant as lions; st. 25). Vagad's poem is dedicated to the family of Fernando de Bolea, and they are named as having descended from the heroic Christian knight of Rodrigo's eighth-century forces. The result of the numerous battles against the Moors is the loss of "España" and a profanation of churches and hermitages by turning them into mosques run by "alfaquís," local religious leaders.[17]

Opposed to the valiant, warrior Christians is the count, who bears more of the blame for what has transpired than the king himself.[18] Fray Gauberto finds it less challenging to believe that someone's individual sin would lead to the punishment of the entire nation than did Díaz de Games, the author who had disputed the idea of national blight caused by an individual's sin, but in this case, the greater sinner is the count, not the king. The epithet "conde malvado" (accursed count) for Julian, as well as the continued references in the poem to the count's "gran traición" (great treason), point to the condemnation of the one who sought revenge, while not excusing the sinner, Rodrigo. The third stanza states plainly that Rodrigo's sin was slighter—"Este pecar fue de hombre" (this was a sin against man)—while the sin against God—"la Ley"—belongs to Count Julian alone. La Cava does not appear again in the poem, and there is no reference at all to Rodrigo's violation of the House of Hercules. On the one hand, that is unsurprising: the poem is about the valor of the Visigoths, metonymically presented in the body of one single knight, who turns out to be the ancestor of the noble Bolea family, to whom the poem is dedicated, and whose valor in the contemporary realm is celebrated. The poem is not a lengthy history of the fall of Spain, nor is it necessary to dwell on any more of Rodrigo's failings than to sum up his sin as "pecar de hombre."

Corral Casts Spain's Founding Myth

What carried the day in the national imaginary was Pedro de Corral's historical romance (c. 1430) and the anonymous *Refundición toledana de la Crónica de 1344* (Revised Toledan chronicle of 1344), composed around 1440.[19] Corral receives all the credit for legendary invention, even though both works circulated around the same time, and the *Refundición toledana* may have preceded Corral slightly and even marginally influenced his work. Corral's manuscript of Rodrigo's downfall and Pelayo's ascendancy spawned several sixteenth-century printings as well as numerous oral poems that enjoyed enduring popularity.

The author of the revision of the 1344 chronicle was a Toledan converso. Critics further agree that the additional description, not present in any early version, of how Rodrigo came to covet the daughter resembles early Christian interpretations of the story of David and Bathsheba: David's victimized gaze from the parapet of his palace into a lush orchard garden in which the lovely Bathsheba bathes, nude, ensnares the king and causes his uncontrollable desire.[20] In this chronicle, the king awakes from a nap and gazes out into the orchard garden, in which a beautiful pool has been constructed. There, much to his delight and dismay, is a nude Caba bathing with another maiden. And because she is so lovely, he is instantly smitten: "E commo aquella donzella Caba, fija del conde don Julian, era de muy gracioso cuerpo e alva como la nieve, fue de súpito el rey della enamorado, en tanto grado que quería morir por ella" (And as that maiden Caba, daughter of Count Julian, had a very pleasing body and skin like snow, he was immediately smitten, to such a degree that he wanted to die because of her; Menéndez Pidal, *Floresta* 149). This particular garden-and-pool landscape does not occur in Corral. The converso author not only casts Spanish history in Biblical terms, a general trend in fifteenth-century historiography, but the Bathsheba figure in Spain's legend—Caba—is a second Eve. And even though modern criticism ignores the probable meaning of the name Caba—Eve—it is unlikely that this escaped the audience of the fifteenth century.[21]

While Corral's version focuses less directly on Biblical imagery than the *Refundición toledana* does, he nonetheless presents Spanish history in providential terms: prophecy correctly predicts the fall, and dangerous woman is the instrument of it; Pelayo's purity, avoidance of women, and devotion to God, Mary, and Christianity inspire miraculous aid to defeat the Muslims in Asturias. By including material on Pelayo from earlier chronicles, and by inventing new, exciting, heroic narratives about him, Corral singlehandedly created a legend of national Gothic origins that inspired pride. In portraying Rodrigo as a flawed hero, but heroic nonetheless, and Pelayo as the divinely ordained successor, Corral made it possible for fifteenth-century Spain to reclaim—or invent—its Visigothic heritage without having to reject Rodrigo as part of that history.[22]

Corral's expansion of the role of the Toledan Jews in the fall of the Visigothic kingdom, their conspiracy with the Muslims and total betrayal of the Christian king and kingdom, and the linguistic linkage between the names Chava and Caba, the fallen woman, evoke his society's anxieties about the Jews and women as threat to community, government, and religion. By emphasizing the Jews, both the *Refundición toledana* and Chronicle of King Rodrigo move the legend of the fall of Spain closer to the story of King Alfonso and the Jewess of Toledo, so that Spanish history begins to be told cyclically. In other words, more than once, Spain has been lost, or has been in danger of being lost, because of a woman, the Jews, and the advantage given to the Muslims when Christian kings engaged in sexual dalliances. Concomitantly, Spanish history recycled stories of the archetypal "helpful Muslim princess," who aids the ruler, often through betraying her own people in some plot or conspiracy, or by bearing the Christian ruler's son. Corral, too, includes such a story when he describes Rodrigo's widow, the former Muslim princess Egilona. In contrast to Caba, who stands for dangerous female sexuality, Egilona, a Christian convert who remains steadfast even after her Muslim kin take over the peninsula, stands for the feminized or sexualized submission of Islam to Christianity.

Both Corral and the *Refundición toledana* fill in the legend's gap about what happened to Rodrigo after his defeat at the Battle of Guadalete with similar stories of his extreme penance involving a snake. The *Refundición toledana* extends its Biblical narrative metaphor by recounting the penance and death of the king in an orchard garden in Viseu, Portugal, where he labored incognito as a hand.[23] In this recreated locus of the Fall, the king breeds a poisonous snake in the orchard-garden, and when it is fully grown, he enters a cave with it and lets it devour him until he dies.

Corral embroiders those elements into a horrendous tale of penitence through excruciating physical suffering. In Viseu, Rodrigo seeks the wise counsel of a hermit, who instructs him to feed a snake into adulthood, and then perform the penitential act of sealing himself in a sepulcher with the snake. Before the physical suffering begins, the king undergoes mental torment when the devil first appears in the form of Count Julian, tempting the king with pride and the return of his kingdom, and then in the form of an alluring, highly eroticized Caba, who offers him her body as she disrobes before him (Corral, 2: 391–96). The king triumphs over the temptations before him, and this serves as mental and spiritual preparation for the physical torture he will soon endure.

After being sealed in the tomb for three days with the famished snake, which has grown two heads, a naked Rodrigo feels the snake slither up his body: "la culebra se levantó de par dél e subióle desuso del vientre e de los pechos. E començó de le comer por la natura con la una cabeça e con la otra en derecho del corazón" (the snake rose up before him and moved up his abdomen to his chest. And it began to eat his genitals with one head, and with the other, his heart; 2: 403). The king interprets the horrific and graphic punishment, calling out that the snake was biting him in the heart, where the sin was born, and in the body part that carried out the sin, which caused the destruction of Spain. This striking imagery of the king's penance and slow, painful death captured the imagination of the public, inspiring one of the most enduring and popular ballads in the Rodrigo cycle.

Both Corral's *Crónica del Rey don Rodrigo* and the anonymous *Refundición toledana de la Crónica de 1344* promote the legend as the downfall of an all-too-human male because of the lustful and seductive properties of women. *Crónica del Rey don Rodrigo* renders complex the role of La Cava by showing her engaged in indecisive conversation with the king over his lustful desire for her, setting in motion the chain of revenge by her letters to her father, her self-condemnation when she realizes what she has set in motion, the manner of her death, and most damagingly for the image of woman, the devil's possession of her body after her death to torment the penitent Rodrigo by appearing to him as the temptress La Cava. Corral clearly intended to make part 1 of his historical romance a text of male successes: a magnificent, well-functioning kingdom is constructed by a trio of men who have bonded, trust each other implicitly, and work together constantly, each doing his part for the welfare of the state. The king, Count Julian, and Bishop Oppas dominate part 1 of the work. Part 2 is dominated by the triumphs of the infidels, the downfall and punishment of the successful men of part 1, and the invented story of the secret marriage of chaste Luz and heroic Favila, parents of the future King Pelayo. La Cava and her mother, Countess Frandina, play a larger role in part 2, where a prevalent theme is the destruction associated with women's speech, by La Cava's revelation to others of what the king had done to her, and by her mother's calls for vengeance. And this is what will predominate in the retellings of subsequent centuries. Both the reprintings of *Crónica del Rey don Rodrigo* and the popular ballad tradition that derived from Corral's work would soon capture the national moral imagination and the nationalistic impulse. These works eclipsed, though never eliminated, the episodes of the king's hubris, the forbidden penetration of the House of Hercules, and the treachery of Julian and the bishop Oppas, in order to highlight the legend as a story of the kingdom that fell because of woman.

Training Isabel, the Princess of Asturias

During her lifetime and afterwards, historians described Isabel of Castile as "more than a woman" and as one who possessed "manly valor" like Joan of Arc. These historians employ the vocabulary found in biographies of female saints, as the reference to Joan of Arc indicates, in which the achievements and sufferings of martyrs and other kinds of saints are said to reach a level of heroism similar to that of men. Along with female saints, the Virgin Mary is often "more than a woman," a model that ensured inspiration and striving in women, and certain failure in the human realm as well. Isabel was a woman so spiritually inclined that she came to rival the Virgin Mary herself, according to her devotees; indeed, they wrote, she was so pure she could have given birth to Jesus. Although contemporary historians credit Ferdinand as the gifted military strategist of the two, and a leader in his right, centuries of testimony highlight Isabel, influencing her portrayal even in our time. For example, her contemporary, the Venetian Andrea Navagiero, praised her military efforts: "Queen Isabel by her singular genius, masculine strength of mind and other virtues, most unusual in our own sex as well as in hers, was not merely of great assistance in but the chief cause of the conquest of Granada" (Fraser 190). Typically, Isabel is shown either in her role as a female archetype of early Christianity, a spiritual mother, or militantly, as a spiritual warrior.[24] In the first instance, her appearance at the scene of battles reputedly brought comfort and added strength to those about to embark on a siege or skirmish in her name. In the second instance, Isabel was Spain's own Joan of Arc, who most ardently desired the conquest of the infidels, but who suffered none of the accusations of sorcery and heretical behavior that plagued Joan throughout her military mission on behalf of France.

As we have seen, interest in illustrious lineages and heroic deeds propelled the popularity of biographies in fifteenth-century Spain, along with catalogs of exemplary men. At the same time, cataloged depictions of women occurred in fiction and nonfiction.[25] Such catalogs of the virtues and vices of women long predate Isabel of Castile. Indeed, writers earlier and later than Boccaccio's *De claris mulieribus* (Exemplary women), one of the most important catalogs of women, assigned ancient and contemporary women to their dialectical categories of exemplary behavior or condemnatory behavior. When Spain found itself facing the unusual state of rule by a woman, Isabel of Castile, poets, historians, spiritual advisers, and politicians all availed themselves of the cultural vocabulary surrounding women to construct how Isabel would be portrayed to her countrymen, and how she would be remembered by posterity.[26] As significant as Isabel is to Spanish history, and as important as it is to understand Spain's intentionally gendered construct of the queen, it is essential to recognize that Spanish historiography and literature dealt with the reality of having a queen rather than a king of Castile by folding her into the larger national project of a return to Spain's Gothic origins. Although the works about Isabel can be analyzed according to specific male anxieties about women and a female ruler, as Barbara Weissberger has done convincingly, I am more interested in how Isabel fits, ultimately, into the larger picture of Spain's historical resurrections of its founding myth through the centuries.[27] History demonstrates that the persistent retellings of the legend always reflect the anxieties of each age and, by virtue of the elements of the legend itself, can always be reduced to male anxieties about female power. David Nirenberg's studies of medieval Spain underscore the prevalence of "feminine coding" to express prejudice and hatred toward the minorities. Spain's challenge in the late fifteenth century, a time of belief in neo-Gothicist ideals and intense anti-Semitism, was to retain such handy coding while exempting Queen Isabel from it.

Even though Ferdinand's name usually comes first when we speak of the Catholic monarchs—Ferdinand and Isabel—Isabel's Castile was the central kingdom in Spain and more important than Ferdinand's realm, Aragon. Although histories promote the view of a joint reign based on mutual respect and equal rule, iconography and some of the same histories cause us to consider Queen Isabel as the figure responsible for launching and continuing the exploration of the New World and as the main ruler of Spain. In the fifteenth century, the national imagination grew to accept—was trained to accept—a woman ruler to the degree she could be effaced as a normal woman. For a people whose polarized view of woman was most frequently Ave-Eva, the reality of a woman as reigning monarch, not just the spouse of a ruler, had to be coupled with the conviction that she was, in fact, Ave, like the Virgin Mary, superior to other women, and ultimately in a category by herself.

No work better illustrates the spirit of the times and the issues facing the political future of Spain in the second half of the fifteenth century than the relatively obscure Fray Martín de Córdoba's *Jardín de nobles donzellas* (Garden of noble maidens). Dedicated to Isabel and written as if the author were an intimate spiritual and political adviser to the princess, the work pertains to the general literary genre of "advice to princes." Written during the controversy of which woman would wear the crown, Isabel, daughter of Juan II and half-sister of Enrique IV, or her niece Princess Juana, putative daughter of Enrique, *Jardín de nobles donzellas* sides with Isabel. It promotes the view that the true nature of woman is virtuous, and that when she strictly adheres to virtue and her best instincts, she is capable of being a good and strong ruler. Harriet Goldberg provides convincing evidence that Martín de Córdoba was probably not an intimate of the princess, and that Isabel appears not even to have owned the book ostensibly written as a didactico-moral guide for her personal development (36–39). Nevertheless, *Jardín de nobles donzellas* paints a vivid picture of the views held in the fifteenth century about women and queens, and enumerates qualities that the future queen was expected to possess, repeated by later writers as facts about Isabel's character and her reign. The treatise emphasizes virginity, modesty, and chaste widowhood as hallmarks of good women everywhere, suggesting for emulation many examples of women from the Bible, folklore, and ancient and modern history. In this regard, Martín de Córdoba draws upon opinions about queens and queenship that previous classical and medieval authorities promulgated generally, as Alcuin Blamires, Paul Strohm, and Peggy McCracken have shown.

Martín de Córdoba is the first writer, I believe, to draw equivalencies between Isabel and the Virgin Mary, which became one of her standard portrayals.[28] Indeed, even in some of the modern histories, such as Prescott's nineteenth- and Walsh's twentieth-century works, the historians speak of Isabel with awe and repeat with unquestioning conviction the views of her contemporary chroniclers that refer to her as superior to women in general, demonstrative of "manly virtue," and comparable to the Virgin Mary. Martín de Córdoba employs the topos of Spain as a paradise and reinforces the fifteenth-century Spanish view that there were two thrones in the universe, God's celestial throne in the East, and in the West, "la silla del Rey de España" (the throne of the King of Spain; 220), which, if politics played out the way the author hoped and expected, would be occupied not by a "Rey," but for the first time by a "Reina." To imply that the queen of Spain would, in effect, be the ruler of the world was not only bold, but prophetic, given her role as mother of an empire. By describing Mary's reversal of the sin of Eve—"E la Virgen María, Nuestra Señora nos paró la visión de Dios, la qual Eua nos quitó, ca por su glorioso parto fue fecho visible el que primero hera inuisible" (And the Virgin Mary, Our Lady, gave birth to the sight of God, which Eve had taken from us, because by that glorious birth was made visible what was before invisible; 162)—Martín de Córdoba suggests that Isabel will do the same for Spain. Poetically, then, and in the national imaginary of Spain, she will be opposed to La Cava, the Eve of Spanish history.

Martín de Córdoba further links Isabel to the Virgin Mary by emphasizing that Mary herself was the daughter of kings: "[L]a señora Princesa, por que es de linaje real, como la Virgen que fue fija de reyes, e por que es doncella, como hera la Virgen cuando concibio al fijo de Dios, e por que espera de ser reyna, como la Virgen que es Reyna delos cielos, señora delos angeles, madre de los pecadores e manto de todos los fieles." (The Princess, being of royal lineage, just as the Virgin was the daughter of kings, and by being a maiden, as the Virgin was when she conceived the son of God, and because she expects to be Queen, as the Virgin is Queen of Heaven, Mistress of the Angels, mother of sinners, and protector of the faithful; 164). The author returns to this theme of shared qualities between the Virgin Mary and the princess when he describes the expected comportment of women who would be rulers. Although all women should incline to piety, as one of their natural virtues, a noblewoman should be the most pious of all ("avn que todas las mugeres sean naturalmente piadosas, pero las grandes lo deuen ser mas que todas"; 199). A ruler needs three qualities, all of them enhanced by an inclination to piety: "Ella es madre e abogada e es escudo" (she is mother, and advocate and shield; 199). Isabel's work was cut out for her; not only did she first have to win the throne, she then had to live up to the impossible standards set by the Virgin Mary.

Martín de Córdoba spells out how Isabel should be mother, advocate, and shield in her future role as queen of Spain. She is "madre nobilísima de sus pueblos" (the most noble mother of her people; 201), who must comport herself with great piety and clemency toward her subjects. In Alcuin Blamires's book *The Case for Women,* in the chapter "Honouring Mothers," he states, "Medieval defence of women often begins with (or soon turns to) an archetypal argument about origins: simply an argument that people—including misogynists—are brought into the world by mothers. It may seem elementary (something 'known far and wide' as one writer puts it) to assert that women ought to be respected and not denounced by those, of whatever status, who are necessarily born of them" (70–71). Martín de Córdoba appropriates a commonplace of medieval defenses of women but broadens it and exalts it by praising Isabel not as future mother of her own children, but as "the most noble mother of her people," as the queen of Heaven is also mother of all the people.

The princess must fight for her people on many levels; as the virgin queen is advocate ("Virgen Reyna es abogada") in the celestial kingdom, so in the earthly kingdom the queen is advocate for the people and is expected to intervene in the king's decision making, particularly if she feels he will suffer a loss of reputation for an incorrect judgment. Martín de Córdoba advises against daily intervention, though he does not indicate how many interventions are acceptable: "no digo que esto se haga cada día, ca enesta manera peresçería el themor dela justicia" (I'm not saying this should be done every day because if that were to be the case, the fear of justice would suffer; 201). Intervention was an expected and acceptable action by good Christian women. In Isabel's own century, Christine de Pizan recognized the role of peacemaker or interventionist as the proper duty of queens and princesses. Blamires finds that Christine perhaps injects a note of scorn for men's inability to control their wrathful and vengeful impulses, but praises women for having this skill: "O God, how many great blessings in the world have been caused by queens and princesses making peace between enemies, between princes and barons and between the rebellious people and their lords! The Scriptures are full of such examples" (51). Paul Strohm discusses the queen as intercessor and finds that men supported an interventionist role for women, because, as Blamires puts it, "it consigned women to a domain where, non-competitively, they could 'supply a male lack'; because it facilitated royal changes of mind; and because the spectacle of the abject, emotional female intercessor helps to 'affirm "maleness"'" (Strohm 103–4, cited in Blamires, *The Case for Women* 88, n.73).

Finally, Isabel is shield, protectoress of her people, especially in guarding the powerless from the powerful. If society is like the sea, in which the rule of law is that large fish consume the smaller fish, the queen will be like the whale (ballena), the largest fish in the sea and will protect the smaller ones, all the members of society who need the queen's benevolent protection.[29] Martín de Córdoba again compares Isabel to the queen of Heaven, this time in the popular iconographic depiction as the protectoress under whose all-embracing cloak the devoted and the needy may take refuge.[30] Additionally, in this assessment of the future role of the princess, the author depicts a ruler not unlike the healing saints such as her distant kinswoman with the same name as Isabel, St. Elizabeth of Hungary, the queen who turned to healing, feeding, and helping the poor and sick, as well as other works of corporal mercy. Blamires includes in his chapter "Honouring Mothers" the commonplace of the praise of feminine healing—part of nurturing—for it enabled women to organize and run households properly and to maintain the proper division between the man's public sphere and woman's world, which was circumscribed in private domestic life (91). No woman had a larger "household" than Isabel, if we consider that Martín de Córdoba is implying that her household is, in fact, the nation. Not expected to remain at home, Isabel's appearances at the sites of military battles was to give succor to the troops in terms of morale and spiritual strength, and was therefore an enormous extension—but an extension nonetheless—of her role as escudo, protectoress, nurturer, and healer.

Isabel married Ferdinand in 1469, five years before she was crowned queen of Castile. The issue of marriage and the role of the wife and wifely tolerance of the husband's failings and foibles, while always a burden for the pious Christian woman, became a particularly difficult one for Isabel. The circumstances of her accession to the throne of the powerful and prestigious kingdom of Castile on December 13, 1474—in hurried fashion the day after Enrique IV's death, at a time when Ferdinand happened to be away at the court of Aragon with his father—apparently caused tensions in the marriage. The political faction that wished to see Isabel crowned queen, before Juana la Beltraneja's supporters could manage to do so for their candidate, hastened Isabel's coronation. Fernández-Armesto, Fraser, and other modern historians claim through evidence from fifteenth-century sources that Isabel always behaved solicitously of Ferdinand's feelings, always ensuring that he would feel that Castile was his as much as hers, and that the joining of the two Christian kingdoms of Castile and Aragon had indeed created one unified political nation, Spain. Ongoing political wrangles over succession to the throne of Castile should Isabel predecease Ferdinand, which is what happened in 1504, made it abundantly clear that many powerful men in Spain did not believe Ferdinand had equal rights to Castile. Ferdinand claimed that he should be king of Castile not only through his marriage to Princess Isabel—an equal partner—but in his own right, through his father's claims to the throne of Castile. In a procession through the streets of Segovia, where Isabel had been crowned, the nobleman Gutierre de Cárdenal preceded the Queen, carrying an unsheathed sword, the symbol of justice. According to a chronicler who much favored Isabel, Diego de Valera, the queen exercised her right in appropriating this symbol for her reign and for herself as dispenser of justice. His contemporary, Alfonso de Palencia, did not share this view. At the heart of the debate was the notion of shared sovereignty by Isabel and Ferdinand and as Elizabeth A. Lehfeldt tells us, a concern that Isabel overstepped boundaries by exhibiting masculine qualities that were the province of kings. Palencia quotes Ferdinand as exclaiming, "Is there any precedent in antiquity for a queen to have been preceded by this symbol, threatening punishment to her vassals? We all know this has been conceded to kings; but I never knew of a queen that had usurped this manly value" (cited in Lehfeldt 40).[31]

But rivalry over "his and her" kingdoms aside, Ferdinand's philandering ways sorely tested Isabel's well-documented "wifely tolerance." Isabel herself would find the amount of tolerance she would be expected to muster for the next thirty-five years to be a heavy burden indeed. Ferdinand had several illegitimate children before and during his marriage to Isabel, and Christian custom expected her not only to accept it silently, but to pray for his soul since women were more naturally pious than men: "es de notar que comun mente las mugeres son más deuotas a Dios que los varones" (It should be noted that typically women are more devoted to God than men; *Jardín de nobles donzellas* 203). It is not clear whether Martín de Córdoba's treatise, with its instructions on the marital duties of the future queen, was written with any knowledge of Ferdinand's proclivities. He speaks of the need for the wife's submissiveness to her husband by tempering all of her activities with compassion and piety, and by honoring the marriage vows. He argues that marriage benefits both men and women with the rewards of fidelity and chastity, and that the sacrament of marriage forbids divorce, keeping the parties together until the death of one of them, which helps them maintain a state of grace in a "cama limpia" (pure bed; 162).

Even though the author does not dwell on the difficulties of married life for women, we can infer that stories of the trials and tribulations of married women and all they endured from brutish, loutish, neglectful, and otherwise misguided husbands may have offered some entertainment and perhaps even comfort to Isabel. An extremely interesting manuscript codex, now housed in the Escorial library (MS h-I-13), is thought to have belonged to Isabel. The untitled manuscript contains nine works, several female saints' lives and several romances, including the *Empress of Rome,* one of the most popular of the type known as the "falsely accused chaste wife or queen." St. Mary Magdalene, in her role as preacher and miracle worker, appears in the collection, as does St. Catherine of Alexandria, whose heroic and learned tour de force debate against the most erudite of the infidels did not save her from martyrdom but did elevate her in the eyes of the adoring medieval public as an intellectual heroine. Although Cristina González has argued that the manuscript was intended for a female public, Thomas Spaccarelli claimed that its audience was medieval pilgrims, male and female alike (25). Though he suggests that the book was carried on pilgrimage, the sheer size of it argues against that idea. Much more convincing is the view of Emily C. Francomano, who supports González's opinion that the manuscript was intended for women and argues that, along with the role models of the four heroic female saints, each of whom illustrate various strengths and talents, the five romances all boil down to one recurrent theme: the necessity for a wife to endure in a marriage, even though trials and tribulations be arduous beyond belief, and even life threatening. The rewards for such a woman are not to be found on earth but, like her saintly sisters, in the celestial paradise that awaits. While there is no consensus that Isabel owned this particularly codex, though several critics have asserted that she did, we know that the works contained within were extremely popular in the fifteenth century, and Isabel undoubtedly would have known them in one form or another. Many of the women who underwent horrific trials in the romances were themselves queens or empresses, and there is little doubt that the enduring and long-suffering wife was a popular category of saintly woman. Isabel, as a queen and pious wife, would only add luster to her already bulging pantheon of attributes, particularly those that associated her with the traits of the Virgin Mary.

Isabel, the Warrior Queen

If the fifteenth-century historiographers before the reign of Ferdinand and Isabel, as divided and factionalized politically as they were, had something in common, in addition to support for political neo-Gothicism, it was the belief that the lofty goals and aspirations of those earlier Christian rulers, who had conquered significant Muslim territories, were continuing to be unwisely neglected by the current kings and the nobility. One romance of chivalry, unusual because the knight is a woman, is *La Poncella de Francia* (The maid of France), that is, Joan of Arc.[32] The work is dedicated to Isabel, believed to have been written as a kind of manual for the princess so that she would be a proper spiritual leader in what would become the military aspect of her role as queen. The likely author, the court chronicler Gonzalo Chacón, positions Isabel as Spain's own Maid of Castile.[33] This would not have been the only occasion for comparison between Isabel and Joan of Arc. Isabel's father, Juan II, had greatly admired the courageous and pious French maid, as had the influential diplomat Rodrigo Sánchez de Arévalo, who had also been secretary and councilor to the king. Isabel's biographer Peggy Liss tells us that the atmosphere of the court, with its open and frank esteem of Joan, would have made her a very likely role model for the young princess (18, 88–89, 98).

The Spanish chivalric romance *La Poncella de Francia* enjoyed great popularity in the sixteenth century, with at least twenty printings in that time, and it continued to be published as late as the nineteenth century. Interestingly, while much is made at the end of the romance of an explicit connection between the maiden Joan and the princess Isabel, it is likely that at the time of its composition—probably not earlier than the late 1460s and not later than 1491—Isabel was certainly not a "doncella," a maiden, but a married woman. By the time of the first printing—Seville, 1512—Isabel was dead, yet the appeal of the work was far from over.

Joan of Arc—Jeanne la Pucelle—was a fifteenth-century incarnation of the earliest Christian women, whose public declarations of their virginity empowered them to enjoy both mobility and leadership roles. While we tend to think of convents as the highest measure of declared piety, enclosure or cloistering as a sign of female chastity was not a feature of the earliest forms of Christianity.[34] In her epoch, Joan's brand of female heroism had little to do with military skill—although history shows that she had that in abundance—and everything to do with the empowering role of her virginity, which gave her superhuman strength and protection from potential advances of men. Marina Warner demonstrates how Joan's fifteenth-century compatriots compared her to the Virgin Mary, whose own images as a warrior stepping on the serpent's head, for example, made her the natural iconographic model for Joan. Among those who provided vivid examples of the protection Joan's virginity afforded her were the so-called rehabilitation biographers, who sought to restore her reputation in the centuries following her death, and they claimed to cite eyewitness testimony from the fifteenth century. As recounted by Marina Warner, one such seventeenth-century biographer, Ceriziers, wrote of Joan's abilities to forestall any impure intentions or actions on the part of the soldiers she accompanied: " 'Whenever anyone looked upon her with impurity or thought dirty thoughts about her, he was immediately struck impotent *forever.*' This accretion to Joan's legend echoes an earlier story, also told by her supporters. A soldier seeing her in Chinon scoffed at her: 'By God, is that the Maid? If I could have her for one night, I'd not return her in the same condition.' Joan retorted: 'In the name of God, you deny him and you so near your death!' An hour later, the man fell and was drowned in the Vienne" (*Joan of Arc* 38).

The image of Joan as the Maid of France was popular in fifteenth-century Spain, as Adeline Rucquoi demonstrates. Although her English foes had already burned

Joan at the stake as a witch and heretic long before the composition of the Spanish chronicle that refers to her, and indeed long before the romance of chivalry under discussion here, the vilification of Joan and the circumstances of her death are never mentioned; the Spanish works present Joan as the pious, virginal, and extremely successful military leader only. One can recognize overt attempts to equate circumstances of Joan's life with that of Princess Isabel, such as in the apocryphal matter of Joan's persistent and multiple suitors.[35]

La Poncella de Francia manifests two political and didactic goals. First, the romance of chivalry presents the quest of France against England as a most noble one and intends to strengthen Franco-Castilian relations through the positive representation of France as the "beloved sister" of Castile (Rucquoi 170). Second, the suggestion that the story of the Maid of France was written as a didactic tool for the Maid of Castile also links the two countries as being led by powerful, but always pious, women. One of the more charming aspects of the romance is the author's role as omniscient narrator who peeks into Joan's bedroom night after night. Spurning love stories, and always turning to God before going to sleep, the young military leader is insatiable in her desire to hear of the exploits of the world's greatest kings and knights from Biblical heroes to Alexander the Great to more contemporary rulers. The narrator intersperses his description of her questions and the didactic answers she receives with remarks that show that he intends these repeated stories now to train the Castilian princess in the stratagems of war.

It is noteworthy that at least two twentieth-century biographies of Isabel focus on her role in the military quest of her country. By the accounts of her contemporary fifteenth-century chroniclers, it would seem that, of the two monarchs—the notion of Isabel as a second Joan of Arc notwithstanding—Ferdinand was, not surprisingly, the military strategist. Of course, images abound of Isabel sanctioning Columbus's journey, wishing him Godspeed in his quest, and launching and supporting the ongoing New World enterprise of domination and conversion to Christianity. Naturally, she does not participate in battles. Antonia Fraser's chapter title for Isabel, in her book *The Warrior Queens,* is telling: "Isabella with her Prayers." What cements Isabel's image as a warrior is her religious relationship to the militant Virgin Mary, in the way that Mary is often depicted iconographically and in miracle collections as the one who vanquishes and puts down the devil, serpents, and other threats to Christian dominion. The statement by the Venetian Andrea Navagiero quoted earlier in this chapter used the language of hagiography, which praised female saints by denying their femaleness and asserting their masculine qualities, in order to praise what he considered to be Isabel's male qualities of mind and of leadership. In Fernández-Armesto's description of 1492 Granada, Isabel arrives at the scene of a battle when her troops are already exhausted from the duration of the fight, but the mere sight of her spurs the men on to defend her honor. William Walsh, even more fulsome in his praise of Isabel than other historians, calls her "the Last Crusader," and describes her unbridled ecstasy at the defeat of Boabdil and the city of Granada on January 2, 1492, and at her awareness that she has brought to fruition the centuries of "Reconquest," putting an end to, among other things, the sexual affronts and indignities suffered by Christian women at the hands of the Other: "Isabel's eyes, very blue that day, were shining with triumph and joy. All her own struggles and sufferings, all the pains and labors and bloodshed of her kingly ancestors, all the wounds and deaths of the thousands of Christian knights who had fought so doggedly for the recovery of this sacred soil, all the shame and agony of Christian women and children who had perished befouled in Moorish dungeons—all the mighty epic of Christian Spain was consummated and justified in that glorious moment. The faith of a woman had prevailed" (*Isabella* 330). Mythically, then, just as the sexual allure and misconduct of a woman had caused the downfall of the nation in 711 in a single act, an inglorious moment, the "faith of a woman," a pious woman without peer in Spain, had righted the wrong, reclaimed the land for Christianity, freed and avenged Christian women from sexual dishonor, all "in that glorious moment."

Even her dealings with Christopher Columbus are painted as Isabel having an affinity with him that is not shared by Ferdinand, an affinity that stems perhaps from like minds or from womanly attraction. Columbus had sought funds for his voyage, and financial circumstances of the nation had obliged the Catholic monarchs to put him off: "Isabel could hardly have failed to sympathize with a man who, like her, refused to be swerved from the road he had taken, and paid no tribute to the impossible. The poet and the artist in her—or was it the woman?—instinctively felt the destiny of this dreamer so facile in images. Where Ferdinand, the cool man of business, detected inconsistencies and small discrepancies, Isabel's more intuitive mind leaped to the central fact of a man of genius willing to risk his life to bring a vast mystery within the limits of actual knowledge" (Walsh, *Isabella* 318).

Walsh utilized some early histories for his accumulation of knowledge about Isabel, but it is clear that he accepted completely the fanciful, flattering verbal portraits and archetypal categories of woman that her contemporaries had constructed for her. Where the real woman falls in all this is difficult to determine even to this day. William Prescott's mid-nineteenth-century history of the reign of the Catholic monarchs, not as floridly written as Walsh's work, is nonetheless extremely flattering in its portrayal of Isabel, accepting the accounts of her contemporaries as nothing less than the truth. He even staves off potential criticism by stating that the accounts may seem to be excessive but most probably are warranted in this case. Although we have reason to believe that Isabel was plain and plump, Prescott waxes eloquent about her looks:

> Her person, as mentioned in the early part of the narrative, was of the middle height, and well-proportioned. She had a clear, fresh complexion, with light blue eyes and auburn hair—a style of beauty exceedingly rare in Spain. Her features were regular and universally allowed to be uncommonly handsome. The illusion which attaches to rank, more especially when united with engaging manners, might lead us to suspect some exaggeration in the encomiums so liberally lavished on her. But they would seem in great measure to be justified by the portraits that remain of her, which combine a faultless symmetry of features with singular sweetness and intelligence of expression. (124–25)

In contrast, Antonia Fraser paints a more conservative portrait, even calling the queen's expression "glum," in a justification for Ferdinand's philandering that is rather remarkable for a book as recent as 1988: "Isabella's portraits show her with a long nose and a down-turned mouth, characteristics not likely to inspire fidelity in one predisposed to philander . . . According to the evidence of their respective suits of armour, Isabella was also taller than Ferdinand by as much as an inch: a superiority not always welcome even in a royal wife . . . Yet in real life, whatever her physical imperfections, Isabella must have been endowed with charm as well as authority; for goodness does radiate its own kind of charm" (188). However her appearance may have been regarded by her husband, his own thoughts on the matter not having been recorded, the strains in the marriage would seem to have sufficient cause in his personal inclinations towards women and in his political views, such as the humiliating rivalry over the rule of Castile, a tug of war continually won by Isabel and her supporters. Such struggles weighed little in contrast to the efforts of the propagandists, among whom were converso poets, who had their own agenda in the queen's favorable portrayal.

In 1486, Fernando del Pulgar's *Claros varones de Castilla* (Great men of Castile) was published in Toledo. A collection of written portraits of important political figures in fifteenth-century Spain, Pulgar's work presents vivid descriptions of the fortunes and fates of "real men," set against the dramatic backdrop of the turbulent court life of fifteenth-century Castile. At the end of the collection, Pulgar includes Fray Íñigo de Mendoza's laudatory poem in honor of Isabel.[36]

Most significantly, Mendoza writes that while our collective human life was lost through the fault of a woman, through God's grace, a woman will redeem us. As

50 excelentes, Seville, 1497–1504. Gold coin. Obverse: portraits of Ferdinand V and Isabel I, with four stars placed between their portraits representing the mint mark for Seville; reverse: their coat of arms. Courtesy of The Hispanic Society of America, New York.

Mary was a "second Eve," in the sense of a reversal of Eve, so too was Isabel, and once again, by implication, a second Virgin Mary.

Mendoza and another poet, Antón de Montoro, are most often invoked in biographies of Isabel and histories of her reign to show the early tendency of chroniclers and poets to compare Isabel and the Virgin Mary. Both are conversos, although few critics mention this. Ian Michael, for example, in explaining other people's surprise that the queen's royal library contained "secular, even racy, material" (104), attributes their shock to the success of Isabel's portrayal as exceptionally pious and devout. That one ought to feel shocked by the possibility that Isabel could have riffled through such books is a tribute to the efforts of all the chroniclers and apologists of her reign to present her, almost from its inception, as a secular version of the Virgin Mary: the Franciscan Íñigo de Mendoza began the dedication to his guide to princes' behavior by comparing Isabel with the Virgin in her specific function of repairer and restorer, the latter of mankind, the former of the realm of Castile, and this idea proliferated in later writers (Michael 104). Antonia Fraser refers to the same poem by Íñigo de Mendoza, and drawing from the history by Felipe Fernández-Armesto, repeats his remark that the poet Montoro declared Isabel worthy to have given birth to the son of God (Fraser 189; Fernández-Armesto, *Ferdinand and Isabella,* 106).

In a most interesting analysis of the poetry of converso authors dedicated to Isabel in the early years of her reign, 1474–1480, Gregory B. Kaplan suggests that socioeconomic and political realities of conversos in fifteenth-century Spain inspired this laudatory poetry in honor of Isabel, in the hope that her wisdom and goodness would impel her to restore the social circumstances of Spanish conversos to an acceptable state.[37]

Bad Women and Good in the Late Fifteenth Century

Two examples point to the solidified view of a culpable La Cava. The first one shows how famous women were viewed in the late fifteenth century, in a didactic letter that includes both Isabel and La Cava. One of Isabel's propagandists, Diego Rodríguez de Almela, wrote letters to Diego de Carvajal in 1484, now contained in a manuscript in the British Library.[38] As David Mackenzie tells us, the eight letters in the collection reflect the author's firm beliefs in the neo-Gothicist "ideals of a united Spain, free from internal strife and infidel occupation" (xvii). The last letter attempts to resolve the issue of the historical role of Alfonso VI's sister Urraca.[39] Legend has it that Princess Urraca was El Cid's lover at one point, and that she famously carried on an incestuous affair with her brother Alfonso, while plotting the murder of their other brother, Sancho. Rodríguez de Almela uses the occasion to reflect on the two archetypal kinds of women, good and bad, and their special significance when the qualities are present in female rulers. He tells us that Urraca was "mala muger," a "bad woman," a sexually sinning harridan, but that her daughter was her maidenly opposite: "la infante dona Sancha que fue noble e virtuosa donzella, por cierto mucho mejor que la dicha reina doña Urraca su madre" (Princess Sancha was a noble and virtuous maiden, certainly much better than the queen, her mother, Urraca; 84). Sancha practices the spiritual and corporal works of mercy, shuns marriage, and embarks on a pilgrimage to Jerusalem, where she is the recipient of a miracle by God on Holy Saturday. After that, "bivio muy casta santa e virtuosamente en toda su vida fasta que murió" (she lived a very chaste, saintly, and virtuous life until her death; 85). There is no historical evidence to support such a dichotomous view of mother and daughter, but in a century obsessed with precisely such categorizations, the presentation is both creative and unsurprising. Because Urraca was a bad woman, he tells us, she found a bad end, as do the men who take up with such women.

Rodríguez de Almela mined stories to reflect the current political views about the efficacy of having a reigning queen of Castile. The author emphasized the notion of a kingdom that fell because of woman, but used the legend of the fall of Spain in the service of proving the moral dichotomy between La Cava, who caused the fall, and medieval Spanish women, who had held their country or province together admirably, reaching a zenith in the reign of the much-praised Isabel the Catholic.

Rodríguez de Almela warns of the dangers of women to rulers, citing as powerful examples the allure of Helen of Troy, and the weakness of the otherwise magnificent ruler, King Solomon. Painting a most unflattering portrait of women in general, and the power of their concupiscence, he refers to Spain's own bad woman: "E dexadas las estrañas corónicas fablando de lo nuestro, esta España por causa de Alataba fija del conde don Julian se perdió, e otras muchas graves cosas" (and leaving aside foreign chronicles to speak of our own, Spain was lost because of Alataba [La Cava] the daughter of Count Julian, and many other grave things occurred; 92). The problem is women's inordinate sexual desire, and men's propensity to seek out such women, always to their own peril. However, Spain has had some notable women, noble and virtuous, with a common trait: although able to govern well, they preferred to be peacekeepers, and most of all, they desired to retire from governance in order to found monasteries and convents, and indeed retire to one themselves. Women who seek power and the throne are no doubt cut from the same cloth as Urraca, while the strongest female rulers are the ones who want it the least. The lengthiest example he gives is Juan II of Castile's sister María (1401–1458), wife of Alfonso V of Aragon and aunt of Isabel the Catholic, who was celebrated as a saintly and pious peacekeeper, and a founder of convents. Rodríguez de Almela casts all the foibles of men as just that, while the sexual desires of women are sins. It is not coincidental that Alacaba leads the list, the one whose sin caused the fall of Spain, and the last to be named is Isabel, she who restored and unified Spain and who, unbeknownst to Rodríguez de Almela at that point, would in just under a decade conquer Granada and then expel the Jews and repress the Muslims.

The second example, an interesting witness to late fifteenth-century Spain's general view of its founding myth, is a biography of an important nobleman, don Rodrigo Ponce de León, entitled *Historia de los hechos del marqués de Cádiz* (History of the deeds of the marquis of Cádiz).[40] In it, the anonymous author blames Count Julian and La Cava, with a passion worthy of a blistering sermon, one for being a traitor, the other a woman who should have remained silent. The author makes no mention at all of Bishop Oppas; and King Rodrigo is excused for his minor offense, an understandable human sin:

> Un rey tan grande y tan poderoso, tan riquísimo y tan esforzado y de tan florecido linaje como fue el rey don Rodrigo, el postrimero rey de los godos en España, y por un pecado tan humano, el cual non alabo, que pudiera ser sofrido o callado, o rescebida enmienda, que fuera bien satisfecho en otras maneras honestas. ¡Oh

mujer malaventurada! ¡Oh conde Julián! ¡Oh entrañas tan crueles! ¡Oh corazones tan duros que quesistes dar tan gran cabsa de tanto cabtiverion, mortandat y destruición en todas las Españas, de tantas gentes, hombres e mujeres y criaturas cristianas! Vuestras ánimas deben ser perdidas en los infiernos. (A great and powerful king, so rich, so forceful, and of such a distinguished lineage as Rodrigo, was the last king of the Goths, and all because of a sin, so human, which I will not elaborate, and which should have been suffered in silence, or could have been recompensed in some other honest and satisfactory manner. O wretched woman! O Count Julian! O cruel entrails! O hearts so hardened that you were willing to cause such captivity, death and destruction in all the Spains, of so many people, Christian men, women and children! Your souls will be lost in hell; cited in Pardo, "Le Roi Rodrigue" 105, n.110.)[41]

The Inquisition and the Holy Child of La Guardia

For commingled reasons—an obsession with blood purity, fear of the economic power of the Jews, and beliefs that the monarchy favored the Jews to the political and economic detriment of Christian Spain—anti-Semitism corroded Spanish society. The mantle of centuries-long, Church-sanctioned anti-Semitism passed from Ferrand Martínez and Vincent Ferrer to the Franciscan friar Alonso de Espina beginning in the mid-fifteenth century. An intellectual and influential member of the clergy, confessor to Enrique IV and his minister of state, Alvaro de Luna, Espina firmly believed himself justified in an inflamed hatred of the Jews and the conversos. His 1454 *Fortalitium Fidei* (Fortress of faith) consisted of four parts, in which each group discussed—witches, Muslims, Jews, and heretics—threatened to endanger and contaminate Christian Spain.[42] In *Fortalitium Fidei*, Espina culled from many sources every known Jewish blood libel in Europe, and recounted stories of Host desecration in Spain, beginning with a case in 1405, along with allegations of ritual child murder, which were never proven. As flowed from Espina's pen, his most demonized enemy, the converso, openly Judaized, consorted with the devil in the practice of witchcraft, and conspired against neighbor and state. His most consistently repeated allegation charged that the Antichrist, whose sole mission is to destroy Christianity, would infiltrate the Church in the body of a converso. He would be born in a time of war of adulterous sexual intercourse between a Christian man and a converso woman, and he would be possessed by the devil, whose vast knowledge he would acquire. Scrutiny and fear of the converso arose from the inability to differentiate by sight the Jew from the converso, who often lived in or near Jewish neighborhoods, and who retained cultural and religious practices that the Church abhorred, fearing that these practices led the convert into the realm of heresy. The story of the Antichrist as converso speaks to the inability to perceive difference in the enemy, the danger of a counterfeit coming in disguise. Espina's efforts, though he was hardly alone, greatly contributed to the formalized persecutions of conversos with the establishment of the Inquisition in 1478.

The belief in the genesis of the Antichrist leads us back to the idea of the converso and sexual danger, and a general preoccupation with sexual liaisons. Like the concubine, who could singlehandedly contaminate the entire city, the converso was an "infection," in the words of Friar Alonso de Ojeda, from the Dominican monastery of San Pablo in Seville. A 1480s political pamphlet, later printed as *Libro del alboraique* (Book of Al-Burak), described the converso as a monstrous hybrid, like Al-Burak, the mythical horselike beast that Mohammed rode from Mecca to Jerusalem and back to Mecca in a single night. In the pamphlet, the anonymous author rails against the false convert, who was almost every converso, accusing them all of pride, hypocrisy, pomposity, cruelty, inhumanity, and of having invented sodomy. Another friar, Andrés Bernáldez, curate of the Church of Los Palacios in Seville, who became one of the chroniclers for Ferdinand and Isabel, following the lead of Espina for whom there were only "public Jews and secret Jews," insisted that there were no true converts, calling the converso the "Jew in disguise."[43]

Some zealous ecclesiastics, like Ojeda and Bernáldez, feared that the Inquisition lacked force, lacked the kind of support from society that it would need to flourish, and their writings and sermons continued to cry out against the injustice and danger visited upon Christianity by an unchecked, growing populace of "heretics." For the first few years, the inquisitorial machine labored to establish itself in cities and towns across Spain, and its establishment in Seville in 1480, and the trials and executions of powerful converso leaders in the city in 1481, including Diego de Susán, about whom we will hear in chapter 6, helped to root the Inquisition there and encourage its spread and implementation elsewhere.

While the legend of the Jewess of Toledo and Alfonso VIII, still popular in fifteenth-century Spain, warned of the dangers to Christian society when the Jews came too close to monarchical power, the case of a murdered Christian child in 1489 or 1490 incited the general populace to fear the Jews and conversos as a pervasive threat to all good Christians. The story of the little boy of La Guardia led to an inquisitorial investigation, a trial, and spectacular executions of the Jewish and converso men found guilty of the crime. Although the story of the martyred child was but one example of centuries-long beliefs in Jewish blood libel, ritual sacrifice, and Host desecration, its impact on Spain cannot be overestimated: modern historians, who generally believe the killing of the little boy never happened, accord this story high significance as the popular impetus for the expulsion of the Jews from Spain in 1492.

Jewish blood libel stems from the belief that the Jews participated in the crucifixion of Jesus Christ, which played a part in the creation of anti-Semitic laws in the Iberian Peninsula as early as the sixth century. Allegations that the Jews engaged in ritual killings, and used the blood of non-Jews, gave rise to gruesome legends of the ritual murder of Christian children, of torturing and crucifying them in a mockery of the Crucifixion, and draining their blood for the making of Passover matzos. Medieval Spain was not the lone European participant in violent anti-Semitism.[44] Medieval England, France, Germany, and Austria all had their legends, from mid-twelfth century England to fifteenth-century Innsbruck, legends that did not abate in later centuries, and that repeated the same narrative patterns. Even Chaucer accuses the "cursed Jewes" of infanticide in one of *The Canterbury Tales.*[45]

Also pervasive were tales of Host desecration, often by stabbing, to crucify Christ again and again: in some miraculous events, the Host would "bleed," spectacularizing the sacrilege of the attackers. The thirteenth-century monk, Gonzalo de Berceo, writes two stories about "true tales" of ritual murder and mockery of Christ, in one case through the stabbing of a wax figure of Jesus. In this collection of *Milagros de Nuestra Señora* (*Miracles of Our Lady*), the guilty Jewish males suffer the penalty of death for their wickedness, described as a blood lust the Jewish people appear unable to control. A recurring feature of these legends revealed the main perpetrator of the evil to be the highest-ranking rabbi of the town or city, to shore up the notion that the Jews were in league with the devil and that gruesome acts against humanity, particularly against Christianity, formed an official part of Judaism, sanctioned by their highest-ranking religious leaders.

Jody Enders describes the popularity of fifteenth-century Parisian performances of a theatrical Host desecration tale, based on a demonstrably invented incident of thirteenth-century Paris. Her assessment of the significance of the play's performance chills the reader: "[T]he Sainte Hostie forges a conceptual bond between drama and real life whose virulence far surpasses the apparent bounds of any stage play. Each time a Christian audience gathered together in the old familiar places of theater to designate Jews as evil and to self-designate their fellowship as virtuous, they reenacted a drama that demanded that [the Jews'] efforts to disembody the embodiment of Christ be avenged by the disembodiment of the Jews" (*Death by Drama* 120). The result of this continual reenacting of "historical memory" is that the "old anti-Semitic legend seemed more real because of theater" (120). And so it was with the legend of the Holy Child of La Guardia, which united Spanish Jews and conversos as evil annihilators of virtuous Christian fellowship.

Spain's first alleged case occurred in 1250, and others followed in the fifteenth century, recounted especially, and with a relish born of great hatred, by Alonso de Espina. But the spectacular elements of the 1490 crime inflamed the national imagination, cementing the view that the Jews, accused killers of Christ, would continue to kill his innocent followers. As Bernáldez and others had continued to insist, Jews and conversos could never be integrated into the social fabric and daily life of Christian Spain, and Spanish Christians would never be safe.

In 1490, so the legend goes, a small child from the environs of Toledo disappeared, murdered by a group of six evil and vengeful Jews and five conversos from the villages of La Guardia and Tembleque, who had witnessed a public burning, known as an inquisitorial "auto da fé," an act of faith, of some Jews convicted of heresy. They decided to enact a horrific revenge on the town by cutting the heart out of a little Christian boy, stealing a consecrated Host, and burning them together. Through black magic, they would turn the resultant ashes into a poisonous mixture that they would use to poison the town's water supply. Juan Franco, a vendor whose comings and goings through the town would not be remarked on, lured a little beggar boy into his cart, having given his blind mother a promise of a better life for her son. Once in the town of La Guardia, they imprisoned the boy and tortured him, while they waited for the perfect day to carry out their crime: the solemn holy day of the Crucifixion, Good Friday, which fell that year on March 31. They reenacted the Crucifixion, from the whipping with reeds to the anointing with a crown of thorns, until they crucified him in a secluded cave near the town. They cut his veins, drained his blood, and began to cut out his heart from the wrong location on his body, whereupon the boy—miraculously—asked what they were doing and directed them to the other side of his chest. At the moment of the tiny martyr's death, they say, his mother instantaneously regained her eyesight.

Meanwhile, the villains still needed a consecrated Host, so a converso sacristan named Juan Gómez provided one. They also solicited the help of some rabbis, who were allegedly well versed in necromancy. While they were putting into place the final details of their plot, one of the Jews entered a church in Astorga, to fool the townspeople into thinking he was a good Christian, but his prayerbook suddenly became illuminated with a light that filled the church. The man fled, but one of the faithful tracked him to an inn, where he was detained and questioned by local authorities. They found the consecrated Host he had hidden, and the inexplicable imprint of a heart on the man's prayerbook, and the plot came out. Though he led the authorities to the cave, they found no trace of the boy. This they attributed to a miraculous disappearance; that is, that God had taken the little one into Heaven, body and soul, as he had his own Son. As with other such tales, no body was ever found, nor did a family report a missing child. But by making the child a fatherless beggar boy, with a blind beggar for a mother, the story solves the problem of why no one in the town knew the family and their lineage, or even the full name of the boy, who later became known as little Christopher, the Holy Child of La Guardia. The Inquisition rounded up the rest of the men, both practicing Jews and conversos, who were tried between December 1490 and November 1491. After subjecting them to long months of torture, during which time confused and contradictory confessions emerged and were subsequently recanted, the inquisitors found the men guilty of murder and heresy, and ordered them burned at the stake in Avila on November 16, 1491.

Historians now believe that Inquisitor General Torquemada played a leading role in engineering this national spectacle of crime and punishment.[46] Haliczer explains that the Toledo tribunal of the Inquisition atypically did not conduct the extended trial. Rather, Torquemada himself convened a special inquisitorial court in the monastery of Santo Tomás de Ávila (150). The story of the Holy Child of La Guardia stunningly and horrifyingly joined the most degraded myths about the Jews—child killers and haters of all things Christian—with the basest desires of the Church, the Spanish monarchy, and its Christian citizenry in late fifteenth-century Spain. What had seemed radical in early fifteenth-century Spain, St. Vincent Ferrer's support for separation and segregation as necessary safeguards against Jewish pollutants ("for he will never be a good Christian who is a neighbor of a Jew"), paled in comparison to late fifteenth-century Spain's conclusion that only extermination and expulsion of the Jews could maintain the country intact and incorrupt.[47] The importance of the trial of the men accused of killing the child martyr to the goals of Torquemada and others to call for, and succeed in obtaining monarchical agreement to, the expulsion of the Jews cannot be overstated. After the trial, Torquemada ordered that priests read from the pulpits of the land descriptions of heretical deeds conducted by conversos, who were, in his mind, nothing but crypto-Jews. Everyone knew about the little child martyr. The Catholic monarchs, who faced ecclesiastical and political pressure to expel the Jews, had wavered for a few years. After being convinced of the Christian public's generally favorable inclination towards such an act, which the story of the Holy Child in no small measure helped to solidify, a month and a half after the execution of those accused of killing the child, the monarchs finally signed the Edict of Expulsion on March 31, 1492, giving the Jews only a few months' time to pack up and leave.[48]

The story of the bloodlusting, Christian-hating Jews and "false converts" captures the anxieties of fifteenth-century Spain, which were sometimes allegorized in a cautionary tale, such as the Jewess of Toledo, and sometimes allegorized into vio-

Hebrew Bible, Spain, 1490–1500. Illuminated manuscript on parchment. Folio 581r: last folio of the book of Nehemiah. Courtesy of The Hispanic Society of America, New York.

lent reality, as in the torture and execution of the Jews and conversos accused of killing the child. The story of the child martyr argues that no one, neither king nor commoner, is safe from the Jew, an anxiety that remained strong in the sixteenth and seventeenth centuries, and that was transferred, in part, to the Muslim in those centuries, who was viewed with increasing suspicion as crypto-Muslims allied with a militant Islam beyond the shores of Spain. In fact, at times of crisis involving the Moriscos, authorities sought to make analogies between the "problem" of the conversos in the matter of the pure expression of Christianity in Spain (that is, free from heretical contamination) and the safety of the Christian individual, for which the memory of the Holy Child of La Guardia could serve a very useful purpose. For example, in the late 1560s, right when the Crown suppressed a Morisco revolt, the first public monument to the Holy Child, a large commemorative tablet, was erected in La Guardia.

The sixteenth century witnessed several important retellings of the story of the Holy Child, and devotion to his cult intensified. According to legend, the hat and socks of the boy were found buried in the cave, the site of his torture and murder, which provided some relics of the little saint. In 1599, the public procession of what was believed to be the consecrated Host from 1490 caused a plague to abate, a miracle attributed to the boy. Lope de Vega's play *El niño inocente de La Guardia* (The innocent child of La Guardia), probably written in 1603, dramatizes the significance of this legend as an allegory of nation building by casting the story within a framework of a dream of national unity based on a purified Christianity in Spain. Lope frames the details of the abduction and murder of the child by scenes of Queen Isabel, fretting about the safety of King Ferdinand in his valorous quests to defeat Granada and the Muslims, and dreaming of unified Christian lands.[49] Today, the town of La Guardia, near Toledo, still celebrates the feast of the child they call Santo Niño Cristóbal, little Christopher, on September 25, where a mass is held in the cave they believe to be the site of the ritual murder. The town church, Our Lady of the Assumption, completed in 1765, contains one chapel dedicated to the child saint.

The Fallen and the Promise

In 1493, Pope Alexander VI bestowed upon Isabel and Ferdinand of Spain the title of Reyes Católicos, that is, the Catholic monarchs. This gesture celebrated the discovery of America, the fall of Granada, and the expulsion of the Jews from Spain, all of which had happened the year before, in 1492. It also granted the Catholic monarchs and their descendants, as well as the king of Portugal and his descendants, total responsibility for evangelization of all the new lands added to their realms. With these declarations, the pope helped set the country on the road to an empire of enormous and unprecedented extension.

Ironically enough, in recountings of the legend of the fall of Spain in 711, the work that was least historical was the one that most shaped the legend in the sixteenth century and beyond, beginning with its first printing in 1499. It is impossible to tell what specific influence it may have had in the fifteenth century itself. But it is abundantly clear that this work invented aspects of and embellished the founding myth in ways that became influential staples of the telling from the early 1500s on. Moreover, and most significantly, Corral had woven together in one work some of the flashpoints of fifteenth-century Spain, including neo-Gothicism and the importance of Pelayo, and the physical, political, and moral dangers posed by women, Jews, and Muslims.

Corral inextricably yoked the founding myth to the treacherous nature of Jews, as open and overt enemies of Christianity and therefore enemies of Spain. Never again could the legend be told without the component of the Jews, not as citizens of Toledo in 711, but as the enemy within. In theory, no Jews had escaped from Toledo to Asturias with Pelayo and the "patricios" (patricians), as Sánchez Albornoz calls them. On the one hand, charging Jewish Spanish citizens with murdering Christian children provided a sensational reason for the need to protect Christianity from them. But Corral brought it all back to a question of origins, by mythologizing, in accessible and popular form, the story of how the Jews not only enabled the fall of Spain in 711, but were never ever a part of the new, eighth-century Spain in Asturias. When Pelayo saves his sister from the clutches of the Muslim prince Munuza, he rescues not only a worthy virgin, but he preserves, by extension, the purity of blood for all of Spain against the Muslim invaders. Munuza embodies the metonymic "sexualized Moor," in which Christian misreadings of the Koran increasingly associated Islam with unbridled sexuality, and therefore a danger to Christian women and men alike.[50] Pelayo kept the Muslims out of Asturias and recovered the girl who might otherwise have mixed Visigothic blood with Muslim blood. Pelayo's acts underscore the fact that the Muslims, like the Jews, had no place in the birth of the new Spain in Asturias. The expulsion of the Jews in 1492 signaled a new beginning for Spain, a return to origins, to the legacy of Pelayo's ethnically pure Visigothic kingdom. For Corral—and for Spain—the girl who was blameless in some stories, or blameworthy on some level simply by being a woman, became Caba, "fija de Satanás," daughter of Eve, and the Eve of Spain. Corral's work showcased two men, Rodrigo and Pelayo, one a judicious Gothic king and one a Gothic Christian nobleman, one whose sexual desire—his tragic flaw—would cause his downfall and that of his country, and one whose heroism and avoidance of women would, at the Battle of Covadonga in Asturias in 718, save all of Europe from the "scourge of Islam." These two men, the fallen and the promise, became intertwined forever at the events that took place on the eve of Spain in 711, when Spain's first Visigothic kingdom was forever lost.

PROMISE AND FULFILLMENT

(1492–1700)

From Don Pelayo the kings of Spain trace their descendancy without ever cutting the line of their royal ancestry, up to the present time; on the contrary, sons have always inherited the crown from their fathers, or brothers from their brothers, which is truly worth noting.

Father Juan de Mariana (1592)

Take from a woman her beauty, take from her kindred riches, comeliness, eloquence, sharpness of wit, cunning in her craft, give her chastity and thou has given her all things.

Juan Luis Vives (1524)

Interlude

It is the time of Spain's artistic Golden Age, the sixteenth and seventeenth centuries, the epoch of Cervantes, the painter Diego de Velázquez, and the architectural marvel the Escorial, King Philip II's sprawling palace-monastery about an hour away from Madrid.[1] The deeds and rule of King Ferdinand, much more than those of Queen Isabel, inspired laudatory commentaries by early modern historians, convinced that he had been the ruler heralded in earlier prophecies of the coming of a kingly savior, who would restore Christian Spain to its former glory. Well into the nineteenth century, historians praised Ferdinand as the one who had fulfilled the promise that started with Pelayo and the Battle of Covadonga in 718: King Ferdinand had achieved the successful restoration of Spain to the purity and greatness of its pre-Islamic condition. Ferdinand, not Isabel, had prepared the country for empire and world dominion. Ferdinand, the Catholic king, set the visionary standard against which his predecessors measured themselves and were measured by others.[2]

But in this Golden Age, set against a backdrop of grand achievement in the visual and literary arts, against prophetic events and timely interpretations that predicted Spain's imperial greatness, against New World expansion, colonization, and evangelization, and against the ambitions of Spain's kings to be the most powerful rulers in the world and the principal defenders of universal Christianity, is the harsh reality of a frequently bankrupt Spain, of the ongoing strife and turmoil produced by the Spanish Inquisition, and of revolts by different ethnic and economic groups, including the Moriscos. The Moriscos in Spain were reminders of the looming threat of Muslim Turkish invasion from outside the country. The Protestant Reformation in Europe, and the discovery at various points during the century of pockets of Protestant groups in Valladolid and Seville, fueled the fear of heresy, a topic of acute anxiety in the sixteenth century. This fear fostered the closing off of Spain, the country's spiritual and intellectual retreat from the rest of Europe, and the efforts of Spain's highly active Counter-Reformation to limit the nation's participation in, and access to, European intellectual advances.[3] Consequently, while no country lends itself to a static profile in any given period, Spain's internal and external fortunes and tensions throughout the sixteenth and seventeenth centuries were particularly volatile, contradictory, dramatic, and dichotomized. The legend of the Fall of Spain in 711, with King Rodrigo's defeat and the start of the Restoration of Spain with "King" Pelayo's victory, emerged time and again during the two centuries. The founding myth, the myth of origins, reflected numerous domestic and international crises and shaped the country's responses to them. Most significantly, the tellings of the founding myth determined how Spain and the Spanish people would define themselves in the modern world. In that sense, though Rodrigo, La Cava, and Julian make for a much more titillating and more frequently told tale, the story of Pelayo mattered more for the future of Spain. The obsession of a blood culture perhaps defined sixteenth- and seventeenth-century Spain more than anything else did. For that reason, along with the increasing emphasis on the nature of monarchy and the role of the monarch, the figure of Pelayo, which allowed tracing both blood and throne to eighth-century Asturias, gained new prominence.

At the end of the fifteenth century, the start of a new century, Spain had found itself a nation poised on the brink of empire. With the Jews expelled, Granada won, and the Granadine Muslims suppressed and moved out of Andalusia to other provinces, the nation could claim something close to a prelapsarian condition—Spain as it was before the fall, before Rodrigo lost it. And yet, if the end of any century impels societal self-contemplation and reflection, Spain at the start of the new century, in spite of the extraordinary achievements of the Crown, was no different in sounding notes of caution—even apocalyptic predictions—amidst the self-congratulatory tone of its court chronicles and reports from the New World. As we will see in the following two chapters, dominant sociocultural and political issues, such as religion, violence, personal and national honor, prophecy, and the view of women, viewed separately and convergently, intersected with nation and empire in fiction and in real life.

Pedro de Corral's *Crónica del Rey don Rodrigo, postrimero rey de los godos* (Chronicle of King Rodrigo, last king of the Goths), the compelling historical romance that audiences accepted as official history, was a perfect tale for the sixteenth century, resonating with important issues of that time. Both the fall and the restoration began with episodes of male personal honor involving the violation of women and were set within a context of religion, violence, and prophecy. These topics gripped the reading public as they entered the new Golden Age, and the issues continued to dominate politics and culture in early modern Spain throughout the sixteenth century. *Crónica del Rey don Rodrigo* did double duty as a testimony of national triumph and as a cautionary tale, a warning not to let down the nation's guard in the ongoing threat of invasion from the Turks, to be vigilant regarding women in general, as well as the Muslims and Jewish converts still within Spain. It served also as inspiration to broaden the fight, in the spirit of Reconquest, with the quest to colonize and

Christianize the New World. The fortunes of Spain would fluctuate wildly through the century-long reign of two important kings, Charles (Carlos) I—later Charles V, Holy Roman Emperor—and his son Philip II, grandson and great-grandson of the Catholic monarchs, while Spain's commitment to world domination and to her role as defender of the faith never wavered.

The sixteenth century was an age of unprecedented interest in, and reliance on, prophecy, which flourished as a lens through which one could regard local, national, and world events. While prophecy and the threats of invasions by infidels were hardly new to Spain or Europe in general, waves of prophecy, portents, signs, and apparitions captivated the cultural and political imagination of sixteenth-century Europe. Prophecy became a tool or mechanism by which cultural and political views could be controlled. Prophecy had always attached itself to the legend of the fall of Spain, and that attachment was heightened by the atmosphere of sixteenth-century Spain. Let us look at brief examples of the significance of prophecy as this century opens onto the age of empire and Spain's self-imposed mission of world Christianization.

Richard Kagan, in *Lucrecia's Dreams,* and Ottavia Niccoli, in *Prophecy and People in Renaissance Italy,* attest to the pervasive atmosphere of dreams, apparitions, monstrous births (a particularly frequent sign), and other kinds of prophetic phenomena in Western Europe. In 1478, Prince John was born to Isabel and Ferdinand, and the hopes of a dynasty rested with him. During the prince's early years, the poet and playwright Juan del Encina reworked into Castilian Virgil's ten Eclogues. The Fourth Eclogue predicts the return to earth of Astraea, virgin goddess of peace and justice. Encina's Sybil prophesies that the monarch who will usher in this new and long-awaited age of peace and harmony is Prince John, while the Virgin Astraea here becomes the Virgin Mary.[4] However, it was not to be, since the prince died in 1497 while the Catholic monarchs were still ruling. Only a few decades later, after the death of the prince, Astraea is linked again to a member of that royal family, Charles I of Spain (1516–1556), on whom fell the hope of world rule.[5] Related to a different prophecy attached to Charles I, Niccoli documents examples of the prophecies surrounding the coming of a second Charlemagne, who would be Holy Roman Emperor and crusading foe against the infidels. An early instance of the prophecy, around 1380, claimed that Charles VI of France was that new Charlemagne. Later reformulated to apply to Charles VIII of France, it then emerged years later attached to Charles I of Spain, who indeed became Charles V, Holy Roman Emperor in 1519, which he held until his abdication in 1556.[6]

The relocation of the former Muslims from Granada throughout the realms of Ferdinand and Isabel did little to assuage the fears of those in power, nor did active campaigns against Islam abate either inside or outside Spain. Isabel had died in 1504,

Charles V, by anonymous Flemish, after painting by Titian,
ca. 1600, Engraving, 26.8 × 19.7 cm. Note the addition of
"Plus Ultra" (there is more), adopted as part of the herald
for Charles V, signifying that more lands lay beyond the
pillars of Hercules, as confirmed by the discoveries of
Spanish explorers. Courtesy of The Hispanic Society of
America, New York.

and Ferdinand was denied the title of king of Castile, but the inquisitor general, Cardinal Cisneros, remained a strong ally and supporter of the king.[7] Cisneros perceived the threat posed by Oran, a city on the coast of North Africa, whose Muslim citizens had welcomed the majority of Spanish Muslims fleeing Spain and forced conversion to Christianity, and who now stood ready to help their religious compatriots fight back. In 1508, four years after the death of Isabel, the archbishop dreamed of a new Crusade, a Mediterranean holy war with Ferdinand, to be joined by his sons-in-law Henry VIII of England and Manuel of Portugal. While that grand plan failed to materialized, Cisneros did persuade Ferdinand to send a force to Oran, which fell to the Spanish Christian army.

Afterwards, a story circulated about Cisneros, that he had found a letter in a church in Toledo before the siege of Oran, which had predicted Christian victory overseas.[8] This news, that Cisneros had uncovered a prophetic document, would encourage Spain and other European countries to face what seemed like inevitable future sea battles against the Ottoman Turks. According to a French diplomat Charles de Bovelles, writing in 1509 and 1510, Cisneros entered the bowels of a Toledan church and discovered in an ark a parchment that showed pictures of Arabs, along with a statement that foretold their demise once the parchment had been found again. Reversing Rodrigo's discovery in the House of Hercules, this prophecy purportedly relied on the same element—a picture of men in turbans—to send the very different message, eight hundred years later, that this time Christianity would prevail. In praising Cisneros, Bovelles writes longingly for a return to the times sung by Virgil, a time of peace and prosperity, and rule by "a single prince" (Bataillon 57).

According to Richard Kagan, in *Lucrecia's Dreams,* the Letter of Toledo was but one of the many doomsday prophecies regularly circulated by medieval astrologers in the Spanish court, this one predicting an era of restoration followed by the destruction of Islam. By providential design, then, the sixteenth-century legend would have us believe that Cardinal Cisneros, almost eight hundred years later, rediscovers a prophetic parchment that reveals that the time had come for the reversal of that fall, and this time, the ones who face imminent destruction are the Muslims. It would not have escaped those who told this fictional tale of Cisneros that, as the current archbishop of Toledo, he would be reversing the treacherous acts of his predecessor Bishop Oppas, the bishop of Toledo during Rodrigo's reign.

A major goal of chapters 4 and 5 in this volume will be to examine some cultural and political paradigm shifts in early modern Spain, which were also prevalent in Western Europe. First is the pervasive tendency to view women in dichotomized fashion, as angel or whore, good or evil, and, as Mary Elizabeth Perry calls them, Magdalenes and Jezebels, reflecting the widespread view that all women are fallen, but some at least—the Magdalenes—can repent. The chastity of a woman was more than virtue; it was her identity. Second, and related to the first point, is the increasingly eroticized political language: when woman is not Eve, seductress of mankind, she is often chaste nation, vulnerable to rape by invaders who threaten the bodies of the populace as well as the Christian body of the nation.

These two developments of the age, or paradigm shifts, reflecting the views of both high and popular culture, are political and religious depending on their individual context, and I will examine them particularly in relation to how they cause the legend of Rodrigo and La Cava to function in different ways from previous centuries.

The portrayals and representations of the dichotomized woman and the gendered nation were staples of early modern Europe, which saw an unprecedented interest in depictions of Ave-Eva, of Mary Magdalene, and in the secular arena, of Lucretia, the Roman matron. Mary Magdalene, a particularly fecund and beloved image in this period, embodied both the fallen woman and the reformed one, never completely able to erase her lascivious past, but a symbol of the convert and the newly pious woman. In painting, literature, and sculpture, the Magdalene represents a former vamp, rehabilitated to the chaste life, and her most frequent posture is that of repentant woman, often in sensual and seductive representations. She is a former Eva, turned to emulate Ave. Along with the fear of women came increased means of controlling them, through enclosure of various kinds. Convents housed those who took the veil as well as many who did not; Magdalen Houses proliferated for unmarried women and reformed prostitutes; marital legislation forbade female ownership of property, limited social freedom of movement, and augmented laws on the subject of widows, whose financial and possible sexual autonomy were a threat. Perry explains the centrality of the notion of women's chastity as a symbol of moral order to political stability in the sixteenth century. There was a "widespread belief in Counter-Reformation Spain that chastity was to be valued above all other virtues for women and that it was the most vulnerable quality. In the peculiar mathematics of Counter-Reformation moralists, the female who lost her chastity acquired in exchange a frightening license to break every other taboo. The unchaste woman, in this view, posed not only a threat to the social order, but a real danger to the salvation of men's souls" (124).[9] Although there is a longstanding tradition of female unchastity and threatened, if not destroyed, political order, Perry is correct that interest in this tradition explodes in sixteenth-century Spain to an unprecedented degree.[10] And it is made manifest in the sixteenth-century evolution of La Cava from blameless victim to willing lover to siren.

Throughout Europe there is increased cultural appropriation of women to stand as symbols of nations, nation building, and destruction of nations. Although an ancient theme, there is a pervasive use of it in the sixteenth century, one that carries into the seventeenth century as well. Elizabeth I of England—the Gloriana, the Virgin Queen—shows how prevalent in this period characterizations of virginity and chastity were as a political model.[11] It is both disturbing and remarkable to realize how many national stories and founding myths depend on the rape of women. Widespread in this time were the representations of the figure of Lucretia, the chaste

Roman matron who killed herself rather than submit to rape and personal and familial dishonor. The rape of Lucretia became the symbol of the birth of humanism, and then the birth of the republic.[12] Later, early modern monarchs, including Philip II of Spain (1556–1598), appropriated this figure as a metaphor for the emergence of his own nation, as he did with paintings of the Rape of Europa (Abduction of Europa). As Marcia Welles points out, scenes of violence against women, rather than being denounced or even regarded as inappropriate in any way, decorated the palaces of Europe.[13]

When we study the figures of various women as they are employed in the renewal of the Spanish state and the birth of the Spanish empire, whose most illustrious figure is Queen Isabel, we see how highly significant was the Spanish pantheon of woman and nation. The interrelation of female sanctity, piety, chastity, and repentance to nation building, as well as its opposite, the interrelation of the impure, impious, lustful, witchlike daughters of Eve to the dangers of national, imperial, and personal destruction pervade the Spanish national and moral imagination.[14] If Isabel came to be seen, even during the time of her reign, and of course beyond, as the maternal nation builder ("wetnurse of the nation," a term also used by political writers about Elizabeth I), La Cava came to be known for her harlotry as the female destroyer of the nation, equated with Helen of Troy for her reckless disregard of the welfare of the state, but infinitely worse than Helen for her added and unforgivable sin of causing the loss of the Christian nation to the Muslims, becoming the quintessential "bad Christian woman."

While fear of heretical practices and crypto-Judaizing threatened the realization of a unified Christian society, the most dangerous and feared enemies, of course, were the Muslims, both inside and outside of Spain, with the English Protestants and French Huguenots a not-too-distant second. Language about these political and religious enemies, especially the Muslims, was eroticized, and comparisons to the female sex were used to disparage the enemy. The Muslims were increasingly characterized as threatening in sexual terms: as effeminate, particularly as sodomites (who would then desire Christian boys), as rapists (leaving unsafe the Christian maiden, wife, and widow), and, since the thirteenth century at least, as morally inferior to Christians and therefore a threat to the entire nation. In the symbolism that saw the country as chaste nation, the Muslims, collectively, threatened to violate the land.

The fear of women converged with the continued revilement of conversos throughout the sixteenth century. Beginning in 1525, the Inquisition pursued with zeal women suspected of sorcery and witchcraft, and of heretical practices such as the movement known as *alumbradismo* (Illuminism), a religious reform that at-

The Apotheosis of the Spanish Monarchy, sketch for a ceiling painting, by Giovanni Battista Tiepolo (Italian, Venetian, 1696–1770). Oil on canvas, oval painted surface, 32⅛ × 26⅛ in. (81.6 × 66.4 cm). From 1762 until his death, Tiepolo worked in Spain for Charles III and decorated several rooms in the Palacio Real, Madrid. This is one of two oil sketches for the saleta adjacent to the throne room. Each shows a female figure of Spain with lions for the province of León, an old woman beside a castle for Castile, and Hercules, the traditional protector of Spain, with a column representing Gibraltar. Courtesy of The Metropolitan Museum of Art, Rogers Fund, 1937 (37.165.3). Image © The Metropolitan Museum of Art.

tracted many women leaders and devoted male followers, who were very often conversos. As Mary Giles explains, Illuminism

> emphasized interiorized Christianity over and against blind adherence to church rituals and belief, with spiritual writers and preachers encouraging individuals to nourish a personal relationship with God through mental prayer and quiet attentiveness to the inner presence of the Divine. Convinced that the Holy Spirit inspired men and women and illumined their way to God, both lay and religious, men and women, learned and uneducated, emerged as spiritual leaders to teach interior prayer and interpret Sacred Scripture. Prominent on the spiritual scene were charismatic women, popularly known as *beatas,* or holy women, who often were accompanied by male admirers and through their ecstasies, visions, and miraculous healing confirmed the power of God to make of the most ordinary person, even an unschooled peasant woman, the channel of his will. (4)

In Spain, another important tool of nation and empire building came from the value placed on relics of saints. King Philip II's devotion to his ever-expanding collection of relics was without peer in Western Christendom, and one of his passions indulged a search for relics connected to the Visigothic period. A special premium was placed on the relics of female saints, particularly virgin martyrs, and the 1587 return to Spain of the centuries-old relics of Leocadia, Toledo's patron saint from the time of the Visigoths, stood as a compelling example of the nation's efforts to become the most visible center of Christianity, and of Leocadia herself to symbolize the nation restored to wholeness and integrity.

Golden Age histories and literature obsessively took up the legend of the fall of Spain and its restoration. The fall inspired seemingly countless imaginative versions and references to the legend, while the restoration, albeit no less fictionalized, simply allowed for fewer embellishments, and quite deliberately excluded any direct dramatization of sex. No genre contributed more to the dissemination of Spain's founding myth than the popular oral ballads. The ballads eroticized both history and political language, indeed as more learned writings were doing, but diffused these views and cemented them in the national cultural imagination. Fecund, "feminized" Muslim towns and cities, like the sexually available Muslim princesses of medieval epic and chronicle, found themselves possessed by forceful Christian men, nobles and commoners alike. The imagery allowed for a dichotomous view of Muslim men. In situations in which they were unable to stave off Christian triumph, Muslim men were painted as effeminate. As marauding barbarians, their lustful possession of Christian women and potential polluting of Christian blood through sexual intercourse, Muslim men were equated with women's dangerous sexuality in

Philip II, 1597, by Giovanni Orlandi (Italian, active ca.
1570–1640). Engraving, 20.3 × 13.5 cm. From Andrea Vac-
caro, *Effigie naturali de i maggior prencipi et piu valerosi
capitani,* Rome, 1597. The golden fleece, which hangs
from the bottom of the herald, is still used today in the
herald of the prince of Asturias, the title of the crown
prince of Spain. Courtesy of The Hispanic Society of
America, New York.

general. Wheatcroft points out in his book *Infidels* that the early medieval recountings of Rodrigo and La Cava made an association between Rodrigo and the Muslims (63). However, early modern tales equated the dangerous sexuality of La Cava
with the sexually unbridled Muslim men. In the early legend, Rodrigo's lust to possess La Cava took precedence over his obligation to protect Christian lands, leaving
them vulnerable to the Muslims, who took possession of them and of the Christian
women they raped. Corral's fifteenth-century book began the shift toward the culpable La Cava, and the sixteenth century capitalized on the association of the leg-

end with minorities and women and their sexually predatory nature. The counterpart to the mythical Astraeas, the mytho-poeticized Isabels and Elizabeths, whose chastity and virginity empowered them to build nations and even empires, and the Leocadias, whose virginity in martyrdom came to represent the nation itself, is the Eve figure of the national legend, La Cava.

During the sixteenth and seventeenth centuries, but particularly in the seventeenth, both Protestant and Catholic reformers focused on the monarch, who in countries such as England and France was regarded more as a quasi-divinity than was the king in Spain. Counter-Reformation moralists, the Spanish Jesuits in particular, began to "reassert . . . the purificatory ideal of the ascetic self. Spearheaded by the new Catholic preaching orders, the Counter-Reformation spread a message of contempt for the world and the flesh, of redemption through denial and mortification . . . As Louis Chatellier has put it, they sought the 'realization of the Christian state' through moral control of the mechanisms of governance" (Monod 51). The Jesuits focused on the nature of kingship:

> [They] argued that kings were responsible to the church, to the pope, perhaps even to the people. Father Pedro de Rivadeneira warned the Christian prince "not to puff himself up with the authority or with the power and sovereignty of the king . . . [kings are] no more than a little dust and ashes." The king should act as the obedient instrument of God and the church: "No king is absolute or independent or proprietary, but is a lieutenant and minister of God . . . [Princes] are guardians of the law of God, but not interpreters; ministers of the Church, but not judges . . . If sometimes, as men, they will fall into some grave crime, they should recognize it and humiliate themselves, and subject themselves to the ecclesiastical canons and the censure and correction of the Church." (Monod 51–52)

In Spanish Baroque culture, the emphasis was on "an outward, practical morality rather than a spiritual interiority" (Monod 130), and writers such as Cervantes and Lope de Vega reflected this model of the king "as the dynamic center of an organic corpus mysticum" (Monod 130), one that focused on action, and less on introspection and self-examination. The sixteenth-century printings of Corral's *Crónica del Rey don Rodrigo* contained a prologue that promoted the importance of confession, and in the story itself Rodrigo submits himself to the mortificatory recommendations of the hermit in order to restore himself spiritually. Here, we can begin to see the seeds of change in the view of kingship, that the ruler must be forgiven by earthly ecclesiastical authorities, as any other sinner would need to do, which also allows society to begin to view the monarch and the nation as separate entities. In contrast, for example, Lope de Vega's play *El último godo* (The last Goth) cares very little for the personal story of the salvation of Rodrigo's soul, turning instead to the actions and monarchical qualities of the nation's savior, Pelayo.

King Rodrigo's sin of lust, even if excused or justified in various ways, fit the concerns of the time. All across Europe, calls for the presence in rulers of the "ideals of the ascetic self" allowed Rodrigo to serve in Spain as a negative example of kingship. This renewed focus on the chastity of the king, or at the very least the ability of the king to control his appetites, was not a new phenomenon.

Chastity, while of paramount significance and importance for women, was important for male leaders and rulers, however much a double standard existed in reality. From early times, sexual restraint symbolized the ability to control one's impulses in general, which would be a good sign of the king's wider ability to exercise caution and prudent judgment in matters of state. In short, chastity and self-control stood in for the ruler's virtue. John Gower, in his fourteenth-century poem *Confessio Amantis* (*A Lover's Confession*), argued that

> the fifth element of statecraft is chastity, which very seldom makes its appearance anywhere these days. Even so, there is no one who can be wholly chaste without an exceptional dispensation of grace. But in view of a king's elevated position, anointed and consecrated as head of the secular order, for the sake of the dignity of his crown he should be more looked up to than anybody of humble rank who is not of such noble consequence. Therefore a prince ought to stop and think before lapsing into debauchery, and beware especially of such infatuation as would transform the quality of his manhood into effeminacy. (Blamires 248–49)

To some extent, Gower's view about the essential role played by the king's own chastity in a successful monarchy resembles the view we have seen from the earliest chronicles of the fall of Spain through the fifteenth century, that decried the decadence of the populace and of the king, when Rodrigo's lust fatally weakened his position as ruler, opening himself and the kingdom to the revenge of both a wrathful father and a wrathful God. But the sixteenth century signals changes in the tale. Rodrigo is not blameless in most of the accounts and will always, from the viewpoint of the obligations of a king to his country, be guilty of a lack of self-control, with widespread and dire consequences. Much more is made of La Cava's role in the fall of the nation than before, and accusations of her lack of chastity pervade the early modern retellings. In the sixteenth century, in large measure inspired by the treatment of the noble Rodrigo in Corral's *Crónica del Rey don Rodrigo,* the fate of the king and his country acquires tragic dimensions. The rape is not seen as debauchery that leads to effeminacy in a ruler, as medieval histories claimed, although adultery is a sin in the Spain of the Reformation and Counter-Reformation. It is seen, rather, as the understandable and inevitable result of what happens when a man is faced with the temptation of a beautiful woman, who is unable or unwilling to guard her own chastity.

Pelayo, on the other hand, is made to reflect perfectly the desirable qualities of a ruler at the same time that he serves as a transitional figure, the blood link between Goths and future Spaniards. He springs into action against the Muslims not when they first subjugate the Christians, but when Munuza abducts Pelayo's sister. Pelayo's character never seems to develop beyond being a reversal of Rodrigo and is painted in very broad strokes. Thus, for example, in all the stories of Pelayo through the centuries, we never hear about his wife until he is dead, and his wife is buried alongside him. Having a wife is of no importance, though having a daughter—who becomes the wife of the first official Asturian king, Alfonso I—becomes essential to the establishment of the monarchical and biological lineage between the Visigoths and the later throne of Castile and Old Christian citizens of Spain.

CHAPTER FOUR

Desiring the Nation

The snake has now bitten / it's biting the part / that deserves the
most blame, / the part that has caused / my misfortune and shame.

"Ballad of Rodrigo's Penance"

The Influence of Pedro de Corral's *Chronicle of King Rodrigo* in the Sixteenth Century

When the fifteenth-century chronicler Pérez de Guzmán roundly criticized Corral's manuscript for its fictional elements that masqueraded as history, he anticipated some of the concerns of sixteenth-century historians and moralists, who believed that the historian's role was a sacred one. Nevertheless, though some historians rejected aspects of Corral's work as largely fictional, much of Corral's plot line already appeared in many histories composed by medieval official court chroniclers. Moreover, some of the features and themes of Corral's popular historical romance held special meaning for the sixteenth-century reading public, indeed for the public imagination of both the literate and illiterate: prophecy; penance; the character development of the king, La Cava, and Julian; the invention of the love story of Favila and Luz; and the birth and upbringing of their son Pelayo.

Although we know that prophecy played an important role in early medieval versions of the legend, Corral expands the role of prophecy. For the sixteenth-century audience, engaged in the triumphs and struggles of national identity, empire building, and ongoing wars, a reminder of the early Christian nation falling to Islam would resonate in particularly acute fashion.

Another feature, Rodrigo's confession and grueling penance, was of great significance to sixteenth-century Spain. We know this from two pieces of evidence. First, the ballads inspired by Corral dwell on Rodrigo's remorse, as he gazes over his devastated army and the field now running with streams of blood, and on his penance. Ballads that derive from longer works traditionally select some high moment of drama and intensify it, such as the ballad lines that serve as epigraph to this chapter. Audiences reveled in the king's confession to the hermit, the hermit's imposed penance, and, most popularly, the dramatic moment when Rodrigo cries out, from within the sepulcher he shares with the snake, that the snake is biting him "where most I sinned!" Second, the 1511 Valladolid edition of *Crónica del Rey don Rodrigo* contains a prologue not found in the earliest printing of Seville 1499, but which reappears in the 1549 Toledo and 1586 and 1587 Alcalá de Henares printings. The new prologue, by an unnamed author, crafts a sermon that encourages the reader to focus on the concepts of sin, penance, penitent, and redemption as they unfold in the tragic tale of the great king. La Cava is referred to as "cruel maiden" (cruel donzella), and the capital letter S in the 1549 printing, which begins the prologue, forms a snake, so that from the very beginning readers are primed to associate Eden with Spain's fall, complete with serpent, a blameworthy Eve figure, and a man who also falls. Corral showcases redemption through Rodrigo's personal penance, and sows the seeds of the nation's recovery and redemption with the actions of Pelayo. We are encouraged as readers to recognize the individual and the universal aspects of the legend. Indeed, the author brings it around specifically to the reader and includes himself: "This was the cause of his terrible and horrifying penance. By means of which example we must all engage in worthy acts of penance since we see that all our sins impede our salvation" (Esto le fue causa dela terrible y espantosa penitencia. Por el qual exemplo deuemos todos hazer dignos fructos de penitencia pues vemos que nuestros peccados del todo impide nuestra saluacion; prologue, edition of Toledo, 1549, n.p.). Unlike the 1499 printing, which ends simply with the inscription on Rodrigo's tomb in Viseu and a statement that the story stands as a lesson to rulers who follow, the sixteenth-century printings all add an additional final statement about the salutary effects of forgiveness of sin and true penance, that says, in effect, pride topples sinners, humility stabilizes them, God forgives them, and Christ, the son of the virgin without stain, brings them to true repentance.

Both the prologue and the brief new ending to the sixteenth-century editions have relevance in the religious context of the time. Although the Lateran Council of 1215 had mandated that confession was necessary for all the faithful, the eve of the Reformation witnessed a decline in trust of the clergy, resulting in a widely held practice of bypassing the clergy in matters of restoring the relationship of the sinner with God. In a climate that emphasized penance but that did not, in the opinion of the Church, sufficiently recognize the role of auricular confession and the absolution that only the confessor could grant upon the sinner, the story of King Rodrigo, his oral confession to the saintly hermit, and rigorous penance devised by the hermit could be seen in a new and significant light. The prologue draws readers into the story of Rodrigo, moving us to equate his individual penitential practice with the universal need for penance for all the faithful. The ending of the work also moves the narrative from the particular to the universal, making exemplary the king's search for the hermit to hear his sins, his willing and humble confession, and his penance.

Stephen Haliczer, in *Sexuality in the Confessional,* a study of confessional and penitential practices in sixteenth-century Spain, illuminates the conflict between the Church's increasing emphasis on sexual sins and the people's increasing—and understandable—reluctance to confess such sins, particularly in light of the general practice of making public those sins during an equally public penance. Moreover, the concept of penance was a site of conflict between the Catholics and the Protestants; as one of the ideas of the Church most protested by Martin Luther, the Church reaffirmed the importance of the sacrament of penance and declared it dogma at the Council of Trent (1545–1564). The *Crónica del Rey don Rodrigo* fits, perhaps in a surprising and unexpected way, concerns of religious practice that consumed the Church of the sixteenth century. The redemption of Rodrigo, told through the expanded story of his remorse, serves to rehabilitate him as a more worthy ancestor of the sixteenth-century "Goths" than earlier portrayals would have done.

Corral's characters express a deep humanity. They go well beyond stereotype, and the four main characters—Rodrigo, La Cava, Julian, and Pelayo—are most articulate and anguished over the events that have occurred and the shape their lives take because of them. Julian at times tries to control his rage but cannot find the means to do so. La Cava yearns to undo what she believes she set in motion by confiding in a friend and in her mother—bringing down a king and a nation. Rodrigo wishes to turn back the clock, but since he cannot, he throws himself into the most grueling penance the hermit devises for him. For his part, Pelayo, groomed from childhood to be an exemplary noble Goth, tries to live under Muslim domination until events dictate that he can no longer reject the mantle of Christian leadership that God's divine plan thrust upon him. We will see in the section on the ballads that admissions of guilt by the characters lend themselves to embellishment and distortion in terms of the blame that can be accorded them. For example, while Corral's La Cava moves the reader deeply by her anguished ambivalence about what has happened to Spain and her own role in it, this very ambivalence inspires the ballads that increasingly accord her blame and a conscious role in seducing the king. When she was mute—as she was for all the versions up to Corral's—La Cava was relatively free from criticism, but once given a voice, she is depicted as a moral agent who chooses her actions. Although she could not have predicted the consequences of her decision to inform her father of the rape, she is nonetheless guilty of setting a chain of events in motion, and for a society inclined to excoriate women's speech, that was enough.

The Woman's Body and the Fate of the Nation

In the 1530s, other representations of the fall of Spain experimented with the link between the woman's body and the nation. Two examples, a poem by Fray Luis de León and a play by Bartolomé Palau, allow us to witness just how culturally ingrained it had become in Spain to focus on sex and the woman's body as a metaphor for both the downfall of the kingdom and inspiration for its rebuilding. While many Hispanists have not read or even heard of Bartolomé Palau, the name of Fray Luis de León is canonical. His poem "Profecía del Tajo" (Prophecy of the Tagus River), which opens with a consensual adulterous relationship between Rodrigo and La Cava, carries weight in the development of the legend of La Cava as a sexually promiscuous and culpable Eve figure. Palau, on the other hand, is little known while nonetheless credited in nineteenth-century histories of Spanish literature as the first national dramatist in Spanish letters—and national drama, as we know from the examples of both England and Spain, was profoundly important in the seventeenth century. Uniquely among all the versions of the fall of Spain in 711, Palau joins the stirring narrative of a virgin martyr, Rodrigo's putative Slavonic fiancée, Orosia, with the most titillating part of the founding myth of Spain, the sexual encounter of Rodrigo and La Cava, but he makes sexual violence the story of both women.[1]

Palau's historico-national drama, *Historia de la gloriosa santa Orosia* (History of the glorious Saint Orosia), composed sometime between 1530 and 1550, but probably before 1542, affords a unique opportunity to witness the direction of the sixteenth-century national imagination, particularly the sexualized imagery surrounding Christian-Islamic confrontations. In 1883, Aureliano Fernández-Guerra edited the play in a volume he entitled *Caída y ruina del imperio visigótico español* (Fall and ruin of the Spanish Visigothic empire). He provides a thorough introduction to the legend of Rodrigo and the fall of Spain and offers what little information is available about the allegedly historical martyred saint Orosia (Orossa or Aurea), reputedly betrothed to a prince of Navarre, but whose caravan was set upon by marauding Saracens. Orosia is still venerated as a saint today in Spain, but whether she ever existed remains questionable. Indisputable is the fact that Palau invents out of whole cloth the engagement of Rodrigo and Orosia. Fernández-Guerra's title—a hit-parade of significant themes about our legend, including the words "fall," "ruin," and the casting of the smallish Visigothic kingdom as a Spanish empire, a notion that develops in the sixteenth-century ballad tradition—reflects the late nineteenth-century enterprise to recover for national attention the lost glory of Spain's Visigothic heritage. Palau combines myth and contemporary phobias to cre-

ate a drama of the legendary scandal of sexual sin and the fear of the sexual intermingling of Christian women and Muslim men.

Palau creates a new and highly inventive version of the legend of the fall of Spain
by showcasing the dichotomized woman, one fallen, one saintly. The five-act play
opens with a discussion of why it is essential for a ruler to be married and the
benefits of having a good and virtuous wife, an important discussion in early modern Western Europe. Rodrigo's adviser first suggests that marriage is necessary to
keep a randy young man free from the sin of fornication. After extolling the virtues
of a good wife, he then repeats the commonplace that the home is analogous to the
kingdom: a ruler who cannot keep a wife and his home in order has little chance of
succeeding on the larger stage of the kingdom. While an ambassador from the Visigothic kingdom travels to Orosia's land to ask for her consent to marry King Rodrigo,
Rodrigo determines to douse the flames of his ardor for Caba. In deference to the
rules of decorum in the staging of plays, Palau refrains from presenting the rape itself. Instead, we hear Rodrigo's tormented lament that Caba ensnares him, and then
we hear her confession to her father that she has been dishonored. She tells her father that she tried to deflect the king's advances by joking lightly with him, but then
describes the rape as dismemberment: "[M]e asió á fuerzas de brazos, / haciéndome
mil pedazos / como rabioso león" (He pinned me with his arms, and made me into
a thousand pieces, like a rabid lion; ll. 1399–1401).

Palau's Rodrigo and Julian clearly err, Rodrigo through lust and Julian through
his betrayal of Christian Spain, but Caba's blameworthiness is representative of the
lot of women in this time. As soon as he hears what happened, Julian swears that the
king's act will cost him as dearly as "el bocado de Adán" (Adam's bite [of apple];
l. 1413). By invoking the king as Adam, Julian ironically casts his daughter as the
blameworthy Eve. Next, he lays out his conspiracy plan to Caba, in which he will
bring "hombres crüeles, / fiera gente y muy extraña / porque destruyan á España,
pues á Dios no son fieles" (cruel men, a people fierce and strange, so that they will
destroy Spain, since they are not faithful to God; ll. 1440–43). Unlike other versions
that chastise La Cava for telling her father, but in which she then regrets it, in this
play Caba cheers her father on, claiming that the destruction of Spain will be God's
gift to them, to satisfy her honor and that of her father. Consequently, she embodies three negative images, the bad Christian woman, the ally of the Muslims, and
the dangerous speech of women.

Implicitly, the invasion is set in motion by the rape at the very time that Orosia
and her party are crossing the Pyrenees and entering Spain. She and her entourage
learn from a shepherd that the land has been overrun by Moors, the king is dead,
and they are likely to be captured by the enemy. Orosia stands firm, declaring that

their faith shall be their defense. As with many tales of young virgin martyrs, Palau's saint is indescribably beautiful and the object of the lustful desires of the non-Christian leader, be he Roman emperor or Saracen king. In this case, the infidel is Muza, one of the two powerful leaders of the Arab invasion. The enraged Muza orders an erotically charged punishment of Orosia, who courageously and defiantly refuses to become his bride, that his men sever her limbs one by one and then decapitate her. Instead of witnessing Rodrigo's vision of the slaughtered masses of soldiers, as the ballads and chronicles relate, the destruction of the nation crystallizes in the juxtaposition of the two women—La Cava, the cause, and Orosia, the saintly innocent victim. It is profoundly significant that the first national drama of Spain is constructed—literally—on the broken bodies of two women, the metaphorically dismembered rape victim of the lionlike king, setting in motion the nation's fall, and the one who is literally dismembered because of the tragedy-inspiring seductiveness of the other woman and the barbarity of the Muslim invader. In terms of the cultural context of sixteenth-century Spain, with its view of women as source of, or at least inspiration for, evil, unless they are saintly exemplars, it is no accident that Palau's inventiveness best expressed itself in this kind of sexualized, dualistic construct. But he also conflates the Muslim king and the Christian ruler as unhealthily and destructively lustful. Rodrigo's character traits and personal qualities had been praised in the first act, in a way that makes tragic his giving in to his baser impulses in raping La Cava. The rape shows him to be virtually indistinguishable from Muza: both are sexual predators, and both participate in the destruction of Spain. Moreover, with the rising anti-Morisco sentiment of Spanish society, coupled with the threat of invasion by the Turks, Palau plays into the deepest fears of Spanish Christians, the sexual threat to the Christian nation by Islam both inside and outside Spain. The play contains many anachronisms, but one of the most striking is the reference to Julian's journey to "Turquía" to conspire with the Muslims about invading the peninsula (ll. 1676–81).

Today, the northern regions of Spain continue to celebrate St. Orosia's feast day on June 25. In the sixteenth and seventeenth centuries, the purported route of her journey into Spain became the site of numerous hermitages. Along the route, near a cave named for Orosia's brother, St. Cornelius (another totally fictitious figure, who is not mentioned in Palau's play), markings in the rock are said to be the imprints of Orosia's knees and of the sword hitting the rock when it decapitated her. According to legend, the Virgin Mary revealed Orosia's remains to shepherds some three hundred years after her death, in a small town called Yebra de Basa. Devotees venerated Orosia's head there, while the rest of her remains was translated to the city of Jaca, where they repose in a chapel in her honor. The translation occasioned the first miracle attributed to Orosia: as the silver urn carrying her remains neared Jaca, all the bells in the city began to peal on their own, signifying the saint's approval of the clergy's decision to move her from Yebra de Basa.[2] Orosia became the patron saint of "los endemoniados," those possessed by devils. Each year, until 1947 when the Bishopric of Jaca prohibited this particular ceremony, the church and town authorities rounded up all those thought to be in the thrall of the devil—mostly women—and subjected them to exorcism, one more example of the pervasive tendency, even up to modern times, to associate women with witchcraft and other dark, supernatural forces.

Fray Luis de León, an intellectual presence in sixteenth-century Spain, is best known for his contemplative poetry and his didactic treatise on marriage, *La perfecta casada* (*The Perfect Wife*).[3] However, "Prophecy of the Tagus River," one of his earliest odes, treats the legend of La Cava and Rodrigo in a powerful juxtaposition of primitive sexual coupling and nature's prophetic commentary on it. The Tagus River, for Spain a kind of River Styx in mythic importance, surprises the philandering couple and accuses Rodrigo of kingly misconduct with impending dire consequences. The anthropomorphic river equates the seemingly simple beauty of the Eve-like Cava with unimaginable destruction for the nation, and the concomitant equation of female beauty and sexuality with evil and malevolence is unmistakable: "Aquesta tu alegría / ¡qué llantos acarrea! Aquesa hermosa / que vio el sol en mal día, / al Godo, ¡ay!, cuán llorosa, / al soberano cetro, !ay, cuán costosa! / *Llamas, dolores, guerras, / muertes, asolamientos, fieros males / entre tus brazos cierras, / trabajos inmortales / a ti y a tus vasallos naturales*" (How many tears does that beauty, born on a fateful day, cause the Goth, alas, and how costly is she to his sovereign scepter! *Flames, suffering, wars, deaths, desolation, and fierce ills are what you hold in your arms, and endless labors for you and your natural vassals;* italics mine).

Prophecy functions in two ways in this poem. The beautiful Cava, "born on that fateful day," is predestined to be the female destroyer, at the same time that the personification of the river Tagus comes forth to inform the neglectful, reckless, and disbelieving Rodrigo that the sexual act and destruction have fused, bringing imminent devastation. Fray Luis ends the poem with the image of an enslaved Christian faithful: "te condena, ¡oh, cara patria! a bárbara cadena" (he condemns you, oh dear native land, to the barbarians' chain).

According to Dámaso Alonso, Fray Luis imitates a Horatian ode that condemns Paris for the abduction of Helen of Troy; for Karl Vossler, the poem adumbrates Old Testament wrathful punishment. Leo Spitzer signals an important difference between Horace and Fray Luis. In Horace's poem, the narrator chastises Paris for the abduction, which will cause a war against the Trojans, while Fray Luis lingers over the sinfulness of the sexual act between the king and La Cava—"en mal punto te goces, injusto forzador"—and locates the blame for the deed in the beauty of La Cava. Perhaps the ghosts of the past inspired the young university student Fray Luis to recall the peninsula's earliest history as he strolled the banks of the river, near Baño de la Cava, the place where she bathed, according to the *Refundición toledana de la Crónica de 1344*.[4] Early modern Spanish recountings of the story of Alfonso VIII and the Jewess of Toledo coincide in the detail that Alfonso abandoned his duties for seven years while he lived with his lover in the Toledan Palacios de Galiana near the Tagus River, the castle named for the apocryphal legend of the young Charlemagne's first wife, the Muslim princess Galiana. By opening his poem with Rodrigo and La Cava luxuriating on the banks of the Tagus River in their ongoing affair, which contradicts every known account of their "relationship," Fray Luis appears to meld the legends of Rodrigo and Alfonso. In addition, the poem offers an excellent example of the identification of La Cava with "Moorishness" in that the baths are associated with Muslim culture. In that sense, like the Jewess of Toledo, she is doubly Other, woman and non-Christian.

Marcelino Menéndez Pelayo calls "Prophecy of the Tagus River" the first Spanish poem to treat a historico-national theme in the classical, or Renaissance Italianate, style. Oreste Macrí, one of Fray Luis's modern editors, notices striking coincidences between sixteenth-century ballads and the poem, in which the emotions and actions of the man and woman become complex, ambivalent, and sinful. Macrí believes that the similarities illustrate a common view of the legend in the sixteenth century (*Poesías* 53, 301–7). This reinforces my argument that there is a marked tendency in sixteenth-century Spain to tilt blame toward La Cava, to cast the fall of Spain in 711 as a second fall from the Garden of Eden, and La Cava as the Eve of Spain, a significantly developed feature of the ballads.

The Loss of Spain in the Oral Ballad Tradition

Ballads in Spain, known as romances, were first printed in the beginning of the sixteenth century, many of them having circulated orally in previous centuries. The first printed edition of ballads, the 1510 *Romancero general* (General collection of ballads), included nine of the earliest poems on the subject of Rodrigo and La Cava. The Rodrigo ballads do not stem from an early medieval oral tradition as so many songs do but derive instead from Corral's work, as do some of the newer ballads, found in the *Romancero nuevo* (New collection of ballads 1530–1587). Although the Rodrigo ballads probably originated in the second half of the fifteenth century, following the circulation of Corral's lengthy historical romance, scholars typically date this first cycle of ballads from 1440 to 1550. The ballads initially circulated in *pliegos sueltos,* "loose sheets," an extremely popular and rapid means of dissemination to an enthusiastic, receptive public. Although sixteenth-century historians differentiated between serious and nonserious history, truth and fiction, the ballads held an ironic place of honor in Spanish society. On the one hand, ballads told fictional stories; on the other hand, they remained the single most effective propaganda tool for teaching history to an unlettered public, and many folks believed them to be minihistories, poetically rendered. No matter how much serious historians challenged or modified details of Corral's work, between the many printings and widely popular ballad cycle it inspired, it remained the standard version of Visigothic history throughout the sixteenth century.

Spain's popular ballad tradition extends to many, many themes beyond gender, but a good number of them do reflect the interest in and fear of women's sexuality, as well as the general trend to cast historical events in gendered language. Lorenzo de Sepúlveda's highly influential 1563 collection of historical ballads, *Recopilación de romances sacados de las Corónicas Españolas, Romanas y Troyanas* (Collection of ballads taken from Spanish, Roman and Trojan chronicles), gave new life to familiar medieval figures. Sepúlveda's goal, to place Spain's history in the context of great kingdoms and empires, impelled him to collect ballads on topics that ranged from David and Bathsheba and other Biblical figures to Alfonso VIII and the Jewess of Toledo; the noble and sexually available Muslim princess, Almanzor's sister, in the *Seven Princes of Lara* cycle; Muslim maidens deceived sexually by Christian men; as well as extensive coverage of La Cava and other "bad Christian women." Particularly powerful ballads in Sepúlveda's collection evoke the fall of Granada in 1492 by casting the defeated city as a conquered and violated woman. In the case of the famous ballad "Abenámar," the female city attempts to dissuade a suitor, the Christian King Juan II of Castile, by pleading her fidelity to her "husband," the Muslim king. The religiosity of the century comes through in a number of ballads that treat the discovery and recovery of relics of the saints from ancient Spain, such as St. Isidro and the Muslim converts Justa and Rufina. New, too, are ballads that emphasize Pelayo's feats, a development that undoubtedly derived from the century's obsession with purity of blood and the desire to cast Pelayo as a Christian Spaniard.

Let us take a close look at the early ballads of Rodrigo and La Cava and how they progress in the negative portrayals of La Cava. The ballads function dialectically in that they both shape and are shaped by evolving public opinion of the culpability of four main characters, Rodrigo, La Cava, Julian, and to a lesser degree Bishop Oppas, who, although still an important presence in sixteenth-century prophetic and historical writings, is almost entirely absent from the ballad tradition. As the century progresses, the ballads foreground La Cava as more culpable than the king, her Eve to his Adam, in the same way that woman is more guilty than man in sexual sins.

Of the three ballads Menéndez Pidal considers to be the oldest, the first, "Los vientos eran contrarios" (The winds were roused), deals with Rodrigo's prophetic vision while sleeping next to La Cava in a bejeweled tent; the second, "Las huestes de don Rodrigo" (Rodrigo's proud army is running away), is a narcissistic *ubi sunt*, in which Rodrigo, gazing on the mutilated bodies of his vanquished army, lying in a field with streams of blood running through it, laments all that he has lost personally; and the third, "Amores trata Rodrigo" (Rodrigo's in love), imagines the besotted king's and the reluctant Cava's verbal exchange before the rape.

In the first and third ballads, in which the daughter is always called la Cava or Cava, several points matter. First, that "the good King Don Rodrigo slept beside la Cava in a sumptuous tent" suggests mutual consent between the king and La Cava, and casts doubt on the act of rape that has been undeniable to this point in our versions of the tale. The ballad, set within the frame of a prophecy pronounced by the maiden Fortune to the king, opposes the feelings of two men and leaves La Cava without voice or agency. The king's desire for La Cava is opposed to Count Julian's portrayal as a man driven by love of his daughter to avenge the dishonor. Significantly, no mention is made of either how the king and La Cava came to be sleeping in the tent together or how Julian came to discover it. What we could consider to be three features in the characterization of the main characters in Corral's work—the concept of the king as a sinner against Christianity, La Cava as victim yet blameworthy as representative of dangerous woman, and the count as a traitor to nation—crystallize in this short poem, "Rodrigo's in love." In other words, unlike other ballads that focus on a single moment or snapshot of the legend, this one covers the narrative from beginning to end, albeit in brief form. This ballad exists in multiple versions, but all maintain the storyline that the king singles out La Cava, parries verbally with her, and despite her wise responses that should have restrained him, rapes her. Nevertheless, in the version quoted below, a curiously ambiguous line appears to throw some doubt on the rape:

cumplió el rey su voluntad	the king exercised his will
más por fuerça que por grado,	more by force than by consent
por lo qual se perdió España	by which means Spain was lost
por aquel tan gran pecado.	on account of that grave sin.
La malvada de la Cava	The evil Cava
a su padre lo ha contado:	has told her father about it:
don Julián que es traidor	Julian has treacherously

con los moros se ha concertado	conspired with the moors
que destruyessen a España	to destroy Spain
por le aver así injuriado.	on account of the dishonor done to him.

What does it mean, logically, that he violated her "more by force than consent?" It does not say "by force, not by consent," but rather opens up the linguistic possibility of some element of consent.

If the early chronicles spoke fleetingly of a "lost *Spain*," the ballads absolutely insist on the identification of Rodrigo's kingdom as "Spain." Here, the invasion is not seen merely as a defeat of the Visigothic kingdom, but a "loss" of Spain, the nation, through sin, and indeed the very destruction of it through conquest. Typically, when a title or a line in a work in early modern Spain employs the word "loss," it is intended to evoke a comparison with the Garden of Eden, original sin, and perdition. "Destruction," on the other hand, while still associated with sin in the sense of the Decadence Tradition and a wrathful God's punishment for the iniquity of a king and his people, focuses on the barbarity of the invaders, the assault as taking place on the eve of Spain, and the subsequent growth as the birth of the real Spain, led by Pelayo.

Alain Milhou makes a convincing case for the widespread use of the term "destruction," and variants of the word in the sixteenth century, arguing that the term infiltrates accounts of New World encounters, of those opposed to strategies of colonization and evangelization, and of those who saw the defeat and elimination of the indigenous population as a necessary cleansing of the vast territory before Spanish occupation could take root and flourish. Milhou cites, in particular, Alfonso the Learned's *Estoria de España* (History of Spain) as the work that cast so many of Spain's battles and wars as one episode of destruction after another. Noting that Corral's *Crónica del Rey don Rodrigo* employs the word "destruction" frequently, he postulates that this is the principal influence on the presence of the word in the ballads created in the late fifteenth and early sixteenth centuries. Not only is Milhou correct about this, but the title changes precisely in 1511 from the 1499 title that merely names the king—*Crónica del Rey don Rodrigo, postrimero rey de los godos* (Chronicle of King Rodrigo, the last king of the Goths)—to one that adds the phrase "with the Destruction of Spain" (*con la destruyçión de España*).[5] Interestingly, though, Milhou believes that a mid-century change diminished the use of the word "destruction" in newer ballads, substituting instead variants of the verb "to lose," *perder,* as the ballads and other works were written as cautionary tales about what was at stake in New World ventures, with its economic and spiritual currency of loss and gain. Even more important than the word "destruction" was the newfound emphasis on the Visigothic kingdom as Spain, once lost, but a recoverable nation.

The expanded version of the ballad "Rodrigo's in love" demonstrates how La Cava fares. Composed and circulating vigorously sometime between 1480 and 1550, this version focuses more specifically on La Cava's physical charms and Rodrigo's understandable vulnerability to them. She flirts with the king: "She still won't agree, and runs off with a smile." This ballad comes directly from Corral. Although she has presumably enjoyed flirting with the king, the sexual act is still rape, not consensual. Afterwards, La Cava loses her beauty day by day, and she finally confides in her friend. The ballad is a poetic summary of Corral's chapters, ending with Julian's determination to avenge his daughter's honor. While the poem does not speak of La Cava in condemnatory language, it nevertheless adds to the popular bank of information that suggests the daughter was aware of her beauty and willing to flirt with the king, although never suspecting an outcome of personal and national tragedy. By implying that she has encouraged the king, the poem contributes to the notion of La Cava as culpable.

In the second class of ballads, composed between 1480 and 1550, prophecy, penance, and Julian's treachery emerge as prominent themes. The ballad that treats prophecy—a description of Rodrigo's penetration of the House of Hercules—has not survived into the twentieth century in the ongoing oral tradition. Still well known today are Rodrigo's severe penance with the snake in the tomb and Julian's moment of ire and weakness that allowed the Arabs to enter the southernmost gates of the peninsula. Quoted at the beginning of this chapter, "Rodrigo's Penance," also known as "Después que el rey don Rodrigo a España perdido había" (After Rodrigo had lost Spain), is a long, narrative ballad whose first line places the agency of the action, the loss of Spain, directly in Rodrigo's hands. Unlike the earlier ballads in which the passive voice is used, "se perdió España" (Spain was lost), here we have no doubt that Rodrigo has sinned as an individual and must make spiritual reparation as an individual. This is a spectacular ballad, so known to the general public that Cervantes includes the most titillating part of it in *Don Quixote*—the hungry snake in the tomb—quoted by a lady-in-waiting, someone who, in the populace of the novel, would not be formally educated.

"En Ceupta está Julián" (Julian is in Ceuta) solidifies the notion of Spain as a nation lost at a time when nation building and national identity are among the strongest forces in Europe. It is, moreover, the ballad that most harkens back to the thirteenth-century chronicles of Ximénez de Rada (El Toledano) and Alfonso the Learned. Rodrigo comes out quite well in the poem as a man who knows he may be beaten, but never defeated, continuing to fight even though he is wounded and his men are down. The poem casts La Cava as a kind of Helen of Troy, and her father and Bishop Oppas as the two traitors to Spain: "Que por sola una donzella / la qual Cava se llamava / causen estos dos traydores / que España sea domeñada" (For the sake of a girl known as La Cava, these two betrayed Spain, which has still not recovered; *Spanish Ballads* 45). Emotions run high in the ballad; when not railing against the treachery of the two men, the poem laments the loss of the motherland as a paradise lost, praising the peninsula as we have seen from as early as Isidore of Seville's historical writings on the Goths: "¡Madre España, ay de ti! / En el mundo tan nombrada, / de las partidas la mejor, / la mejor y más ufana, / donde nasce el fino oro / y la plata no faltada, / dotada de hermosura / y en proezas estremada" (Oh Spain, our poor country, renowned through the world, the best and the proudest, a jewel, a pearl, where gold can be found, and silver as well, whose beauty's renowned, whose virtues excel; *Spanish Ballads* 44). The actual transgression of the king is not mentioned, nor is La Cava blamed, a view that not only is unusual in the sixteenth century, but is overshadowed by the ballads of more vivid description of sexual scandal.

According to Menéndez Pidal, the final ballads of the first half of the sixteenth century have a special internal unity, each focusing on a specific scene of the legend, rather than trying to cover many episodes in few lines as the earlier poems do. The earlier poems, for the most part, offer a fairly sweeping overview of the legend from the king's attempts to seduce La Cava to the consequences when her father and, sometimes, the bishop take action. Two ballads should be mentioned here. The more important, for our purposes, is the widely circulated one that begins, "Gran llanto hace la Cava" (La Cava's lamentation), which, while deriving in part from Corral by casting her as an Eve figure, intensifies her role as destroyer of the nation, aware of her overt and innate culpability as woman. La Cava laments the tragedy provoked by her beauty and bemoans ever having been born (a view of her the public undoubtedly would have shared). As in Corral's graphic rendering of the effects of defeat, La Cava anguishes over the mutilation of mothers, children, and even nuns by the marauding barbarians. While calling the king a great, but unfortunate, man, she further denounces herself by calling herself "Spain's perdition":

Tú eres perdición de España,	You are Spain's perdition,
fuego que todo lo apura,	a fire that destroys everything,
de ti quedará memoria	you will forever be remembered
para siempre en escriptura,	in writings,
unos te llamarán diablo	some will call you devil
otros te llamarán diablura,	others will call you devilish,

| otros te llamarán demonio, | others will call you a demon, |
| otros que eres su hechura. | others that you are his witch. (*Floresta* 2: 44) |

One aspect of the dichotomization of women in this era was the escalating view of women and witchcraft in the sixteenth century, women in league with the devil, "the source of evil," which reached astonishing proportions in Counter-Reformation Spain, as María Helena Sánchez Ortega tells us. Another aspect was the emphasis on the woman's open mouth—and garrulity—as proof of a lack of chastity. As Peter Stallybrass says, in a statement that applies as much to the misogyny of Spain as to that of England, "Silence, the closed mouth, is made a sign of chastity. And silence and chastity are, in turn, homologous to woman's enclosure within the house" (127). Although it has always been part of the legend of La Cava that she informed her father of Rodrigo's deed, an example of direct speech has been rare. It is ironic, but not coincidental, that the increased examples of La Cava speaking—pleading, lamenting, informing, reasoning—all coincide with her emergence as central to the legend, and culpably so. The voice of agency that she acquires in Corral's *Crónica del Rey don Rodrigo* becomes the very complex, morally suspect, and then completely unchaste voice of the sixteenth-century ballads. As Diane Wolfthal demonstrates in "Women's Communities and Male Spies," the prevailing medieval viewpoint of women's talk as frivolous gossip, and then as potentially harmful gossip, evolved in the sixteenth and seventeenth centuries to the firm belief that gossip leads women to violence (126). She points out many examples of woodcuts and drawings that showed chatting women grouped in gardens and other ostensibly semiprivate settings, while men peer at them, unseen, spying and eavesdropping, not unlike the scene of King Rodrigo gazing at La Cava, his wife, and the other women of the court. While in real life men who spied were breaking the social code, Wolfthal tells us, male justification for doing so abounded, as women might have been revealing secrets about their husbands or even plotting nefarious deeds.

"Cuán triste queda Castilla" (How sad Castile is) points to increased national feeling in the sixteenth century. Specifically, it serves as a popular example of what Henry Kamen describes as the sixteenth-century tendency to perceive Castile and Spain as identical, especially among emigrants to various parts of the growing Spanish empire: "[T]he history of voyage, discovery, conquest and war was written up by official historians in a way that gave all the glory to Castile. In a sense this was not new, for other European nations also were trying to discover their own identity through an exploration of their past" (*Empire* 333).[6]

The ballad bears no relationship to Corral's work but arises out of purely contemporary emotions and concerns. Like "En Ceupta está Julián," it focuses on the nation itself, metonymically Castile, which will be the symbol for all of Spain in later Rodrigo ballads as well, as the suffering victim of the treachery of Julian and Oppas. After this brief introduction to the reason for destruction, some ten lines, the ballad demonstrates its affinity with current events—the sixteenth-century wars against the Turks—by describing in painful detail the slaughter of innocent civilians. Worse than the physical slaughter is the horrible affront to Christianity: churches are profaned by the Muslim invaders, bishops are martyred, and violated Christian maidens renounce their faith and embrace Islam. Without mentioning La Cava, the ballad cleverly combines two themes, which in fact have been intertwined ever since the daughter of Julian was introduced into the history of the 711 fall of Spain: sex and the fall of the nation. We have come a long way from the early recountings of the defeat of the Christian Visigothic kingdom, which carefully refrained from naming the religion of the invaders, preferring instead to focus on their geographical provenance, to avoid the impression that, while God was indeed punishing his Christian people for their sins, He was in any way favoring Islam over Christianity. Sixteenth-century Spain showed no such restraint. Among the many horrors of defeat by enemies of Christendom, the poem suggests the revulsion felt by a Spanish society obsessed with "purity of blood" to know that their Christian maidens were now willingly engaged in sexual intercourse with the Other, the Muslim, and renouncing Christianity to do so. The sexual act between La Cava and Rodrigo may have set in motion the chain of events that led to the fall, but the result is more sex, which continues the downward moral, spiritual, and political decline of the nation. With two new sets of "infidels," the invading Turks in Europe and the Amerindians in the New World, one enemy to be kept from the shores of paradisiacal Spain, the other ripe for conversion in the new Garden of Eden across the seas, the legend of La Cava and Rodrigo found renewed meaning, which the ballads both reflect and reinforce.

A new interest in Spanish history resulted from the increase in national sentiment, and the "romances eruditos" (learned ballads), such as those found in Sepúlveda's 1563 collection, offered unique opportunities to provide names, places, and historical episodes, which helped to teach national history to a generally unlettered public. In one case, a ballad demonstrates a tendency that will become more pronounced in the seventeenth century, the insistence on Rodrigo as the end of a line of rulers, and the emergence of his successor Pelayo as the king to whom all the subsequent monarchs of Spain trace their lineage and right to rule. The poem "De los nobilísimos godos que en Castilla habían reinado" (On the most noble Goths who ruled Castile) accomplishes in a few short lines the linking of Hercules as the first of a line and Rodrigo as the last, while Pelayo holds onto "las Esturias," both the remnant of the past and the seed of the future Christian kingdom, which will be restored by the efforts of each of the kings who follow. A second poem, "Triste estaba don Rodrigo, desdichado se llamaba" (Sad was don Rodrigo, wretched he was called), reinforces the fact that the Catholic king Ferdinand appeared to matter more in sixteenth-century historiography than Isabel did. The poem not only sweeps the centuries in its movement from the fall in 711 to Ferdinand's triumph in Granada in 1492, but it emphasizes Rodrigo's actions as a history and defeat separate from the national history of recovering Christian lands from the Muslims, and it casts La Cava as blameworthy. She is referred to, variously, as the one who inspired the king to "bestial amor," as "maldita Cava" and "malvada hija" (bestial love, accursed Cava, evil daughter), and she is cursed directly in the poem: "¡Maldita sea la tu hija, / que de tan gran mal fue causa!" (Accursed be your daughter, who caused such great evil!). Rodrigo is emphasized as the last Visigoth: "¡Oh mal venturoso rey, / postrer godo que reinaba, / hoy pierdes tu tierra y reino" (Oh unlucky King, last Goth who ruled, today you lose your land and kingdom). It remains for Pelayo to emerge as the first ruler, a kind of Biblical typography, in which the new man overturns the old, the new law reverses the old law: "diole Dios muy gran victoria" (God granted him a great victory). The final stanza moves from the eighth century to the end of the fifteenth: "Otros reyes sucedieron / que lo perdido ganarán, / hasta el quinto Fernando, que el Católico llamarán, / que con su esfuerzo ganó / el buen reino de Granada" (Other kings followed, who won what had been lost, until Ferdinand V, called the Catholic, who with his mighty effort won the good kingdom of Granada).

Menéndez Pidal calls the next chronological group of ballads "romances artificiosos nuevos," new "artificial" ballads composed for the specific period, the second half of the sixteenth century, as opposed to ballads that either derive from historical or fictional longer narratives or that existed centuries earlier until being recorded in the sixteenth century.[7] In general, these ballads reflect issues within the culture of sixteenth-century Spain and are a good marker for what interested the public, as well as revealing people's attitudes toward women and their nation. Except for three ballads that deal most directly with La Cava, they focus on the monarch and national history. Once again, Rodrigo is emphasized as "el postrer godo de España" (the last Goth in Spain) in the opening line of one ballad, and "el último rey godo" (the last Gothic king), in the second line of another. In this current age of empire, the ballads heighten and dramatize the loss by the repetition of España, "Spain," and by referring to Rodrigo's kingdom anachronistically as "todo el imperio de España" (the entire Spanish empire) now "y en manos de tus enemigos" (in the hands of the enemy infidel). By reinforcing Rodrigo's place as the last Goth and the last Gothic king, Pelayo emerges as the first king of a new Spain and the first Spaniard.

Two fascinating ballads highlight the Spaniards' lively interest in deciphering La Cava's role in the fall of Spain. "Cartas escribe la Cava" (La Cava writes letters) and "De una torre de palacio" (From a tower in the palace) postulate two opposing views of the daughter of Julian: is she the honorable victim Lucretia or the seductive Eve? In the first forty-six-line poem, La Cava's letter—her own first-person voice—comprises thirty-six lines of the total number. It is the poem that presents her and women's words in the most dignified, indeed, almost regal, manner. She addresses her father with appropriate courtesy: "Muy ilustre señor padre, / el mayor que hay en Castilla" (Illustrious father, the greatest one in Castile). While La Cava builds to the high point of the drama, the moment of rape, she never resorts to a harsh or injudicious voice. Moreover, this is the ballad that most exculpates her: not only does she refuse to answer the king at all when he reveals his feelings to her—as the noble Julian's daughter, she is greatly offended at the king's disrespect to her lineage and her virginity—but he enters her room when she is sleeping and rapes her. La Cava is not blamed for her failure to dissuade or otherwise fend off the king. The ballad ends with an implied comparison of Rome and Spain, and her exhortation to her father to avenge her honor: "Debéis de vengar, señor, / esta tan gran villanía, / y ser Bruto, el gran romano, / pues el Tarquino se hacía; / si no, yo seré Lucrecia, / la que dio fin a su vida" (You must avenge, sir, this great affront, and show yourself to be Brutus, the great Roman, since he [Rodrigo] acted as Tarquin; if not, I will be Lucretia, who ended her own life).

As we saw earlier, the rape of Lucretia began to represent the impetus for the birth of a nation during the time of humanism. Indeed, one of the most important paintings in Philip II's collection was Titian's spectacular *Rape of Lucretia,* commissioned as a gift for the king. During this time of nation building and, indeed, empire building, it is no surprise that some ballads dramatize the moment of La Cava's Lucretia-like challenge to her father to act as a brave Brutus, heightening the tension between rape and vengeful action. A curious feature is the fact that La Cava's suicide is not a given, as Lucretia's always was. La Cava threatens to kill herself unless her rape is avenged, as if there could be some restoration to honor for a deflowered maiden, whereas for Lucretia, the vengeance she seeks does not in any way deter her from suicide, so certain is she that a raped woman's dishonor is irreparable.

La Cava was not granted the moral high road for long: circulating at the same time as her "Lucretia" ballad is the one that derives in part from a work we will consider in the next chapter, the Morisco Miguel de Luna's late sixteenth-century *Verdadera historia del rey don Rodrigo* (True history of King Rodrigo), "De una torre de palacio." This ballad, often printed with the title "Fatal desenvoltura de la Cava" (La

Cava's fatal immodesty), offers an example of how a later title, not found in the poem itself, guides the reader's interpretation of the poem. La Cava, a fun-loving young woman out in a garden adjacent to the palace, laughs and plays uninhibitedly with other young maidens. She winds a yellow ribbon up her legs, which emphasizes their porcelain whiteness and beauty. Although the girls think they are alone, the king peers through the dense ivy. When the king summons La Cava to his room and propositions her, the ballad moves from the court of the king to the court of public opinion. Using the third-person voice, the ballad ends with contrasting opinions: "Dicen que no respondió, / y que se enojó al principio; / pero al fin de aquesta plática / lo que mandaba se hizo. / Florinda perdió su flor, / el rey quedó arrepentido / y obligada toda España / por el gusto de Rodrigo. / Si dicen quién de los dos / la mayor culpa ha tenido, / digan los hombres: la Cava, / y las mujeres: Rodrigo" (They say she didn't answer, and that at first she was angry. But at the end of his proposal, she did what he ordered. Florinda lost her flower, the King became repentant, and Spain yoked, all because of the pleasure of Rodrigo. As to which of those two was more blameworthy, the men say: "la Cava," the women say: "Rodrigo"; Menéndez Pidal, *Floresta* 2: 68). The line about sexual intercourse is a play on words, since as we can see from the Spanish quoted above, flower—flor—is found in her name as well, Florinda, literally, Lovely Flower, Flor[l]inda, who has now been deflowered. The ballad not only suggests consent, vitiating the traditional view of the king as a rapist, but ends with a kind of poll that divides along gender lines: men believe La Cava to be the more guilty, while women blame Rodrigo.

A second version of this ballad is even more overt in its attempts to depict the king as helpless for being hopelessly smitten, while La Cava consents to have sex with him. In this version, she shows more than just her legs. When she disrobes completely to bathe in the fountain in the heat of summer, her body eclipsing the others in loveliness, Rodrigo is inflamed with love. Florinda lost her flower, the ballad recounts and then, in the "public opinion" section of the poem, offers direct contradictions: "She said he forced her to it, / He said she gave full consent." Then follows the poll again, suggesting the never-ending debate between men and women as to who is more to blame.

Philip II's Chronicler, Ambrosio de Morales, and the Development of the Heroic Pelayo

Sixteenth-century Spain was not alone in its overwhelming interest in historiography and the unique mission of the historian. The Spanish humanist Juan Luis Vives, who lived in England while the Catholic monarchs' daughter, Catherine of Aragon, was married to Henry VIII, was but one of many Europeans who wrote eloquently and passionately on the role of the historian to be truthful, edifying, and morally above reproach in his writings. It is only a slight exaggeration to say that this century produced as much writing on the subject of how to write history as it did historiography itself.[8] Eyewitness historical accounts were particularly valued, and the writer who had access to such accounts, or even better, could claim to be an eyewitness to historical events, was special indeed; hence the abundance of court chroniclers appointed by Holy Roman Emperor Charles V and his son King Philip II to witness and record the realm's significant activities. But the history of early Spain, as well as any history of the distant past, posed obvious challenges. How did early modern historians justify as truth their own writings about ancient deeds they could not have witnessed, and in the face of contradictory accounts of those deeds?

In some cases, they asserted their lack of political agenda as evidence that they would be truthful writers, though one would be hard pressed to find a chronicler without some kind of ideological agenda. In other cases, they spoke of the need for the historian to be an exemplary Christian and to allow himself to function as a kind of empty vessel into which God would pour his sacred truth, which would emerge through the historian's pen. Pertinent to both arguments was the exhortation to the historian to conduct careful, intelligent, and dedicated research to ensure that he had found all extant evidence about an event, and that he could determine, even if only by counting the number of times an event was recorded in a certain way, what the truth of a matter might be.

The stakes were high for the Spanish historian for two reasons. First of all, Antonio de Nebrija, in his 1492 *Gramática castellana* (Castilian grammar), had exhorted learned men to write elegant and well-researched histories in Castilian rather than in Latin. Given the widespread belief that Italians wrote better Latin than Spaniards did, when the Latin histories of ancient Spain circulated in Europe, they were often the product of non-Spaniards, especially Italians. Equally widespread among Spaniards was the belief that these histories took delight in diminishing and even mocking Spain's past. Nebrija believed that Castilian historians needed to take control of their own national enterprise of historical recounting and create a pure, consistent, and high-quality Castilian that would enhance the telling of glorious deeds and would create a body of edifying work for learned readers, too often found wasting their time "leyendo novelas o istorias envueltas en mil mentiras e errores" (reading fiction or histories full of a thousand lies and errors; 6–7). Second, the writing of history not only brought the past to the present, but it strove to guide readers' future behavior. Naturally, the use of the vernacular, Castilian, would make these histories accessible to a wider public. As Mary Gaylord tells us:

> History, whose mission it is to transform deeds that deserve to be remembered into words, necessarily grounds itself on the symbiosis of doing and saying, of acting and reporting. Yet, at the same time that writing serves as record or repository of memorable acts which have already occurred, exemplary history is also charged with using language to incite its readers towards exemplary deeds of their own. In this way, history uses present discourse to link past and future orders. This projection into the future of exemplary and monumentalizing historical narratives can take the form of implicit promises or openly prophetic utterances about the future of persons, dynasties and nations. [Early modern chronicles] had continual recourse to the prophetic mode, which both first- and third-person historians used to confer significance on the deeds of their historical actors and to confer authority on their own written accounts. Promises, based on Spain's providential history and of noble genealogy, serve not only as framing premise, but as part of the compelling subject of these histories. ("Pulling Strings with Master Peter's Puppets" 137)

But the lot of the sixteenth-century Spanish historian was not an easy one. Given the century's and the country's propensity for prophetic writings—their authenticity doubtful and their fictionality often demonstrable—the potential was great for philosophical and ethical dilemmas for the upright moral historian, whose duty included reporting events of prophetic fulfillment and recording prophecies he may well have known to be purely invented. Prophecies and miracles engendered particular challenges for the historian because their very nature as wondrous and supernatural events made their veracity questionable. At the same time, the lines between history and fiction continually blurred (as they had in previous centuries), and theorists and moralists sought out the truthful to excoriate those who wrote not lying fictions, but lying histories. This is the era of the nationalist "falsos cronicones" (false chronicles) and their critics, a polemic that in large measure inspired Cervantes' masterpiece *Don Quixote,* with its multiple invented layers of story and history.[9] Indeed, on some level even the sixteenth-century prose romance *Historia de los dos enamorados Flores y Blancaflor* (History of the two lovers Flores and Blancaflor), a version somewhat different from the thirteenth-century one mentioned in the prologue, could have been criticized as intentionally defrauding the reading public. Instead, *Flores y Blancaflor* enjoyed great popularity and multiple early modern printings, for this kind of pro-Christian invention was sanctioned by the unspoken code that if it furthered Christianity in some fashion, its edifying qualities outweighed its potential dangers to a gullible public. Far more dangerous in the opinion of moralists such as Juan Luis Vives and Pedro de Rúa, to name but two, were the works purporting to be "true histories," written by those who should not have been engaged in such deceit, at least in the view of their opponents. Clever and imaginative authors, such as Antonio de Guevara, the bishop of Maldonado, who was one of the authors most translated in Elizabethan England, and whose fictional history of Marcus Aurelius in the 1520s went so far as to include letters allegedly written by the Roman himself, found themselves condemned by their contemporaries, who believed such betrayal of the truth to be reprehensible.

Not only prophetic material or the sifting out of truth from fiction in the false chronicles proved problematic for scribes of historical deeds. Ironically, in the sixteenth century, Corral's historical romance, with its largely fictional element, was praised implicitly and explicitly as the principal account of La Cava, Rodrigo, Julian, and Pelayo, with rightful claim to truth-value. Historians of recent decades "have recognized how much fiction there is, not only in stories like those of Rodrigo and Gaiferos, but in the whole notion of 'Reconquest'" (Gaylord, "Pulling Strings" 131). But even medieval historians noticed the contradictory details in the tellings of historical events of the fall of Spain in 711 and its aftermath, such as El Toledano's and Alfonso the Learned's pointing out the uncertainty about whether the king had raped Julian's daughter or wife, and Díaz de Games' *El Victorial* (The victorious one), which refuted the entire story of La Cava and the king. So, when "In the sixteenth and seventeenth centuries, King Rodrigo and his namesakes turn up everywhere" (Gaylord, "Pulling Strings": 132), historians turned ever more faithfully to scholarly investigation to deduce the version of the past that most, in their opinion, reflected sacred truth.

A royal chronicler during the reign of Charles V, Florián de Ocampo, produced the first early modern edition of Alfonso the Learned's *Estoria de España* (History of Spain) in 1543, designed to promote the telling of history in Castilian, as Nebrija had urged at the end of the fifteenth century, and to comb the sources to compile the most accurate and authentic recounting of early Spain. Ocampo may well have been the one to circulate the story of Cisneros and the putative discovery of a prophecy of imminent defeat for the Muslim enemy in 1509. Ocampo took up the challenge of writing Spain's early history with zeal, ending with the Roman conquest of the peninsula in 209 C.E., but he confused facts and mixed up names and episodes, which was only to be expected given the "thousand lies and errors" that, according to Nebrija, lay embedded in the medieval chronicles.

One of the most serious and respected historians of the sixteenth century, Ambrosio de Morales, appointed royal chronicler to Philip II in 1563, a post he held until his death in 1586, grappled with these issues when he undertook the massive project of continuing the history begun by Florián de Ocampo. To verify the material in Alfonso the Learned's history, Morales returned to early Latin and Castilian sources, most notably Rodrigo Ximénez de Rada's *De rebus Hispaniae* (*History of the Deeds of Spain*) and the *Crónica de 1344*. However, when it came to telling the founding myth of the fall of Spain, Morales relied on both Alfonso the Learned's and Corral's story of La Cava and Rodrigo for his source texts, and on what he believed to be the Arabic chronicle of Rasis, the Moor.[10]

In continuing the story of early Spain, whereas Corral invented a fanciful tale of Pelayo's origins, the mysterious early years of the hero, Ambrosio de Morales expanded—invented—material about the years of Pelayo's reign in Asturias. Although Pelayo was certainly known and celebrated in the sixteenth century through Corral's popularity, through some neo-Gothicist poetry and political writings of the fifteenth century, and through the popular ballad, Morales's lengthy account of Pelayo's deeds cemented his position as the first king of the new Spanish era. Morales employed the literary convention of the reluctant hero to explain the gap between the fall of Spain to the Muslims and Pelayo's leadership in the Battle of Covadonga. As we know from folktale and other primitive narrative constructions, when the principal hero fails for any number of reasons, his successor reluctantly accepts the mantle of authority, and usually does much to avoid facing his inevitable responsibility and fate.[11]

If the fifteenth century encouraged neo-Gothicism, seeking to confirm Spain's Christian Gothic heritage, the sixteenth century thoroughly embraced these Gothic roots. Morales, like some of his compatriots in the history-writing enterprise, asserted the veracity of his writings by emphasizing his research skills and his belief in God's will that these heretofore hidden truths about the early Spanish kings be brought to light. For example, he expresses great pride in how much he expanded the truthful material on Pelayo:

> Pues yo (á Dios sea la gloria de todo) he extendido bien á la larga esta parte de
> nuestra historia que aquí escribo . . . y acrecentando mucho en ella: pues donde
> nadie ha escrito cincuenta hojas, yo la prosigo por quasi quatrocientas. El mucho
> trabajo y las exquisitas diligencias con que se ha comprado esto, y el sacar á luz
> con buen fundamento de verdad muchas cosas de estos tiempos de que ántes no
> se tenia ninguna noticia: harto claro se parecerá por toda la Corónica, y cada uno
> las podrá considerar en ella. (I—though all the glory belongs to God—have
> greatly expanded this part of our history, adding much to it. Whereas no one had

written fifty pages before, I extend it to almost four hundred. This was paid for by hard labor and exquisite research; this, and the bringing to light on a foundation of truth many things from those times, which have never before been seen, all of this will be apparent in my chronicle, and each reader will be able to ponder these things; vol. 7, prologue: 3–4.)

Wherever possible, Morales cites eyewitness testimony, if not of the deeds themselves, then of the trace evidence of their existence. For example, while weighing whether the king raped Julian's daughter or wife, and recounting the various historical claims of her name, Morales informs us that he saw the pole in Málaga inscribed with La Cava's name, to mark the spot from which the ship embarked to return her to Africa, proof that she existed and, by extension, proof of other aspects of the story, including her name and kinship to Julian.

Morales links Pelayo to predestruction history, suggesting that this nobleman had been a cousin of Rodrigo and already an heir to the Visigothic throne (vol. 6, bk. 12, chap. 67). This will be of particular importance as the national drive intensifies to establish actual bloodlines back to the Visigoths. Subscribing to the Decadence Tradition, Morales revisits the earlier authorities on the sins of Witiza and the debauched clergy and general populace of Spain. According to Morales, and not found in earlier chronicles, because of Witiza's cruelty to Pelayo's father and the potential for wrath to be visited upon him and because he was offended by the disgraceful moral state of the kingdom, Pelayo went on pilgrimage to Jerusalem, returning when Rodrigo became king. One of Witiza's greatest sins against Christianity was to allow the Jews back into the kingdom, and to give them great privileges (vol. 6, bk. 12, chap. 65). How, Morales asks, could divine justice have been temperate in the face of "tan enormes pecados" (such enormous sins)?

Morales suggests that Pelayo had been a royal member of the king's bodyguard, perhaps the captain of the king's sword-bearers, and one of the few survivors of the Battle of Guadalete: "En esta batalla creo yo cierto que se halló el Infante Pelayo; pues siendo tan deudo del Rey, y teniendo tan principal oficio en su casa, no le faltaria en tal jornada. Escapó con la vida, porque lo guardaba Dios para el bien universal de toda España." (In this battle I am certain Prince Pelayo was found; given that he was so loyal to the king and the holder of such a singular office in his household, he would not fail the king on that day. He escaped with his life because God was protecting him for the universal good of all Spain; vol. 6, bk. 12, chap. 69).

In placing Pelayo at the moment of the fall of Spain, he parts company from Corral, according to whom Pelayo, though a relative of Rodrigo and already a prince of northern Spain, the son of the duke of Cantabria, was not present in Rodrigo's court.

In fact, Morales discredits and discounts Corral, calling his work fictional (vol. 6, bk. 12, chap. 64). Morales sifts through the older chronicles, asserting which facts he believes to be true, combining and resolving various competing traditions. Julian is to blame, indeed, but he was aided by the sons of Witiza, who traveled to North Africa, and by Bishop Oppas, who may have been the brother of Julian's wife. For Morales, the king erred in raping La Cava, but the entire population was decadent and merited God's punishment (vol. 6, bk. 12, chap. 69), culminating in the Battle of Guadalete, which Morales places not in 711, but on September 9, 714. Morales accepts the view that the king simply vanished from the battle, and that subsequently his engraved tomb was discovered in Viseu, Portugal. In short, after having praised Rodrigo for his many personal strengths and that of his court, Morales wastes very little time on Rodrigo and La Cava, and only slightly more on Julian. Well into the story of Pelayo, Morales returns to the ultimate fate of Julian. According to Morales, Munuza believes that Pelayo and his men defeated the Muslims in Asturian battles only because of the treacherous help of Julian and the sons of Witiza. Although Morales does not specify what Julian reportedly did to warrant the label of traitor to the Moors, he recounts the seizing and beheading of the three Christian men by Munuza's men.

Morales ties Pelayo to the most significant symbols of the birth of Spain, the relics of saints contained within the Cathedral of Toledo. By having Pelayo present at the battle in which Spain fell, and by having him accompany Bishop Urbano and the sacred books and relics to the Asturias, Morales makes concrete the continuation of the old, fallen Visigothic kingdom in the Muslim-free area of Asturias, site of a newborn Spain.

In the ninth-century *Crónica de Alfonso III* (c. 866–910), the earliest recounting of Pelayo and his reign, the Muslim ruler Munuza abducts and marries Pelayo's sister while Pelayo is away, and there is nothing he can do about that. Corral rewrites history so that Pelayo rescues his sister, thereby preventing a mixture of Visigothic and Arab blood. Morales, too, subscribes to the rescue story, though he says no more than that Pelayo took her away from Munuza by a clever stratagem, thereby engendering Munuza's wrath and desire for revenge. Like El Toledano, Morales uses this enmity between the two men to lead into a lengthy preamble to the miraculous battles that launched what Morales calls the "Restauración," the Restoration of Spain.

As we know, miracles abound in this part of the legend. Pelayo and his men strategize in a cave they have dedicated as a church and shrine to the Virgin Mary, and here the men elect Pelayo as the new king. But Morales makes this part of the legend the occasion for prophecy. A man who committed a homicide tried to hide in the cave, but Pelayo and his men found him and nearly killed him on the spot. A hermit who dwelled in the cave begged Pelayo not to profane the sacred space, which is a refuge to all, by violence and bloodshed because Pelayo might one day need to seek the sanctuary of that holy place. Pelayo considered the hermit's remarks to be "a secret prophecy" (secreta profecía) of his future victory, a view Morales shares by declaring that it took place on the very spot where Pelayo later triumphed over the Muslim militia.

Morales often provides dates of events, such as Pelayo's election as king in 718, and whenever possible emphasizes both the line of continuation from the Visigothic kingdom—the bloodline—and the rupture between the fall of the Visigothic kingdom and the mobilizing military efforts of Pelayo and the other Asturians in 718, seven years characterized mostly by cooperation with the ruling Muslims and a covert resistance. When the abduction of Pelayo's sister provides the impetus the Christians need to decide that they must not continue in the shadow and service of the Muslims, Morales paints a vivid picture of what they faced to overcome the enemy. Alcamán, one of Tarik's four principal army captains, led a brigade of many thousands, while Pelayo had only a few hundred men. Bishop Oppas reappears as the archetypal traitor to Christendom, sent as an emissary of Alcamán, clambering up the rocks to call out a warning and an offer to Pelayo. If Pelayo would reconsider the impending battle and recognize that they stood no chance of winning because of the number of men arrayed against them—164,000—and because the rock-mountain terrain left them little opportunity for hiding or for deft footwork in battle, he, Oppas, would serve as intermediary with Alcamán. Pelayo's contempt for Oppas and trust in God guide his response: "Ni me juntaré jamas en amistad con los Alárabes, ni seré su súbdito . . . yo confío en Dios, que deste pequeño agujeruelo que tú ves, ha de salir la restauracion de España, y de la antigua gloria de los Godos" (I will never befriend the Arabs, nor will I be subject to them . . . I have faith in God that from this little mouth of the cave that you see must come the restoration of Spain and the former glory of the Goths; vol. 7, bk. 13, chap. 3). The enemy attacks the Christians at the site of the holy cave, but miraculously the tens of thousands of arrows heading toward Pelayo's men turn around in midair and land on the "Pagans" (Paganos), killing fully half of them.

Morales sifts through the authorities to clarify the source of the miracle, determining that the most convincing historical testimony attributes the miracle to the most holy Virgin Mary, "cuya Iglesia aquellos Infieles con tanta violencia profanaban" (whose Church the Infidels profaned with such violence; vol. 7, bk. 13, chap. 3). The changes Morales introduces may be nuanced, but they are significant nonetheless. The ninth-century Asturian chronicle also claimed that the cave was a sacred space in honor of Mary, but that God performed the miracle. Here, the attribution

The Battle between Christians and Moors at El Sotillo, part of an altarpiece, ca. 1637–1639, by Francisco de Zurbarán (Spanish, 1598–1664). Oil on canvas; arched top, 131⅞ × 75¼ in. (335 × 191.1 cm). In 1370 the Spanish forces were saved from a night ambush when a miraculous light revealed the hidden Moorish troop. This picture of the miraculous occurrence was painted for the Carthusian monastery of Nuestra Señora de la Defensión in Jeréz de la Frontera and formed part of a large altarpiece fifty feet wide and thirty feet high, comprising twelve paintings. This is a good example of the centuries-long tradition of attributing aid in battle against the Muslims to the Virgin Mary. Courtesy of The Metropolitan Museum of Art, Kretschmar Fund, 1920 (20.104). Image © The Metropolitan Museum of Art.

of the miracle directly to Mary resonates with the climate of the century, which identified victories and defeats with women, and particularly in Spain and Latin America, victories were identified with the Virgin Mary. Regarding the instantaneously crumbling mountain in which the rest of the Muslims die, Morales urges doubting readers to recall God's miracle when the Red Sea parted only for the chosen people, drowning the Egyptians who attempted to follow them. Asturians also tell of the miracle of the Cross that day: a crucifix appeared in the sky, a sign of the victory to come. Pelayo fashioned a cross of oak, and used it as his standard that day, as did the kings who followed him in battle against the Muslims. This image of Pelayo leaning on the cross of victory appears as a woodcut in many works, and as a frequent subject of nineteenth-century paintings.

Morales then recounts how Spain began its restoration, as "Goths" came in increasing number to Asturias. With the death of Pelayo on Friday, September 18, 737, after a reign of nineteen years, and a burial in the church of the virgin martyr Eulalia, his son Favila became the ruler. Shortly after ascending the throne, Favila was killed by a bear while hunting, and his children were too young to rule. The daughter of Pelayo, wed to Alfonso, who according to Morales was an Asturian of royal blood, became the concrete link between the old Visigothic line and its continuation, and her husband became Alfonso I of León. Later histories debate whether Pelayo had ever been king formally and officially, though all histories accord him the role of continuing Iberian Christian blood after the fall of Spain, and of initiating the Reconquest. Morales takes particular care to contradict the history of another of Philip's chroniclers, Esteban de Garibay y Zamalloa, who had asserted that Pelayo was not a Goth.[12] Not only does Morales beg to differ, but he points out that Spain is the envy of Europe for she possesses an unbroken line of kingship more than eight hundred years old at the time of his writing: "No hay Nación ninguna que considerando bien esto, no lo tenga por una incomparable gloria de la real sangre de España" (There is not a single nation that, considering this point well, would not agree that the royal blood of Spain possesses incomparable glory; vol. 7, bk. 13, chap. 6).

Philip II and the Power of Prophecy

An event from the last part of the sixteenth century demonstrates how important its Visigothic history was to the Spanish nation. In addition, the event—the translation of the remains of the fifth-century virgin martyr St. Leocadia to Toledo in 1587—underscores the importance of relics and religion to Spain's early modern nation building and growing national identity, as well as the intersection of women's bodies and nation building. One year later, Protestant England handed Catholic

Spain a most devastating and stunning naval defeat. In the background, and span-
ning the years 1587 and 1590, stands the curious story of Lucrecia de León, the
Madrileña whose nighttime dream visions, collected in an enormous set of Inquisition notebooks known as "dream registers," predicted the downward spiral of the
country as well as the downfall of the king personally. According to Inquisition documents, Lucrecia predicted the defeat of the "Invincible Armada" a year before it
sailed in 1588. As Kagan tells us in his fascinating book *Lucrecia's Dreams,* Lucrecia
was unusual in that she was not a nun guided by spiritual stirrings, nor was she known
as a political figure or someone close to the court in any way. Although not of the
nobility, she was nonetheless a young woman of some means, though she had more
in common, apparently, with the street or marketplace prophets, who appeared in
times of political unrest and economic crisis to preach millennial scenarios (8). In
the 1520s and 1530s, following the prophecy in which Holy Roman Emperor Charles
V was heralded as a second Charlemagne, the street prophets "proclaimed Charles V
the Last World Emperor, the ruler destined to unite Christendom, conquer Islam,
and prepare the world for the Day of Judgment" (8).[13] The 1580s were a hotbed of
doomsday predictions for the court of Spain and King Philip II personally, spurred
on by the "crisis of confidence that beset Philip's court in the late 1580s" (88). Embedded in this national story of burgeoning unrest is the triumphant moment of the
return of the remains of Toledo's beloved daughter, the patron saint, Leocadia.

Relics of saints were not only required in order to sanctify every church, they
were a marketable commodity from the early days of Christianity. Relics authenticated the mission of monasteries and convents, attracted pilgrims (and pilgrim
dollars) eager to venerate the remains of their favorite saint, and in a less cynical or
commercial vein, appeared to move deeply the public who saw them as a local or
national symbol of community. Patrick Geary's engrossing history of the widespread
theft of relics in the Middle Ages documents the transactions, both overt and covert,
that testify to the cultural and social contexts that impelled this thriving spiritual
and economic commerce.[14] Geary's work entertains not only because thieves—often
clerics—went to enormous lengths to obtain authenticated relics as well as to claim
authenticity in the face of the most dubious evidence, but because the stories of the
saints' complicity in the theft or restoration of their own remains often rival any
Boccaccian novella for humor and tall tales.

In 1567, Pope Pius V granted Philip permission to unearth, buy, or recover by any
means necessary the relics of saints to protect and centralize them at the physical,
political, and metaphorical heart of the Spanish empire. Philip had moved the court
from Toledo to Madrid in 1561, but he nevertheless greatly preferred the austere but
imposing monastic refuge of El Escorial, north of Madrid, and his reign was marked

by a relentless drive to bring as many relics as possible there. And although patron saints and holy relics were of undeniable importance to Spaniards in general, Philip was an unrivaled collector of saints' relics, whose passion bordered on the fanatical, as Carlos Eire tells us: "He continually asked for [the relics] to be placed against his eyes, mouth, head and hands, driving his *relicario* [relic curator], Fray Martín de Villanueva, to distraction. Philip became obsessed with them and was driven nearly mad" (*From Madrid to Purgatory* 268). While others dreamed of gold, silver, and other booty from the New World, Philip longed for such treasures as the body of Spain's patron saint, Santiago de Compostela, and the legendary hairs of Mary Magdalene, two grand quests that remained unfulfilled to him, one because the clergy in Galicia refused to cede the body and the other because, though much sought after, no one knew where any hairs might be found.[15] At the time of Philip's death in 1598, he had amassed close to eight thousand sacred objects.

For Spain, in the time of its nation building and empire building, the veneration of the remains of a female saint had special resonance. Counter-Reformation Spain's climate of deep religious sentiment, the focus of sixteenth-century Spain on the cult of the Virgin, the special place of her mother, St. Anne, in the pantheon of saints, the overwhelming popularity of the sensually portrayed penitent Magdalene in print and the plastic arts, and even the implication of the special importance of female martyrs in the nationalist play we examined earlier in this chapter, Palau's *Historia de la gloriosa santa Orosia* (History of the glorious Saint Orosia), all point toward and derive from the same cultural practices. Spanish Catholicism even had its version of "the helpful Muslim princess" in the figure of St. Casilda. According to legend, the eleventh-century Casilda, like the father-defying Muslim princess Galiana, associated with stories of Charlemagne, was the daughter of a Muslim ruler of Toledo, a king who, in keeping with the narrative conventions of these tales, hated all Christians and the Christian faith. Instead of a conversion to Christianity inspired by the love of, and in order to be with, a man, as in the stories of Galiana and Alfonso VI's concubine or wife Zaida, Casilda fell in love with Christianity itself. In her demonstration of love, rather than bestow it on a single person, Casilda chose Christian love, *caritas,* defying her father by secretly feeding the Christian captives. She escaped her father's wrath and fled to the countryside, where she lived, after a Christian baptism, as an anchorite near Briviesca in Burgos. The Prado Museum houses the most famous painting of St. Casilda—who is still venerated in Burgos, Zaragoza, and Toledo, and invoked in war—Zurbarán's rendering of the Saracen maiden with roses in her lap.

In the early 1570s, Philip sent his chronicler, Ambrosio de Morales, on a hunting and collecting spree of books and relics in Spain, which Morales used as the basis for

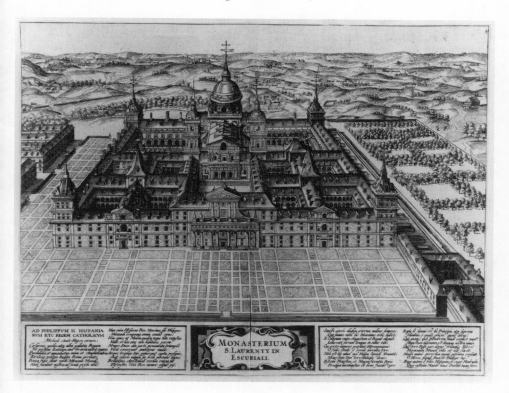

View of El Escorial, 1572–1593, by Joris Hoefnagle (Flemish, 1542–1600). Engraving, 36.5 × 46.5 cm. From Georgius Bruin and Franz Hohenberg, *Theatre des cites du monde* (Civitates Orbis Terrarum), Trans. unknown, [Brussels: ca. 1572–1593]. Courtesy of The Hispanic Society of America, New York.

his 1575 *Antigüedades de las ciudades de España* (Antiquities of the cities of Spain). As explained earlier in this chapter, Morales explored and wrote about León, Galicia, and Asturias, especially the areas that pertained to Pelayo and the early Asturian kingdom. Morales's investigation of the legend of Pelayo increased interest in Leocadia, the patron saint of Toledo, especially the part of the legend that attributed the rescue of her relics by Pelayo.

For her refusal to renounce Christianity, St. Leocadia had been imprisoned in a well, where she fashioned a cross from sticks and spent the time in prayer until her death there. Her remains rested in a church in Toledo, until her bones were translated from Toledo to Asturias. There is ample historical evidence of Leocadia as patroness of Toledo and the early Christian church in Visigothic Spain, and thirteenth-century chronicles do mention Pelayo as a translator of some saints' relics. However, it is important to emphasize that the specific claim of Pelayo as protector of the remains of Leocadia is an early modern creation, which served the needs of the monarchy and historians in the sixteenth century. In the early ninth century, the Asturian king, Alfonso II (791–842), known as el Casto (the Chaste), built a church in honor of St. Leocadia in the royal city of Oviedo, and to house her relics, where they rest today. Alfonso may have translated the relics from Toledo, as some historians believe; it is unlikely that Pelayo rescued them from Toledo during the invasion, as sixteenth-century historians, like Morales, asserted. In a fascinating chapter in Morales's *Corónica general,* he discusses the relics and sacred objects that he examined in the cathedral in Oviedo, opining on their provenance and authenticity (vol. 7, bk. 13, chap. 40). In addition to bodies of saints, the chasuble miraculously presented to St. Idlefonso by the Virgin Mary, and Pelayo's gold and jewel-encrusted cross, Morales describes the most precious sacred object of all, the small, blood-stained linen cloth known as the Holy Sudarium of Oviedo that, to this day, many people believe covered the head of Jesus after the Crucifixion.

Morales recounts the story of a miracle associated with the relics of Leocadia when they were still in the Cathedral of Toledo, a miracle first recorded by Cixila, the eighth-century archbishop of Toledo and biographer (c. 775) of St. Ildefonso. The seventh-century bishop of Toledo, Ildefonso, wrote a treatise on the virginity of Mary. One day, while praying before the sepulcher of Leocadia, Ildefonso beheld the levitation of the sepulcher's stone covering, which "30 men could not have lifted," and the appearance of the saint herself, who cried out, "O Ildefonso, por ti vive la gloria de mi Señora" (O Ildefonso, through you lives the glory of my Lady! vol. 6, bk. 12, chap. 39: 224). The Visigothic king Recesvindo, also a witness, gave Ildefonso a knife with which to cut a piece of the saint's mantilla, which Morales claimed to have seen himself in the Toledan cathedral. Morales tells us that Alfonso the Learned brought to the cathedral the remains of kings Wamba and Recesvindo, and, he believes, the remains of "the king, don Pelayo." In 1575, Philip journeyed to the cathedral to venerate the holy bodies of St. Ildefonso, the Visigothic kings, and Pelayo.

A fifteenth-century witness of the status of Leocadia's legend, Fernán Pérez de Guzmán, wrote the poetic *Loores de santos* (In praise of saints), which exists in eleven extant poetic songbooks (*cancioneros*), testifying to its popularity; he praises Leocadia as "defenssora y patrona / de la ynperial cibdad / que fue de la magestad / gótica trono y corona" (Defender and patroness of the former imperial city of the majestic Gothic throne and crown; Maguire and Severin 165). In the longest of the six saints' lives recounted in the hymnal, Pérez de Guzmán calls Leocadia a virgin, holy from birth, and, anachronistically, "born in the Castilian kingdom" (naciste virgen muy santa / en el reyno castellano), when there was no such kingdom. The poet makes much of her rejection of the value and recognition accorded earthly notions of high lineage, both her own and that of the Roman emperor. She rejects the amorous advances of Emperor Dacian, telling him that she prefers the lineage and love of Jesus Christ. Although Dacian expects her to weaken after lengthy incarceration, she resists, winning her martyr's crown and the enduring adoration of Toledans. In preparing their edition of these fifteenth-century poems, Fiona Maguire and Dorothy Sherman Severin had to rely on a seventeenth-century collection of saints' stories to relate the lives, which indicates how difficult it is to find versions of the legend of Leocadia that may have circulated in the Middle Ages.[16] At any rate, although Pérez de Guzmán did situate Leocadia in a Castilian realm, and indeed, in a very early example of the later tendency to do so, refers to the Visigothic kingdom as an empire, he makes no reference to Pelayo or the translation of her relics, or any other importance of the saint beyond the city of Toledo.

Leocadia's remains had long been housed in the monastery of St. Gislenus in Flanders; the Jesuit priest Miguel Hernández had negotiated their release in 1582 (Forcione 317). How they moved from Asturias to Flanders is not clear. The intimate relationship that a believer experienced with a favored saint is demonstrated by the manner in which royal chronicler Esteban de Garibay y Zamalloa describes his own efforts to free the saint, as if she were a damsel in distress. Before Hernández secured the agreement from the pope to allow the saint's remains to be returned to Spain, Garibay y Zamalloa had pleaded with the archbishop of Toledo and Philip II to "save the saint by removing her from a land where she is 'surrounded by heretics' and placing her in the secure kingdom of Spain, where Catholicism is flourishing" (quoted in Forcione 317). The translation of relics sometimes inspired slow processions, allowing for the veneration of the saint along the way by a fervent and adoring public; it took five years for the saint to arrive in Toledo from the Flemish monastery.

In 1587, a long-awaited and grandly conceived and executed spectacle moved and delighted the Toledan crowds that lined the streets for a chance to glimpse the procession and the reliquary carrying the remains of their beloved patron saint, Leocadia.[17] The following passage, which Forcione assembles from the writings of Francisco de Pisa, Hernández, and Garibay, allows us a small window into the magnificence of the event for the population hungry to witness miracle and spectacle:

> While the astonished populace expressed its jubilation with "all kinds of music, vocal and instrumental, with dances and games, and a thousand types of merry-making," the *regidores* [town councilors] carried the holy burden beneath canopies of "gold and silk" through the streets of the city, sacralizing the spaces of their daily

lives by touching them with wonder-working relics. At various predetermined points on their route the celebrants halted to allow the citizens to offer their tribute to the saint in the form of "triumphal arches, and large images of saints and kings, with their elegant inscriptions written in Latin verse and in prose" . . .

[In] a culminating epiphany, King Philip II, the royal family, and the grandees of Spain emerged from the house of the archbishop to escort the litter on the final stage of its passage . . . They approached the church and the magnificent representations of the glories of "many saints of Toledo, and kings of Spain, and other princes," which the architects of the city had created for the celebration . . . On the following morning the cardinal conducted a pontifical mass, the coffer was opened, the authenticating documents, "instruments and testimonies" were examined, and, following their approval, King Philip locked the coffer and delivered the key to the treasurer of the church. A solemn procession bore the bones to the sacristy and their permanent abode, "a place which was appropriate for them, as it was the very palace of Our Lady the Virgin." (318–19)

The festivities occasioned no fewer than three lengthy recountings, one in the memoirs of the diplomat Garibay, and religious histories by Francisco de Pisa and by Miguel Hernández.[18] There existed a vast public demand for this kind of work, as we see in the ship registers of books sent to the Americas, which also contained great numbers of spiritual biographies and devotional texts. But if we consider the staggering quantities of materials that testify to the popularity of such events as the arrival of St. Leocadia in Toledo, as well as the quantities of materials that informed the daily lives of the faithful, we begin to sense the magnitude both of religious practices in the daily experience of the people and of the enormous honor accorded Philip, as well as the nationalistic and imperialistic propaganda, of being portrayed as the monarch who brought the patron saint home, fulfilling the promise of Pelayo almost nine hundred years earlier.

In 1587, the year before the defeat of the Spanish Armada, the power and popularity of the king as unifying symbol of Spanish nationalism was at its peak. Philip, of the Spanish Hapsburg line begun by his father, is equated with Pelayo, the first Asturian king: Philip's actions fulfill and bring closure to the promise begun hundreds of years earlier by Pelayo; both men protect Leocadia from the barbarians, Pelayo by taking her away from Toledo when she needed rescuing, Philip by arranging for her return. Rather than focus on the idea of the new kingdom overturning the old Visigothic kingdom, as chroniclers had done at least since the twelfth century, Francisco de Pisa bypasses the link of the Spanish monarch to the vanquished Rodrigo, the "last" of his line, in order to connect Philip with Pelayo, and to the

view of history as a pattern of promise and fulfillment.[19] The mental image of Leocadia's mutilated body serves as a symbol of the desecration Spain suffered during
the Muslim invasion, while her remains were transformed into a holy object. The
return of her bodily remains to Spain stands as yet another metaphor that employs
the woman's body as the restoration of Spain. St. Leocadia has been invoked even in
the twenty-first century in the Church's 2000 pastoral letter from the archbishop of
Toledo, a recent call for Spain to revive the "raíces cristianas" (Christian roots) of its
national identity.

The return of Leocadia's remains offered a symbolic triumph that brought mo-
mentary respite from the realities of a nation that feared invasion. Contributing to
the country's vulnerability to attack by the Turks was that, despite its new position
as a world power and global colonizer, Spain had never developed a strong navy. The
1571 victory against the Turks in the Mediterranean, the Battle of Lepanto, celebrated equally in Spanish history and fiction as one of the most glorious triumphs
of Christendom, should have incited a more concerted effort to build a powerful
navy, but it did not. In addition to the constant Turkish threat, Spanish galleons to
and from the New World suffered crippling attacks by the English fleet, especially
by the legendary Sir Francis Drake. Because of this ongoing and costly piracy, Philip
consented to send the Armada toward England, designed to put a stop to the piracy,
and retake the Netherlands in the bargain. For Philip and Spain, this constituted another holy war, the opportunity to take on the "Protestant Scourge" and defeat them
once and for all. Along with the Spanish ships, private fleet vessels from Naples and
Portugal, carrying gunpowder from Germany, 130 in all, set out from La Coruña on
July 22, 1588, under the leadership of the duke of Medina-Sidonia. The English
roundly defeated the armada at Calais, destroying many ships and killing thousands
of soldiers. Many more sailors died off the coast of Ireland, when their ships fled the
English onslaught. The duke returned to Santander in the third week of September,
having lost about one hundred ships and fifteen thousand men.

To conclude this chapter, let us return to the story of the prophetic Lucrecia de
León. She was not formally educated: according to Kagan, she received training only
in "rudimentary reading skills," and her lover, Vitores, "testified [at her trial] that he
never saw any books in the León household" (24). Nevertheless, Lucrecia's dreams
registered a fairly detailed knowledge of Spanish history. Kagan offers an intriguing
explanation for how she could seem so knowledgeable:

> In the sixteenth century oral culture was almost as rich and diversified as that
> available in print. Oral transmission, for example, may well account for Lucrecia's
> knowledge of the Cid, the medieval hero who appeared in her dream of 13 July

1588. Although various versions of the chronicle of the Cid's life had been available in print since the end of the fifteenth century, he was best known through the *romances* [ballads], the cycle of old chivalric tales and *chansons de gestes* that began to be published in the course of the sixteenth century. These ballads may also account for much of Lucrecia's historical knowledge, notably that concerning King Roderic, Spain's last Visigothic ruler, who appears in the dream of 20 April 1590. (24)

If we combine Kagan's opinion with our knowledge that the ballads of Lucrecia's time were the learned and historical ones filled with names, places, and details, and that one goal of the ballads was to teach history to, or provoke national sentiment in, an unlettered public, the idea that oral tradition supplied Lucrecia's wellspring of historical data that informed her dreams is even more probable.

Kagan believes that Lucrecia's dreams—especially her own prominent role in many of them—suggest that she "was engaged in a form of mythmaking in which an otherwise neglected adolescent appears larger than life" (74). She records several dreams in which she is both a victim of the Turks and "a Spanish Joan of Arc, a *doncella guerrera* or warrior woman who helps to rescue Spain from its enemies" (74), and provides additional contexts in which she is portrayed as the savior of Spain. Given that so many of her dreams focus persistently on the loss of Spain in the near future, and that they return to the story of Rodrigo and the fall, she appears to be juxtaposing herself—a new Joan of Arc—as a savior of Spain to the female figure who had lost Spain, La Cava. By the same token, her implication in 1590 that Philip II was an imminent Rodrigo, about to lose his empire, was hardly received with enthusiasm, least of all by Philip, so recently celebrated as a Pelayo, not a Rodrigo. In this climate of anti-Muslim fervor, Lucrecia's prophetic equation of Philip with Rodrigo terrified the political and ecclesiastical powers, who feared a repeat of the legendary loss of the Christian peninsula to the victorious Muslim armies. As Henry Kamen tells us, at this time Spain and Philip inspired a widespread lack of confidence in the overseas empire: "The king's own secretary informed Philip II in a confidential document that 'the people are full of complaints and many say that things are not going well'. 'I am astonished at what they tell me about Castile', commented a Spanish resident of faraway Lima in 1590, 'that it is finished, and I believe it from what people say here. Here we go neither hungry nor thirsty, nor do we lack for clothing.' Another, writing from the same city to relatives in Jérez de la Frontera, was alarmed by news of 'the hardship that you suffer in Spain. Since we want for nothing over here, we can hardly believe it'" (309–10).

Whatever the true source of Lucrecia's prophetic dreams, she had correctly predicted, a year before it took place, the defeat of the armada in 1588. The Inquisition took note: "The dreams' prophetic quality, their immediate relevance to the future of Spain, and their source—divine or diabolical—these were the aspects of Lucrecia's dreams that captured the attention of . . . the Holy Office" (74). Lucrecia was arrested and tortured—during which time she confessed to many of the charges brought against her—and was sentenced ultimately to "one hundred lashes, banishment from Madrid and a two-year seclusion in a religious home" (155). As harsh as it sounds, Lucrecia's sentence was relatively light compared to the number of women who would not have fared nearly as well faced with the same charges of having dreams instigated by the devil himself.

This is the climate near the end of the century: continuing faith in the powers of prophecy to describe the present and help shape future action, and tremendous reliance on the symbolism of bodies, particularly female bodies, to reflect both the woes and the triumphs of Spain as nation and empire. Linked to this symbolism is a boundless anti-Morisco and anticonverso sentiment among the Christian populace, and uncertainty about the reign of a king who, only months before, during the celebration of the translation of the remains of St. Leocadia, was seen as a savior of the nation and as a king divinely ordained to lead the world to Christianity. Philip faced the humiliation of the defeat of what came to be known, tauntingly by the victors, as the "Invincible Armada," amid growing national unrest, by retreating even more to the hermetic solitude of El Escorial.[20]

CHAPTER FIVE

Here Was Troy, Farewell Spain!

How sad Castile is . . . and what Spain felt the most / and
what caused the most pain / was to see the churches / profaned by
the Moors
> Seventeenth-century oral ballad about the Fall of Spain, 711

A Tale of Tales

Throughout the sixteenth century, the Church and state view of Spanish Moriscos as a national problem intensified, and the fear of invading Ottoman Turks had increased significantly. Illusions of tolerance disappeared: after the fall of Granada in 1492 to the Christians, Ferdinand and Isabel had pledged to allow Muslims to maintain their customary daily life in Spain, including the use of Arabic, traditional Muslim dress, and religious practices, but by 1499 the Muslims were subjected to mass baptisms or faced expulsion from the country. Emperor Charles V and King Philip II issued numerous edicts against the Moriscos and the use of Moorish dress, language, and customs.[1]

It was typical in this time to cast the enemy as a sexual one, and misogyny served a useful purpose in that endeavor. Medieval Spain identified the lust of King Rodrigo with the desires of the invading Muslims, but early modern Spain linked La Cava to the Muslims. Manuela Marín, in her article, "Marriage and Sexuality in Al-Andalus," explains the origins of the over-sexed Muslim male, which led him, legendarily, to insatiable lust for both women and men, particularly young boys. This view was heightened dramatically in the sixteenth century and is therefore never absent from the discussions about Islam and the fear of invasion by the Turks or by the Moriscos who remained in Spain. As Richard Trexler points out, the accusations hurled at Muslims and Jews in Iberia, as beings consumed by sodomy and other acts considered to be debauchery, were clearly prevalent in Christian society, and of much concern to lawmakers and the clergy.

In the 1560s, Spain warred against the Ottoman Empire, but increasingly the collective national Church and state authority perceived little, if any, difference between the Morisco uprisings in the peninsula (to protest stringent penalties and lack of basic liberties) and the Muslim enemies in the Mediterranean Sea. Islamic religious practices had been forbidden in the edicts of 1501, 1502, 1524, and 1526. In 1567, Philip II issued a ruling that forbade speaking and writing in Arabic, as well as possession of Arabic books, regardless of quality or kind. These brutal measures of religious and cultural effacement contributed to the Moriscos' rebellion in late 1568 in the mountainous region outside of Granada known as the Alpujarras. Authorities accused Spanish Moriscos of adhering to the tenets of Islam, of being false Christians, and of continuing loyalties to Islamic rulers far from Spain. The Christian triumph in the Mediterranean Sea's Battle of Lepanto in 1571 may have buoyed Spain's conviction of divine support against the infidels, but no one expected comprehensive victory, inside and outside of Spain, without protracted bloody conflict. The most heavily populated Morisco communities, especially Valencia and other port cities on the Mediterranean, stockpiled ammunition for corsairs and pirates, aiding those who would attack Spain's shores. While it is clear that some of these activities indeed occurred, they were not nearly as pervasive as the Crown and Church alleged, but as with the Jews a century before, the accusations shored up the view that Spain harbored a viper in its bosom.[2] To both Church and state, the Muslim inhabitants of Spain moved from being enemies of the faith, whose conversion might allow for assimilation into Spanish Christian society and customs, to being Morisco enemies of the state, a threat to national security. Ironically, throughout the sixteenth century, the always inventive and flourishing ballad tradition developed and then embellished the romanticized figure of the "noble Moor," a character of great valor and chivalric qualities.

Official history intended to record the Muslims and Moriscos as interlopers, occupants of nine hundred years, but not real Spaniards and not part of the real Spain. As Francisco Márquez Villanueva points out, a powerful minority—the nobility of Castile—charted a future for Spain that would transform it into the nation they desired, homogeneous, Catholic, and secure from outside influences (*El problema morisco* 199).

Some twenty years before the official Edict of Expulsion of the Moriscos from Valencia, a discovery rocked Philip II's court. Shocking to those clergy, politicians, and noblemen already hoping and planning to expel the Morisco population from Spain was the March 18, 1588, discovery of a lead box underneath a Granada minaret, which workers demolished in preparation for a new part of the grand cathedral built there. The box contained some relics—a bone, a piece of cloth, and an image of the Virgin Mary—and a parchment with prophecies written in Arabic and Castilian (with an additional inscription in Latin), known today as the Tower of Turpin manuscript, which foretold the end of the world.[3] In addition to the shocking prophetic

Battle of Lepanto illustration in Jerónimo Corte Real,
*Felicissima victoria concedida del cielo al señor don Juan de
Austria, en el golfo de Lepanto de la poderosa armada Otho-
mana.* Lisbon: Antonio Ribero, 1578. Folio 170v. Courtesy
of The Hispanic Society of America, New York.

content of the manuscript, the fact that it was written in Arabic and Castilian implied a connection between Arab and Christian Spain, or between Islam and Christianity, that deeply unsettled Church and state authorities. Allegedly written by
John, one of the four gospel writers, this prophecy underwent tremendous scrutiny
by religious authorities during a decade that saw countless prophecies of doom,
some of which seemed to come to pass, such as Lucrecia de León's prediction of the
defeat of the armada in 1588. However, nothing prepared the authorities for the 1595
unearthing in Sacromonte in Granada of nineteen thin circular tablets made of lead,
each about the size of a communion wafer, causing a stir comparable to the discov-

ery and questions of translation and authentication of the Dead Sea Scrolls in the twentieth century (L.P. Harvey, *Muslims in Spain* 8). Officials charged the Moriscos Alonso del Castillo and Miguel de Luna, Arabic interpreters to the court of Philip II, with the portentous task of translating the leaden tablets. To guard against fraud, they allowed Luna to translate first, and then Castillo, without Castillo's having seen what Luna had done (López-Baralt 213, n.7).

Significantly, these tablets, allegedly from the first century, combined religious beliefs of Christianity and Islam in an attempt to create religious syncretism. The goal, in short, was to stave off the ever-increasing policies against the Moriscos in Spain by demonstrating the importance of Muslims to Spain, and of their shared religious history with Christianity, as attested to by these tablets. They contained prophecies that, if believed, might have given religious and state authorities pause in continuing down the path toward the Moriscos' expulsion from Spain. Although these relics were authenticated in April 1600, enough influential disbelievers remained to render the tablets useless against the inexorable tide that swept away whatever resistance remained in the peninsula to the notion of the need to expel the Moriscos. In September 1609, town criers in Valencia announced the first Edict of Expulsion, which had been signed a few days before, ordering Valencian Moriscos to leave the country. The ongoing process and additional edicts for other regions of Spain continued until 1614, when more than 275,000 Moriscos had been forced to abandon their homeland.[4] As López-Baralt aptly concludes about the counterfeit tablets: "There is some suspicion that the controversial pair Alonso del Castillo and Miguel de Luna, who took part in the 'official' translation of the lead tablets, were in fact their authors, aided in their singular and utilitarian theological venture by persons with some interest in the opposing religion. The false chronicles and the Tower of Turpin manuscript are today seen as pathetic in their theological naiveté and tragic in their total failure to halt the Moorish expulsion and to lend dying Spanish Islam some last prestige" (201).[5] Darío Cabanelas and others provide convincing evidence that Castillo's and Luna's participation is not a suspicion but a fact.[6] The straddling of Christianity and Islam, with the aim of creating a believable syncretism between the two religions, formed part of a larger strategy for Luna.

In this cultural and political context of anti-Islamic sentiment and quest to discover national origins, and almost immediately following the defeat of the armada, Luna claimed that on November 30, 1589, he had finished translating another "found text," this one an eighth-century history from Arabic into Spanish. Printed in 1592, the first book of his two-part *Historia verdadera del rey don Rodrigo, en la qual se trata la causa principal de la pérdida de España y la conquista que de ella hizo Miramomelin Almançor Rey que fué de Africa, y de las Arabias* (*True History of King*

Philip III, 1687, by anonymous Flemish. Engraving, 19.8 × 16.4 cm. Courtesy of The Hispanic Society of America, New York.

Rodrigo, in which is treated the principal cause of the loss of Spain and her conquest by Emir Almanzor, a king of Africa and the Arabias), purported to be the eyewitness account of Abulcaçim Tarif Abentariq, who had served with Almanzor and Tarik during the invasion of the peninsula against Rodrigo. Moreover, Luna's alleged find painted a much more admirable portrait of the Muslim rulers than of Rodrigo.

For Luna to counter with a "true history" Corral's fifteenth-century laudatory "history" of Rodrigo, to say nothing of disputing the favorable view of Rodrigo proffered by the sixteenth-century learned historians, shook the court to its core, and later centuries continued to feel the reverberations. And yet, he clearly remained trusted and in favor, or he would never have been asked to translate the leaden tablets in 1595. Luna followed up this first part of his "history" with a second part printed in 1600, which described the enlightened and judicious rule of the Muslim kings in Spain. Luna's own version of the founding myth of Spain supported what might be called a political syncretism, when he portrayed Pelayo and the Muslim rulers of Spain as attempting to find an acceptable coexistence. For Luna and like-minded others, what had existed before could exist again, especially if their founding myth attested to indissoluble national origins of one Spain, a Muslim-Christian country.

The famed Jesuit moralist and political theorist Juan de Mariana published his Latin history of Spain, *De Rebus Hispaniae* (*General History of Spain*), in the same year that Luna published his *True History of King Rodrigo,* 1592. Mariana's Castilian translation of his work, *Historia general de España,* which would have circulated among a much wider reading public than the Latin history, appeared in 1601. In contrast to the widespread negative criticism heaped upon Miguel de Luna's inventiveness, we find highly favorable views accorded Father Mariana's history, even though it is acknowledged that he infuses his account of the legend of the fall and Pelayo's reign with invention and borrowings from something other than historical chronicles. This raises interesting issues. First of all, while Mariana's reconstruction of history needs to be placed within the context of what was considered a proper and reasonable inventiveness for a sixteenth-century historian, what he selected to incorporate into his history about La Cava portrayed her as less moral and less of a victim than other historical authorities did, whose chronicles Mariana relied on.[7] Interestingly, Menéndez Pidal praises Mariana for the elements that he borrows from Corral that are not absolutely historical, but "novelesque fictions" (ficciones novelescas), which he claims contribute to the history's "estilo historial clásico, de reposada andadura, matizado de suave penetración psicológica y moral, salpicado de advertencias críticas fáciles y complacientes con el sentir del lector, adornado con cartas y arengas elegantemente dilatadas bajo la pluma de la Cava o en boca del rey godo y de Tarif" (classical historical style, of appropriate length, lightly colored by moral and psychological penetration, spiced with timely and appropriate critical commentary for the reader, adorned with elegantly rendered letters and dialogues from La Cava's pen or from the mouths of the Gothic king and Tarif [Tarik]; *Floresta* 2: xlix). Although they wrote centuries apart, Juan de Mariana and Menéndez Pidal held in common the goal of shaping their national history in a particular way that favored Christianity and excluded Jewish and Muslim cultural, social, and political contributions. Mariana's history of Spain casts events of the fall of Spain and its aftermath specifically in terms designed to speak volumes about nationalism in Mariana's own time. In 1605, two literary works were published. One of them, part 1 of *Don Quixote,* has enjoyed unparalleled acclaim, celebrated worldwide in 2005 for the four hundredth anniversary since its first printing. The other, *Pelayo,* a twenty-canto epic poem based on the Restoration hero's deeds, remains justifiably unknown and almost impossible to find anywhere: in 1949, Marcelino Menéndez Pelayo labeled it "uno de los más insulsos y fastidiosos que pueden encontrarse" (one of the most insipid and fastidious works one could ever find; *Obras completas,* 3: 49).[8] Ironically, the first work, about a crazy but idealistic middle-aged man who thinks he is a knight, sprang from the genius of a writer fairly unheralded in his time, a jailbird and near-pauper, Cervantes, while the second man, Alonso López Pinciano, author of the most important work of literary theory of early modern Spain, the 1596 *Philosophia antigua poetica,* took as his subject Spain's earliest hero, the putative founder of the Spanish throne.[9] Two years later, in 1607, Cristóbal de Mesa published an epic poem about Pelayo called *La Restauración de España* (The restoration of Spain). A friend and disciple of Italy's great epic poet Torquato Tasso, Mesa included Tasso as the third of great epic writers, after Homer and Virgil.[10] Neither López Pinciano nor Mesa measured up to their Greek, Roman, and Italian literary counterparts, and unsurprisingly, the Spanish historical epic proved to be no match for the imaginative genius of Cervantes. Nevertheless, Pelayo did become a favored figure with many neoclassical and Romantic writers, who turned frequently for source material to the history written by Juan de Mariana.

What all four of these works—Mesa's *La Restauración de España,* Cervantes' *Don Quixote,* Luna's *True History of King Rodrigo,* and Mariana's *Historia general de España*—had in common can be summed up by a single word: prophecy. The control of prophecy meant, quite simply, the control of history. While prophecy was of the utmost importance as a tool for creating a Christian nationalist history and sentiment in Spain, for the Moriscos it was the last hope and the only path they could discern to cultural—indeed, literal—survival.[11]

As we saw in the previous chapter, the historian in the early modern period was understood to perform a sacred duty of casting events in terms of their truth-value and exemplarity. Because of his unique ability to interpret the past and employ his own knowledge to put the events in their proper moral and philosophical context, the historian was also a kind of prophet. His writings should interpret the past in such a way as to inspire a path for the future. According to Juan Luis Vives, the sacred duty required the historian to provide his own opinion, his own moral commentary on the past.[12] Ironically, the late sixteenth century's two most enduring retellings of the legend of Spain's fall and restoration, both printed in 1592 but used time and again by later writers of history and fiction, could not have been more different in intent: Luna's *True History of King Rodrigo* and Mariana's Latin *De Rebus Hispaniae.* But in style, there is a marked similarity: both avail themselves of the role of the historian to provide moral commentary on past events in order to manipulate and guide the future. And most significantly for seventeenth-century Spain, both authors assess, evaluate, promote, and attempt to influence the ideal portrait of a king and the unsavory portrait of his opposite, the corrupt, despotic, or tyrannical king.

Women continued to play an important role in the legend of the fall and restoration of Spain. The language of desire in the sixteenth century metaphorically locates the legend of the fall and restoration as part of a large enterprise of nation building, on the bodies of women, especially La Cava and Pelayo's sister and his daughter, and on the dual depiction of the feminized and eroticized Muslim enemy. Magdalenes and Eves continued to dominate the seventeenth-century cultural landscape as women were typecast socially, politically, and religiously, and the good woman continued to be represented by the Virgin Mary. The interest in defining the monarch and the monarchy, according to Frederick De Armas, encouraged renewed emphasis on another female figure, Astraea, the goddess of justice, though she had never disappeared from the political scene: in the late fifteenth century, even Queen Isabel the Catholic was called the new Astraea. Margaret Ferguson, in *Dido's Daughters,* analyzes the importance of the figure of Astraea in terms of theories of gender and empire building for early modern Europe in general. The celebration of exemplary and mythic women as models did little to enhance the reputation of real women, since the good woman was seen to be as elusive and ephemeral as the goddess of justice herself often seemed to be.

Instead, seventeenth-century Spain showcased the role of La Cava as emblematic of the dangers of women and female sexuality in general, and in a particularly compelling context, as danger to the role of the monarch. While earlier legend found Rodrigo blameworthy for his moral laxity and lustfulness, certainly dangerous traits in a ruler, the seventeenth century turns its attention, both because of international common concerns and of internal national disillusionment, to the nature of the monarch, the powers of the monarchy, the idea of the nation or the republic, and specifically the origins of the Spanish monarchy and the essence of Spanish nationalism. And for that self-examination, the figure of the heroic, incorruptible, and unswervingly Christian Pelayo proved indispensable.

This chapter focuses on a few works that best capture the seventeenth-century views of the legend of the fall of Spain, some that precede the expulsion of the Moriscos and some that follow it. In addition to Miguel de Luna's *True History of King Rodrigo* and Juan de Mariana's treatment of the same material, I also look at the historical ballads that developed during the first half of the century. Next, I look at two of Lope de Vega's plays, *El último godo* (The last Goth), performed in 1618, and *Las paces de los reyes y judía de Toledo* (The peace of kings and Jewess of Toledo), printed in 1617 but probably written between 1610 and 1612. As examples of works from after the expulsion of the Moriscos that continue to treat legendary material of early Spain, I briefly consider the anonymous *Casos notables de Córdoba* (Notable cases of Córdoba, 1618), a collection of stories and anecdotes about Córdoba's role in the building of Spain, and Diego de Saavedra Fajardo's two important works, *Idea de un príncipe político-cristiano* (Idea of a political Christian prince, 1640) and *Corona gótica, castellana y austríaca* (Gothic, Castilian and Austrian crown, 1646).[13] Saavedra's treatises measure the dangerous significance of the past for the present. He casts the legend of the fall of Spain in 711 in terms understandable to a seventeenth-century audience, concerned with the powers of the king and the legitimacy of rule, and his essays demonstrate, once again, the flexibility of the legend for political propaganda. Unconcerned for the most part with the specific need to equate the fall in 711 with the contemporary threat of the Ottoman Turks to inspire continued religious warfare, as other writers and politicians did, Saavedra Fajardo instead weaves a persuasive argument in his essay "O subir o bajar," (Either rise or fall) for the necessary moral and ethical character of a ruler, the absence of which can lead to any kingdom's defeat.

Miguel de Luna and Spain's Prophetic History

What, specifically, was Luna's contribution to the development of the history and legend of the fall? Although *True History of King Rodrigo* provoked hostile and even virulent reactions from his contemporaries and from later critics and historians of his work, it remained influential to subsequent versions of the legend, despite all efforts to suppress and discredit it. In terms of the figure of La Cava, we owe to Luna the name Florinda La Cava. Up until then, she was La Cava or Cava or Caba alone, or in the even earlier versions, Alataba or Alacaba. Luna says her first name was Florinda, which in Spanish would mean beautiful flower, and that La Cava is Arabic for "la mala muger," the evil or wayward woman. He is, of course, correct and is the first writer to spell out clearly that "caba" is (and remains today) the Arabic word for prostitute.

In addition, borrowing from the poignant scene in the popular work *Celestina,* in which the dishonored young woman Melibea—albeit dishonored by a consensual sexual relationship, not by rape—throws herself from a tower because she cannot live with the shame, Luna's Florinda does the same. She blames herself for the loss of Spain, for the dishonor she has brought to her family, and is horrified that her name will live in infamy eternally.[14] Luna creates a linguistic connection between the city of Málaga and Florinda La Cava. Before she plunges to her death, she cries out that the city she lives in, Villaviciosa, should henceforth be known in notorious honor of "la más mala muger que ubo en el mundo," (the worst woman the world has ever known) and, in a name deriving from "mala muger," called Málaga by the Christians and Malaca in Arabic (chap. 18: 82–83).

There is little difference between the voice Corral gives La Cava and the one Luna endows her with: in both, she articulates her self-condemnation as she blames herself for the downfall of Spain, which the ballad tradition perpetuates. But Luna's work condemns La Cava more powerfully because he insists that her very name means "evil woman." Moreover, he eliminates all the scenes that Corral created of La Cava's attempts to convince her father to spare fair Spain. Rather, La Cava is now unequivocally Eve, representative of dangerous and seductive woman, unsparing in her ability and desire to topple a king and nation. Luna's work influenced the *romancero,* which in turn influenced histories and other nonfictional recountings, particularly in having La Cava increasingly carry the blame for the downfall of the nation. English writers especially favored Luna's account of the legend.

The ballads about La Cava often focus on the letter to her father informing him of her dishonor. Luna adds to the storehouse of episodes by inventing a clever letter, purportedly written by Florinda, and discovered by Luna during his "archival research": "teniendo yo esta sortija, que va dentro de esta carta, con esta engastada esmeralda, sobre vna mesa suelta, y descuydada (joya de mi, y de los mios tan estimada, como es razon) cayó sobre ella el estoque Real, y desgraciadamente la hizo dos pedaços, partiendo por medio la verde piedra, sin ser yo parte de remedialla. Hame causado tanta confusion este desastre, qual jamás podria mi lengua significar en el discurso de mi vida" (chap. 4: 17). This late seventeenth-century English translation, *The History of the Conquest of Spain by the Moors,* is slightly different from the Spanish but is still excellent and was a version that circulated widely in multiple printings: "You must know, then, my dear Father, that I had, heedlessly, left upon a Table the Ring I send you in this letter; and was not so careful to lock up close this precious Jewel, which I esteem'd more than my Life, and which you and my Mother had so earnestly recommended to me: But the King, having a desire to it, impetuously threw himself to take it; and seeing I would not give it him, he drew his Sword, and gave it so many hacks, that whatever screams and strugglings I us'd to hinder him, he has, as you see, cloven it in two, both the Ring and Emerald enclos'd in it" (1687: 27–28). As in the early chronicle in which Alataba sends her father a rotten egg within a box of splendid objects, the count immediately understands the sign intended by this now broken jewel, which was a common euphemism for virginity.[15]

Luna portrays a very different king from Corral's, one whose sole interest is saving his own skin. Rodrigo appears in battle and disappears when all are vanquished. Tarik, determined to find him, sends out a search party. They return with a bewildered-looking man dressed in king's garb, who turns out to be a shepherd wearing Rodrigo's clothes. Rodrigo, having exchanged his clothes for a shepherd's rustic outfit, was last seen heading to Castile and is never heard from again. Given that many of the histories, including Ambrosio de Morales's and Juan de Mariana's, concur that Rodrigo's fate—death in battle or disappearance—is not verifiable, one might wonder why Luna's depiction was challenged. Simply put, as Luna paints the picture, the cloak of cowardice covers this despotic ruler; there is little suggestion that his disappearance results from unbearable grief and guilt at what he has wrought, and even less suggestion that he will spend his remaining time as a Christian penitent. Julian, for his part, out of his mind with grief over the suicide of his daughter, stabs himself in the heart. The narrator tells us that Florinda's death was God's "castigo por sus [Julian's] grandes peccados" (punishment for his grave sins). The countess dies a painful death of "una cancer incurable, que le dió en el vientre" (an incurable cancer in her chest; chap. 18: 82).

Luna's lengthy *Verdadera historia* has not been studied extensively, though Francisco Márquez Villanueva, Luce López-Baralt, and James T. Monroe made brilliant contributions to what López-Baralt calls Luna's "historical melodrama." It is beyond the scope of this book to provide the kind of analysis the work deserves. However, the use of prophecy merits mention. Unique to Luna's version of the legend of the fall are three prophecies, complete with astrological signs and wonders, which, by an odd route, brings us back to the story circulated in the first decade of the century about Cardinal Cisneros, and of course to the lead tablets found in 1595.

As in Corral's version, when Rodrigo penetrates the enchanted edifice, he discovers a room with a statue in the middle of it. Unlike Corral's House of Hercules, though, in which great silence prevails throughout, Luna's version packs a punch. As the king enters swaggeringly, and his men, fearfully, the torches are suddenly extinguished by some unseen force, and a most thunderous noise frightens them all, which turns out to be the statue itself, using a battle-ax to strike the floor in repetitive movements. Visible is a prophecy: "Por estrañas naciones serás desposseido, y tus gentes malamente castigados" (chap. 6: 24; Thou shalt be Dispossessed by foreign Nations, and thy Subjects shall be punisht as well as thee, for all their Crimes; 43). Luna combines the Decadence Tradition, in which all the population is culpable, with the early modern emphasis on the nation. Earlier prophecies had predicted a conquest by "men who looked like this," clearly Arab figures. Luna makes the prophecy allegorically relevant to late sixteenth-century Spain by focusing on the conquest by "foreign Nations" at a time when Spain constantly battled England, France, Portugal, and the Turks, and had just lost the Spanish Armada to England only a year before Luna introduced this work to the court. Even though Rodrigo insists that the cave be sealed and no one speak of it, "nevertheless, it was immediately buzz'd about all the Court" (44), not unlike the court gossip surrounding Philip II and the increasing lack of confidence he enjoyed nationally and even in the New World.[16] Calling his astrologers and other wise men to read other signs, the king hears that the time had come to take up arms.

The next chapter's prophecy relates to Tarik, here known as General Tarif, the Muslim leader of the invasion. His forces notice a woman on the battlefield waving a white cloth, and, after bringing her to their leader, she begins to speak:

> "Signior, I am born in Spain . . . I remember that about sixty years agone, when I was very young, I heard my Father relate, as I was in the corner of his Chimney, a Prophecy, importing that the people of our Religion should lose the Government of our Country, which was to be conquer'd by the Moors: And among other things, it was precisely mention'd that the Captain who was to make this Conquest, should be very brave, and have on his Right Shoulder a Mole very hairy, of the bigness of a Pea, nay, and that his Right Hand should be much longer than his other; insomuch, that without stooping, he might cover all his knee with that hand. He who made this Prediction is an honest Religious, for whom we Christians have a singular veneration. I earnestly conjure you, in case you have these marks I have newly specified, in recompence for the good News I bring you, to save our Lives, I and my Children; and to hinder any injury from being done to their Persons or Goods."
>
> Tarif having caus'd what this Woman had newly said, to be explain'd by a Christian Interpreter he had with him, was overjoy'd to hear these things. He strips himself immediately, in the presence of Count Julian, and of all his People, and having caus'd the place the Woman instanc'd to be view'd, they found there the Mole she had mention'd, and the Right Hand longer than the Left, tho not quite so long as she had said. (55–56)[17]

The mole as identifying mark of a hero or heroine can be found in folktales, romance, and even contemporary works. Cervantes parodies this scene by having Don Quixote search his body for just such a mole, to see if he really is the famous knight errant foretold by legend and chronicle. The feature about Tarik's right hand being larger than the left, a prediction fulfilled by a look at Tarik's own two hands, comes right out of folklore and popular culture, in which the size of the hand signifies a man's valor and sexual prowess by standing for the size of the penis. Given that the enemy—the sensual Muslim male—is greatly eroticized in this period, and the domination of the land also signifies sexual domination and superiority over the defeated, Tarik's sheer size—the "giant" as sexually forceful being—emphasizes his power and the very real threat of conquest. Curious, though, is the slightly inaccurate prediction of the pious man, as recounted by the Christian woman, that the right hand, while indeed larger than the left, "was not so large as she had said." What are we to make of this? When Kagan discusses in *Lucrecia's Dreams* the sheer quantity of prophetic material in the Middle Ages and early modern period, he mentions that prophecy was not exempt from humorous treatment, so this could be a parody of prophecy. However, Luna's work is serious, so another possibility is more likely.

The prophecy Rodrigo discovers in the enchanted edifice typically predicted the fall of his kingdom, with no limit placed on the quantity of territory that would fall to the invading Muslims. The hand covering the entire knee symbolizes the Muslims' incomplete domination of Spain in the eighth century. That the hand is not quite so large as the earlier prediction would have it reflects the fact that Pelayo and his band of Christian survivors hold just enough territory from Muslim control as to ensure that the dominion of the Moors over the peninsula will not be a complete one.

Near the end of part 1 of Luna's work, astrological signs of impending disaster abound; comets shoot through the skies, clouds rain blood on the heads of the people, there is a famine of corn, and people develop great sores in their groins and behind their ears, which "knock'd off a very great number" (203–5; murió infinito numero de gentes; *Verdadera historia* chap. 27: 124, 127). What would a reader in Spain at the end of the 1500s make of that? Ibn 'Abd al-Hakam, from whose ninth-century chronicle Luna had already borrowed, tells almost a similar prophecy, but it foretold the Muslim victory in 711. Luna's prophecy points to a future beyond the Muslim conquest, and he brings this section of his book in line with a well-known apocalyptic prophecy that had circulated since the twelfth century, that had found new life and notoriety in 1480 Florence, and that had circulated in Europe in varying formulations. The view it promotes, that Christianity and Islam would merge, anticipates the kind of syncretism between Christianity and Islam that Luna promotes in his *Verdadera historia* and, most importantly, that the apocryphal lead tablets of Sacromonte, forged by Luna and Castillo, precisely testified to.

In 1902 the historian Moses Gaster studied the "Letter of Toledo," a doomsday prediction sent in 1184 by astrologers in Toledo to Pope Clement, in which they foretold a series of catastrophic events that would threaten the inhabited world in 1186. Gaster points out that this very prediction, and echoes of it, can be found in chronicles throughout Medieval Europe, and that it was copied and modified for centuries. In the 1480 Florentine version, between the years 1447 and 1510 Christianity would be subjugated to Islam, whose power would prove the strongest in Spain, but after a series of astrological signs, the Muslims would join the Christians, and a mighty Roman emperor would be raised anew. In subsequent retellings and reworkings of the letter, the necromancers and astrologers of Toledo are replaced by other kinds of authorities, and in the Florentine version of 1480, which bears, I suggest, remarkable similarities to Luna's *Verdadera historia,* the prediction is made in the form of a letter "from a pious hermit from behind Mount Sinai, and also from a certain Rasis of Antiochia, who have both got their information from Arabic writings" (Gaster 127).

Almost more interesting than Luna's *Verdadera historia del rey don Rodrigo* itself is the ire it provoked among Luna's contemporaries, and the disparagement it received by cultural historians of the nineteenth and twentieth centuries. Part of what inspired rage and dismissiveness was Luna's claim of having found the text by a Muslim eyewitness, and that this counterstory to Corral was the *true* history, which portrayed Rodrigo in such a negative light, Pelayo as less than effectual, and the Muslim rulers as judicious kings who best embodied the soul and essence of Spain. Moreover, the unflattering apocalyptic parallels of Rodrigo's reign with that of Philip II played very poorly as prophecy, not least because the parallels hit too close to an undeniable truth.

On one level, Luna's work is but a pro-Muslim contribution to the sixteenth-century flood of invented histories of Spain's illustrious past, the aptly named "falsos cronicones" (false chronicles) which were designed to inspire national sentiment. Luna wrote during a climate highly sensitive to invention masquerading as history, but one that at the same time zealously embraced the creation of national history, indeed—it cannot be overstated—a centralized Christian national history of Spain. The legend of the fall of Spain was already steeped in fiction; many sixteenth- and seventeenth-century writers explored the exchange of history and fiction to much acclaim. But the fact is, in Philip's court in late sixteenth-century Spain, Luna remained religiously and culturally suspect, an outsider, even as he was, as Philip's interpreter, a political insider, with a good number of powerful supporters who believed that he was faithful to Christianity. Luna was a Morisco, a New Christian, a member of the vulnerable group under siege, and he dared to challenge a Spanish national foundational myth and to portray Rodrigo as a despot. In contradistinction to Corral's highly favorable portrait of the king, Luna's Rodrigo plots against his own nephew, whom he envies and fears, and the nephew's mother swears never to rest until she sees successful vengeance against the king for his "traiciones y maldades" (chap. 2: 10; in the English translation, "calumny and treason" 13). Its message—that Rodrigo, as repository of Visigothic values, still present and cherished, was instead tyrannical, debased, and cowardly—was an intolerable insult to the current project of a centralized, Christianized national history. Luna counted on his prominent position in Philip's court to showcase the work, but he undoubtedly also counted on public acceptance of it as one more "found text," particularly in light of the other discoveries that had been made in 1588 and would be made again in 1595. We are so accustomed to thinking of the "found text" as a literary device or pretext that it is difficult to keep in mind that many people did in fact believe Luna when he wrote that he was merely the translator of the Muslim Abulçacim's eyewitness—and surely biased—account.[18]

For example, one firm believer in Luna's claim to be merely the translator, not the author, was Gregorio López Madera, who later would participate in the organization and official expulsion of the Moriscos in 1609–1614. A prominent jurist in Madrid and a nationalist, a strong believer in the idea of the origins of Spain in its Visigothic and even pre-Visigothic roots, López Madera joined other prominent men who convened in 1600 to determine—once and for all—the authenticity of the relics and lead tablets that had been found in Sacromonte, which, ironically, modern critics believe to be the forgeries of Luna and his father-in-law, Alonso del Castillo. In 1601, López Madera celebrated the conclusion of his colleagues, that the holy objects and sacred writings were indeed authentic, in *Discursos de la incertidumbre de las reliquias descubiertas en Granada desde el año 1585 hasta el de 1598* (Discourses on the uncertainty about the relics discovered in Granada between 1585 and 1598). The author discusses much more than the discoveries of Sacromonte, ranging from his belief that the Castilian language in the Iberian Peninsula predated Latin and was, therefore, an independent language to his ruminations on what he viewed as the unrelenting problems caused by the Jews over the centuries. Lamenting that the Jews already inhabited the peninsula at the time of the Muslim invasion of 711, López Madera cites as historical proof of the large Jewish population what he believes to be Arabic sources: "los muchos [judíos] que hallaron quando entraron en España los Moros, segun el dicho Rasis, y el autor de la perdida de España, que traduxo agora del Arabigo antiguo Miguel de Luna" (chap. 17: 52; "the Moors found many Jews when they entered Spain, according to Rasis and the author of the loss of Spain, newly translated from the ancient Arabic by Miguel de Luna").

Corral had invented a backstory for Rodrigo's wife, an African princess whom he called Eliata, instead of the more frequently found Egilona. In Corral's narrative, an accord between Rodrigo and Eliata's father determines their marriage. Luna reverts to the popular storyline of the sexually available Muslim princess with its metaphorical association of besting the enemy by appropriating what is his. According to Luna's version (chap. 3: 14–15), the powerful African king Mahometo Abnehedin longed for legitimate heirs to his lands, so he planned to marry his daughter Zahra Abnalyaça to an appropriate suitor. But before he could arrange a match, Zahra and her ladies-in-waiting were amusing themselves on the shore, and they climbed aboard a docked ship to rest. Heavy winds launched the ship and they, along with bad fortune, hurtled the boat across the strait until the ship struck the Spanish coast, where Zahra and her company were taken prisoner. Presented to King Rodrigo, Zahra falls in love, and Rodrigo is equally smitten. After converting to Christianity, Zahra marries Rodrigo and allows those maidens to stay with her who also convert, while the others return to Africa. Those who went home informed Zahra's father of her marriage to the Christian king: "El qual de oir esta nueva se cayó muerto de su estado. Y como no tenía otros hijos, ni herederos, sucedió en su Reyno . . . Almançor, Rey de las Arabias" (Upon hearing the news, the king fell dead from the shock. And, as he had no other children, nor heirs, he was succeeded by Almanzor, king of the Arabias; chap. 3: 15). In this way, Luna presents a slight variation of the theme as we have seen it in earlier chronicles. The Christian king does not gain lands by taking the female representative of those lands, but the taking of the Muslim king's only heir still deprives him of a legacy to control his lands.

In *Verdadera historia del rey don Rodrigo,* Luna played into some of Spain's deepest fears by including in his narrative a law that Christian women must now marry the Muslim men who had invaded the peninsula. By asserting that there was much sexual intermingling and intermarriage between Christians and Moors after the fall in 711, Luna's work offered a picture of the past that would alarm and even outrage the seventeenth-century obsession with *limpieza de sangre,* "purity of blood." Many Spaniards believed that the early modern Moriscos descended from the Muslims who had overrun Spain, just as they believed themselves to be latter-day Christian Visigoths. Common sense and a look into their own families would have confirmed the present and past sexual intermingling, but society clung to the legend with good reason. Having converso blood reduced one's status in society, and Moriscos were on the precipice of expulsion.

Another powerful element of Luna's story was having Rodrigo's daughter, here named Egilona, marry a Muslim prince. This is a particularly interesting development in Luna's rendition of the legend.[19] López-Baralt mentions the marriage as an example of Luna's yearning for a pluralistic society in that Egilona remains Christian, and Abdelasis, Muslim (244). However, that is not Luna's innovation, for the marriage of Abdelasis and Rodrigo's widow Egilona comes from the earliest Asturian history, the ninth-century *Crónica de Alfonso III* (Chronicle of Alfonso III), and both Morales and Mariana make the same point about the tolerance of their respective religions after marriage. Luna's real innovation is the return to a ninth-century Arabic chronicle in which Egilona is the daughter and not the widow of Rodrigo, as she is in Christian chronicles. In Ibn 'Abd al-Hakam's chronicle, the earliest extant Muslim perspective on the events of eighth-century Spain, Rodrigo's daughter encourages her husband to wrest Seville from the caliphate and rule over it himself. A widow would have had no claim to the throne. But if Rodrigo had had a daughter, she would have been the legitimate heir to the Crown in the sixteenth-century view, not Pelayo, a more distant relative, if a relative at all.[20] Thus, the Moriscos themselves, through the marriage of one of their own to the Visigothic princess, could lay claim to the Spanish throne and preempt sixteenth-century Christian claims that a differently named daughter, Pelayo's Ermesinda, links the monarchy to its beginnings.[21]

In her essay on "Moorophile" literature of early modern Spain, the curious body of works in which Muslims appear as beautiful, noble, and brave, Luce López-Baralt discusses what she calls the "doubleness" of Luna. His history of the fall of Spain in 711 strikes some real blows at the myth of the good, Christian, Visigothic king Rodrigo. Simultaneously, Luna goes to great lengths to show himself to be an orthodox Christian by criticizing Islam and Muslim beliefs, although he sometimes appears to take issue, subtly, with certain elements of Christian dogma (212–21, at 217). López-Baralt concludes that Luna's *Verdadera historia del rey don Rodrigo* is full of contradictions and inconsistencies. Márquez Villanueva, more certain that the doubleness reveals the writer's true leanings, writes in "La voluntad de leyenda de Miguel de Luna," "There may be some controversy as to what sort of Muslim Miguel de Luna was, but there can be none as to the fact that he was no Christian" (390; cited in *Islam in Spanish Literature* 217). The talented Luna played a dangerous game with his literary forgeries. During the Inquisition, conversos continued to be tortured, tried, and convicted as heretics, but the numbers of Moriscos brought before the Inquisition soared, especially after 1550 or so. Had he been found out as a forger, Luna surely would have been executed. The crime of forgery would have been bad enough, but the fact that the lead tablets promulgated a syncretism of Christianity and Islam in statements that represented pure heresy in Christianity's terms would have led inquisitors to the conclusion that Luna was a crypto-Muslim, a danger to the Crown and to Christianity. Fortunately for him, his defenders' power outweighed that of his enemies. He continued to work in Philip II's court, and after the king's death in 1598, Luna translated in the court of Philip III in spite of the shadow of suspicion that remained over him for the rest of his life (and well beyond!). When he died in 1615, his enemies claimed that he had eschewed hallowed ground to be buried in virgin land, as Muslims did. The rumor persisted so vigorously that, in 1618, it caused the archbishop of Sevilla, Pedro de Castro, to rise up in defense of his late friend. He issued a declaration that said, in part, "El Miguel de Luna era hombre de bien, de habilidad e ingenio. Vivió católicamente; murió con todos los sacramentos en casa del secretario Alonso de Valdivia" (Miguel de Luna was a gentleman of talent and intelligence. He lived as a Catholic; he died having received all the Sacraments in the home of secretary Alonso de Valdivia).[22]

Ironically, although much despised and criticized, Luna's work greatly influenced subsequent tellings of the legend, and his hand appears elsewhere as well. For example, La Cava's suicide becomes a staple of the telling, as in this seventeenth-century version. In the midst of the battles in the Iberian Peninsula against the Muslims, historian Gabriel Rodríguez de Escabias claims, Julian attempts to flee with his daughter "Florinda, que los moros llamaban Caba, e tambien Hecuba que es tanto como mala fembra e desaventurada" (Florinda, whom the Moors call Caba, and also Hecuba, because she is such a bad and wretched woman; *Crónica do Mouro Rasis* 360), but the Moors turn on him, kill him and leave him unburied. This is what his daughter regrets, not the fall of the monarch or the fate of the nation, but the loss of her father, which impels her to commit suicide: "And when Florinda found out, she was in great despair, crying and cursing herself, such that those with her were unable to shelter her or help her. And one night, when everyone in the castle was asleep, she climbed to the highest point of the castle and threw herself down. And in the morning, they found her dead, and eaten by beasts. For this reason, they call the place where she killed herself Julian Way, and the Castle of la Caba." This suicide description, an excellent example of the infiltration of pure fiction into a historical chronicle, replicates that of the lovestruck heroine Mirabella, in Juan de Flores's fifteenth-century sentimental romance *Historia de Grisel y Mirabella* (History of Grisel and Mirabella), who killed herself after the death of her lover, Grisel, which served as Luna's inspiration for this episode.[23] Luna's other enduring contributions to the legend, in addition to popularizing the Toledan "baño de la Cava," where La Cava supposedly bathed, is the connection of her name to the city of Malaga.[24] Though the inspired and desperate creative efforts by Luna and other crypto-Muslim and Arab historians failed to change the fate of Moriscos in Spain, his *Verdadera historia del rey don Rodrigo* remains, along with Corral's, the most influential recounting of the legend.

Father Juan de Mariana and Early Modern Nationalism

Mariana's *Historia general de España* includes much of the same material as Ambrosio de Morales's, especially regarding Pelayo as a cousin of Rodrigo and therefore a noble Goth, though he disagrees with Morales on various historical points. Differences between the two historians have more to do with tone and what they intend to emphasize than with factual disagreements. For example, Morales expanded the historical material about Pelayo both to emphasize the unbroken lineage of the Spanish monarchy from Pelayo to Philip II and to highlight the motif of the restoration of Spain. Mariana, while a believer in those ideas, juxtaposes the actions of the two kings, Rodrigo and Pelayo, to paint a picture of good and bad qualities of a ruler, and to describe religious conflict as the impulse for nation building. Mariana's work was greatly respected in his own time and beyond, and his treatise on kingship influenced political theorists well into the nineteenth century. Menéndez Pidal and others credit him with trying to produce as objective and accurate a portrayal of events as possible. Yet, even though he frequently cites El Toledano, as Morales before him had done, it is very clear that, for Mariana, El Toledano's insistence on the general iniquity of the king and of the Visigothic people, inspired though it may have been by the debauched king Witiza, and the blamelessness of the unnamed daughter of Count Julian, could not be perpetuated in the seventeenth century. Instead, Mariana appropriates some of the information that developed in the ballad tradition. For example, he suggests that La Cava immodestly revealed too much of her body, implying both the innate licentiousness of woman and that she herself set in motion the events that led to the king's and the nation's fall. Although Mariana refers to the king's desires as sinful and wrong, he nonetheless hints at the incapacity of the king—or of any man—to resist the lust that ensnared him when he saw La Cava's beautiful flesh through the window.

Mariana judges that Rodrigo "se despeñó a sí y a su reino en su perdición, como persona estragada con los vicios y desamparada de Dios" (hurled himself and his kingdom into perdition, like a person ravaged by vice and abandoned by God; bk. 6, chap. 21: 193).[25] Mariana had tremendous liberty to promote the historical accuracy of whichever version of events he fancied, but significantly he chose to portray the call for vengeance as a challenge from daughter to father, from woman to man, almost, we could say, from Eve to Adam. In an era of Jezebels and Magdalenes, Eves and Marys, while the Morisco "falsifier" Luna painted the remorseful and repentant Magdalene, Father Mariana instead saw Jezebel: "If you are truly men," La Cava writes in Mariana's history, "Vos si sois varones hareis que . . . no pase sin castigo la burla y befa que hizo á nuestro linaje y á nuestra casa" (you will not rest until you have avenged the dishonor done to our lineage and our home; bk. 6, chap. 21: 193). Mariana includes a good amount of invented direct testimony by the characters of the legend, with lengthy letters and speeches by La Cava, Rodrigo, Tarik, and Pelayo.

A comparison of how Corral, Morales, and Mariana treat a particular episode in the legend underscores how Mariana achieves his goal of focusing on the monarchy and nationalism in particular ways. On the eve of the decisive Battle of Guadalete, Corral portrays the religious preparation that precedes it. Rodrigo prays alone in the church, confesses, and takes Communion. He expresses deep concern for his own salvation, and more importantly, for the souls of the men he will lead into battle. In Morales's description, the king appears not to be anything but a defeated figure from

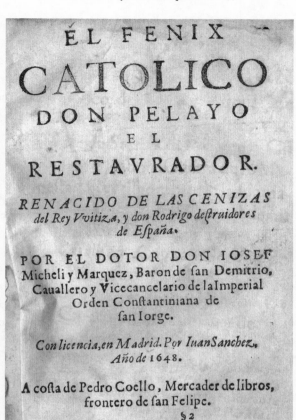

ÉL FENIX
CATOLICO
DON PELAYO
EL
RESTAVRADOR.

RENACIDO DE LAS CENIZAS
del Rey Vvitiza, y don Rodrigo deſtruidores
de Eſpaña.

POR EL DOTOR DON IOSEF
Micheli y Marquez, Baron de ſan Demitrio,
Cauallero y Vicecancelario de la Imperial
Orden Conſtantiniana de
ſan Iorge.

Con licencia, en Madrid. Por Iuan Sanchez,
Año de 1648.

A coſta de Pedro Coello, Mercader de libros,
frontero de ſan Felipe.
§ 2

Title page of José Micheli y Márquez's *El fénix católico don Pelayo el restaurador*. Madrid: Juan Sánchez, 1648. Beginning in the fifteenth century, historians insisted on Pelayo as the immediate successor to Rodrigo, but with the difference that Pelayo's rule became the seed of modern Spain. The title (The Catholic Phoenix don Pelayo the Restorer) alludes to the rebirth of Spain and the Spanish monarchy out of the ashes of the ruined Visigothic empire. Courtesy of The Hispanic Society of America, New York.

the time the Arabs enter the peninsula, who attempts to stave off the inevitable by sending his valorous young nephew into battle before he himself goes out with the troops to the battlefield. The nephew, Sancho, is killed, and the king realizes defeat is imminent. The troops fought listlessly for, as Morales opines, what chance did they have when God had ordained that their iniquity would be punished by this loss?

For his part, Mariana makes the most of this moment in a brilliant narrative move. Both Rodrigo and Tarik address their men, attempting to inspire them to the most valorous fighting humanly possible. But Rodrigo is all about God and Christian nation, while Tarik is all about greed. When Rodrigo broke into the locked edifice, Mariana assailed the king's lack of "reason and prudence," not as a man proud or greedy, as earlier accounts had cast him. But now, close to the moment of destruction, Mariana's king rises to the occasion in a lofty rhetorical marriage of nation and religion:

> Mucho me alegro, soldados, que haya llegado el tiempo de vengar las injurias he-chas á nosotros y á nuestra santa fe por esta canalla aborrecible á Dios y á los hom-bres. ¿Qué otra causa tienen de movernos guerra, si no pretender de quitar la libertad á vos, á vuestros hijos, mujeres y pátria? . . . Hasta ahora han hecho guerra contra eunucos: sientan qué cosa es acometer á la invencible sangre de los godos . . . Tomad ánimo y coraje, y llenos de confianza acometed los enemigos, acordaos de vuestros antepasados, del valor de los godos: acordaos de la Religion Cristiana debajo de cuyo amparo y por cuya defensa peleamos. (I am gladdened, soldiers, that the time has come to avenge the injuries done to us and to our holy faith by the swine so abhorrent to God and to men. What other cause could move us to war than the attempt to take away your liberty, your children, wives and country . . . Up until now they warred against eunuchs. Let them feel what it is to come up against the invincible blood of the Goths . . . Take heart and have courage, and full of confidence attack the enemy, remembering your ancestors, the valor of the Goths, remembering the Christian religion under whose protection and in whose defense we fight; bk. 6, chap. 23: 195.)

On the contrary, Mariana tells us, Tarik, while invoking Mohammed, reveals more base motives, that his people have always wanted to extend their empire, and this battle will allow them to become lords of Spain and enjoy rewards, riches, and immortal renown (bk. 6, chap. 23: 195–96).

Like Morales before him, Mariana explains that several years pass before Pelayo realizes the impossibility of coexistence with the Muslims. The main difference between Morales's account and Mariana's, apart from disagreements on a few minor details, is that Mariana takes every opportunity to insert in the narrative that the Christian survivors were "godos," and to refer to their military actions as a benefit for "la patria" or "el imperio." While the Christians are treated well enough by the Muslims, Pelayo exhorts them to realize that there are worse things to fear than what the enemy might do to you if you resist, and that they must:

aplicar algun remedio á la enfermedad, dar muestra de vuestra nobleza, y acordaos
que sois nacidos de la nobilisima sangre de los godos . . . las adversidades y trabajos nos aviven y nos despierten. Direis que es cosa pesada acometer los peligros de
la guerra: ¿cuánto mas pesado es que los hijos y mujeres hechos esclavos sirvan á
la deshonestidad de los enemigos? (apply some remedy to the illness, give sign of
your nobility, and remember that you are born of the noble blood of the Goths;
let adversities and hard deeds revive us and awaken us. You will say that it is a difficult thing to take on the risks of war: how much harder is it that our enslaved children and wives serve the dishonor of the enemy? bk. 7, chap. 1: 203.)

Mariana consistently focuses on the monarchy as the patriarchy it was. No other
historian alludes to a last will and testament left by Pelayo, but Mariana asserts that
the will called for his son-in-law and daughter to rule. By making Alfonso I a descendant of the Visigothic king Recared, who had converted to Roman Catholicism
in 589 C.E., the history of the Spanish monarchy remains Gothic, male, and the result of divine providence, as Pelayo's own reign had been. For example, much later
in Mariana's history, in the sections in which he describes the reign of the Catholic
monarchs, he emphasizes Ferdinand rather than Isabel, as did so many of Mariana's
contemporaries and predecessors, although Isabel comes in for her own share of
praise. In describing how they appeared after the conquest of Granada, Mariana
writes: "Los Reyes Don Fernando y Doña Isabel con los arreos de sus personas, que
eran muy ricos, y por estar en lo mejor de su edad, y dexar concluida esta guerra, y
ganado aquel reyno, representaban mayor magestad que antes. Señalábanse entre
todos, y entre sí eran iguales: mirábanlos como si fueran mas que hombres, y como
dados del cielo para la salud de España" (Mariana bk. 25, chap. 18; King Ferdinand
and Queen Elizabeth being richly clothed, in the prime of their Age, and having
conquered that Kingdom, seemed to appear more Majestik than before. They
seemed above all others, and were equal as to themselves. Everyone looked upon
them as more than Human, and sent from Heaven for the glory of Spain. They restored Justice and Religion and rewarded their subjects by merit, stirring them to
virtue and learning; *General History* 458).

Although in the fifteenth century, Isabel was compared to the Virgin Mary, and
here, both king and queen are "more than Human," in terms of the monarchy, Mariana makes Ferdinand the real ruler. Mariana asserts that "fué diestro para las cosas
de la guerra, para el gobierno sin par: tan amigo de los negocios que parecia con el
trabaxo descansaba" (in Martial Affairs he was expert, in Matters of Government not
to be paralleled; he loved business; bk. 25, chap. 18).[26] Isabel, meanwhile, was
described not in terms of her skills and accomplishments, but of her relationship

to her husband: one noted in her "la gravedad, mesura y modestia de su rostro singular . . . tenia amor á su marido, pero mezclado con celos y sospechas" (bk. 25, chap. 18; "singular Modesty and Gravity in her looks . . . She bore her husband affection, but mixed with jealousie; *General History* 458). Womanly jealousy is a theme with Mariana, who also found that Rodrigo's wife, Egilona, suffered from jealousy when her husband turned his attentions to other women.

In the eighteenth century and beyond, Mariana received wide praise from Spanish authorities, but also in England. In 1777 John Bowle, who wrote extensively about Cervantes, seconded the praise of Mariana offered by another eighteenth-century scholar, Benito Jerónimo Feijóo, the Benedictine philosopher, moralist, and literary historian: "Give me leave to add to the just elegies of [Mariana's *Historia general de España*] by Padre Feijóo this testimony: that though a Spaniard, he [Mariana] held rational, manly notions of liberty, and though a Jesuit, he has all the appearance of candour and honesty."[27]

Spain's Second Helen

The ballads composed between 1590 and 1640 dramatize the relationship between Rodrigo and La Cava, adding numerous examples of the link between the sexual act and the fall of the nation. As we saw in earlier ballads, La Cava laments the loss of her virginity, and when her father avenges her honor through means that jeopardize the Christian kingdom of the Iberian Peninsula, she regrets it, tries to prevent his actions, and rues the certainty that her name will forever be linked with the downfall of a just king and a beloved nation. In the extensive set of seventeenth-century ballads, comparisons are made between Troy and Spain, and Visigothic Spain is often anachronistically referred to as an "empire," reflecting the double view by seventeenth-century Spain of the greatness of its own empire and the recognition of the precarious tension between success and failure: the empire could fall, or be "lost," as had happened in 711. Another important measure of the focus on the ruler himself is the presence, and increasingly fanciful portrayals, of Pelayo. He is the new king who emerges like a phoenix from the ashes of the reign of Rodrigo, as Lope states at the end of his play *El último godo* (The last Goth), to become the natural successor to the failed Rodrigo and the new leader who protects and nurtures the fragile remains of Christianity in the peninsula. Given considerable emphasis in this century is Rodrigo's epithet, "last King of the Goths" and the "last Goth," while Pelayo is the "first," the initiator of the new line of kings and the first Spaniard. These ballads derive from the prevailing sixteenth-century sensibility to distance the

Pelayo illustration in José Micheli y Márquez's *El fénix católico don Pelayo el restaurador.* Madrid: Juan Sánchez, 1648. Woodcut. Page 127. Courtesy of The Hispanic Society of America, New York.

current monarchy from Rodrigo and his fall, focusing instead on Pelayo and his victory in the Asturian region of Covadonga as the birth of the new Spain.

These seventeenth-century ballads, often elegant in their composition, reflect to some extent the trends developed in Golden Age poetry—especially amatory poetry—from Garcilaso, in the mid-sixteenth century, through the seventeenth century, becoming more and more ornate, exotic and, indeed, befitting the name often given to it, baroque. One interesting example is the poem known as "El baño de la Cava," because it manages to combine well-known conceits, a resemblance to Milton's Eve in *Paradise Lost,* and the identification of La Cava with Arabic customs. La Cava is relaxing in a glorious fountain: "Sobre el cuello de marfil / lleva esparzidas las hebras, / que como sirven de lazos / tambien al cuello se acercan" (Above the ivory neck are scattered threads, which also draw near the neck to ensnare it; *Floresta* 2: 71–72). First of all, Muslim or "Turkish" baths were popular in Spain, and the public would make the connection between La Cava's arrival in Toledo from Muslim North Africa and her unsurprising attraction to Arabic customs. Second, a commonplace of the period was the equation of a woman's lush curls, spiraling in all directions, with alluring and captivating sexuality. The operative word, perhaps, is "captivating." Just as an onlooker would be smitten by this vision of wanton loveliness, the tendrils and curls loop around the neck of the women, as if ensnaring the neck itself, and of course metaphorically ensnaring the amorous onlooker. Such descriptions of hair invited comparisons with the labyrinth, the dangerous structure that ensnares and does not release, another image that had great currency in the seventeenth century. The next stanza of the ballad shows the eyes of La Cava reflected in the pool of water, "un segundo Narciso" (a second Narcissus), and this image of her hair falling wildly, while she regards her reflection in the water, strongly resembles the description of Milton's Eve using the water as mirror, an ambiguous figure who projects at once girlish innocence and awareness of her allure.

Immediately following this description of La Cava, the ballad turns to Rodrigo, who is peering at her through shrubbery, and who, in his mind, equates Troy and Helen with Spain and La Cava, which implicitly casts the woman as blameworthy. In another ballad, "El rey fugitivo" (the fugitive king), Rodrigo blames both himself and La Cava:

> Amada enemiga mía,
> de España segunda Elena,
> ¡oh si yo naciera ciego,
> o tu sin beldad nacieras!
>
> . . . .
>
> Fuerza fue la que te hice,
> mas también mirar debieras
> que tu beldad poderosa
> usó conmigo de fuerza.
> Eres mar tempestuoso,
> y entendí que Cava eras;
> más lo uno y lo otro fuiste
> pues que me acabas y anegas. (*Floresta* 2: 91–94)

(Beloved enemy of mine, Spain's second Helen, would that I had been born blind, or you without beauty! While I admit I forced you, you must admit that you used your powerful beauty on me by force. You are a tempestuous sea, and I understood that you were Cava, but you were both since you kill me and deny me).

He may have forced her, he admits, but resorting to reverse blame by casting the woman as metaphorical rapist, he claims that her powerful beauty—elsewhere called "infernal"—forced itself on him. Calling her a tempestuous sea and a "cava," playing with the name, he claims that she destroyed him and took him in, another example of the increased and specific use of the body—La Cava's body—and the fall of the king and of the nation. The overt sexuality and Freudian implications of the cave as vagina—both dark, damp apertures—would not be lost on a public accustomed to ballads and other poems of sexual double entendres. The phrase "me acabas," which visually contains the name Caba, literally means "you are finishing me," "you are killing me."

In another ballad, one of the few newer ones that return to the topic of Rodrigo's penance, the baroque play on words links La Cava, death, and the snake. One stanza says: "Púsome en su guerra amor / la Cava, fué lance fuerte, / y a fuerza vencí la fuerza / y no pude a mí vencerme" (La Cava roped me into her love-war, she was a strong lance, and by force I vanquished the force, but I could not overcome myself; *Floresta* 2: 97–99). So La Cava, the initiator and, metaphorically, the phallic lance and by extension, therefore, the metaphorical rapist, captured him, and the irony of his overcoming the force that assailed him is that, of course, he was not controlling himself. Rodrigo places himself and his lack of control at the end of a fairly long line of overwhelming forces, which serves to vitiate his guilt. Each octave is followed by the same refrain, the playfulness of which the English translation cannot quite capture: "¡Cava, me acaba! / Acaba, culebra, muerde. Descubre la pintura de la muerte" (Cava, you are finishing me! Finish, snake, bite. Reveal the portrait of death). The use of the verb "acabar," to terminate, to finish, here, to kill, used both with Cava and "culebra" (snake), and the smooth way the word-sounds run into each other, link the woman and the viper, as well as the sex act and the act of killing. A different poem, "La Cava al rey forzador" (La Cava to the rapist-king) showcases the fate of the monarchy, when a sweaty and disheveled Cava tries to fend off the king, by using words that announce his impending downfall as king. This differs from earlier ballads, in which she attempts to deflect his attention by praising him or begging for her honor to be left intact:

"Y si la ley, Dios, honra y padre
no estorban vuestros deseos,

soy Cava, y seré principio
de vuestros daños eternos."
Rodrigo, que sólo escucha
las voces de sus deseos,
forzóla y aborrecióla,
del amor propios efectos.
Quedóse dando suspiros,
porque al fin de tales hechos,
si con extremo se ama,
se aborrece con extremo. (*Floresta* 2: 72–74)

("And if the law, God, honor, and father cannot restrain your desires, I am Cava, and I will be the architect of your eternal suffering." Rodrigo, who heard only the voices of his desire, raped her and hated her, the proper effect of love. He stayed there, sighing, because, at the end of such deeds, if he had loved excessively, he also hated excessively).

A particularly dark poem, it is probably also one of the most humanly astute and accurate. Casting Rodrigo's feelings not as love, but simply as "deseos," desire, the poem shows him to be driven to achieve his goal, which is to take La Cava by force if she does not give in to him. He forces her and ends up despising her, the poem tells us, which is the "proper or natural effect of love." Although today we know that rape is an act of anger and power, and not of love or sexual desire, and this poem still uses words like "passionate love" as the inspiration for extreme hate, it takes an almost modern view. On the one hand, it is true that many medieval works emphasize the male pleasure of the conquest and the loss of continuing desire once the goal has been achieved. However, this poem, unlike many of its predecessors, never casts Rodrigo's desires as love, which would be like medieval models, but more as a demonstration of power. His rape of La Cava leaves him feeling not without interest but actively angry toward her, a fairly modern confirmation of rape as an angry act of power, not of love. In *El último godo,* Lope de Vega most likely appropriates his depiction of the king's anger from this ballad, and has his Rodrigo thunderously proclaim not only that he wished he had killed Florinda earlier, but that he still might do it.[28]

The ballads cast La Cava, variously, as a wronged woman seeking justice, a jealous lover who feels the king's attentions are now straying, and a woman who led the king on willingly. Where she differs from her earlier portraits is that in all these cases, she determines to seek vengeance herself, writing in one ballad to her father, "venganza de Rodrigo te demando" (I demand that you seek vengeance on Rodrigo) and "pidiendo a Dios justicia, a ti, venganza" (I ask God for justice, you for vengeance;

Floresta 2: 77). In the first instance, by far the least prevalent of the depictions, we can see that the emphasis is on La Cava's honor, but also that the king has not behaved as a king should. In the other ballads that depict La Cava as evil and vengeful and possibly jealous, there is a dual poetic emphasis. The king has allowed himself to be distracted from the business of governing, from the exemplary and model behavior the monarch should embody, and women are trouble, particularly this woman. By tying La Cava to Helen of Troy, La Cava is faulted for her dangerous beauty, her intentionally seductive comportment, or both.

The sixteenth-century ballad that ended with an "audience poll" of which one was more to blame, Rodrigo or La Cava, receives new life in the seventeenth century, but with emphases appropriate to the evolving concerns about the monarchy and views of the inevitably blameworthy woman.[29] The poem opens with a somber reminder that Spain was "lost" because of a vengeful woman and a man vanquished by love, a feeling that in ancient times was not punished. La Cava's call for vengeance, which immediately follows the poet's declamatory statement that such acts of love are usually excused, situates her as the one who causes the fall of Spain, linking her to poisonous vipers. The "public" in the ballad, a kind of Greek chorus, call out that by the "lightning bolt" of two women, Spain and Troy are the same, destroyed: "'Here was Troy,!' men, women and children cry in one voice." The poem equates La Cava with the basilisk, a viper catalogued in medieval bestiaries as having a Medusa-like poisonous gaze, and her voice with the siren song of classical mythology, which brought sailors to ruin. La Cava publicizes the king as lascivious and the act as a rape, but she does so to enhance the validity of her accusation, which "perhaps, was consensual ardor." Going further, and taking an Augustinian view, here popularized, that there is no such thing as sex without even some tiny moment of womanly consent, the poem suggests not only that women can stave off attacks, but that her current response may well reflect her sense of guilt for having given in.[30] Both parties are blameworthy, say the words of the poem, although clearly more lines have dealt with the guilt of La Cava than with that of the king, and the poem ends with the now-familiar poll, divided along gender lines: "when asked which is more to blame, the men say La Cava, the women, Rodrigo." Finally, Troy reemerges as a touchstone for the seventeenth-century view of the fall of Spain. In another popular oral ballad, the belatedly self-aware Rodrigo contemplates his kingdom in ruins, while his bloodied and almost demolished troops continue to rally to battle cries of "¡Guerra, al arma, arma!" (War, to arms, to arms!). The king—for once facing reality rather than denying it—follows their cry with one of his own: "Here was Troy! Farewell, Spain!" (¡Aquí fue Troya, adiós, España!; Menéndez Pidal, *Floresta* 2: 87–88).

Lope de Vega and the Stage of King and Nation

Lope de Vega was the first dramatist to show an interest in the fall of Spain since Bartolomé Palau's *Historia de la gloriosa santa Orosia*.[31] Lope de Vega's plays, in which a monarch figures prominently, have long been thought to show him as the ultimate political conformist, as in Melveena McKendrick's summary of the prevailing critical view of Lope as "a lackey of the system, a jobbing genius who tamely sold his soul to his political masters, uncritically swallowing all the ideological platitudes of the day." Deviating from this view, she demonstrates most convincingly how Lope negotiated "a path of prudence between the acceptable and the unacceptable in political commentary in the commercial theatre" (*Playing the King* 12). Specifically, McKendrick extends to Lope's own plays the commonly held view that Spanish plays in the early modern era manifested a distinct capacity to speak with multiple voices, sometimes propagandistic, sometimes subversive; that Spanish theatre could criticize king and country; and, that "Spaniards could harbour doubts about a king's ability to rule without wavering in their commitment to monarchy, which was for contemporary Spanish theorists the logical and most effective form of government in the face of the mutability that characterized all human existence" (6).[32]

Lope clearly found the gendering of national history to be an effective strategy for examining that history and its relevance to the present, including views on the monarchy, on women, and on national identity. The two plays to be examined here, *El último godo* (The last Goth) and *Las paces de los reyes y judía de Toledo* (The peace of kings and Jewess of Toledo), both highlight, expand, or otherwise create gendered conflicts in material that we know well from the many versions we have considered in this study.

El último godo allows Lope to explore a variety of contemporary issues through the lens of sexual behavior. His main source for *El último godo* is Miguel de Luna's *Verdadera historia del rey don Rodrigo* (True history of King Rodrigo), and our knowledge of this work and other legendary versions enables us to gauge the significance of some of Lope's innovations. *El último godo* focuses on conversion, betrayal, and vengeance in a package of sexual activity, with an emphasis on three women, the Muslim princess Zara (also Zahra), Florinda La Cava, and Pelayo's sister, here called Solmira.[33] In having Rodrigo marry Zara, the sexually available Muslim princess who defies her father to convert to Christianity, Lope borrows directly from Luna, while also returning to a prevalent theme from early Castilian chronicles of the thirteenth and fourteenth centuries. Lope clearly found social and political value in exploring the sexual and marital relations among Christians, Jews, and Muslims. In fact, in a new twist on the legend, Zara is the daughter of the man who will later conquer Spain, Tarik. The story unfolds so that two fathers, the Christian Julian and the Muslim Tarik, seek vengeance against the same man, Rodrigo, for the same act, sexual relations with their daughters.

All three women show their strength and virtue: Zara by welcoming Christian martyrdom after Rodrigo's defeat, La Cava by her shameful recognition that she will be reviled by history even though technically innocent of any wrongdoing, and Solmira, who fends off Muslim attackers who attempt to rape her. Lope shows that women are dangerous to the Crown and nation, just by being who and what they are, though he invites us to compare, and ultimately to judge, the three women in contexts of sexual conquest. Lope does accord Florinda some dignity and a degree of innocence, which popular balladry had effaced in favor of the portrayal of La Cava as seductress. Nevertheless, the prevailing cultural view was, in fact, that a woman who did not want to be raped could manage to avoid it; such is the vivid visual testimony of Solmira's feisty wielding of a knife to save herself from a sexual threat. The Muslim Zara becomes a Christian wife, in spite of her father's opposition, and then a Christian martyr. Solmira, the sister of the new King Pelayo, staves off sexual conquest by a Muslim, symbolically maintaining purity of blood in Asturias. But the Christian maiden, Florinda, cannot fend off King Rodrigo, and we should recognize that the public at that time would have both a degree of sympathy for La Cava and a suspicion about her culpability. Renato Barahona, in his study of sex crimes and lawsuits in early modern Spain, claims that a woman's "honestidad" (honesty) was linked to chastity and to her ability to fend off attackers. In other words, a woman's "honesty" gave her much physical power whenever it should be needed (*Sex Crimes* 125). Indeed, Pelayo himself judges La Cava as "la vil Florinda" (the vile Florinda). Ambiguities abound in Lope the playwright, as they do in life, and McKendrick suggests that the genius of Lope's plays lies in the way he constructs ambiguity through a conflict between what the characters say and what the characters and spectators see happening. The audience understands Julian's anger as a father, at the same time that they know he is in the wrong: even the Muslim leader comments that any man who would betray his country cannot be trusted.

In the opening scene of the play, the king accidentally drops crown and scepter to the ground. While the other characters and the audience immediately recognize this as a very bad sign, the king incorrectly interprets this as a good sign. Throughout the centuries of the legend's recountings, Rodrigo has been a bad interpreter of the prophetic warning in the enchanted edifice or House of Hercules, and here, Lope simply extends the king's flaw throughout his play: in contrast, Pelayo, whom Lope casts as Rodrigo's cousin, as Morales and Mariana did, interprets prophecies correctly; Pelayo stands for everything Rodrigo is not.

Mariana and other political theorists supported the hereditary throne, although they recognized that not all relatives would be fit to govern. Some could be trained to govern—hence the plethora of manuals devoted to the education of the prince—but some were irredeemably flawed. With obvious valor and suitability, Pelayo, the new ruler, dramatically counters the unsuitability of his cousin Rodrigo, characterized by his sexual unruliness. As in Corral's *Crónica del Rey don Rodrigo,* Lope's Pelayo is warned to avoid the snares of women. In the third act, Pelayo venerates the relics saved from desecration by the marauding invaders, the relics that serve as symbolic cornerstone of the building of the renewed Christian nation. In fact, in much of this act, Pelayo shows himself to be a chaste and devout Christian, and the play focuses on his reverence to God and his saints. Monod tells us that the early modern descriptions of kings in prayer typically reflected pleas for a successful outcome in battle or for some other public and national good, rather than for an individual boon. Where Rodrigo succumbed to his personal gratification, Pelayo puts the nation first, indivisible from Christianity. Ultimately, Lope supports the notion that, while the monarch may fail, the monarchy itself will survive as long as the new king does not fall into the same traps as his predecessor.

In his monumental epic poem *Jerusalem Conquered* (1609), Lope devotes book 6 to Rodrigo and the fall of Spain. Epic poetry, specifically "epopeya trágica" (tragic national epic), as Lope calls it, characteristically depicts a world of men, even if an act involving women may initiate the chain of events for nations, such as Paris's abduction of Helen of Troy. Florinda is compared to Helen of Troy, and in discussing the rape of La Cava, the poetic narrator says that feminine weakness simply gave in, so she is not completely blameless. There is little mention of La Cava, and no mention of Rodrigo's wife, who plays such an important role in *El último godo.* Instead, the poem highlights the relationship between the king and Count Julian (Menéndez Pidal, *Floresta* 2: 131–32). Like the loss of sacred lands in the Far East, the emphasis here is on the loss of Spain and on her vulnerability and submission to the infidels, not on the development of the legend post-sex act or of the fate of Julian and Florinda. Rodrigo simply disappeared from the battlefield and "died in secret." Lope's use of the legend in two genres, with their own differing narrative conventions, indicates his awareness of the legend's potential for manipulation to fit specific needs and aims of the author and the public.

Another great dramatist, Calderón de la Barca, also took up the legend, however briefly and tangentially, in his play *La Virgen del Sagrario* (the Virgin of the shrine, or sanctuary), in which La Cava's reputation fared poorly.[34] Downplaying the culpability and sexual nature of Rodrigo's actions, Calderón dramatizes the king's penance in the tomb with snakes who bit his torso or chest, bypassing the graphic plot of the ballads that claimed that the snake had bitten him "in the part where most I sinned." Rodrigo's literary redemption emerges as the penitent monarch, and blame is placed squarely on the woman:

Ya sabéis que la causa lastimosa
de la tragedia que lloráis en vano
fué de Florinda la deidad hermosa,
a quien Cava ha llamado el africano (Menéndez Pidal, *Floresta* 2: lxii)

(You all know that the unfortunate cause of the tragedy that you lament in vain was Florinda's goddess-like beauty, who is called Cava by the African).[35]

In addition to the story of Rodrigo and La Cava, Lope turned his hand to another legend of kingly dalliance, that of the captivating beauty of the Jewess of Toledo, which ensnared King Alfonso VIII. Lope takes an already gendered national story even further by focusing the conflict on the two women, the Jewess and the queen, one whose very existence threatens the country, the other whose womanly jealousy sparks the country's salvation from potential ruin. *Las paces de los reyes y judía de Toledo* (The peace of kings and Jewess of Toledo) was composed between 1604 and 1612, most likely between 1610 and 1612, and printed for the first time in 1617, according to James Castañeda, in his edition of the play (130). The title refers to the marital rupture between Alfonso and his wife, Queen Leonor, during the king's seven-year affair with the Jewess, here named Raquel, and specifically to the action of the third act, when Alfonso and Leonor commit to each other again, bringing "peace" to their marriage, which will redound to the good of the kingdom.[36] Though little studied compared to many of Lope's plays, *Las paces de los reyes y judía de Toledo* nicely fits what Stephen Gilman referred to as Lope's vision of Spanish history as a three-act play. The first act suggests the medieval values that Alfonso, the child-king, would want to prepare for and grow into; the second act, the abandonment of those values, as Lope and earlier historians believed that many rulers of the fourteenth and fifteenth centuries had done, until the Catholic monarchs—and late-fifteenth-century neo-Gothicism—returned to the mission of reconquest and what they lauded as core values of Pelayo and his followers, a return to mission that Lope engineers by Queen Leonor's design in the third act.[37]

As David Darst points out, Lope's play demonstrates that Alfonso can hardly be capable of taking care of his own lands and conquering Muslim territories when he cannot conquer his own sexual appetite (4). The historians Ambrosio de Morales and Juan de Mariana link the loss of the Battle of Alarcos to God's punishment of Alfonso for his sins with his lover. Linking a sexual sin to the inability to hold on to Christian land crafts Alfonso's story as a repetition of the loss of Spain in 711. Lope makes this connection explicit in several places, including at the close of the second act, when a mysterious shade warns the king: "Mira, Alfonso, lo que intentas, / pues desde que fuiste niño, / te ha sacado libre el cielo / entre tantos enemigos. / No des lugar desta suerte, / cuando hombre, a tus apetitos: / advierte que por la Cava / a España perdió Rodrigo." (Consider, Alfonso, what you are planning, since from the time of your childhood Heaven has kept you free from many enemies. Do not give in, now that you are a man, to these appetites. Beware, on account of La Cava Rodrigo lost Spain; ll. 1841–48). Undeterred, Alfonso offers the excuse that "Amor me quita el juicio, / y perdida la razón / conozco el daño y le sigo." (Love steals my judgment from me, and with reason lost, I know the danger and I follow it; ll. 1900–2).

The play explores the "otherness" of women on a number of levels. Queen Leonor is foreign, from England, but Christian. Raquel calls herself a Spaniard, though not a Christian. However, she identifies her blood through her Jewishness, not through her Spanishness, saying to her sister that Christians flee from people of "our blood" ("como vemos los cristianos huir de la nuestra sangre"; ll. 1148–49). Leonor, though foreign born, shares Alfonso's "Christian blood." Raquel asserts her superiority as a woman by invoking the early modern Spanish commonplace of the cold northern European juxtaposed to the passionate, vital, hot-blooded southern European. The queen is cold and icy, according to Raquel, who exhibits the passion that captivates the king. Although Castañeda claims that "Ultimately, [Raquel's] only guilt is that of beauty" (50–51), the play-text demands that we recognize deeper guilt, linked to the connections of woman, nation, and religion. Raquel is the stereotypical seductive female, and she is an adulteress. When they first marry, Leonor sees in Alfonso a gallant gentleman, and he appreciates her beauty and grace. Lope insists on bonds between this husband and wife that go beyond the fulfillment of political duty. Like La Cava in the ballad tradition, Raquel is called a basilisk (ll. 1264–65), the poisonous viper with the deadly gaze. Queen Leonor refers to Raquel as "aquella hebrea hermosa, / segunda Cava de España" (that beautiful Hebrew woman, second Cava of Spain; ll. 1961–62). After the queen exhorts the nobility to show themselves to be of "Gothic blood" by murdering Raquel (l. 2017), one of the noblemen, Beltrán, urges them on: "Hoy ha de morir la Cava, que de nuestro mal se goza" (Today, La Cava must die, she who so delights in our misfortune; ll. 2323–24). The female figure directly associated with the fall of Spain to the Muslims conflates with that of a Jewish woman whose amorous enslavement of the king results in similar consequences of Christian lands lost to, or left in the control of, Muslims. The blameless La Cava of early legend is long gone, and Lope avails himself of the dichotomization of bad woman, who makes kingdoms fall, and good woman, whose fidelity and commitment to her marriage and adopted country protect the collapse of both. But Leonor is a formidable woman, every bit as dangerous as Raquel, though in different ways. One might argue that Lope reinforces the notion that the truly dangerous woman is one left uncontrolled by marriage and society. While Leonor is on the side of right according to the play, demanding that the adulteress, non-Christian Raquel be killed in order to restore to the queen and to Spain her husband and its Christian king, Spanish society surely sought to keep such manly strength firmly in check: hence, the "peace" of kings, the return to the status of the household in which the man is king.

Early modern chronicles include the "awakening" motif, when the angel appears to Alfonso, shaking him from the spiritual darkness that began with his sexual enslavement. One of Lope's other innovations is to focus on the king's recommitment to Spain and to the fight for Christianity against the Muslims and Jews through the lens of the sacrament of marriage and his renewed vows to Leonor. As Yvonne Yarbro-Bejarano discusses in her study of Lope's plays, often "the national mission of battling the infidel provided the ideological glue for unification and, later, justification for imperialist hegemony" (232). Lope's play goes further. The metaphorical defeat of the sexualized enemy—Jews and Muslims alike—occurs when the Catholic monarchs Alfonso and Leonor reaffirm their marriage vows. By killing the Jewess, purging the king's marriage of this blight upon it, by identifying blood with religion, and by demonstrating his renewed, now potent, efforts against the Muslims, the play reaffirms a national identity based on Christian blood and a national history built on the alienation of minorities from it. Like the diptych of national legend created by associating the fall with La Cava and the building of the new Spain with Pelayo's outrage over the abduction of his chaste sister, Lope too finds such a diptych to be compelling national history in his version of Alfonso and the Jewess of Toledo.

The Legend of the Fall of Spain after the Expulsion

If the name of King Rodrigo enjoys little approbation in Lope's plays and epic poem, he fares better in another, anonymous version of the legend, which proclaims him a valorous and virtuous native son of Córdoba. The little-known collection of anecdotes entitled *Casos notables de Córdoba* (Notable cases of Córdoba, 1618) purports to be about famous heroes and heroines and local notables, all of whom had some connection to Córdoba. On one level, *Casos notables* is just one more literary example of the widespread interest in origins, in questions of individual and national identity, in defining one's present by determining the essence of the past, even—and especially—if that definition involves recasting the events of the past. What makes it worth considering here is that it attempts to efface history, Muslim Córdoba as "the ornament of the world." As the seat of the caliphate of Muslim Iberia, Córdoba indisputably shone as a center of learning, culture, and opulence. Not so in this book, written right after what we might call the official end of Al-Andalus, Muslim Spain, with the last of the Morisco expulsions in 1614.

Within the collection of anecdotes, one that tells the history of Rodrigo's loss of Spain is unusually long and full of detail. The narrator, Lonsario, cites Ambrosio de Morales and Rasis, the Muslim chronicler, as the sources of his tale.[38] Significantly, the history opens with an emphasis on nationalistic concerns. The story is sad, Lonsario says, because the loss was so great, but it is nonetheless enjoyable to hear about "because it is about our nation, and the king from our homeland" (por ser de nuestra nación, y el Rey de nuestra patria; 261).

The powers and accoutrements of a king, according to seventeenth-century standards, pervade the description of Rodrigo and his reign. In addition, Rodrigo's accession to the throne welcomes optimism and hope for the nation, for this new king possesses the qualities and virtues needed in a ruler and so sorely lacking in his predecessor, Witiza. The coin that bears Rodrigo's face and seal and Latin motto, his known talents and diplomatic skills, and the many written documents about him and his reign all bear witness to the grandeur of his sovereignty. However, being overwhelmingly human and desiring what he should not, none of his honors or innate kingly qualities deter him from raping the young woman he desired. One difference between this and many other versions is that the downfall of Spain was set up before the rape by the king's enemies, the sons of Witiza, who have already approached a dishonored Count Julian with plans to betray the king. Because the king had reneged on a promise to marry the daughter, Witiza's sons knew they would find a kindred spirit in Julian. The rape offered the specific occasion for the count to begin to exercise his plans for revenge.

In this version, Rodrigo breaks into the locked edifice impelled by "una indiscreta curiosidad" (an unwise curiosity; 266). This description, brief as it is, makes a paradigm shift between the expression of the Middle Ages and the early modern period. Pedro de Corral had described Rodrigo's desire to enter the House of Hercules as an act of "cobdicia," covetousness or greed, a sin of overweening desire for possession of the treasures within. Curiosity, in seventeenth-century usage, referred to an improper seeking of knowledge, improper because God has separated what humankind may know from the knowledge that belongs to God alone. Recognizing the difference between the two is a constant human struggle, to be dealt with through prayer and humility. The Rodrigo of *Casos notables,* however, suffers from the same illness as Cervantes' character Anselmo in *Don Quixote,* the husband whose insistence on testing his wife through trials only God should be permitted to design earned him the name "el curioso impertinente," the man of foolish curiosity.[39]

Casos notables, with its specific intention of showcasing important historical figures and events from Córdoba's rich past, glosses over the king's particular flaws to levy all blame on the treachery of Julian, who, unlike Rodrigo, was not a Cordoban native. This short tale leads from the disappearance of Rodrigo on the shores of the Guadalete River during battle to the humiliating servitude of the city under Muslim rule. Rodrigo's disappearance, as his entire army is slaughtered all around him, and which he carries out by leaving his clothes, crown, scepter, and horse by the banks of the river, is not characterized as cowardice, a flight to save only himself, but surprisingly, and unconvincingly, as "una de las más notables estratagemas de guerras que se describe de reyes vencidos para deslumbrar sus enemigos" (one of the most notable stratagems of war ever told of defeated kings in order to fool their enemies; 268).

In the previous chapter, we saw how the notion of the loss of Spain gave way to emphasis on the violent destruction of the nation; *Casos notables* employs the notions of loss and of destruction in an interesting and localized way. Accordingly, the result of the invasion and battles was the destruction, not of the nation, but of the magnificent city of Christian Córdoba, which, according to *Casos notables,* suffered more at the hands of the Muslims than any other city in Spain, especially evidenced by the city's history of Christian martyrs. Churches were destroyed, bishops driven out, many citizens renounced Christianity, but fortunately, a bishop of Córdoba did remain, as did some nuns and monks, although they paid dearly for their refusal to deny Christ. Christianity is portrayed, necessarily, as the underdog religion, struggling to continue to exist and to reemerge; therefore, it is unsurprising that persecutions of Christians and the resultant martyrdom, the earliest form of witnessing for Christianity, play such a prominent role in the history of the earliest decades following the victory of the Muslims and the defeat of the Christians.[40] In other words, if Córdoba had been "the ornament of the world," it was when the Christians held it before the invasion, not once the Muslims ruled it.[41] The story ends with the narrator saying that this is all he knows and has read of King Rodrigo, "con todo lo demás que he sabido de la pérdida de España" (along with all I know of the loss of Spain; 270). In this version, while Spain may have been lost, Córdoba was destroyed, and the city functions as a microcosm of the nation, which also allows the narrator to highlight and underscore the valor of the Christian Cordobans and the heroic virtue of her eighth-century martyrs.

Diego de Saavedra Fajardo, one of the most important politicians and political theorists of the seventeenth century, treated the legend of the fall twice, in his "mirror of princes," *Idea de un príncipe político-cristiano* (Idea of a political Christian prince, 1640), one hundred essays on the monarchy and the role and qualities of a ruler, and in his history of the Castilian throne, *Corona gótica, castellana y austríaca* (Gothic, Castilian, and Austrian crown, 1646). Saavedra Fajardo referred to the first work as political theory and to the second as a demonstration of those theories in historical practice: "En la *Idea de un príncipe político-cristiano* presente a vuestra alteza la teórica de la razón de estado, y agora ofrezco la prática advertida en la *[Corona gótica, castellana y austríaca]* . . . Es la verdad la que más importa a los príncipes, y la que menos se halla en los palacios" (In the Idea of a political Christian prince, I presented to your highness the theory of the reason of state, and now I offer practical advice in Gothic crown . . . Truth is what is most needed by princes and what is least found in palaces; *Corona gótica* 269).

The sixtieth essay of *Idea de un príncipe,* "O subir o bajar" (Either rise or fall), demonstrates the Baroque view of a kingdom as an ordered cosmos with the monarch at the center. It also reveals the author's view—shared by many—that the king and his kingdom were under God's keenly aware governance:

> Many are the causes of the rise and fall of monarchies and republics. He who attributes them to chance, or to the movement and influence of the stars, or to Plato's numbers, or to climacteric years, denies the concern of divine Providence for the things of this world. God did not disdain to create these orbs, nor does He disdain the governance of them . . . Kings reign through Him; by His hand are scepters granted. Although He lets man's inclinations, whether innate or learned, influence the preservation or the loss of kingdoms (trans. John Dowling, *Saavedra Fajardo* 86–87; Muchas son las causas de los crecimientos, i descrecimientos de las Monarquias, i Republicas. El que las reduce al caso, ò àl movimiento, i fuerza de los astros, ò à los numeros de Platon, i años climactericos, niega el cuidado de las cosas inferiores à la Providencia Divina. No desprecia el govierno destos orbes, quien no despreciò su fabrica . . . Por el reinan los Reyes. Por su mano se distribuyeron los ceptros . . . [D]eja correr las inclinaciones naturales, que ò nacieron con nosotros, ò son influidas . . . disponiendo con nosotros las fabricas, ò ruinas de las Monarquias; *Idea de un príncipe* 60: 418).

Saavedra Fajardo attributes the decline of nations to varied events that fit four categories: religion, honor, life, and property. In discussing honor, he uses the examples of Julian and Rodrigo as two different kinds of honor. Julian took offense because the king dishonored him, and a king who does not comport himself in a fashion worthy of a prince is not worthy of the obedience of vassals. Second, Saavedra Fajardo writes, "the greatest infirmity of a republic is incontinence and lasciviousness. From these vices are born sedition, the downfall of kingdoms, and the ruin of princes, for they blemish the honor of many other men, and God punishes them severely. Because of a single lecherous act, Spain was buried in ashes for seven centuries" (*Saavedra Fajardo* 88; La mayor enfermedad de la Republica es la incontinencia, y la lacivia. Dellas nacen las sediciones, las mudanças de Reinos, y las ruinas de Principes, porque tocan en la honra de muchos, y las castiga Dios severamente. Por muchos siglos cubriò de cenizas à España vna deshonestidad; 421).

In *Corona gótica,* Saavedra Fajardo opens the final chapter—the defeat of Rodrigo and the fall of what he calls the "Gothic Empire"—with the insight that it takes a great deal to bring down a nation. For him, the defeat of the Goths was unlikely due to Rodrigo alone, but the seeds of the downfall were sown in the political actions of the earlier corrupt rulers, particularly Witiza. This viewpoint, while objective and startlingly modern—historians today agree that the kingdom was unstable for some time—contradicts his statement in "O subir o bajar" that attributed the fall of the Goths, perhaps poetically, to "a single lecherous act." But the author accomplishes two things in his history. First, he shows himself to be weighing a number of earlier authorities, presenting differing opinions about what happened, while typically indicating which opinion he believes or supports, such as the historicity of Florinda (wife or daughter of the count), and discounting others, such as the veracity of the enchanted palace legend (377b). Second, his account of the conspiracies, the acts of the king and others, the strategies of the Muslims, the assaults on Christian lands are told with the talent, imagination, and fervor of an author of a romance of chivalry. In *Don Quixote,* one character who pronounced on the quality and value of various literary genres, the Canon of Toledo, suggests that a prudent reader would be inspired by the fascinating events of history and the Bible, and not need to resort to reading the "lying fictions" of invented knights. If all historiography were as suspensefully told as Saavedra Fajardo's rendition of the legend, the Canon just might have been right.

Just as Lope incorporates references to practices and beliefs about the monarchy that reflect seventeenth- rather than eighth-century views, Saavedra does the same: for example, he invents a letter from Florinda to her father, in which she laments that feminine frailty is no match against "la violencia y tiranía de un rey" (the violence and tyranny of a king; 375b). Customarily, King Rodrigo had not been referred to as a tyrant, but Juan de Mariana and other contemporary theorists had much to say on the general subject of the tyranny of kings. Another contemporary concern is the king's abandonment of his public duties for his private passions, a betrayal of his subjects' well-being, which is a major flaw in a ruler, as Saavedra writes: "Estas

pérdidas, y el descuido de don Rodrigo, desacreditado por su poca atención al gobierno y aborrecido de todos por sus pasiones y vicios, obligaban a los buenos a
tratar de asegurar sus vidas y retirarse a otras provincias por no hallarse a la vista de
la ruina de sus mismas patrias." (These losses, and the negligence of Rodrigo, who
was disgraced by the little attention he paid to government, and was hated by all for
his passions and vices, obliged the good people to try to save their lives and flee to
other provinces in order not to witness the ruin of their own native lands; 377b).

Pelayo appears as a fit ruler: "En don Pelayo ardían espíritus reales y generosos"
(In Pelayo burned royal and generous spirits; 381a). Saavedra devotes a fair amount
of space to the translation of relics, including those of St. Leocadia to a monastery
in Flanders, and the salvation of church objects, treasures, and the sacred vestments
of the priests. The author describes the waves of invasions by the Muslims, the
beauty of Spain and the disgrace of her subjugation, and his hope that the present
populace and future rulers will learn from God's punishment of, significantly, "the
Spanish nation" and other peninsular realms: "Grandes fueron los trabajos y calami-
dades con que Dios apuró la constancia de la nación española, primero en el yugo
de los romanos, después en él de los bárbaros, y últimamente en él de los africanos"
(Great were the labors and calamities with which God afflicted the Spanish nation,
first with the yoke of the Romans, next with that of the barbarians, and finally with
that of the Africans; 385b). He ends with a moralizing note on the fragility of empires and the duties of rulers: "Lo que nos muestra la experiencia y el orden natural
de las cosas es que los imperios nacen, viven y mueren, y que aún los cielos (corte
del eterno reino de Dios) se envejecen. Lo que conviene es que la virtud, la pruden-
cia y la atención de los reyes hagan durables sus reinos." (What experience and the
natural order of things teach us is that empires are born, live and die, and that even
the heavens [the court of the eternal kingdom of God] age. What is needed from
kings is virtue, prudence, and attention in order to make their reigns last; 387b).

Saavedra reinforces the belief that Visigothic blood flows through the veins of
Spain's kings, and that their monarchical line must be differentiated from Rodrigo
and the Visigothic kings who preceded him. He tells us that Rodrigo's epitaph in
Viseu read: "Aquí yace Rodrigo / Ultimo rey de los godos" (Here lies Rodrigo, last
king of the Goths). Saavedra interprets this for the reader: "Lo que en él se refiere,
que don Rodrigo fué el último de los reyes godos, no se debe entender en la sangre,
sino en el título, porque don Rodrigo y sus predecesores se llamaron reyes godos, y
sus sucesores reyes de Astúrias, de Leon y de Castilla; habiendo caído con don Rodrigo el imperio gótico, porque de allí adelante, quedando casi extinguida la nacion
goda, solamente la Española mantenia dentro de los montes la libertad, y allí levantó
otro nuevo ceptro en la misma sangre real de los godos, eligiendo por rey à don

Pelayo con diverso título, armas y insinias reales" (Rodrigo was the last king of the Goths, but one should not understand that to mean the last in blood, but in title, because Rodrigo and his predecessors were called Gothic kings, and his successors, kings of Asturias, of Leon and of Castile; the Gothic nation [in this sense, a people] was almost extinguished by the fall of the Gothic empire with Rodrigo; from that point on, only the Spanish nation kept liberty alive in the mountains, and it was there that another scepter in the royal blood of the Goths was raised, when Pelayo was elected king with a different title, arms, and royal insignias; 380a). Saavedra carefully distinguishes between what remains buried with the Visigoths at the death of Rodrigo and what engendered the birth of Spain: Pelayo, who started a new monarchy but continued the "royal blood" of the Goths.

From the time of Saavedra Fajardo until the work of the influential Benedictine monk, philosopher, and critic Benito Jerónimo Feijóo, no truly important work treats the legend of the fall of Spain. Curiosities did appear, such as the "false chronicle" that purports to be the story of one of the legend's minor and definitely fictional characters, who had yet to have his memoirs told: the confessor who counsels the penitent king. However, in this mid-seventeenth-century telling, copied by José Pellicer in 1646, and then disseminated in a widespread manuscript tradition, the king seduces both mother and daughter and has a child by La Cava. The confessor, sensing that his time was better spent with the hope of the future than with the specter of the past, flees to the Asturian mountains with Pelayo, and nothing is related of the death or flight of Rodrigo. A version of the legend by Cristóbal Lozano, called *David perseguido* (David persecuted), mixes information from Juan de Mariana and Miguel de Luna, several ballads, and other medieval folkloric sources to form an odd tale that has Rodrigo break off his formal engagement to La Cava, defends La Cava's anger at the king's offensive behavior, and introduces La Cava's jealous mother, whose own lust causes her to substitute herself for her daughter in the king's bed.

Either Rise or Fall

Our story could end here. Golden Age writers of history and fiction cemented the elements of the national myths of Spain's origins, of the "Loss of Spain in 711" and the victorious moments of her "Restoration." There was no more to tell, or at least, little left to invent. Sepharad had died in 1492, though the Inquisition in the sixteenth and seventeenth centuries condemned many new Christians and their descendants for heresy and Judaizing. Al-Andalus had died multiple deaths, first militarily and culturally, from the conquest of the major cities, beginning in 1085, with the retaking of Toledo, to the surrender of King Boabdil of Granada in 1492. Religiously, the choice of forced baptism or expulsion, between 1499 and 1502, and the diminishing right to retain or practice any aspect of Arabic culture in the sixteenth century, dealt the final blow to any dream of a shared Spain, which culminated in the official departure of the last of the Moriscos in 1614 from the shores of Spain.

Diego de Saavedra Fajardo wrote at a time of national bewilderment. The greatest empire in the world always seemed to be bankrupt, and quality of life in the country very poor. Plagues beset the nation, as they did England and other parts of Europe. But Spain was supposed to be God's chosen nation and people to rule the world. John Elliott captures the problematic mixture of sentiments that swept through Spain in the seventeenth century, a combination of deep despair and renewed hope for a salvation:

> The Castile bequeathed by Philip IV to his four-year-old son was a nation awaiting a saviour. It had suffered defeat and humiliation at the hands of its traditional enemies, the French. It had lost the last vestiges of its political hegemony over Europe, and seen some of its most valuable overseas possessions fall into the hands of the heretical English and Dutch. Its currency was chaotic, its industry in ruins, its population demoralized and diminished . . . Castile was dying, both economically and politically . . .
>
> Was there, then, no hope of resuscitation? Castile, which had lived for so long on illusions, still clung to the most potent of them with the tenacity born of despair. A Messiah would surely arise to save his people. (*Imperial Spain* 356)

That Spanish messiah never did appear. Philip IV died in 1665, during a time of deep financial crisis for Spain. The long wars with France and England had cost Spain dearly, and the country not only declared bankruptcy several times, but lost its treasure ship to France at one point, leaving Spain without any deliveries of silver from the New World for two years. At the time of Philip's death, Spain had entered war with Portugal over Portugal's fight for independence, and that country enjoyed the military support of France and England, who sent troops to fight Spain on Portuguese soil. In June 1665, three months before the death of Philip IV, Spain lost the decisive battle of Villaviciosa, and with it, all hope of winning back Portugal. Elliott's final assessment of the waning years of Philip's reign is significant:

> [Philip's] later years had been as melancholy as those of his Monarchy, for whose misfortunes he considered his own sins to blame. His first wife, Elizabeth of Bourbon, had died in 1644, and his only son, Baltasar Carlos, in 1646. His second mar-

riage in 1649, to his niece, Mariana of Austria, brought him two sickly sons, of whom the second, Charles, by some miracle survived to succeed his father at the age of four. This last pallid relic of a fading dynasty was left to preside over the inert corpse of a shattered Monarchy, itself no more than a pallid relic of the great imperial past. All the hopes of the 1620s had turned to dust, leaving behind them nothing but the acrid flavour of disillusionment and defeat. (*Imperial Spain* 353)

A fascinating and early opinion of Philip's reign, a marginal note found in a copy of a first edition of Mariana's *Historia general de España* (1601) that I consulted at the Hispanic Society of America, demonstrates how strong the impulse was to read the past—especially the Visigothic defeat—through the lens of present struggles, conflict, and threats.[42] Mariana recounts Rodrigo's accession to the already troubled Visigothic throne in Spain:

> que ni las voluntades de la gente se podian soldar por estar entre sí diferentes con las parcialidades y bandos . . . ellos por sí mismos tenian los cuerpos flacos y los ánimos afeminados á causa de la soltura de su vida y costumbres. Todo era convites, manjares delicados y vino; . . . y á ejemplo de los principales los mas del pueblo hacian una vida torpe y infame . . . juntamente desbarataron toda la disciplina militar . . . con todo esto no faltaron quien por satisfacer á sus antojos y pasiones con corazones endurecidos pretendiesen destruirlo todo (bk. 6, chap. 21: 191–92). (The Kingdom was full of Distractions, by reason of the several Interests, the People were grown Effeminate, giving themselves up to Feasting, Drink, and Lewdness; and the Military Discipline was quite lost, and the Kingdom of the Goths was now running headlong to Destruction; *General History* 97.)

In the margin of the 1601 Spanish book, at the line about the people's habits, is written in brown ink: "este es el estado en que oy nos allamos 1666!!!" (This is the state in which we find ourselves today 1666!!!).[43] Clearly some passionate reader blamed Spain's contemporary plight, a year after Philip IV's death, with its fiscal ruin and resounding losses to her bitter enemies, on a population possessing the moral equivalent of the iniquitous Visigothic populace who was about to lose Spain in 711. And, it is an excellent example of a single reader doing what centuries of chronicles had done, interpreting the present by means of analogy with the past. The idea of the "effeminate" Spaniard, whose weakened moral core also hindered the effective defense of his country, was widely noted, as *De Monarchia hispanica discursus* (Discussion of the Spanish monarchy), by Italian political theorist Tommaso Campanella, illustrates: "[T]he periodic failure of Christian armies to defeat the Turk was probably due to a progressive 'weakening of the semen'" (qtd. in Pagden, *Spanish Imperialism*

Juan José de Austria as Atlas Supporting the Spanish Monarchy,
1678, by Pedro de Villafranca (Spanish, 1615?–1684). Engraving,
25 × 17 cm. During this time of crisis for the Spanish monarchy
after the death of Philip IV, his illegitimate son, Juan José de Austria, struggled with Mariana, Philip's widow, for control of the
country. He served as prime minister for a short period. Courtesy
of The Hispanic Society of America, New York.

60).[44] In *Sex and Conquest,* Richard Trexler's study of the homophobic and otherwise eroticized language commonly used to describe the Muslim enemy, which later
became the language of the New World encounters, he demonstrates how the language and laws of the Iberian Peninsula reflected homophobic fears and the association of homosexuality with political defeat. To control sexuality would be a means

not only of ensuring the morality of the people, but of strengthening the nation as well: "In 1623, a law took effect that rewarded men who married at 18 years and punished men who were still single at 28. The law was clearly aimed in part against homosexual acts in a society where marriages were thought to be failing. Then in 1635, Fray Francisco de León, prior of Guadalupe, denounced 'men converted into women, soldiers into effeminates, who are haughty and full of airs, sport toupees, and for all I know wear women's cosmetics'" (59). While warding off rampant homosexuality, such laws also return to and underscore the continuing relevance to Christian society and empire of the notions expressed in Augustine's *The City of God,* that the conjugal bed was the seedbed of the city. Spain found the control of male and female sexuality to be crucial in this time of empire building, forged against the tensions of threatened, vulnerable, and even crumbling structures of Spanish society and government.

The peripatetic historical events of loss and renewal, and the tendency to regard such events in the Biblical pattern of a fall and a redemption, pervades Western narrative, both fiction and nonfiction, and always when recounting the events of 711 and its aftermath. Indeed, such casting of historical events is not confined to Spanish retellings of the story. Captain John Stevens's 1699 English translation, with his personal commentary, of Juan de Mariana's history ends the first volume with the following passage:

> Thus Spain was destroy'd, and thus ended the kingdom of the Goths. The kingdom and nation of the Goths were thus subverted, in my opinion, by a peculiar Providence, that out of their ashes might rise a new and holy Spain, greater in strength and dominions, to be the defense and bulwark of the Catholic religion. This was the opinion of F. Mariana, and not without reason; for he writ when Philip II of Spain was Lord of the East and West Indies, by the Addition of the king of Portugal, as he mentions in this place. To what a low ebb the affairs of Spain are reduced since, will appear by the sequel of the History, when we draw near our times. Let us conclude the Book, to begin another with the Resurrection of Spain after these mortal calamities. (*General History* 101)

Stevens, as well as Mariana, casts the fall of Spain in 711 in both mythic and religious terms. Here, the Reconquest and later imperial quest of Spain are a Resurrection, but the English translator joins the collective lament of Spanish historians that the present time, as Spain entered the eighteenth century, reflected a greatly diminished nation. If the anonymous Christian chronicler of eighth-century Spain, in his *Crónica mozárabe de 754* (*Mozarabic Chronicle of 754*), could bemoan the Muslim invasion and Visigothic loss as "the Damnation of Spain" (Damna Spanie), surely this lamentable evaluation had returned—with a vengeance—to close the seventeenth century and usher in the eighteenth as a disillusioned Spain confronted her shattering dreams of empire.

Our story could end here, but it does not. Spain entered a long period of disillusionment and decline, though still building and administering an overseas empire, and fighting enemies in every corner of the world. The "enlightened ones" of the eighteenth century continued to recount and debate Spain's history, but nineteenth- and twentieth-century Spain—as well as England and the United States—truly brought to life, as if they had never left, the legendary figures of the histories and fictions of medieval and early modern Spain. To do so, they returned to the very documents, fictional and historical—the manuscripts, the early printed editions, the compilations of oral ballads—whose contents we have seen for ourselves in the first two acts of this three-act play of history.

IMAGINING SPAIN

(The Enlightenment to the Present)

CHAPTER SIX

Ancestral Ghosts
and New Beginnings

I say that the loss of Spain gave Spain the occasion for her supreme
splendor. Without that fateful ruin Spain would not have achieved
such a glorious restoration . . . No other Nation can glory in
having won so many triumphs throughout the centuries as ours
did in the eight that were spent on the total expulsion of the
Moors.

> Benito Jerónimo Feijóo, *Teatro crítico universal,* bk. 4,
> "Discourse 13.xvi: Glorias de España," 1726–1740

I can never think about the loss of Spain without another feeling
that adds to the sorrow of that great calamity, about the injustice
done to the most blameless instrument of it. I am speaking about
the daughter of Count Julian, who, having been violated by
King Rodrigo, told her father how she had been injured . . . On
her they place all the blame of our ruin. Oh happy Lucretia! Oh
unfortunate Florinda! . . . Why is Lucretia celebrated and Florinda
detested?

> Benito Jerónimo Feijóo, *Teatro crítico universal,* bk. 4,
> "Discourse 13.xv: Glorias de España," 1726–1740

Who is Spanish? Who may live in Spain? From the earliest Christian chronicles
about the invasion of Spain by the Muslims even to very recent writings about the
problems of immigration, these deceptively simple questions appear, implicitly and
explicitly, over and over, having inspired through the centuries enormously contested
answers. The search for answers, based on the continuing search for origins, consumed academics and other intellectuals in the nineteenth and twentieth centuries.
In many profound ways, that search did not remain in the realm of the theoretical,
but reached out to touch ordinary lives, as it had done in centuries past.

Paloma Díaz-Mas, in her book *Sephardim: The Jews from Spain,* movingly recounts the struggles of one influential Spaniard, Angel Pulido Fernández, to lobby for the lifting of the 1492 Edict of Expulsion to allow for the return of the people he called "Spaniards without a Homeland," descendants of exiled Spanish Jews, whom he had encountered by chance for the first time while traveling on a ship from Budapest to Serbia. An elderly couple on the boat spoke a strange kind of Spanish, but recognizable as Spanish nonetheless; to the astonishment of the Pulido family, it was Ladino, the Spanish spoken by the Jews of the fifteenth-century expulsion. As Pulido's son wrote, "My father . . . was so astonished and happy to hear them that his life changed direction right there" (cited in Díaz-Mas 74).[1] Pulido came to believe that, like the couple he met, Enrique Bejarano and his wife, all the Sephardim, many of whom lived nearby in Jewish communities in North Africa, longed for the country—the homeland—that was lost to them. An active group of "filosefarditos" (lovers of Sephardim), as Spanish society referred to them, studied Jewish culture and history of Spain, and lobbied the government for the Edict of Expulsion to be rescinded. But not all Spaniards viewed this renewed contact with the Jews with equanimity or enthusiasm, to judge by the example of the Spanish Franciscan writer who used the pseudonym Africano Fernández, for his 1918 book *España en Africa y el peligro judío* (Spain in Africa and the Jewish peril). Notwithstanding formidable opposition, Pulido's publications and unflagging political activism led directly to Primo de Rivera's December 20, 1924, law, in which he proclaimed that "former Spaniards or their descendants and, in general, members of families of Spanish origin" could seek citizenship in Spain if they applied before December 30, 1930. During the time of Pulido's campaign for restorative justice, "for the first time the Sephardim became a matter of public consciousness in Spain. Some of the ideas of the campaign are still alive today" (Díaz-Mas 159).

This chapter and the epilogue point in several directions. The goals are fourfold, though easily summed up as a demonstration of the profound persistence of medieval and early modern cultural practices, concerns, and texts in the modern period. I look at the artistic manifestations of the stories of Rodrigo, La Cava, Julian, and Pelayo from the Enlightenment to the present and, of particular note, their popularity in Spanish and English Romanticism, in the heyday of the movement known as Orientalism. I show how the myths of origins of Spain contributed to the national debate about the essence of Spain and Spanish national identity in the nineteenth and twentieth centuries, and where contemporary resonances of the ancient past now exist. Pelayo and his legendary achievements continued to be important, particularly in the nineteenth and twentieth centuries. Not only was Pelayo intriguing to Spanish, English, and American authors of the nineteenth century, but his story became inextricably connected to the world of politics in Francisco Franco's dictatorship and in the current monarchy. I revisit legends discussed earlier in this book, such as the Holy Child of La Guardia, the cult of St. Leocadia, and Alfonso VIII and the Jewess of Toledo, to see how scholars, politicians, and the Church manipulated the stories into new service. For many readers, the examples contained in these two final parts of the book will suffice to answer the question, "What ever happened to . . . ?" But what I hope, above all else—the same hope that I harbor for other parts of the book—is that I will have provided any number of intriguing avenues, out of the vast array of texts examined and referenced in the present study, to pique the reader's curiosity for future study and reading pleasure.

The Challenge of Foundational Myths in the Age of Enlightenment

One of the greatest thinkers of the Spanish eighteenth-century Enlightenment was the Benedictine philosopher-critic Benito Jerónimo Feijóo. In his *Teatro crítico universal* (Universal theater of criticism), a collection of essays published separately between 1726 and 1740, Feijóo writes about the "glories of Spain," which revolve greatly around the evangelicalism of the monarchy. He praises the Catholic monarchs, particularly Ferdinand, for having purged the nation of "la Morisma," the Moorish peoples, presumably through the mass conversions of 1499–1502. Like the early modern historians Ambrosio de Morales and Juan de Mariana, Feijóo admires Ferdinand's military prowess and arts of government, calling him the "great Teacher of Politics," and attributing much of Spain's later success to the paths forged by the king. That does not mean Feijóo ignores Isabel: "Isabel, a woman, not only more than a woman, but more than a man, on account of which she has ascended to the level of Heroine" (bk. 4, discourse 13: xxiii).[2]

A number of Feijóo's essays manifest deep concern over the power of popular culture to persuade the public to incorrect religious, moral, and political beliefs and to hold views that are ultimately detrimental to the advancement of society. Feijóo found mystifying, and culturally and politically stultifying, the persistent belief of the national imaginary in superstitions, apocryphal saints, and certain parts of the national founding myth, particularly in blaming Florinda La Cava for the fall of Spain. Time and again, he tackles long held and even cherished beliefs, hoping to counter by logic and rational explanation why these beliefs are incorrect. But just as his essays on the absurdity of some of the miracles attributed to popular saints did little to erase the public's belief in those miracles and the power of saints, both can-

onized and purely legendary, Feijóo's spirited defense of women in general, and
Florinda La Cava in particular, did not change the long-term collective view of her
as the nation's female destroyer. He writes in "Defensa de las mujeres" (Defense of
women):

> Ya oigo contra nuestro asunto aquella proposición de mucho ruido, y de ninguna
> verdad, que las mujeres son causa de todos los males. En cuya comprobación,
> hasta los ínfimos de la plebe inculcan a cada paso que la Caba indujo la pérdida
> de toda España, y Eva la de todo el mundo. Pero el primer ejemplo absolutamente
> es falso. El conde don Julián fue quien trajo los Moros a España, sin que su hija
> se lo persuadiese, quien no hizo más que manifestar al padre su afrenta . . . El se-
> gundo ejemplo, si prueba que las mujeres en común son peores que los hombres,
> prueba del mismo modo que los Ángeles en común son peores que las mujeres;
> porque, como Adán fue inducido a pecar por una mujer, la mujer fue inducida por
> un Ángel. No está hasta ahora quien pecó más gravemente, si Adán, si Eva; porque
> los padres están divididos. Y en verdad que la disculpa que da Cayetano a favor de
> Eva, de que fue engañada por una criatura que no ocurrió en Adán, rebaja mucho,
> respecto de éste, el delito de aquella. (I hear the proposition, full of noise but lack-
> ing in truth, that women are the cause of all evil. As proof, even the lowliest ple-
> beians constantly invoke that La Cava brought about the fall of Spain, and Eve, of
> the whole world. But the first example is absolutely untrue. Count Julian was the
> one who brought the Moors into Spain, without his daughter having to persuade
> him to do it, and all she did was tell him of the injury done to her. The second
> example, if it proves that all women are worse than men, it also proves that all an-
> gels are worse than women because Adam was led to sin by a woman, but a
> woman was led to sin by an angel. We still cannot agree which one sinned more,
> Adam or Eve, because the Church Fathers themselves were divided; indeed,
> Cayetano's pardon of Eve for having been deceived by a creature superior to her
> in intelligence and wisdom, which cannot be said of Adam, greatly diminishes her
> guilt in comparison to his; *Teatro crítico,* bk. 1, discourse 16: i.)

In a later political and sociocultural essay on the essence of Spain and Spanish
nationalism, from which this chapter draws its epigraphs, and in which Feijóo
praises the Catholic monarchs, he tackles in a different way the national imaginary's
condemnation of Florinda La Cava. Feijóo believes firmly in the historicity of the
founding myth; what he challenges is the interpretation of it. Apparently, he received harsh criticism for having exculpated La Cava in "Defense of Women,"
which he alludes to in this next attempt to reason with the public. First, he states

that God punished the entire nation for "los desórdenes del rey" (the unruliness of the king), which aligns him with seventeenth-century historians such as Juan de Mariana and Diego de Saavedra Fajardo, as well as with such literary figures as Lope de Vega. Next, he continues to defend La Cava, saying that she was not responsible for her father's actions, nor should she be castigated for telling her own father what the king had done, when the Roman rape victim Lucretia is praised for having revealed King Tarquin's rape of her:

> sobre ella cargan todo la culpa de nuestra ruina. ¡Oh feliz Lucrecia! ¡Oh desdichada Florinda! ¿Qué hizo esta española que no hubiese hecho primero aquella romana? Una y otra recibieron la misma especie de injuria: una y otra la revelaron: aquella, al esposo; ésta, al padre; una y otra deseaban la venganza, y que ésta cayese sobre el príncipe que había hecho la ofensa. ¿Por qué, pues, es celebrada Lucrecia y destestada Florinda? Sólo porque el común de los hombres, ni para el aplauso ni para el vituperio, considera las acciones en sí mismas, sino en sus accidentales resultas. Fue saludable a Roma la queja de Lucrecia; fue funesta a España la de Florinda. (What did the Spaniard do that the Roman had not done first? Both suffered the same kind of offense, both revealed it; the former to her father, the latter to her husband; both desired vengeance on the prince who had done the offense. Why, then, is Lucretia celebrated and Florinda detested? Only because men do not consider the actions themselves, to either applaud or deride them, but the accidental consequences of the actions. Lucretia's complaint benefited Rome; Florinda's was fatal to Spain.)

The passage continues:

Pero del bien y el mal fueron autores únicos el esposo de una y el padre de otra, sin intervención ni aún previsión de las dos damas. Y aún el que la venganza fuese fatal para una república y útil para otra dependió menos del designio de los autores que de las circunstancias y positura de las cosas . . . Espero me perdone el lector esta breve digresión, por ser en defensa de una principal señora española, a quien algunos porfiados maldicientes persiguen aún, después de la apología que por ella hice en el *Discurso* último del primer tomo. (But the only authors of the actions, for better or worse, were the husband of one and the father of the other, without the intervention or even foreknowledge of the two ladies. And even though the vengeance proved fatal for one republic and useful for another depended less on the authors' designs than on the circumstances and outcome of things. I hope the reader can excuse this brief digression since it is a defense of an estimable Spanish lady, who some perfidious evil-speakers continue to pursue, even after the apologia I wrote on her behalf in my essay on the defense of women; bk. 4, discourse 13: xv.)

Thus, if the republic (as he often refers even to the early manifestations of the country in his work) had flourished rather than fallen, Florinda would be heroine, not harlot or traitor, in the retellings of the founding myth.

Significant also for the evolution of the legend and notions of the essence of Spain and Spanishness is Feijóo's characterization of Florinda as "the Spaniard." It is one thing to argue that the Castilian throne began with the Visigothic kingdom, a point many versions of the legend have sought to bolster. But it is quite another to refer to Rodrigo, Florinda, Julian, and Pelayo as Spaniards, and to insist, as Spanish national history has done from the fifteenth century to the present, that Spain was born in 589 C.E. when King Recared and the Visigoths converted from Arian Christianity to Roman Catholicism. Calling them "Spaniards" stoked the fires of the great nineteenth- and twentieth-century debates about Spain's national identity.

Fallen Women Take the Stage

Eighteenth-century censorship, justified as new views of decorum, meant that the portrayal of Rodrigo as rapist fell out of fashion in the eighteenth century. In Madrid in 1770, ecclesiastical and royal authorities announced a prohibition against a particular play, *La pérdida de España* (The loss of Spain), by Eusebio de Vela, stating that it was indecorous to refer to the king, the bishop, and even the Spanish nation in the ways in which the telling of this tale insisted; moreover, conspiracies and treason against the king were not suitable themes for representation on the stage (Menéndez Pidal, *Floresta* 3: 17). Partly for that reason, some writers sought new angles through the less explored women of the legend, specifically Pelayo's sister and Rodrigo's widow, although the resultant works were minor indeed. In the 1770 play *Hormesinda,* the playwright Nicolás Moratín cast Pelayo's sister as Florinda's rival in the court, while another, Antonio Valladares y Sotomayor, wove a tale in which Muza's son Abdelasis names Rodrigo's widow and former African princess, Egilona, as the new queen of Spain.[3] Picking up a strain of sixteenth-century attempts to argue for an ancient Gothic-Arabic Iberian throne, as we saw in Miguel de Luna for one, Valladares y Sotomayor also anticipates many of the nineteenth-century academics' discussions about a shared Iberian and African racial and cultural heritage, which they used to justify a range of beliefs, from Spain's right to colonize North Africa to the ever-continuing disputes about Spanish blood purity.

One of the very few women to treat the legend of the fall, María Rosa Gálvez succeeded in 1804 in returning Rodrigo to the stage after decades of censorship had silenced tellings of the legend. Her play, *Florinda, tragedia en tres actos* (Florinda, tragedy in three acts), convinced the censors to include the legend in the category of "classical tragedy," lifting the ban that had suppressed the story for being indecorous to a Spanish ruler. Gálvez casts Rodrigo as lovesick over Florinda but locked in a loveless marriage to Egilona. Not one to transgress the holy sacrament of marriage, initially at least, he pines for Florinda and longs for the marriage he would have happily honored. The king laments that God and the Church have made the bonds of matrimony indissoluble. Among Gálvez's innovations, in addition to a slight exploration of social issues as the first writer to suggest the possibility of divorce to solve Rodrigo's problem, an idea taken up later by English Romantics, here Pelayo is in love with Florinda, to whom he is about to become betrothed. Rodrigo's sexual jealousy impels his rape of Florinda. While it is clear that the eighteenth century, and even part of the seventeenth, clearly favored the story of Pelayo and the renewal and restoration of the nation, rather than focus on its destruction and demise except as a warning to rulers, Gálvez's take on this is completely new: Rodrigo's actions stem more from his rivalry with Pelayo than from his strong feelings for Florinda. In other words, it is implied, had Florinda not been the beloved of the king's cousin and rival, Pelayo, the king's attentions may well have focused on another woman, or no other woman, and Spain's historical path might have been very different.[4]

Upon learning that, however unwillingly, Florinda has indeed been with the king, Pelayo spurns and curses her; on the battlefield, seeing the havoc wrought by the avenging of her dishonor, Pelayo cries anew: "They will curse the detestable name of the odious Florinda!" (¡Maldecirán el detestable nombre de la odiosa Florinda!; Menéndez Pidal, *Floresta* 3: 32). For her part, Florinda vacillates between blaming herself and blaming Rodrigo: "Rodrigo was the cause, I was just unlucky" (Rodrigo fue la causa, yo fui sólo infeliz; *Floresta* 3: 34–35). Like her Roman predecessor Lucretia, Florinda stabs herself, crying out that both she and Spain perish at the same time and that she will bear the eternal blame. Earlier in the play, Gálvez had included a moment when a politically astute Florinda becomes excited at the prospect of the bloodshed that will signal her revenge. In most cases, when La Cava hopes for some retaliation by her father, it is either acknowledged or implied that she expects action only against the king and not against innocent people. Here, she first asks for personal revenge, then becomes excited by the prospect of the entire treason planned, and then returns to her previous view that innocent people should not suffer for Rodrigo's offense.[5] When she kills herself, her father comes upon the corpse, an agonizing moment, and the Muslim leader Tarik sums up the situation by casting blame on Julian: "Crime, treason, and vengeance always merit such payback" (El crimen, la traición y la venganza siempre tal recompensa merecieron; 35).

Given that Menéndez Pidal never bothered to counter any negative portrayals of La Cava by earlier authors, such as Juan de Mariana, one of his favorites, it surprises that he praises Feijóo's essayistic defense of La Cava as intellectually bold and courageous. But, in fact, he does so as a means of criticizing María Rosa Gálvez, claiming that she fails to recognize the potential in endowing the heroine with tragic qualities. Quite simply, he attributes this to a lack of talent: "The spectator of María Rosa's tragedy sympathizes much more with Julian's daughter than the author does, who, in this drama, gives one of many proofs of the affective dryness characteristic of so many poetesses" (Así que el espectador de la tragedia de María Rosa compadece a la hija de Julián muchísimo más que la autora, que en este drama da una de tantas pruebas de la sequedad característica de tantas poetisas; *Floresta* 3: 32). He recounts that another minor author justifiably, in his opinion, rewrites Gálvez's ending to have Florinda rail against men and the injustice she has suffered. Further, he suggests that Gálvez, affective dryness notwithstanding, might have benefited from further research before composing her play: "How Rosa Gálvez needed to read what Father Feijóo said about Florinda!" (¡Cuánta falta le hizo a Rosa Gálvez leer lo que el padre Feijóo había dicho sobre Florinda! *Floresta* 3: 32). Admittedly, both play and characters appear overwrought, so Menéndez Pidal's aesthetic judgment is not without merit. Nevertheless, one cannot help noticing that only in the case of the Morisco Miguel de Luna had he felt impelled to take the author to task, and now he chooses this single instance to speak up in defense of Florinda, peremptorily sending back to her studies the only woman author we have seen thus far.

In Gálvez's play, precursor to Romanticism's great interest in Rodrigo, Julian, La Cava, and Pelayo, Florinda La Cava emerges as a figure in her own right, after centuries of portrayal as the powerless victim or as the site of evil through woman's inherently evil nature. While the nineteenth-century portrayals are not exactly feminist advances, authors do attempt to rehabilitate La Cava's reputation and, at the very least, develop the one-dimensional character who was so often relegated to the role of pawn or seductress.

An exile from the court in Madrid, Vicente García de la Huerta, composed a particularly important neoclassical drama, a tragedy in one act, *Raquel,* the name given in the seventeenth century to the Jewess of Toledo. García de la Huerta worked as the archivist for the duke of Alba and in time became the official court poet for Charles III. A run-in with a powerful nobleman ended with García de la Huerta's exile to the North African city of Oran (known to modern film goers as the setting of *Casablanca*). While there, he wrote *Raquel,* a play based on the legend of Alfonso

VIII and the beautiful Jewess, which had its premiere on January 22, 1772, followed by productions in Barcelona in 1775 and Madrid in 1788, the year after the playwright's death. Literary historians laud the author for having successfully crafted a Spanish tragedy on a nationalist theme according to neoclassical precepts—not an easy feat, judging by the vast number of truly dreadful plays from this period in Spain. García de la Huerta's sources, the poem and drama by the seventeenth-century Luis de Ulloa and Juan Bautista Diamante, respectively, followed Lope's lead and the seventeenth-century emphasis on the duties, responsibilities, and obligations of the monarch to his country, and the sanctity of the sacrament of marriage between the king and queen as a metaphor for the well-being of the Christian state.

As we've seen, women's stories and the stories of their bodies—the fates of La Cava, Egilona, and Ermesinda in particular—stood for the fate of the nation. La Cava, the most ambiguous, is sometimes the woman betrayed by her own king, more often the cause of his downfall. Rodrigo's widow, Egilona, though now married to the Muslim prince Abdelasis, holds fast to her religion and seeks ways to win the country back for the Christians. Early materials disagreed about whether Egilona was a North African Muslim princess or a Goth, or whether Rodrigo had a wife at all. When a work portrays her as African, she is the helpful Muslim princess, a Christian convert, eager to betray her people for the sake of rescuing and protecting Christian lands; when she is a Goth, her portrait merges with that of Ermesinda. That is, Pelayo's sister, as the strong, pure, and inviolate Christian Gothic–Spanish maiden, often chooses suicide by poison rather than marry Munuza, and when she does marry him, she eagerly looks for ways to escape.

Orientalism, Romanticism, and Visigothic Spain

Orientalism means at least two things to us today. First, it refers to a movement—almost a fetish or obsession—in nineteenth-century Europe, which placed great value on the exoticism of the Far East. Familiar to many people through beautifully lavish paintings (Delacroix, for example) and tales of swashbuckling Christian heroes battling the adherents of Islam, Orientalism romanticized the "East"—which, despite their location in Europe, included Moorish Spain and gypsy culture—delighting in scenes of white desert sands, harems and toilettes, exotic marketplaces, brooding men in flowing tunics, and sensuous, mysterious, dark, and beautiful women. In addition to collecting Islamic and Chinese *objets d'art*—*turquoiseries* and *chinoiseries*—it became fashionable for the rich to have their portraits painted while they posed in Eastern dress. In academic circles, Orientalism refers to the cultural phenomenon Edward Said analyzed so brilliantly in the 1980s, in which he argued that the West

"La Alhambra. Patio de los Leones," by Charles Clifford (1819–
1863). Albumen photograph, 42.3 × 32.5 cm. From *Album de
Andalucía y Murcia,* 1863. Courtesy of The Hispanic Society
of America, New York.

remained largely ignorant of the East, and that Orientalism therefore was a fiction,
constructed by the West. Moreover, this Western construction of "the Orient" au-
tomatically views the West as more civilized and the East as exotic and less sophisticated. His general conclusion, which has led to the creation of academic theories
of "postcolonialism," argues that colonizers—as the West has been—always place
the observers' culture in a superior position to that of the observed.

For Spain, Orientalism, and Europe's fascination with it, cut two ways. On the
one hand, Spain, which remained steeped in Moorish influence in spite of attempts
to efface it through the centuries, basked in Europe's appreciation of its beauty and
the richness of its culture, as in the Muslim and gypsy-influenced Andalusia of Pros-

per Mérimée's 1846 *Carmen,* for example. European interest in Moorish Spain began earlier, though, as María Soledad Carrasco Urgoiti tells us: "Pérez de Hita's book [the 1595 *Guerras civiles de Granada* (*Civil Wars, I*)] crossed the Pyrenees early in the seventeenth century and eventually gave rise to an almost mythical interpretation of Moorish Granada as an exquisitely refined European court where précieux sophistication had first bloomed" (140). Pérez de Hita's work had romanticized the decline of Boabdil's Granadan kingdom in the late fifteenth century, and it, along with the sixteenth-century ballad tradition in particular, inspired much European and American literary production that capitalized on the sentiments of melancholy and longing for a lost and glorious past.

Many towns in Spain held, and continue to hold today, annual celebrations known as "fiestas de moros y cristianos" (celebrations of Moors and Christians), consisting of re-enactments of battles between the two religions.[6] Posters announcing exhibitions—world fairs—in the nineteenth and twentieth centuries underscore that Spain participated in the fostering of Spanish Orientalism as much as any foreign nation did. On the other hand, the insistence that Spain was Africa, that Africa began in the Pyrenees, distanced Spain culturally and intellectually from the rest of Europe and contributed to the view that Spain was backward, unsophisticated, and uncivilized.[7] The saying "Africa begins in the Pyrenees" became popular in nineteenth-century France. Its origins are unclear, though some attribute it to Napoleon, as a statement of his sneering disparagement of Spain.

Nineteenth-century British, Continental, and American travelers toured Spain, and many found it an alluring place for extended sojourns. In that age of diaries, travel journals, and occasional poetry, it sometimes seemed that everyone was a writer. From Washington Irving to Samuel Longfellow to Walter Scott, not only did male poets and novelists live in Spain, but the culture fed their art. They weren't alone. Bridget Bigatel-Abeniacar describes the very interesting contributions of some American women, who offered opinions on everything from Spanish politics to America's superior housing. From Kate Field's 1875 *Ten Days in Spain,* which she wrote after coming to Spain to interview the eminent politician Emilio Castelar: "Latin drawing-rooms resemble our hotel parlors in small, and as Spanish families move whenever there is a death among them, they exist without roots. Though Americans move oftener than the English, our homes are the prettiest, most comfortable and convenient in the world." Apart from Castelar's deplorable taste in home furnishings, Field found him to be naive, "not a man of the world," and simply not up to dealing with the cutthroat world of politics.[8] After penning *Three Vassar Girls Abroad: Rambles of Three College Girls on a Vacation Trip Through France and Spain for Amusement and Instruction, With Their Haps and Mishaps,* and pub-

Florinda, 1853, by Franz Xaver Winterhalter (German, 1805–1873). Oil on canvas, 70¼ × 96¼ in. (178.4 × 245.7 cm). This painting was shown in the Paris Salon of 1853. It is a replica of a version of the same size given by Queen Victoria to Prince Albert in 1852. The king can be seen on the left, peering through the shrubbery. Courtesy of The Metropolitan Museum of Art, Bequest of William H. Webb, 1899 (01.21). Image © The Metropolitan Museum of Art.

lishing it in 1883, Elizabeth (Lizzie) Williams Champney's three Vassar girls followed it up in 1885 with a tour of South America. Champney continued to travel the world and write about it until her death.[9]

Myths about Spain's national origins by their very nature of conflict between Christianity and Islam became a favorite subject of Orientalism. Romantic operas celebrated, in the nineteenth-century vein of showcasing women of these historical legends, the tragic stories of Florinda and Raquel. The famous Austrian dramatic poet Franz Grillparzer wrote a play in 1855, *The Jewess of Toledo,* based on Lope de Vega's drama. Although a German favorite, he had had one humiliating experience in which one of his plays was laughed off the stage; after that, he refused to show his work. After his death in 1872, *Die judin von Toledo* was found among his papers and staged in the 1880s; the work was translated into English in 1953. A stunning example of Orientalism and Romanticism, now housed in the Metropolitan Museum in New York, is Franz Xaver Winterhalter's *Florinda*. Exhibited at the Paris Salon of 1853, the painting is a replica of one Queen Victoria had presented to Prince Albert the year before. In the painting, Florinda and maidens luxuriate in the gardens of the palace, though Florinda, alone of all the women, looking young and shy, pulls her shawl tightly around her, while several of the women sprawl in various stages of undress. Off to the side, the king spies on the women. Another painting, visually arresting for its brilliant colors, is Horace Vernet's mid-century rendering of the epic event of the Reconquest, Alfonso VIII's victory at the Battle of Navas de Tolosa in 1212, several years after the murder of Raquel.

Much to the dismay of Spanish critics, philosophers, politicians, and historians who sought to turn the indignity of the fall of Spain in 711 into a more glorious defeat, the fall before the rise, as it were, the work that most influenced writers abroad in the seventeenth, eighteenth, and nineteenth centuries was Miguel de Luna's *Verdadera historia del rey don Rodrigo* (True history of King Rodrigo).[10] The ballad tradition, which tended to cast La Cava most often as a siren, and the king as noble and judicious but felled by a fateful and dangerous passion, ran a close second.

Nineteenth- and twentieth-century critics have judged Luna harshly. Take, for example, Menéndez Pidal, whose monumental effort to document all works dealing with Rodrigo demonstrated the wildly different versions of the legend, which certainly should have armed him with the ability and objectivity to regard Luna's work as one more fanciful version. Instead, ignoring the fact that up through the fifteenth century, historiography almost always called itself "chronicle," and that even Corral's own historical romance pretends to be an eyewitness account of the events, Menéndez Pidal exempts Corral from criticism by claiming intentional authorial fictionality, that he wrote a historical novel, while Luna is excoriated for having written "una historia falsificada" (a falsified history; *Floresta* 2: xliv).[11] Conveniently forgotten by Menéndez Pidal, the fifteenth-century Pérez de Guzmán had railed against Corral's disseminated manuscript, accusing him of lying, which Mariana quotes in his own history when he discredits Corral. Aghast that Luna claims to have discovered the text—a literary strategy that only a few years later Cervantes used in claiming that his *Don Quixote* was the work of the Moor Cide Hamete Benengeli, and that he himself was merely the translator—Menéndez Pidal appears particularly riled that Luna asserts that Abulcaçim Tarif not only witnessed the fall of Spain, but also had access to King Rodrigo's private papers, and that he had discovered a cache of letters by La Cava and Pelayo (xlv). Considering the nineteenth-century agenda to forge a Christian national identity based on theories of eighth-century origins, Menéndez Pidal had every reason to despise Luna's work, which would serve as a source to many more English Romantic writers interested in Spain's origins than Corral's work would.

Earlier, in 1854, in his history of Spanish literature, the dedicated Hispanophile George Ticknor described Corral's work as "chiefly fabulous" and "imaginary," a work that naively claims but cannot support historicity, as these "old chronicles" typically do: "the circumstances related are, generally, as much invented as the dialogue between its personnages, which is given with a heavy minuteness of detail, alike uninteresting in itself, and false to the times it represents. In truth, it is hardly more than a romance of chivalry" (212–13). But he defends such efforts: "The principle of such a work is, of course, nearly the same with that of the modern historical romance. What, at the time it was written, was deemed history was taken as its basis from the old chronicles, and mingled with what was then the most advanced form of romantic fiction, just as it has been since in the series of works of genius beginning with Defoe's *Memoirs of a Cavalier*" (214). Ticknor goes on to say that he finds admirable the depth of feeling such authors included in their fanciful works:

> these old Spanish chronicles, whether they have their foundations in truth or in fable, always strike farther down than those of any other nation into the deep soil of the popular feeling and character. The old Spanish loyalty, the old Spanish religious faith, as both were formed and nourished in the long periods of national trial and suffering are constantly coming out; . . . and thus, in this vast, rich mass of chronicles, containing such a body of antiquities, traditions, and fables as has been offered to no other people, we are constantly discovering, not only the materials from which were drawn a multitude of the old Spanish ballads, plays, and romances, but a mine which has been unceasingly wrought by the rest of Europe for similar purposes, and still remains unexhausted. (215–16)

Refusing to grant Luna any space in the main body of his literary history, and after having acknowledged repeatedly the fictional element in other purportedly truthful accounts of Spanish history (not to put too fine a point on it, Corral's *Crónica del Rey don Rodrigo*), Ticknor relegates him to this remarkable footnote:

Another work, something like the [*Crónica del Rey don Rodrigo*], but still more worthless, was published, in two parts, in 1592–1600, and seven or eight times afterwards; thus giving proof that it long enjoyed a degree of favor to which it was little entitled. It was written by Miguel de Luna, in 1589, as appears by a note to the first part . . . Southey, in his notes to his "Roderic" (Canto IV), is disposed to regard this work as an authentic history of the invasion and conquest of Spain, coming down to the year of Christ 761, and written in the original Arabic only two years later. But this is a mistake. It is a bold and scandalous forgery, with even less merit in its style than the elder Chronicle on the same subject, and without any of the really romantic adventures that sometimes give an interest to that singular work, half monkish, half chivalrous. How Miguel de Luna, who, though a Christian, was of an old Moorish family in Granada, and an interpreter of Philip II, should have shown a great ignorance of the Arabic language and history of Spain, or, showing it, should yet have succeeded in passing off his miserable stories as authentic, is certainly a singular circumstance. That such, however, is the fact, [critics] Conde . . . and Gayangos . . . leave no doubt, —the latter citing it as a proof of the utter contempt and neglect into which the study of Arabic literature had fallen in Spain in the sixteenth and seventeenth centuries. (214n–15n)

While many Christian writers through the centuries had opined that Rodrigo governed poorly or, at the very least, showed remarkably poor judgment in his rape of Julian's daughter, it would seem that Luna had no right to offer such an unflattering view of Spain's past, of Spain's early king, even the king who had "lost" Spain in 711. The depth and hypocrisy of Ticknor's and other critics' unexamined prejudice against the Morisco author, manifested in their undisguised anger toward him and his work, is striking even today. Nevertheless, the anger is understandable because Luna's work defied the nineteenth-century political and nationalist agenda, which was manufactured in no small measure by writers such as Menéndez Pelayo and Menéndez Pidal. George Ticknor, like others of the nineteenth century, sought to find and define true Spanishness and the essence of Spain, solidifying a modern national identity based on eighth-century Gothic origins, and tracing it through a linear development of Christian writers. They considered the contrary contribution of a Morisco like Luna to be an unwelcome intrusion, to put it mildly. For if Rodrigo were indeed a despot, rather than a noble and tragic king, and Christian purity of bloodline through the centuries a complete myth (although it is exactly that), then the nineteenth-century arguments of the birth of Christian Spain in 589 C.E. and its continued Christian history through the centuries could not but collapse. And this could not be permitted under any circumstances.

The tarnished Rodrigo of Luna's telling survived the journey north to become a notable character in English Romanticism: in the hands of Robert Southey, Walter Scott, and Walter Savage Landor, both Rodrigo and Julian are reinvented as tragic heroes.[12] Rodrigo is restored to a dignity first seen in Pedro de Corral's *Crónica del Rey don Rodrigo* and Julian in particular is raised to a level of dignity unseen in any of the Spanish versions through the centuries; Pelayo the Perfect needed no rehabilitation.[13]

English interest in the study of Spain's origins as a nation-state extended well beyond casual intellectual curiosity, and the nobility with which English writers endowed the stories of Spain's Asturian Christian origins, as well as celebrating an even earlier race of pure, pre-Visigothic "Spaniards," in turn reinvigorated Spanish intellectuals to recount ever more insistently those origins in their own nineteenth-century histories and fictions. English writers not only felt at home in Spain, but they discovered in it "a land that was simultaneously real and open to constant reimaginings. Above all, it was a space onto which Romantic writers, male and female, projected their own concerns—their hopes and fears about their own individual, gender and national identities" (Pratt par. 5). For Michael Ragussis, England's fascination with the Spanish Inquisition and the conversions and persecutions of the Jews in particular allowed for explorations of its own "Jewish question," which was at the center of the English national agenda in the mid-nineteenth century. Such works fared well with a reading public that demanded narratives of the exotic and thrilling deeds of the Visigoths and the Moors, the women they fought over, and the acts of patriotism and religious fervor that filled the tales.

Robert Southey first took up the legend of the fall of Spain in a poem in 1802, but he ruminated on the richness of the subject for some time before returning to the theme in 1808, this time to tackle a lengthy poem about the king and issues of national identity. *Roderick, the Last of the Goths,* printed in 1814, was inspired by the War of Independence between Spain and France.[14] While working on the poem, Southey wrote to a fellow poet: "That which at present employs the little time I can afford for poetry, is upon the foundation of the Spanish Monarchy by Pelayo. It had long appeared to me a fine subject, and the deep interest which I take in Spanish affairs induced me at this time to select it because the circumstances sufficiently resemble those of the present contest to call forth the same feelings" (*New Letters,* 2: 14–15, cited in Saglia). Apparently, Southey first meant to call his work *Pelayo* but decided that King Rodrigo's tragedy was at the center of his interests and his work, even though he went on to exalt Pelayo's origins and character traits as man and king.

The poem opens with Rodrigo's flight from the battlefield, ending up in a monastery in which his penance, which we saw in Corral and in the ballad tradition, is transformed into heroic sanctity, and Rodrigo is ordained a priest. Returning to Córdoba in priestly garb, and unrecognized by Pelayo, the king advises him to accept the crown. Southey's portrait of Rodrigo shows a man whose fall from grace— from power and the throne—results in a dramatic demonstration of humility before the man who will be his successor. As an example of the tremendous religiosity of the work, the author has Pelayo and Florinda meet the disguised Rodrigo on the road to Asturias. Not recognizing King Rodrigo in priest's clothing, Florinda confesses to him that, while she did not consent to have sex with the king, she had allowed herself to fall in love with him—a married man—when he told her how he had married Egilona for reasons of state, and how unhappy he was. They pray together after he hears her confession.[15]

In the convoluted telling of the personal fortunes and misfortunes of the main characters, Southey embeds theories on national identity. For example, the poem offers a view of nineteenth-century Spain and Spaniards as an unbroken line of racial purity that predates the Goths themselves. For Southey, Pelayo's coronation righted a wrong in that he believed—or at least posited—that Pelayo had been both a Spaniard and a Goth, between which Southey greatly distinguished. Southey theorized that a pure race of Spaniards had existed prior to the kingdom of the Goths, from which Pelayo descended. Thus, as the link between the defeated Visigothic kingdom and a man of purer lineage than King Rodrigo, and certainly one of better personal qualities, Pelayo embodied the traits of his ancestors, "a better race, always praised and feared and respected by the Romans, loyal and faithful and true and reasonable" (xlv).[16]

Sir Walter Scott's *The Vision of Roderick* (1811) offers a tragic king and a shrewd Florinda, whose screams were pure design to hide her complicity in the sexual activity, indeed to disguise her role as seductress of the hapless king. Landor, also in 1811, wrote *Count Julian,* a five-act tragedy in which the sons of Witiza are the guilty conspirators with the Moors, rather than the falsely accused and long-suffering Julian. Decorum prevented the representation or even direct reference to the rape of La Cava, and an interesting innovation to the legend, shared by Landor and Southey, is the alleged sterility of the queen, Rodrigo's wife, Egilona, which justifies the king's attraction to La Cava, called in this play Covilla. Rodrigo repudiates his wife and offers to marry the now-dishonored Covilla, but Julian rejects the king's idea, enraged in a manner depicted as extremely noble. In battle, the count has the opportunity to kill the king but discovers that his wrath has dissolved, and he pardons him instead. Both men overcome their passions to behave heroically, in the context of the tragic hero of Romanticism.

English Romanticism influenced *Florinda,* the semi-epic poem in royal octaves by the duke of Rivas, Angel de Saavedra, which represents the most significant contribution to the legend by Spanish Romanticism. Saavedra composed partly in London—the first two cantos of five total are signed "London 1824"—during which time he came into contact with the English Romantic representations examined above. The third canto was composed in Malta (1826), and the work was published in Paris in 1834, along with Saavedra's reworking of the medieval legend of the seven princes, *Siete infantes de Lara,* called *El moro expósito* (The foundling Moor). The latter poem made the duke of Rivas famous. As we saw in chapter 2, the seven princes of Lara, one of the founding myths of Castile, employed the motif of the sexually available Muslim princess who goes to the prison to "comfort" the father of the slain princes, which resulted in the birth of the half-Castilian, half-Arab avenger of the murder of his seven half-brothers. In the climate of European and Spanish appreciation of the exoticism of Moorish Spain, the tale of the ethnically hybrid hero, who fits into neither community completely, found an approving audience.

Saavedra's Florinda lives in her own palace and entertains openly as Rodrigo's lover. A smoldering, disguised stranger casts a pall on the banquet, and the mask removed reveals Florinda's disapproving father, who is then thrown into prison by Rodrigo. A Gothic atmosphere of shadows, phantasms, prophecy, and the predictions of a Jewish necromancer shape and direct the poem far more than the characters do. Florinda never abandons her love for Rodrigo, and all three main characters behave heroically on some level, each accepting blame for the impending fall of Spain. The poem has not been well regarded by critics, although E. Allison Peers praises it for its nascent Romanticism, making it one of the earliest manifestations of that movement in Spain. As a contribution to the legend of Florinda and Rodrigo, it serves to foreground Florinda's consent in the sexual affair, but its lack of popular and critical success probably contributed very little to the public's awareness of the legend.

Many Spanish authors, in Spain and abroad, tried their hand at the legend of the fall of Spain, and just as many turned to the legends of the Middle Ages. While the proponents of nineteenth-century Spanish liberalism held no monopoly on Spain's medieval national history, they often took up Spain's myth of origins with vigor. For example, a Spanish liberal expatriate, Telesforo Trueba y Cosío, published *The Gothic King* in London in 1830 in a romanticized history of Spain that included the legend of Rachel, "the Fair Jewess," so called because her complexion did not exhibit "the olive hue of her race" (*Romance of History* 210).

The Search for Spanish National Identity in Medieval Spain

> Christianity gave its unity to Spain . . . Thanks to it, we have been
> a Nation, even a great Nation, and not a multitude of individuals.
> Concluding line to Marcelino Menéndez Pelayo's
> *History of Spanish Heterodoxy* (1880–1882)

Most Spanish elites preferred to equate "the idea of Spain" with other European countries, and not with a land and peoples whose customs and religion they had spent centuries trying to excise from their own national history. Nevertheless, nineteenth-century European Orientalism ironically helped to legitimize Spanish academics' own interest in investigating, recovering, and appreciating aspects of its Semitic past, even though the ultimate goal of a national, Christian, linear history did not seek to include medieval Jewish and Muslim Spaniards as their real ancestral countrymen.

In the late eighteenth century, Hebraists began to publish some linguistic studies of ancient and medieval Hebrew writings. The first chair in Judaic studies, specifically in Hebrew philology, founded in 1837, was held by Antonio María García Blanco, who inspired a number of intellectual disciples. From 1843 to 1881, the great scholar of Arabic Pascual Gayangos y Arce held a chair at the same institution. The first two books on the history of Spanish Jewry to be printed in Spain were Adolfo de Castro y Rossi's *Historia de los judíos* in 1847 and Jose Amador de los Ríos's 1848 *Estudios históricos, políticos y literarios sobre los judíos de España*. The liberal government, in power since the 1812 constitution of Cádiz, with its objective of educational reform, fostered Hebraic and Arabic studies, but that did not imply the existence of an open and newly tolerant society, for the 1812 constitution insisted on Catholicism as the religion of Spain. While Orientalism romanticized Spain's Moorish past, the rescue of Jewish culture remained, for the most part, the intellectual endeavor of the academy, within universities and Spain's royal academies, such as the Real Academia de la Historia (Royal Academy of History). Kamen documents the many inquisitional autos-da-fé against New Christians accused of Judaizing in the seventeenth and early eighteenth centuries, though there were relatively few after 1730, with the last occurring in Toledo in 1756, and the last prosecution of a case taking place in Córdoba in 1818 (*Spanish Inquisition* 283–304). Following the vote of the

Cortes of Cádiz in 1812, the monarchy abolished the Inquisition in 1813, again in 1814, and, for the last time, on July 15, 1834, just three years before the founding of the Hebrew chair at the University of Madrid. Anti-Semitism pervaded the culture, which continued its social obsession with lineage and purity of blood. Moreover, not every scholar who wrote about the Jews did so to castigate the treatment they had received: Amador de los Ríos, for example, the author of one of the mid-century histories of the Jews in Spain, opined that the Catholic monarchs had been justified in expelling the Jews.

The second half of the nineteenth century experienced an unprecedented explosion in scholarship, as happened in other European countries. Alvarez Junco considers the 1850 publication of the first of Modesto Lafuente's thirty-volume *History of Spain* to signal the start of this very creative period in scholarship, which was followed by at least a "dozen other national histories published until the end of the century" ("The Formation of Spanish Identity" 20). Lafuente's history became an important school textbook, and "as a result of the Romantic taste for historical painting, the images of the main historical feats were being created in the form in which they would be transmitted to the twentieth century; even today, most illustrations of history schoolbooks come from the period 1850–1880" (20). Important books on anthropology, science, educational reform, agricultural development, and history occupied scholars, particularly in the last two decades of the nineteenth century. Hundreds of editions of medieval texts accompanied vast histories of literature; German scholars in particular joined Spanish scholars in these endeavors. The extraordinary quantity of scholarly output of the Spaniards Marcelino Menéndez Pelayo, a champion of Catholic conservatism, and slightly later, Ramón Menéndez Pidal, would cause them to become synonymous with the creation of a Spanish literary canon that has dominated university curricula, including in the United States, until the last two decades of the twentieth century.[17] Often embedded, and sometimes overt, in these scholarly excursions was national soul searching for the essence of Spain and an answer to the question, "What is Spain?" which acquired urgent intensity after the loss of Spain's last colonies abroad in 1898. Marcelino Menéndez Pelayo's *Historia de los heterodoxos españoles* (History of Spanish heterodoxy), reprinted many times, gave weighty testimony to the belief in the nationalist narrative of a Spain that was Catholic from its very beginnings. During this time, El Cid emerged as the national hero of Spain, the thirteenth-century Riojan monk Gonzalo de Berceo became celebrated as the first true Spanish writer, and Cervantes' *Don Quixote* came to stand for everything that was right and wrong with Spain. The scientific scrutiny to which everything was submitted resulted, of course, in different judgments. Intellectuals shored up the cases of some historical figures, while debunking others. The Royal Academy of Spain awarded a prize to Ramón Menéndez Pidal for his 1893 study of *The Poem of the Cid*. Not everyone saw nineteenth-century medievalism as a positive advancement of Spanish interests. A short time later, Joaquín Costa, who had attributed what he called "the mischief of Spain" to the country's inattention to educational and agricultural reform, lamented that the tomb of El Cid would need seven locks on it or he would haunt Spain forever (cited in Giménez Caballero 2).

The scholars of the nineteenth and twentieth centuries pored over medieval and early modern historical documents, manuscripts, and books in their quest to understand and to clarify some puzzling, contradictory, or disputed facts about Spain's early history. One legend that came under scrutiny was that of little Christopher, the Holy Child of La Guardia. Interestingly, this will lead us to yet another invented, gendered story that places a woman at the center of it, the story of the Beautiful Woman of Seville, who allegedly betrayed her father to the Inquisition by telling her Christian lover about a converso plot against representatives of the Inquisition.

In 1889, American historian and enthusiastic Hispanophile Henry Charles Lea submitted to the English-speaking world for their judgment the fullest examination thus far undertaken of the Inquisition trial documents and subsequent historians' assessments of the legend of the Santo Niño, the Holy Child of La Guardia. As we saw in chapter 3, Torquemada and the Inquisition used this spectacular scandal—that a group of Jews and conversos had ritually murdered a small Christian boy in order to cut out his heart, mix it with a consecrated Host, and use the mixture to poison the town's water supply—to push the Catholic monarchs closer toward signing an Edict of Expulsion of the Jews. Lea's lengthy article contained his trademark scholarship, a thorough examination of primary sources and a balanced assessment of the evidence within, but his main goal was to showcase the work of a Spanish scholar, Father Fidel Fita. As Lea states admiringly, "This celebrated case, which has been embroidered with so many marvellous legendary details, can at length be studied with some approach to scientific accuracy, through the publication by Padre Fidel Fita, S.J., in 1887, of the records of the trial of one of the victims by the inquisition of Ávila."[18]

In Lea's study, what comes through heartbreakingly, in the words of the trial documents themselves, is the fear of the accused, who had been tortured and imprisoned for a year before their final confessions. The testimonies of the accused contradict each other left and right, and individual testimonies change over time, as the mental and physical torture impelled them to say anything that might bring them any measure of relief. Though the inquisitors attempted to reconcile the many discrepancies in testimony, they finally gave up:

On 16 Nov. 1491, they held a solemn *auto,* in which were read the sentences of condemnation, framed so as to excite the liveliest popular horror, and to bring into special prominence the proselytizing efforts of the Jews and the judaising propensities of the *conversos.* The victims were "relaxed" to the secular arm. At the *Brasero de la Dehesa*—which long remained as the inquisitorial *quemadero,* or burning-place—Juce Franco and his aged father were torn with hot pincers and burnt to death. The three deceased Jews were burnt in effigy. The *conversos* had a milder fate. By professing repentance and begging re-incorporation in the bosom of the church, they obtained the privilege of being strangled before burning. (243)

Lea lists the many records and hagiographies, from the first written account by Damián de Vegas in 1544, which Fita also prints in his own study, to one just five years before Lea's own article, all of which he believes overstate, if not outright fabricate, the case. Neither Lea nor Fita dismisses the possibility that the accused men (or a few of them) were guilty of something, perhaps even dabbling in sorcery. Nonetheless, following Fita, Lea firmly states: "In thus reviewing the evidence it is difficult to avoid the conclusion that the Santo Niño [Holy Child] was a mere creature of the imagination, begotten by torture and despair" (242). Moreover, he shares Fita's view that most certainly Torquemada and others exploited the "crime" for propagandistic reasons to advance the cause of expulsion.

Certainly, it is little surprise that one or two scholarly articles had no effect on popular beliefs about the Holy Child. Their work might have affected the opinion of Church authorities in Spain, which clearly it did not. What does surprise, however, is that Fita's and Lea's compelling scholarship failed to convince subsequent historians as late as the 1930s, as the vituperative polemic between William Walsh and Cecil Roth demonstrates.

William Walsh published his extremely popular biography *Isabella of Spain* in New York and London in 1930, and he repeats as fact the stories of Host desecration and ritual murder. He casts Isabel as a heroine—his breathless description of her at the conquest of Granada was cited in chapter 3 of this study—caught in a real-life quest of good versus evil, in which the saintly queen must do battle with the villainous conversos. Although he admits that no evidence exists that diabolical practices, such as child sacrifice, formed an official part of Judaism, he adds, "It does not follow, by any means, however, that Jewish individuals or groups never committed bloody and disgusting crimes, even crimes motivated by hatred of Christ and of the Catholic Church; and the historian, far from being obliged to make wholesale vindication of all Jews accused of murder, is free, and in fact bound, to consider each individual case upon its merits . . . One must admit that acts committed by Jews sometimes furnished the original provocation" (440). He follows this with a twenty-eight-page account of the Holy Child of La Guardia, dismissing the work of Fita and Lea, and accusing Lea of intellectual dishonesty for suggesting that unwarranted torture had impelled false confessions. Instead, according to Walsh, the torture responded to specific bad acts of the accused, and his conclusion, ultimately, is that evidence points to the historicity of the little Christian martyr.

The respected Jewish historian Cecil Roth answered Walsh in a 1932 article in the *Dublin Review,* in which he asserted that Walsh "reads Spanish history with the eyes of the wildest anti-Semite . . . and places the most complete credence in any anti-Jewish libel, however absurd, however far-fetched, and however discredited . . . Thus the work repeats, and may even do something to popularize, certain gruesome allegations, long discredited, which have never seriously been repeated in this country during the present generation" (219). Roth returns to the scholarship of Fita and Lea to counter the points Walsh made, and to signal where he believed Walsh deliberately ignored evidence that debunked the legend of the martyred child. His long-term concern, partly stated above, was that Walsh could bring renewed life to ugly and false allegations. In addition, Roth reminds the reader, "The whole question is not, even after all this lapse of time, a mere literary polemic. The cult of El Santo Niño de la Guardia is still alive in Spain. Monuments have been erected to his memory; miracles are said to have been worked by his means; a religious work has been published at least as recently as the second half of the last century describing his martyrdom and achievements; while the great Lope de Vega wrote a play on the subject, which is still read" (250).

The same issue of the *Dublin Review* includes Walsh's pull-no-punches response to Roth. Walsh marshals an impressive array of materials to counter Roth's charges, but his bottom line appears to be that he will not succumb to what he considers Roth's and the Jews' bullying tactics to force him into indefensible scholarship. Far from backing away from any of his statements in *Isabella of Spain,* Walsh adds that Roth and the late Lea share an unholy disregard for the truth, unfairly impugn the reputation and piety of Torquemada, and that Lea had ulterior motives in defending the Jews. In this last part, he seems to be alluding to the fact that Catholic authorities in the United States had criticized Lea for his attacks on the Church in his other writings on the Inquisition, and to be implying a collusion of sorts, in that Lea knew, corresponded with, and was praised by Jewish scholars and religious authorities for his treatment of the Jews in his scholarly works.[19] Walsh remained on slightly surer ground while defending his scholarly position, because even if one disagreed with his interpretation, he nonetheless based his statements about the medieval incidents on Biblical sources and medieval documents. The footing turns rocky when Walsh asks Roth why he should back away from his firm belief that the Jews commit detestable crimes:

> when I see evidence in the world around me that Jews do commit detestable crimes; when I see a Chicago judge convicting two young Jews, sons of two of the wealthiest Jews in the United States, of the fiendish and cold-blooded murder of a boy; and when I see a jury in the town of my birth convict a Jew of having his store burned by another Jew to collect insurance, and causing two little Christian boys, who lived over the store, to be burned to death in the night, I am not willing to admit, without a critical study of the facts, that, when a Christian judge or a Christian bishop in the Middle Ages condemned certain Jews to death, the judge or the bishop must always of necessity be guilty of barbarous injustice, and the Jews must be innocent.

What makes Walsh wrong about the guilt of the Jews in the Holy Child case is that the more convincing scholarship of Fita and Lea proves him wrong. That he saw the challenge to his scholarship as a Jewish conspiracy becomes all the more understandable, if shocking, when he openly examines the medieval events through a contemporary lens that relies on all the centuries-long stereotypical views of Jews: rich, driven by the desire to acquire money, merciless in their pursuit of it, and willing to sacrifice Christian boys, a detail that, in Walsh's telling of the incidents, becomes highly significant. After all, the death of any little boy in such an accident would be tragic; why inflame matters by insisting on the boy's Christianity?

The Catholic Church has never recognized as a saint the Holy Child of La Guardia, nor has it ever canonized any child allegedly martyred by Jews through ritual practices. Nevertheless, the Holy Child of La Guardia remains an important popular icon of slain innocence. In parts of Spain, the feast day is celebrated in September, and the town of La Guardia holds annual commemorative events in honor of the little child. In anticipation of the four hundredth anniversary of the publication of *Don Quixote* in 1605, the town carried out an entire month of events throughout September 2004 that celebrated both Cervantes and the Holy Child, culminating, at the end of the month, in a procession through the town in honor of the child.

Beginning in the middle of the nineteenth century, histories began to refer to a story about a converso conspiracy in Seville in the 1480s, which attempted to justify why the Inquisition had been a necessary institution for Church and Crown. In his voluminous *History of the Inquisition*, Lea recounts the story of Susanna, the "Beautiful Woman" (the Fermosa or Hermosa Fembra) of Seville, with no challenge whatsoever to the historicity of the tale and unquestioning fidelity to the slightly earlier sources (vol. 1, bk. 1: 162–64). One such source was Matute y Gaviria's 1849 *Relación histórica de la Judería de Sevilla* (Historical account of the Jewish Quarter in Seville). In 1480, Diego de Susán, a rich merchant, prominent converso, and leading citizen of Seville, galvanized other powerful members of the converso community to fight against the arrival of the Inquisition to Seville. He and other men of the threatened group decided on a plan of armed resistance. They began stockpiling weapons. At the first sign of trouble, as they saw it, the arrest of a converso, the men would carry out a massacre of the inquisitors and anyone who helped them. Diego had a daughter, Susanna, so lovely that the whole city called her the Beautiful Woman, Hermosa Fembra. She and a young Christian aristocrat were in love and carried on a secret affair. Susanna, weighing the risk to her beloved should a riot ensue, and deciding that true love trumped loyalty to her father, revealed the conspiracy to her lover, who ran to the magistrates. Soon, the inquisitors were in full possession of the details, including the names of all the converso conspirators. The first to be arrested was Susanna's father and his closest associates. The trials were prompt, as were the executions, in which six men and six women were burned at the stake on February 6, 1481. A second auto-da-fé occurred shortly after, in which Diego de Susán reportedly perished, though he died "a good Christian."

Citing Lea, Walsh tells the same story, apparently finding Lea a far more reliable source on the stories of wayward women than on stories of an unholy Inquisition. Here is how Walsh describes what befell Diego de Susán's daughter after her father's execution in 1481: "*La Hermosa fembra* found herself penniless, since her father's property had been confiscated. She was hated by Jews as a parricide; but the Bishop of Tiberias took an interest in her and obtained admission for her to a convent. Her voluptuous nature eventually led her out of the cloister to a life of shame. Age withered her marvellous beauty, and she died in poverty, requesting that her skull be placed over the door of the house in the Calle de Ataúd [fittingly, street of the coffin] where she had plied her trade, as an example to others and a punishment for her sins" (280). In this story, Susanna fits into no community whatsoever, is a slave to her passions, but appears to believe that she is dirty and evil, hence the self-awareness that her sorry life could serve as a negative example to others. The "example," as it were, need be no more delineated than to beware the fate of a fallen woman.

In accepting the story without challenge, Lea's usual sensitivity to stereotypes failed him completely in this case, though it does go to show how firmly certain stereotypes about fallen women continue to pervade Western culture: the fallen woman remains the quintessential outcast. Indeed, in addition to those legendary staples about women and sexuality, both Lea and Walsh would have recognized another perennial one, and a particular favorite of the nineteenth century, the re-formed prostitute. Susanna should have been a "heroine," by exposing the conspir-acy that threatened the start-up of the Inquisition in Seville. Yet, she is, first and foremost, both woman and converso. The age-old tendency to promote a woman's flaws through exaggerated sexuality and sexual transgressions comes together with Susanna's converso status, and her inability to commit to the convent demonstrates at once her inflamed sexuality and true status as a Jewess and not a true Christian converso.

Late twentieth-century scholarship points to more invention than simply Su-sanna's story. Modern studies support the historicity of Diego de Susán's execution but dispute the legend of converso conspiracy. Netanyahu asks, "How can one ex-plain the general credulity displayed by so many eminent historians toward the claims and accusations of the Spanish Inquisition?" (1146). As one example of such credulity, he examines this legend, the so-called Converso Conspiracy of Seville, concluding that authorities had feared that powerful men of the city might, through their opposition to the Inquisition itself, threaten the work and effectiveness of that newly created institution. According to Netanyahu, the Inquisition tried, convicted, and executed Diego de Susán and others for being Judaizers, not conspirators (1149–1154). He does not even mention the legendary daughter, apparently having rejected it, justifiably, as pure invention. Kamen adds, "The whole story about the plot and betrayal was in reality a myth: Susán had died before 1479, the plot is undocu-mented, and there was no daughter Susanna" (*Spanish Inquisition* 47); he does not comment on the invention of a gendered narrative.

The historians who discuss the conspiracy and Susanna all cite Andrés Bernáldez, the converso-hater and chronicler to the Catholic monarchs, who described the ar-rest and death of Diego de Susán some twenty years after the event, in the first decade of the sixteenth century. The implication in most modern histories is that the story of Susanna comes from him. But, in fact, there is nothing of the kind; Bernáldez mentions neither a conspiracy plot nor a daughter, though he does say that Diego de Susán was a prominent converso, one of the first to be executed by the Inquisition in Seville, and that most of the conversos who were executed were wealthy men whose property was confiscated by the state. While the legend of Su-sanna may have originated before the nineteenth century, the earliest account I found comes from the 1849 *Relación histórica de la Judería de Sevilla,* which subse-quent scholars, among them Lea, Walsh, and Kamen, all use as their reference for the story of Susanna.

It is clear that the story of Susanna developed long after the execution of Diego de Susán, and quite possibly centuries afterwards. Why invent a fallen woman story?

I suggest that the invention of the figure of Susanna, with the particular contours of her story, neatly encapsulates the fear of women and female sexuality, and it would not be the first time we have seen a fallen woman become central to the recounting of a historical event. The creation of Susanna is a particularly powerful commentary on the ability of a culture to shape misogynistic myths in the same way, over and over, out of very few elements, or even out of whole cloth, while scholars have rarely even questioned its veracity.

Pelayo, the Role of Women, and Contemporary Spain

> Here lies the holy King D. Pelayo, elected in the year 716, who in
> this miraculous Cave began the restoration of Spain. The moors
> vanquished, he died in the year 737, and his wife and sister join
> him here.
>
> Late eighteenth-century epitaph on Pelayo's sepulcher by the
> altar of the Most Holy Virgin in the Cave of Covadonga

In addition to being a frequent literary subject, Pelayo was painted many times in the nineteenth century. One of the most famous paintings, Pelayo leaning on a large cross of victory as he addresses his men, by Luis Madrazo y Kuntz, won first prize at the National Exposition in 1856. The "Spanish fever" within the Orientalism that gripped Europe spread to the United States as well, with the popularity of Washington Irving's *Legends of the Conquest* and *Tales of the Alhambra,* inspiring a number of novels about Pelayo, including Anna Cora Ogden Mowatt's 1836 *Pelayo or the Cavern of Covadonga,* W.G. Simms's 1838 *Pelayo: A Story of the Goth,* and Elizabeth T. Porter Beach's 1864 *Pelayo.*

At the same time that intellectuals and artists inside and outside Spain obsessed about Spain's national identity, the religious devout, especially rich Asturians in Spain and in Cuba, sought to connect with the past in a more concrete way, with money, through the renovation and restoration of the shrine at the Cave of Covadonga.[20] As Carolyn Boyd explains, Covadonga had served the Bourbon dynasty in the eighteenth century as a symbol of the national restoration they claimed to have promulgated, the Bourbons as new Pelayos ("Second Battle" 41).[21] A fire destroyed the shrine in 1777, and though wealthy Asturians began its restoration, it fell into disrepair until the late nineteenth century. Amidst the anguished years of national soul searching following the loss of Spain's last colonies in the Americas and the Philippines, renovations prepared the area around Covadonga in 1910 for the twelfth centenary of the 718 battle. However, Boyd tells us, Covadonga became a battleground in the early twentieth century between those who asserted its religious connection to a myth of continuity and those who saw its future as a secular symbol of a fresh start; it remained a contested ground for decades (56).

Francisco Franco indulged in overt gestures to link his government with symbols of early modern Imperial Spain, such as the adoption of the national coat of arms of the Catholic monarchs, with some modifications. The Hapsburg king Charles I, who became the Holy Roman Emperor Charles V, had added the imperial Pillars of Hercules to signify the empire that had gone well beyond the markers long symbolizing the end of the known, civilized, and navigable world. Franco maintained the pillars, but he replaced the fleur-de-lis in the center of the later Bourbon kings' herald with the Sacred Heart of Jesus. Returning to another symbol of the Catholic monarchs, he surrounded the entire crest with a giant eagle, known as the Eagle of St. John. As the animal associated with the evangelist John, the eagle in the crest stood for Spain's total identification with, and fidelity to, Catholicism; this was the shield of Spain from February 2, 1938, until 1981. Ferdinand's and Isabel's royal symbol, also in their herald, a band of arrows yoked together, was placed in the lower right corner of Spain's post–Civil War coat of arms. Like King Philip II, Franco developed a fanaticism for relics; he reputedly slept with the hand of St. Teresa of Avila, the saint most identified with the Franco regime.

However, Franco's shrewd exploitation of the myths and legends of early Spain depended on material much older than the time of the Catholic monarchs. Many names and places associated with the Spanish Civil War (1936–1939) take on new meaning when one understands their connection to Spain's founding myth. As we know, Américo Castro considered the civil war to be a religious one waged on the claim of the name "Spain" and "Spaniard." One need only consider the Spain of the 1930s and the associations made between that period and Pelayo, as historical and legendary figure; Covadonga, the cave in which Pelayo and his men planned to drive the Muslims back; and the province of Asturias, the cradle of Spain, to see how correct Castro was, and how inextricably linked such a view is from an awareness of what took place in eighth-century Spain.

Through the centuries, Asturians have maintained pride that their land had never been dominated by the Muslims after the fall of Spain in 711. When, in 1934, there was a revolt by Asturian miners, Franco's Nationalist forces moved north to crush it. At that point, the forces included the Moroccan Foreign Legion, which Franco deemed the "Hispano-Moroccan Brotherhood," a fraternity quickly forgotten when it came to his later policies and fanatical dedication to the National Catholic Right. To inspire a united call to arms against the encroaching army, the Asturians distributed leftist flyers that conflated the eighth-century enemy with the current one, announcing alarmingly, "Moors in Covadonga!"[22] A great irony, that the person who brought "the Moors" to Covadonga would cast himself as a "new Pelayo": "In Nationalist discourse, the Civil War was a 'Crusade' against 'those without God and without Patria,' and Franco was a new Pelayo, the leader of the 'Second Reconquest of Spain'" (Boyd, "Second Battle," 57). Franco's regime installed the oft-photographed statue of Pelayo holding the Cross of Victory, which is in a plaza in Oviedo near the cathedral.

A triumphant moment for the Franco regime occurred with the return of the image of the Virgin of Covadonga, which had disappeared from the shrine in the 1930s:

> The discovery of the lost image of the Virgin of Covadonga in the Spanish embassy in Paris provided the occasion to celebrate the recovery of the "true" Spain from the foreigners and "bad Spaniards" who had betrayed its essential values. On June 11, 1939, the image of the Virgin arrived at the border city of Irún, where it was received with maximum military honors and a massive popular reception presided over by the Bishop of Oviedo and Doña Carmen Polo de Franco, the Asturian-born wife of the dictator. From the frontier the image processed through urban and rural Asturias before being enthroned once again upon her altar in the Holy Cave. (Boyd, "Second Battle" 56–57)

But the link to Pelayo is even stronger than Boyd indicates. First of all, Pelayo not only initiated the Reconquest, but sixteenth-century historians had credited him with rescuing relics and other treasures from Toledo during the invasion of Spain and hiding them in Asturias, from which they disappeared, only to reappear centuries later in Flanders. Thus, as we saw in chapter 4, when Rome authorized the return to Spain of the remains of the martyr St. Leocadia, patron saint of Toledo, the country cheered Philip II as the "second Pelayo," who had saved the maiden from the Protestant "heretics" of the North, just as Pelayo had saved her from the "infidels" of North Africa. And, like St. Leocadia, whose return occasioned triumphant processions from Flanders into Toledo, and then all through the streets of Toledo for the faithful to witness, the Virgin of Covadonga processed from Paris to her mountain shrine. Franco not only brought the Virgin home, he did so as both a new Pelayo and a new Philip II.

Franco's particular brand of politics, which equated Spain with a National Catholic ideology, was known as "covadonguismo." He mandated the participation of adolescents and young adults in youth groups, and school curricula reflected the indivisible link between Church and state. Hearth and home, Church and state all functioned together, and every citizen had his or her contribution to make to the

Catholic nation. Teenage boys belonged to a mandatory group called "the Pelayos."[23] A weekly magazine, *Pelayos,* contributed to their formation and education as young Pelayos who would emulate the Christian warrior-king's tenacity, courage, endurance, bravery, and devotion to the Virgin.[24]

In Franco's Spain, the ancient dichotomy between bad women and good women proved to be neither ancient nor without potential for exploitation. Much has been written in recent years about the Sección Femenina, in which Franco encouraged girls to choose Queen Isabel and the Virgin Mary as role models. As Barbara Weissberger has shown convincingly in her analysis of Isabel in the Franco years, the general nourished a deep regard for the Catholic queen, while shamelessly exploiting her image as a model for the repression of Catholic girls and women, and as a propagandistic tool for various general political goals not specifically related to women.[25]

Drawing the parallel between woman and state, schoolbooks showed the peninsula as the crowned head of Queen Isabel (cited in Weissberger 191). Unlike the sixteenth-century renderings of Europe as a sovereign woman, whose head was Spain and whose crown the southernmost part of the peninsula, the Pyrenees served as the queen's crown. While school curricula, indissoluble from the teaching of the theory and practice of Catholicism, promoted the joys of following the model of "good women," and for boys, the need to venerate their mothers and later marry "good girls," other areas, such as public health campaigns, employed the model of the temptress, the "bad woman," to encourage sexual abstinence. Civil War posters provide striking examples of one such campaign, in which women clearly bear the burden of spreading disease, and men are portrayed as victims, lured into a sexual deathtrap. At the top of one poster is the warning, "Avoid venereal disease," and at the bottom, beneath the picture of the prostitute and soldier, "as dangerous as enemy bullets." Linguistically, since both enemy bullets and the adjective "dangerous" are feminine in Spanish, and the words begin on the poster almost as an extension of the woman's arm, the message hits the reader squarely that "WOMEN" are as dangerous as enemy bullets. Another poster evokes Eve and the fall. A naked woman with a snake around her waist faces a hapless soldier, whose arm raises up in defense against the head of the serpent, which lunges toward him, mouth open, ready to strike. In this case, the words read "a discharge [from military service] for venereal disease is desertion." Undoubtedly, the diseases generated by unregulated sexual behavior, especially between prostitutes and itinerant soldiers, and the loss of fighting men to disease, proved to be a real problem for the military. But my point is more culturally broad than that: the most potent images about sexual relations, even in the 1930s and beyond, cast women as Eves, luring men to their downfall.

The Founding Myth and the New Millennium

For close to thirteen centuries, historians, theologians, politicians, and the Spanish national imaginary in general accepted what Peter Linehan refers to as the "big bang hypothesis" (74) of the fall in 711, that the change from Christian kingdom to Muslim domination was instantaneous and dramatic, the almost overnight turning from a Christian kingdom to a Muslim caliphate that characterizes the national founding myth through the centuries. The date of the invasion—711—remains legendarily fixed, and the decisive Battle of Guadalete did take place on July 19, but historians now believe that the conquest of the peninsula occurred gradually, over the course of about three years, with city after city surrendering, and without noticeable change in the daily lives of the people. As the present study has shown, the legend of the fall of Spain, especially in its neo-Gothic aspirations, engendered issues of raging debate from the fifteenth century on, and especially in the late nineteenth and twentieth centuries, such as whether the Visigoths as a people ended in 711 along with the Visigothic kingdom or survived to continue their lineage unbroken in the early Asturian kingdoms to the present; what the character and nature were of "homo Hispanus"; whether God, in his wrath, had punished the people of Spain for their sins and the sins of their king; what role the Jews and Muslims played in the life of the peninsula; and to what extent they could be excluded from the evolving definition of "Spaniard."[26] But what do late twentieth-century and early twenty-first-century historians now believe to be historically true about the events of the fall of Spain in the eighth-century Iberian Peninsula? What is still regarded as historical and what is fiction?

First of all, the historicity of the various figures in the legend has been widely disputed. Roger Collins, whose views appear to be shared by most modern historians, dismisses as nonhistorical some contributions of the Arabic chronicles, including the rape of the daughter and the penetration of the enchanted edifice, which he calls fantastic elements. Tackling the issue of the historicity of Julian, he states, "Even the most romantic of historians have tended to pass by the rape story, but the existence of Julian himself and his role in abetting the Arab conquest have received an extraordinarily high level of credence" (*Arab Conquest* 36). The possibility of the historicity of Count Julian is something he cannot discount completely, though he finds wanting the arguments put forward by historians. The earliest Christian recountings of the Muslim invasion attribute divine punishment for the iniquity of the Visigothic kingdom as the reason for the Arab victory; there is no mention of Julian and an act of vengeance. Many modern historians argued, counterintuitively, that the details of Julian found in later chronicles reflected earlier sources now lost, rather than the more likely trajectory, supported by Collins, of added embellishment to the later works (35–36).[27]

On the dismissal of the rape story and the figure of the count's daughter, I would inject a note of caution, for I find the Arabic inclusion of the raped daughter very intriguing. While it is true that the earliest record of the invasion fails to mention any such event, that should not surprise us since that history, the *Crónica mozárabe de 754* (*Mozarabic Chronicle of 754*), ascribed the defeat of the Visigoths to the Decadence Tradition in general, and not to any single iniquitous deed. And even though the first Arabic chronicle to make mention of the violation of a woman occurs some distance in time from the event, there is something about the absence of fanciful detail in the account, something about the straightforward statement that an act of sexual dishonor had incited the broken bond between lord and vassal, that is compelling in its simplicity, to say nothing of the fact that such things do indeed happen in real life. As I look back on the centuries of material, it seems to me at least worth arguing that, if the Arab historians were to invent something out of whole cloth, they might have done a better job of it than the scant mention the violation receives. While the lack of embellishment suggests to me to keep in mind that part of every myth is true, and the difficulty lies in figuring out which parts, I am also aware that for me, Florinda La Cava became real through the tellings of her story, and quite simply, I may be loath to let her go.

Recent historians focused their research on what might have caused such a rapid disintegration of Rodrigo's kingdom, given that he ruled no more than three years. One of the most respected historians, Bernard F. Reilly, who wryly comments that because of the number of studies produced in the 1980s and 1990s by British historians, "the Visigoths have gone somewhat out of style these days except perhaps in England" (*Medieval Spains* 211), dismisses the likelihood that we will ever recover a full accounting. Nonetheless, he opines that the story is as full as it needs to be to address why Visigothic Spain fell in the early eighth century: historians already possess sufficient information about the military skirmishes and political infighting that pervaded the peninsula and about the constant turmoil and instability that marked the governance of various Visigothic kingdoms. As he puts it:

> The conquest of the Roman Empire in the west by the Germanic tribes two centuries earlier is a real conundrum in that a more primitive people conquered the more advanced one and it is precisely the condition of civilization that ordinarily confers an insuperable advantage in such contests. But at the beginning of the eighth century in Iberia two relatively backward peoples met and one of them was

vanquished. Unless one posits a much higher degree of sophistication for the Visigoths than the observable facts warrant, no greater crisis or decline need be descried than the one which had been gradually turning Roman society into a Germanic one for the past three centuries. (*Medieval Spains* 49)[28]

Through the centuries, declarations by writers who sought to reflect on Spanish national identity and its glorious origins, that this had been a sophisticated society, have skewed our perspectives on the period and the notion of a coherent, civilized, and perhaps even cultured court. Although we know relatively little about the reign of Rodrigo's immediate predecessor, Witiza, from 703 to 710, we do know that the time was "marked by famine and plague in the peninsula . . . [and] that the weight of the coinage declined sharply" (Reilly, *Medieval Spains* 49). We know that the ninth-century Asturian chronicles—the earliest Christian chronicles to craft a narrative of the quest to reverse Muslim domination that began historically with the hero Pelayo—tended to portray Witiza as corrupt, and his sons as even more so, part of attempts to rationalize and justify how a weakened Spain could have fallen to the Muslim army.

Historians remain unsure about the relationship of Witiza's father, King Egica, to Rodrigo's father, Teodofredo. The early accounts differ, some not mentioning the father or any connection at all, others claiming that Egica blinded him and then exiled him. Rodrigo's succession to the throne was not achieved amid the universal acclaim of all the powerful nobles and minor rulers, many of whom supported the succession of Witiza's son Agila, whom Witiza had named to follow him. No small part of the dispute derived from the disagreement among the Visigoths about whether a king should inherit the throne through familial links, be chosen by his predecessor, or be elected by the nobility. It remains unclear whether the nobility clashed over the choice between Agila and Rodrigo because of the men in question or to protest the process of accession to the throne:

A portion of the nobility . . . chose Rodrigo (710–711), who had probably been *dux* of Baetica, as their king. Agila managed to retain the loyalty of Septimania and the Tarracoensis but Rodrigo was recognized in the remainder of the kingdom despite the presence in Seville of Bishop Oppa, brother of Witiza. Both claimants were in fact dethroned by the Muslim invasion of the following year which toppled Rodrigo immediately and Agila somewhat later when they penetrated to the north . . . Even so the Muslims were unable to conquer the peninsula, less able than the Visigoths for that matter. The Basque country remained beyond their world. Asturias they penetrated but briefly. Galicia and northern Lusitania they occupied for perhaps forty years. The basin of the Duero they were to abandon almost as quickly. But for four centuries they were to hold its coasts and the river basins of the Guadalquivir, the Guadiana, the Tajo, and the Ebro. The Iberia that had always mattered was theirs. (Reilly, *Medieval Spains* 49–50)[29]

Not all contemporary historians agree with Reilly, of course, although for many, the disagreement is one of degree, not of kind. Those who would vigorously disagree are those Spanish historians and literary historians, even in the twentieth century, who have accepted the legend of Rodrigo, La Cava, and Julian as fact, as the driving principle of the Muslim invasion and Iberian defeat, and of the legend of Pelayo as the history of the start of Christian resistance and reconquest. Their own arguments were nuanced, often challenging one historical point or another, depending on what particular aspect of nation building, of the shaping of a Spanish national history based on the foundation myth, they were supporting, defending, or disputing. Even today one finds a remarkable level of belief in the historicity of Spain's founding myth, especially as it relates to matters of the throne, the relationship between Church and state, particularly when certain religious figures are celebrated for their connections to nationalism, and to the continuing popular belief that the areas of Asturias and Galicia constitute a more "pure strain" of Spaniard than any other region.

The politics of Restoration that has characterized the ongoing construction and revision of the founding myth continues to the present day, though the particular circumstances that inspired a grand nationalist historical narrative have changed from century to century, as has the definition of what it means to be a Spain "restored." It is fair to say that the current monarchy and government still struggle to find a balance between the opposing views of Covadonga as the site of a myth of exclusionary national origins, the continuation of a Christian kingdom, and as the symbolic site of a new beginning. Moreover, complicating the struggle, as Carolyn Boyd points out, many Spaniards remember "covadonguismo" as repressive cultural politics that they are happy to have moved beyond ("Second Battle" 59). Clearly, though, King Juan Carlos I and the government wish to rescue the national symbol from its negative association with the Franco years and reinterpret it for a democratic Spain. The national coat of arms adopted on December 19, 1981, returns to that of the Hapsburg-Bourbon dynasties, although the eagle of St. John has disappeared, as has the Sacred Heart of Jesus that Franco had added.

But in 2001, a commemorative year, the fiftieth anniversary of the establishment under national and royal patronage of the Marian shrine at Covadonga, the planning of festivities and events shone a spotlight on this problem of the blurred lines between Church and state, as Asturian politicians, crowding into the cave shrine

Commemorative stamps on the early history of Spain by political cartoonists José María Gallego and Julio Rey, released September 22, 2000.

and lobbying for political issues, literally and metaphorically elbowed Church officials aside during the royal visit there. That same year, the king authorized a new coat of arms for his son, the prince of Asturias, Crown Prince Philip, a modified version of the national coat of arms, with the addition of the collar of the Golden Fleece that hangs from the bottom of it, which had been part of the herald of the Catholic monarchs. In January 2004, Prince Philip visited Covadonga again, this time to celebrate his thirty-sixth birthday, accompanied by his then-fiancée Letizia, now his wife. Church and state blended once again when the couple attended a liturgical celebration in the Holy Cave, where they met with both Church representatives and local politicians, including the president of the Parliament of Asturias.

This renewed interest by the government in the history of the links between the Crown and Asturias has proved worrisome for many Spaniards and popular with others. The myth that the eighth-century Asturian mountains witnessed the birth of the Spanish monarchy cannot be easily divorced from the part of the legend that claims that also born at that time was the authentic Spaniard and the modern Christian nation. But this national dialogue, this awareness of the power of symbols and myths, is also sign of health and progress, and of a spirit of "convivencia," whose dream existed in the works of Américo Castro and other visionary thinkers, but whose reality seemed unimaginable even in the not-so-distant past. Democracy and humor represent but two indicators of Spain's continuing advancement in the modern world. Enjoying a career that would have been all but impossible in the Franco years, the highly regarded political cartoonists Gallego and Rey produced a series of drawings for the 2001 commemoration that brought to caricatured life all the figures of Spain's early history, and poked fun at some of Spain's most cherished beliefs about itself. José María Gallego and Julio Rey, who draw for *El Mundo,* hold honorary posts as professors of humor at the venerable University of Alcalá de Henares, birthplace of Cervantes. Their irreverent drawings satirize everything from Spain's demonization of the Arabs to Pelayo's stratagems to trick the Muslims, to the ultimate futility of Spain's former imperial dreams. A culture that can laugh at itself and its myths of origins can use that vision to see beyond the limitations imposed on it by its history, as Spain is now committed to doing.

Epilogue
Cultural Dialogues

I began with a story, so let me end with one.

A 1998 film from director José Luis Garci, *El abuelo* (*The Grandfather*), garnered numerous awards in Spain and was nominated for an Academy Award as Best Foreign Film. Based on a nineteenth-century novel by the realist writer Benito Pérez Galdós, *The Grandfather* explores a crisis in a single family, and in so doing, challenges the provincial investment in Spain as a pure, Christian society. The film refers to the founding myth of the fall of Spain directly, though fleetingly, and makes it relevant today. A proud, elderly aristocrat from northwestern Spain, living in South America, learns of his only son's death. Returning to Spain, where his son has left him a letter that reveals a family secret, he discovers that one of his two granddaughters is illegitimate, the product of his foreign-born daughter-in-law's affair with an artist, a man considered beneath them socially. This adds to the grandfather's suspicions about his daughter-in-law, Lucrecia Richmond, whose foreign nationality—her "otherness"—combines with the view of her as a fallen woman, an adulteress. But the revelation adds a catch to the shocking news: his son, hoping his father will love both girls, does not tell him which is the granddaughter who carries his "pure" blood and which one is "tainted." As we now know, northwestern Spain, Galicia, and Asturias, "the cradle of Spain," symbolize quality of lineage, which is defined as much, if not more, by Christian blood than by money and titles of nobility, because the latter can be acquired, while blood cannot. The grandfather, named Rodrigo, symbolizes the old world and old order: though almost penniless, he is driven by enormous pride in his bloodline.

When his daughter-in-law, fed up with the provincial town, plans to move to Madrid and take the girls with her, the grandfather pleads with her to leave his true granddaughter. She refuses to divulge the secret. Just before the departure, one of the girls, whose tender solicitude of her grandfather and love of her home make her a most sympathetic figure, insists upon staying with Rodrigo and her family's long-time servant, the intellectual, low-paid, but Old Christian tutor to the girls. The proud aristocrat finds love in unexpected ways, once love breaks through the barriers of prejudice based on his beliefs of superior blood and lineage. The odd little family—grandfather, elderly tutor as old as the grandfather, and young girl—begin a new life together. While the story reveals that the girl who stays behind is the illegitimate granddaughter, the fact is that this allegory of Spain and Spanish society writ large hopes that we, like the newly enlightened Rodrigo, will not care. Like Lily in Virginia Woolf's *To the Lighthouse,* who realizes at the end of the book that "love has a thousand shapes," so, too, Rodrigo realizes before it's too late that love and acceptance transcend blood, and that there are many ways to define a family and a society other than through blood and claims of lineage, a needed and timely lesson for Galdós's, and perhaps even Garci's, Spain.

At the end of the film, the little girl begins reciting from memory the names of all the Visigothic kings of Spain, delighting her elders, who congratulate each other on the intelligence of "their" daughter. The name of Rodrigo, the last Visigothic king, whose reign signaled the end of an epoch for Spain, and who, not coincidentally, shares the name with her grandfather, hangs in the air as the camera pans over the exquisite landscape of verdant hills and proud, rocky mountains, at once lush and forbidding. The elderly pair start over with mutual understanding and hope for the future, as the aristocrat and the tutor plan, almost giddily, to share in the life of the young girl who so needs them. And so, too, Spanish society today exhibits pride in its Christian, Muslim, and Jewish cultural heritage and embraces the racial and ethnic mix of its people, although not without some sociocultural tensions.

In 1998, the German Historical Museum mounted an exhibition entitled Myths of Nations, to which many European countries contributed paintings that best exemplified their collective sense of national identity. Spain submitted four paintings, all nineteenth-century compositions of significant historical moments. One painting depicts the second-century, fourteen-year siege by the Romans of the Celtiberian city of Numantia, near the present-day Soria in Castile-León. When the Romans held their ring of ramparts around the city, the Numantians chose collective suicide rather than life under Roman rule. Through the centuries, Spaniards celebrated their "ancestors" for their noble pride and love of freedom, traits they believed the Numantians passed on to them. Another painting, the *Second of May, 1808,* when Napoleon crushed a rebel group that refused to leave Madrid after the Spanish king had been forced to abdicate, again celebrates the bravery and heroism of the Spanish, and their unwavering commitment to freedom. The other two paintings relate to Spain's founding myth: *Don Pelayo and the Battle of Covadonga* and *The Surrender of Granada, 1492.* The Covadonga painting was Madrazo y Kuntz's prize-winning canvas from the National Exposition of 1856. Unlike the first two examples, which portray moral victory in a time of military defeat, these two paintings depict the military victory of Spanish Christianity over Islam. What frames the founding myth is not fall and redemption, but promise and fulfillment, Covadonga as the seed of Spain, the surrender of Granada as completion of the re-Christianization of the peninsular kingdom.

The prologue to *The Eve of Spain* suggested why the legends of the past matter today. We care about what was written and believed in the earlier centuries because people in the nineteenth and twentieth centuries cared about what had been written, believing as they did, that those earlier centuries were formative for modern Spanish national identity and the origins of the nation. We care about the earlier centuries because people today still experience the sentiments, beliefs, and consequences of actions taken long ago. The Myth of Nations exhibit in Germany is not a nostalgic reminder of no-longer-held beliefs of the origins of European countries and their people; rather, it reminds us that many of those beliefs are still held today. More importantly, the exhibition reminds us how fervently communities created— and are still creating today—stories of collective identity designed to foster a sense of unity, and that in so doing, they also create stories of who will be left out—or shut out—of that collective identity.

At the end of the last chapter, I mentioned a new kind of coexistence in Spain in the way that Spain recognizes itself as a multicultural society. Signs of this abound in politics and culture, though many challenges remain.[1]

Artistic production recovers and, in brilliantly evocative and imaginative rememberings, reconstructs Spain's past to offer lessons for our present. Historical novels in the 1980s and 1990s invited the lost voices of women and minorities to speak, and audiences responded enthusiastically. The contemporary novelist, essayist, and literary critic Juan Goytisolo has often examined the intersection of Christian and Muslim cultures in Spain, the fragments and remnants of Muslim culture, and the suppression and oppression of Spanish Islam. In the name of forging a national identity of the Spanish people and creatively defining—through erasure of difference and a defining of what Spain is not—an "essence of Spain," Goytisolo challenges his country to confront its deep-seated anti-Islamic beliefs and sentiments. In other beautiful works, Antonio Gala novelized Boabdil, the last ruler of Granada, and Antonio Muñóz Molina painted a haunting verbal canvas of Jews and Spain, entitled *Sefarad*. Novels by Ángeles de Irisarri and Magdalena Lasala, for example, explore the world of medieval women, including, in their joint novel *Moras y cristianas* (Muslim and Christian women), daily life and the things—besides religion—that bring us together and separate us.[2]

In some creative changes to longstanding cultural activities, many towns have redesigned their annual festivals of Moors and Christians, the reenactments of medieval and early modern battles between Muslims and Christians. Some towns decided that the foregone conclusion to the battle—the Christians always defeat the Muslims—did not need constant reinforcement, no longer represented Spanish society, and alienated rather than united a contemporary, multicultural Spain. Redesigned, the festival becomes a way of celebrating cultural aspects of their shared heritage. Some towns and cities retain the original structure of the festivals, which provokes another area of lively debate among the citizens.

I mentioned the Prince of Asturias Award in the prologue, and the speech by one of the 2002 winners, Edward Said.[3] Said praised what he calls Spain's successful negotiation of its pluralist society: "what was once suppressed or denied in Spain's long history has received its due, thanks to the recreative efforts of heroic figures such as Américo Castro and Juan Goytisolo." Pioneers they were, but they are far from alone today in the quest for a dialogue of cultures and peoples, within Spain and with the world. I can think of no better symbol of this than the Prince of Asturias Award itself, which is given in arts, letters, communications and humanities, concord, sports, technology and scientific research, and international cooperation. Originally established as a way to link the idea of Asturias with a new beginning, as Asturias had represented in the eighth century, but frequently given to Spaniards in the early years of the award, the Prince of Asturias Foundation has grown in stature and scope, by finding excellence and achievement, champions of compassion and innovation, in every corner of the world. Indeed, Spain is a model for the world in other ways. In a country whose national history reflected so much religious intolerance, the majority of the citizens now embrace tolerance and human rights in admirable, forward-thinking ways. And yet, Spain faces complex challenges, as we saw in the prologue to this book. Spain struggles with problems of the twenty-first-century globalized world, such as migration, specifically in the form of immigration from North Africa, and the impact of this immigration on the rest of Europe. On another front, current realities in Spain make a rather startling connection with the fifteenth century, when Ferdinand and Isabel set about trying to invent and establish a Spanish national identity that would override regionalist identities. The concept of Spain and a single nationalist identity fragments and splinters as the people increasingly recognize the cultural-political regionalist struggles of multiple Iberian identities, with regionalist politics, languages, and cultures. The country as a whole is confronting their lingering historical prejudices and the new challenges that put Spain in the forefront of some of the most pressing geopolitical issues of today.

Chapter One · *Setting the Stage*

1. In *The Virgin and the Bride,* Kate Cooper discusses the commonly held view that the sexual enslavement of rulers and leaders did not bode well for the public good: "[Plutarch's] treatment of Antony's politically disastrous attachment to the Ptolemaic queen of Egypt, Cleopatra VII, is a case study in the addiction by which a man subverts his political and military obligations, succumbing to the whims of the woman by whom he is bewitched. Antony's intemperate and self-destructive behavior is shown to have had repercussions not only for his public standing but for the Roman state itself" (9).

2. The reputation of a culpable La Cava lives on. The program for the musical version that opened in London on May 22, 2000—*La Cava*—informs us, "legend has it that the fair Florinda's actions at King Rodrigo's court were the direct cause of the invasions of Spain and the overthrow of the Spanish Empire by the Moors in 711." In this contemporary, and largely ahistorical version, Florinda falsely accuses Rodrigo of rape, thereby solidifying her reputation as a Potiphar's wife, a treacherous Delilah, a seductive and politically minded Cleopatra, a femme fatale Helen of Troy, while exonerating Rodrigo, the politically overwhelmed but morally upright ruler.

3. For more on this topic, see chapter 5. In addition, for a fascinating discussion of how Morisco historians attempted to inscribe their history and culture into the dominant Christian one of Spain, see Barbara Fuchs, *Mimesis and Empire,* especially chapter 4, "Virtual Spaniards."

4. Chapter 6 will examine more fully the robust nature of Spain's search for origins in the nineteenth and twentieth centuries.

5. Students of various genres of Hispano-medieval literature have come to realize, over the last thirty years or so, how exclusionary the Menéndez Pidal canon truly was. In the last quarter of the twentieth century, the Hispano-medieval canon greatly expanded, and many formerly neglected texts and authors are receiving their due. Nevertheless, the effects of the early and strict canon are still being felt, and scholars continue to lament the power Menéndez Pidal wielded in the formation of the canon. See, for example, Catherine Brown, "The Relics of Menéndez Pidal."

6. An exhaustive study by Peter Linehan of the earliest history of Spain recounts the ways in which contemporary historians debated, interpreted, and reinvented those early centuries.

History and the Historians of Medieval Spain provides a fascinating account of how the Visigothic kingdom and the reigns of the earliest Leonese-Castilian kings of Spain provoked some of the most vigorous, and even bitter and virulent, debates among nineteenth- and twentieth-century historians about the origins of Spain and Spaniards, and what those writers believed was at stake in winning their arguments. Disarray and disagreement confused the debates, and much history was simply unverifiable, but that did nothing to diminish the intensity of the arguments, which continue to affect Spanish history even today.

7. In addition to drawing on speeches and writings of the Spanish Civil War, Goytisolo cites a later example of anti-Islamic sentiment—offered by European Orientalist Raymond Charles in his 1960 work, *L'Evolution de l'Islam*—to demonstrate the pervasive and prevailing view of historians who accepted the belief that Muslims exhibited violence and uncontrollable lust: "For almost eight centuries, Spain served as an outlet for the destructive rage, the thirst for blood and the lasciviousness of its Islamic invaders—for its *Schadenfreude,* a product of a physiological necessity based on sexual anxiety—and the spasmodic convulsions, the sensual frenzy that at times have an enervating effect, and at others stimulate the modulated laments and paroxysmal invocations of Flamenco, express, even more directly than Goya, the age-old embrace of the Moor, in which tirelessly rekindled lust excludes any and every intervention of the spirit" (228).

Confirming, if nothing else, that the "sexual anxiety" is in the eye of the beholder rather than an ethnic or racial fact of being, Charles and Goytisolo also chronicle without comment the shift from the lusty King Rodrigo's own sexual scandal—and any discussion of the hatred heaped on the woman of the legend—to the obsessive focus on the invaders themselves. Consequently, the "collective anti-Moorish discourse," as Goytisolo names it, may have gone unchallenged until his own novels began to question long-held cultural assumptions, but until the present study, so had the antifeminist discourse of the founding myths, especially the one that casts La Cava as the national harlot, the Eve of Spain, purported cause of the loss of the peninsular earthly paradise.

8. Shahrazad is translated variously as city person, city dweller, and city freer, or savior of the city.

9. For an analysis of Shahrazad's clever regulation of the king's sexual desire through her control of his desire for narrative, see Fedwa Malti-Douglas, *Woman's Body, Woman's Word.*

10. Augustine's grave concern about, and frustration over, his own inability to prevent involuntary erections and nocturnal emissions appears in the *Confessions* and is but one of many examples of his ongoing—and unwinnable—struggle to control all aspects of his own body (bk. 10, chap. 30).

11. The tales in this collection range from three or four lines to several pages and derive from classical stories, folktales, hagiography, and history. Some critics believe the collection to be a supply of sermon topics, although John Keller and others argue that the tales of adulterous wives and gullible husbands were not suited to the pulpit, but rather were intended for the edification and pleasure or entertainment of lay and clerical readers or hearers (Sánchez de Vercial 4–5).

12. For a penetrating analysis of how national histories use the stories of their past for contemporary purposes, see Gabrielle Spiegel, *Romancing the Past,* whose book studies the relationship of French medieval chronicles to the earlier history of France.

13. Krappe's work is impressive for the many examples he cites of such legendary falls of nations and cities; nevertheless, his conclusion, that the presence of the legend in Spain is the result of Germanic Christian influences and not Arabic chronicles, is incorrect. Krappe, along with Menéndez Pidal and others, felt a strong need to justify the development of the legend of La Cava and the king in Spain as coming from other Christian precedents and not from Muslim historians. Such is the powerful draw of founding myths, that many historians went to great lengths to establish a long historical trajectory of Christian predecessors so as not to, in their opinion, de-legitimize or de-Christianize one of Spain's most enduring foundational legends.

14. Sometimes even continents can be virgins or kept women. Ramírez's nineteenth-century speech still astonishes for its breathtaking sexism, as in the following description of pre-Columbian Mexico as a virgin of the Americas that God, the harem keeper, attempted to hide from his other concubines, Asia, Africa, and Europe, but left impregnated: "niegue siquiera la historia que el cielo estrechó entre sus brazos un día a la virgen América, y la dejó fecundizada, alejando sus amores para ocultarlos del harem donde prodigaba sus caricias al Asia, al Africa y a la Europa, y declárense razas expósitas todas las que poblaron en los primeros tiempos el Nuevo Mundo" (Deny even the history that one day Heaven clasped the virgin America in his arms, and left her pregnant, hiding his love from the harem in which he caressed Asia, Africa and Europa, and declare the early races who populated the New World in her early years abandoned races).

15. Although studies abound on the topic, one of the earliest and most informative introductions remains Katharine M. Rogers, *The Troublesome Helpmate.*

16. Some Western queens are portrayed as peacekeepers and appropriate interventionists in their nations' politics, and these are usually consorts of a king, rather than rulers in their own right. See Strohm (*Hochon's Arrow*) and Blamires (*The Case for Women*). Slightly different cases are Isabel I of Castile and Elizabeth I of England, the former because she was both wife to a king and a queen in her own right. Isabel is sometimes portrayed as the peacekeeper and interventionist in her husband's political dealings and sometimes as an activist. Elizabeth I was, of course, queen and ruler of a powerful nation. As activists, both were successful in large measure because of the public's perception of their goodness and chastity, and in the case of Elizabeth, her own public declaration of virginity. But the Christian male master narrative favored the retellings of the inverse of the chaste woman, the female destroyer of the nation, because the ongoing eroticization of political language, the prevailing power structure, and the misogyny that flourished in Western cultures reinforced reliance on that narrative.

17. For excellent studies on the pivotal role women played in the early Christian Church, as well as what could be called the power of virginity, see works by Elm, Salisbury, and McNamara. Also, for an excellent biography of Elizabeth I, see David Starkey, *Elizabeth.*

18. The versions often overlap and intertwine, and much confusion results from attempts to sort them out logically. Moreover, so many manuscripts are lost that it is impossible to determine with certitude what medieval chroniclers may have known, which is no longer extant, and therefore which versions influenced others. For example, while we have manuscripts that purport to recount the work of a historian in the tenth century, these manuscripts date from the late fifteenth century, and it is not possible to ascertain what really came from the tenth century and what were later additions.

19. Many civilizations choose to remember defeat and destruction as resulting from the moral turpitude of their rulers, decadence that pervades the entire society, or a plague or other natural disaster sent by a wrathful God to punish iniquity. Boniface's characterization of the Muslim victory as a result of "the harlotry of Spain" is perfectly in keeping with tradition. Nevertheless, the British historian Roger Collins (*The Arab Conquest of Spain, 710–797*) views as curious the insistence on the violent overthrow of the Visigothic political order and its connection to the notion of underlying moral causes for the defeat of kingdoms. Although beliefs in other societies' decline for reasons of moral lack have been roundly scotched by historians, the fall of the Visigothic kingdom to the Arab invasion has been particularly vulnerable to a moralizing perspective. Collins takes the view that Spanish historians have been understandably caught up in trying to explain later events through an understanding of its earliest history, leading to questions of national identity, but that non-Spanish historians should have had no vested interest in perpetuating fictions about the history. Collins finds the dominance of the Decadence Tradition among non-Spanish historians something of a mystery, which he says can be traced back at least to "an English Presbyterian minister, the Reverend Dykes Shaw, who in 1910 was among the earliest of the proponents of the decadence explanation for the fall of Visigothic Spain" (6–7). See also Kenneth Baxter Wolf's chapter "An Asturian Chronicler," 46–60. The full chronicle can be found in *Crónica mozárabe de 754*, ed. José Eduardo López Pereira.

20. The *Crónica mozárabe de 754* was little known and even less appreciated until Roger Collins called attention to it in 1989, despite López Pereira's 1980 edition of it. After vigorous debate by historians, it is now accepted as a work of Spanish origin, whose date of composition is soon after the last events recounted in 754: "It is thus the only detailed peninsula witness of the Christian origin to the Arab conquest and its aftermath. Moreover, as has been suggested, it considerably predates not only the earliest surviving Arab accounts, but also many of the traditions upon which the latter were to be built up" (Collins, *Arab Conquest* 27). The consequences of ignoring this chronicle have made for dubious history in the foundational myths of Spain but great storytelling, with significant political impact.

21. *Medieval Iberia*, ed. Olivia Remie Constable, selection from *Mozarabic Chronicle*, trans. Kenneth Baxter Wolf, 30. Both Wolf (*Conquerors* 40) and Collins (*Arab Conquest* 61–63) discuss the importance of the author's reticence to delineate "the recent conquerors of the peninsula, who differed from him in both race and religion" (61). Collins points out that the three groups mentioned—Mauri, Arabes, and Sarraceni—held little difference for, say, Isidore of Seville, whose own seventh-century writings were a major source for the *Crónica mozárabe de 754*, but that the differences between the Berbers (Mauri) and Yemeni Arabs (Arabes), and Sarraceni (Syrian Arabs and those of the north of the Arabian peninsula) should have held considerable significance in the first half of the eighth century, when the *Crónica mozárabe de 754* was composed (62). Nor does the chronicler refer to the religion of the conquerors: the above names are religiously neutral—not heretics, infidels, and pagans, as is so often found in later medieval writings—and refer instead to ethnicity. While Collins ascribes these omissions to such assumptions as the audience's obvious awareness of such differences and the relative unimportance of spelling it out, or of the author's own fear of the consequences of reviling the Prophet (by the ninth century a capital offense, although probably an earlier prohibition, beginning with the time of Muslim domination), it seems to me more in

keeping with the Christian chronicler's desire to focus on the iniquity of the Visigoths and God's justifiable punishment of them, while disavowing that God allowed any special privilege to, or recognition of, Islam.

22. From the thirteenth century on, the legend names the Bishop of Toledo Oppa or Oppas. In the *Crónica mozárabe de 754*, the treacherous Oppas is not an ecclesiastic at all but a son of King Egica, and the faithless Bishop of Toledo is called Sindered. Wolf, in his book *Conquerors and Chroniclers of Early Medieval Spain*, translates the anonymous Christian author's withering assessment of Sindered: "A short time after the invasion of the Arabs, [Bishop Sindered] lost his nerve and, like a hireling rather than a shepherd, and contrary to the precepts of the ancients, he deserted Christ's flock and headed for his Roman homeland" (131). Muza ibn Nusayr was the Muslim governor of the Maghreb (modern Tunisia, Algeria, and Morocco), and Count Julian appears to have become his vassal at some point after 700 C.E. Muza named the Berber chieftain, Tariq ibn Zayad, governor of Tangier, and Tariq (Tarik and sometimes Tarif) conducted the raiding parties and reconnaissance tours that convinced Muza a successful invasion was possible. According to Derek Lomax (10–16) and other historians, it was Tarik who carried out the invasion, arriving in the capital city of Toledo in October 711, only to find that the archbishop and most of the inhabitants had fled. Muza, meanwhile, landed at Algeciras in the fall of 712 and proceeded to conquer most of the south, including "the great city of Seville, which he entrusted to a garrison of the city's Jews; for those Jews who had survived Visigothic persecution welcomed the Muslims as liberators and offered them help" (Lomax 13).

23. From the translation by Kenneth Baxter Wolf. This chronicle followed the model of the encyclopedic chronicles of Eusebius and Jerome in the fourth century, and then of John of Biclaro and Isidore of Seville in the seventh century. For a discussion of these earlier chronicles, see Wolf, *Conquerors and Chroniclers of Early Medieval Spain*, and the works of Roger Collins and Derek Lomax.

24. While there are many discussions of various Arabic sources and chronicles of the early history of the peninsula in the modern histories by Derek Lomax, Bernard Reilly, Roger Collins, Thomas Glick, and others, they are also examined by Menéndez Pidal in his two works on Rodrigo, *El rey Rodrigo en la literatura* (King Rodrigo in literature) and the three-volume *Floresta de leyendas heróicas españolas: Rodrigo, el último godo* (Collection of heroic Spanish legends: Rodrigo the last Goth). Other important references are Sánchez Albornoz's article, "San Isidoro, 'Rasis' y la Pseudo-Isidoriana," and a book by Julia Hernández Juberías, *La península imaginaria* (The imaginary peninsula). In terms of our legend, while most contemporary historians find both episodes, the story of Julian's daughter and the penetration of the enchanted edifice, to be purely fictional, Menéndez Pidal was inclined to believe in the historical veracity of the rape, but not in that of the enchanted edifice. In discussing the *Ajbar Machmua,* an anonymous Arabic compilation of the eleventh century, Menéndez Pidal notes that the overall lack of fantastic and marvelous elements makes him believe that the chronicle is aiming for historicity. If we accept this, he points out, we should take seriously that the *Ajbar Machmua* includes references to Count Julian's entrusting of his daughter to the court in Toledo, and Rodrigo's rape of her, but does not make any reference to the House of Hercules episode, or any such fortified edifice penetrated by Rodrigo.

25. The earliest extant manuscripts of Ibn 'Abd al-Hakam's history are later than the ninth

century, but Lomax and other historians believe that the later manuscripts correctly reflect the content of the now-lost earlier history. Even if they are wrong and the later manuscripts have somehow included material that derived from a different source, this does not diminish the two arguments that are important for my study, that the material about La Cava is not in the manuscript testimony that is closest to the historical events (as we saw from the lack of reference to her in *Crónica mozárabe de 754*) and that the legendary material that relates to La Cava and to the episode of the enchanted edifice come from Arabic, not Christian, sources.

26. The richly designed and jewel-encrusted Table of Solomon became a legendarily sought-after object, even appearing in the *Thousand and One Nights,* among many other tales. For a discussion of the sources and diffusion of the legend, see Julia Hernández Juberías, *La península imaginaria.* Much of the remaining portion of Ibn 'Abd al-Hakam's account of the conquest of Spain focuses on the recovery of the table and Tarik's triumphant return to his homeland with the treasure.

27. Sixteenth-century Muslim historiographers latched onto this detail about the daughter's marriage to a Muslim prince, instead of the widow of Rodrigo, because they tried to argue that the former could be the legitimate heir to the throne, which a widow would not have been. By extension, they could argue that the Muslims had a legitimate connection to the throne ever since the eighth century. The intention was not to convince anyone that a Muslim merited the throne of Castile in the sixteenth century. Rather, they hoped to establish both a history of convivencia and to recall the figure of Abd al-Aziz as a fervent and true Christian convert, in the hopes that these memories would stave off what they feared was imminent, an edict of expulsion from Spain, as the Jews had suffered several decades earlier.

28. This English translation is by David A. Cohen, in Constable, based on the Arabic edition of Charles C. Torrey of Ibn 'Abd al-Hakam's *Futūh Misr'.*

29. Linehan, however, disputes that the *Crónica de Alfonso III* can be considered a continuation of Isidore since there is a gap of several decades between the years at the end of Isidore's chronicle and where the ninth-century chronicle takes up its story: "It is far from being the case, as has been alleged, that the *Crónica de Alfonso III* is a 'continuation' of Isidore of Seville's *Historia Gothorum* [*History of the Goths*]. Isidore's narrative had ended in 625–6. Yet it is neither there nor at Catholic Spain's baptism in 589 that the Chronicle begins, but with the exaltation of Toledo on the occasion of Wamba's anointing in 672" (95). For Linehan's full discussion of the manuscripts of the *Crónica de Alfonso III* and its relation to the story of the fall in 711, see especially 76–82.

30. The chronicle exists in two manuscripts that do not always agree with each other, known as the Roda and Oviedo versions. Historians believe that the Roda text is earlier and therefore more accurate; the manuscript dates from the reign of one of Alfonso III's sons, Ordoño (914–924), but historians believe it was likely written in the early 880s, and definitely during the reign of Alfonso III (866–910). Another chronicle from this time, but less important than the *Crónica de Alfonso III, Crónica de Albelda,* also promotes the theory of Asturias as the legitimate inheritor of the Visigothic kingdom.

31. For this part, I rely on historian Kenneth Baxter Wolf's translation and study of the *Crónica de Alfonso III* in *Conquerors and Chroniclers of Early Medieval Spain.*

32. Throughout the centuries, there exists a confusion between the names Muza and Munuza. Muza was the second-in-command to Tarik. Munuza was reputed to be the Arab

ruler of the area in Asturias near Covadonga. Some fictions and chronicles say that Muza abducted Pelayo's sister, but most make a distinction between the initial invader of Spain, Muza, and the Arab who fought against Pelayo some years later, Munuza.

33. In this chronicle, Pelayo's abducted sister is unnamed; in later histories and literary works, Ermesinda or Ormesinda is often the name of the sister, but this is not a consistent feature.

34. For more specific information on Rasis and why even modern critics tend to think they are citing Rasis, when they cannot be doing so, see chapter 5.

35. The argument is that Ibn al-Kittaya had family reasons for avoiding any criticism of Witiza's reign. A brief selection from the work of Ibn al-Kittaya, who died in Córdoba around 977 C.E., appears in Menéndez Pidal's *Reliquias de la poesía épica española* (relics of Spanish poetry). This history, written in Arabic and translated into Castilian by J. Ribera and included in *Reliquias,* offers evidence that the story of the edifice, the prohibition against entering it, and the rape of the daughter of the count appear early in the Arabic accounts of the fall of the Visigoths. Ibn al-Kittaya shows the penetration of the house to be linked to the purported assertion that Rodrigo illegitimately usurped the Gothic crown, "hecho que el pueblo cristiano no aprobó" (a deed the Christian people did not approve of). Inside the house, Rodrigo found the ark and the inscription within, predicting the invasion and domination of Spain by figures resembling those painted on the materials contained within the ark (*Reliquias* 10).

36. When he goes to the court to take his daughter back home, feigning to the king that her mother was ill and missed her company, the king, in passing the time in conversation with Julian, asks him if he has any birds of prey. Julian affirms that he does, saying he will bring them back to Rodrigo, God willing. And, the narrators tell us, Julian thought that these birds of prey were the Moors that would soon be unleashed upon the kingdom. Once again, the king is completely unaware that he has failed to read a sign or warning correctly.

Chapter Two · Granada Is the Bride

Epigraph: The quotations from Alfonso the Learned and 'Abd Allah are cited in O'Callaghan (5, 9); translation O'Callaghan.

1. No one places any credence in this legend today. However, for centuries the legend circulated in tandem with one that claimed his father and mother both came from Norman aristocracy. Hence, the "à" that often accompanied his name, as in Thomas à Becket. More recently, historians believe that Becket came from humble family origins on both sides of his family. What remains unchallenged is the belief that his mother encouraged Thomas's devotion to the Virgin Mary.

2. This version of the young Charlemagne legend comes from a fourteenth-century manuscript of Alfonso the Learned's *Estoria de España,* the only known copy that contains the trilogy of *Flores and Blancaflor; Berta, the Mother of Charlemagne;* and *Mainete* (the manuscript is in Madrid's Biblioteca Nacional, 7583 [olim T-233], and is one of the main subjects of my book *Floire and Blancheflor and the European Romance*). Popular contemporary collections still relate the story of Galiana and Charlemagne. See, for example, A. Santos Vaquero and E. Vaquero Fernández-Prieto, *Fantasía y realidad de Toledo,* 2002, and L. Moreno Nieto, *Leyen-*

das de Toledo, 1999. Other continental versions of "Charlemagne's first wife" explain that he constructed a palace in her honor in Burgundy, which became known as Galiana's palaces.

3. See Stith Thompson, *Motif-Index of Folk-Literature,* in which the ogre's daughter (6532), helps the hero against her father. The motif appears in a Spanish epic, the story of Garcí Fernández, a count of Castile. Garcí Fernández journeys to France, rescues a beautiful young woman from an intolerable situation, and kills her father (the "ogre"). The twist in the tale comes from the fact that this heroine, after marriage, decides that her husband is as inconvenient to her as her father had been, and she contrives a way to kill him. For an examination of the folk motifs in this epic, see Deyermond and Chaplin, and my article "Private Man, Public Woman."

4. Other chronicles stand between the ninth century and the grand national histories of the thirteenth century. For example, the first Christian chronicle to refer to Count Julian is the *Crónica silense,* written after the reconquest of Toledo by a Toledan Mozarab around 1115. The Asturian line of argument that blamed Witiza principally for the iniquity of the Visigoths and the evils that subsequently befell Spain under Rodrigo's reign also demonstrated a hostility toward Julian and his role as traitor to his faith and his king, views that continue to resonate in the historiographies of El Tudense (Bishop Lucas de Tuy, 1236), El Toledano, and Alfonso the Learned. In his 1298 *Libro contra la seta de Mahomath* (Book against the sect of Mohammed), St. Pedro Pascual (c. 1227–1300), a Christian bishop writing in southeastern Spain in the thirteenth century, attributes the rape of the count's daughter to Witiza himself, the king who preceded Rodrigo, but still blames Julian for his offensive behavior in conspiring with the Moors. El Tudense and El Toledano condemn the debased reign of Witiza but do not attribute the rape to him. All the Arabic sources that treat the story of the rape uniformly attribute the deed to Rodrigo, with the exception of Ibn Jaldun's excoriation of Witiza in the fourteenth century, although it is unclear if he has been influenced by St. Pedro Pascual or by court writings in the southern kingdom of Granada. Menéndez Pidal believes that the attribution of the rape to Witiza originated with lower-class Mozarabs in the eleventh century, and that the upper-class Mozarabs, who had more direct and frequent contact with the Muslim historiographers, always maintained the storyline that Rodrigo had committed the rape.

5. For a discussion of how rape was viewed in the Middle Ages, and how contemporary feminist theories on rape can skew our interpretations of these early texts, see Evelyn Birge Vitz's article on rape and political correctness. See also works by Gravdal, Barahona, and Baines.

6. For a brief but extremely informative biography of El Toledano, and the reasons for his significant role in the Christian kingdoms' military expansion, see the introduction to Juan Fernández Valverde's edition of *Historia de los hechos de España.* El Toledano's predecessor by a few years, Bishop Lucas de Tuy (El Tudense) wrote a history in 1236 that is one of the most important sources for the histories of El Toledano and Alfonso the Learned. However, Fernández Valverde's excellent source study of El Toledano's history shows us that El Toledano gives us a fuller account of the reign of King Rodrigo than El Tudense gives us, and that it comes from El Toledano's extensive consultation of Asturian and Mozarabic sources, including *Crónica de Alfonso III* and *Crónica mozárabe de 754,* as well as ecclesiastical sources such as records of the Councils of Toledo, and Arabic chronicles.

7. For an excellent study of the importance of El Toledano in the construction of the Castilian kingdom, see Lucy K. Pick, *Conflict and Coexistence.*

8. In a fine analysis of the Visigothic kings' episodes in Alfonso the Learned's history, Alan Deyermond argues that the narrative pattern is one of death and rebirth, of a fall that opens the way for an ensuing redemption, in a double sense of spiritual rejuvenation and the eventual rebirth of the nation. I would point out that the story of Rodrigo is always such a story, not simply in Alfonso the Learned but in all its manifestations. What changes is the manner of crafting the fall and redemption through the narrative details and the varying figures of culpability.

9. Fraker describes the "Gothic thesis" as "the proposition that the kings of Spain are the successors of the Goths, and that they form a single line" (38). Early Christian chronicles argued for Pelayo as a Visigoth and therefore the immediate successor to Rodrigo, which allows for an unbroken line between the Visigoths and Pelayo as first king of the Asturias. Next, the *Crónica albeldense* (Chronicle of Albelda, coetaneous with the chronicle of Alfonso III) recounts a translation of the former splendor of Christian Visigothic Toledo to Oviedo, in León. The seat of the kingdom is then moved by Ordoño II to the city of León in 914. While Bishop Lucas de Tuy, El Tudense (1236), retains the importance of León to Spanish history, El Toledano (1243) reworks this material in order to highlight Castile and make direct links to the former glory of Toledo (Fraker 38–40). All of this works together to enable Alfonso X to avail himself of the newfound emphasis on Castile and maintain the Gothic thesis to include his own reign.

10. On the topic of lamentations over "lost Spain," a staple of fall of Spain narratives and which Alfonso the Learned included in his history, see Olga Tudorică Impey.

11. According to Fernández Valverde, three sources form the pillars of El Toledano's narrative, St. Isidore of Seville, Jordanes, and Lucas de Tuy. Although important as a source for El Toledano's general narrative, the 1236 Hispano-Latin *Chronicon mundi* of Bishop Lucas de Tuy, while exceedingly influential in other spheres, is the least important in terms of any enduring contributions to the legend of the fall of Spain. There were plenty of searches for scapegoats to justify the fall in 711, and for Lucas de Tuy, the Jews were the most significant contributors to the loss of the capital, Toledo, as he calls them the "purulent ulcer" of Hispania (Linehan 66). The earliest accounts of Rodrigo's reign did not cast the Jews in such a prominent role, and El Toledano ignores El Tudense in this regard. Instead, he turned to Arabic sources, which make no such claim; nor does the *Crónica de Alfonso III,* which focuses on the Decadent Tradition of the populace and not on conspiring Muslims and Jews. One can see in El Toledano the scholar at work: instead of dismissing accounts or facts he believes to be untrue, he weighs varying reports in order to determine what is likely or more probably true. Thus, in his telling of the fall of Rodrigo's kingdom, he gives the information as he finds it in differing reports. For example, on the matter of Oppas, the treacherous bishop, usually called bishop of Toledo, but occasionally bishop of Seville, he states: "Algunos afirman que Oppa fue hijo de Witiza, otros, hermano del conde Julián, pero es más cierto que fue hijo de Egica y hermano de Witiza; pero de cualquier manera que fuera, lo seguro es que fue arzobispo de Sevilla" (Some affirm that Oppa was the son of Witiza, others, a brother of count Julian, but he was likely the son of Egica and brother of Witiza; at any rate, what is certain is that he was the Archbishop of Seville; *Historia de los hechos,* bk. 4, chapter 2: 162). This is not to say that the earliest days of Christendom in the Iberian Peninsula were not virulently anti-Semitic. Linehan records examples of pervasive anti-Semitism, particularly once the Visigoths

accepted Roman Christianity in 589 C.E. The point is that the Jews, while undoubtedly will-ing to accept the change of landlord, which they believed would result in better treatment of them, and while perhaps submitting willingly to Muslim invaders once it became clear that the Visigothic kingdom was no more, were neither the instigators of the invasion nor more blameworthy than the Christians who were defeated, or who simply surrendered when the Muslims arrived at each succeeding unconquered town and city.

12. A glance at the previous two books, before arriving at book 3 and the recounting of the Visigothic kings from early times to the destruction of Spain, shows that much material derives from the Toledan *Crónica mozárabe de 754* (*Mozarabic Chronicle of 754*). Book 3 shows a change, a narrative history framed by paraphrasing from Genesis, as the story approaches the reign of Witiza through the loss to the Arabs and the praise of Spain. The earlier chapters of book 3 have an occasional Biblical paraphrasing, but chapter 16, "Sobre los crímenes y las ar-timañas de Witiza" (On the crimes and dirty dealings of Witiza), begins with a quotation from Genesis, which explains why God found no pleasure in the Visigothic kingdom and its people, and the section on the Visigoths ends with another quotation from Genesis, which denounces the consequences of rage and anger, and tells how the people were dispersed into the twelve tribes of Israel. The first quotation that frames the history of the Visigothic kings comes from a chapter in Genesis that describes God's displeasure at the iniquity of the sons of Noah, and his willingness to smite the entire race in order to start over. The connection to the devastation of the line of Visigothic kings is obvious. The lamentation over lost Spain and the praise of her wonders contain many references drawn from the biblical book of Lamentations, Jeremiah, Isaiah, as well as references from the New Testament, one from Mark and one from Corinthians II.

13. On the women whose sexual appetites and bloodlust inspired much of the action in the chronicles of the counts of Castile, the earliest rulers of the heart of Iberia, see, for ex-ample, articles by Deyermond, Bluestine, and my article "Private Man, Public Woman."

14. See *The Romance of Adultery.*

15. Kathryn Gravdal, in *Ravishing Maidens,* discusses the etymology of the word "es-forçar" and the evolution of its usage in Romance languages. We know the word "esforçar" was used in this way at the time of *Crónica de 1344,* with multiple evocations of manliness, and in fact, Rodrigo uses it when he laments the death in battle of his nephew Sancho: "E vos érades el valente, e vos mi sobrino, érades el esforçado, e vos érades el piadoso" (And you were valiant, my nephew, forceful and pious; chapter 88: 130).

16. However much this Christian chronicle and other later chronicles declare themselves to be faithful translations of the lost Arabic sources from which they purportedly derive, this is a good example of something that cannot logically be other than a later, Christian addition.

17. See Charles A. Knudson, for example, on the Saracen princess in medieval French tales.

18. Louise Mirrer's book *Women, Jews, and Muslims in the Texts of Reconquest Castile,* an-alyzes this poem (17–25), and offers insightful analyses of portrayals of the "Muslim princess," especially in the medieval ballad tradition.

19. Two of the most important books on Alfonso VI and his era are by Bernard F. Reilly, *The Kingdom of León-Castilla under King Alfonso VI, 1065–1109* and *The Kingdom of León-*

Castilla under Queen Urraca, 1109–1126. For an interesting study of Yusuf, see Miriam De-Costa, "Historical and Literary Views of Yusuf, African Conqueror of Spain."

20. For a discussion of the "beautiful Jewess" theme in a poem by Alfonso the Learned, see Mirrer 31–43, and as a topic in Hispano-medieval literature in general, see Aizenberg.

21. Of the seventeen manuscripts collected of Alfonso's *Estoria de España* that Menéndez Pidal dated as closest to the time of Alfonso himself, only two include the marginalia about Alfonso and the Jewess. Nancy Joe Dyer's extremely interesting analysis of the literary properties of Alfonsine historiography discusses the appearance of this story in different manuscript traditions in the late medieval and early modern periods.

22. As did so many of his contemporary fifteenth-century historians, the chronicler Lope García de Salazar attributes the devastating defeat of eighth-century Spain not to Rodrigo's specific failings, but to the cumulative weakening effect on the country of the atrocities of Rodrigo's predecessor, Witiza, in conjunction with the unrelenting efforts of those who remained loyal to him and opposed to Rodrigo's accession to the throne. For García de Salazar, this history ensured Rodrigo's inevitable loss, the foretelling of which was the penetration of the House of Hercules. It stands to reason, then, that to the extent to which a historian or poet adheres to this view, the less important La Cava is to the legend.

23. Dyer does not include García de Salazar's work in her article but explains that "evil Jewess" and an accusation of sorcery first appear in late fourteenth-century chronicles (156).

24. Henry Charles Lea, the first modern historian to recognize the prominent role Martínez played in the uprisings against the Jews, published his findings in 1896 in the *American Historical Review.*

Chapter Three · *Blood Will Out*

Epigraph: "Los godos ignoraron el adagio popular castellano: *no hay enemigo pequeño.* Lo han ignorado con frecuencia muchos grandes pueblos. Y los judíos nunca han sido además pequeños enemigos" (105).

1. See chapter 6 for the nineteenth- and twentieth-century polemic about these Spanish examples of Jewish blood libel.

2. As Nirenberg tells us, "By the late fifteenth century, many Christians considered the conversions a disaster that threatened the spiritual health of the entire Christian community. The converts and their descendants were now seen as insincere Christians, as clandestine Jews, or even as hybrid monsters, neither Jew nor Christian. They converted merely to gain power over Christians, to degrade, even poison, Christian men and to have sex with Christian women. Some went so far as to see this insincerity as a product of nature. Baptism could not alter the fact that the Jews' blood was corrupted by millenia of mixture and debasement, indelibly saturated with a hatred of everything Christian. Hence purity of blood laws were needed to bar the descendants of converts from any position of power or privilege, and 'natural Christians' were encouraged not to intermarry with them" ("Conversion, Sex, and Segregation" 28).

3. As Netanyahu tells us, for quite some time the only piece of evidence was an entry in Fernando del Pulgar's biographies of great men of Castile, in which he includes Torquemada

as a recent Christian (431). Other chroniclers followed suit, and it is now accepted as fact. For excellent studies of the Inquisition, and Ferdinand's and Isabel's role in it, see Netanyahu, *The Origins of the Inquisition in Fifteenth-Century Spain,* Henry Kamen, *The Spanish Inquisition,* and John H. Elliott, *Imperial Spain.*

4. For the study of Spanish historiography and humanism, the works of R.B. Tate remain essential. For an important, recent study of the character of Spanish humanism in the fifteenth and sixteenth centuries, see Homza, *Religious Authority in the Spanish Renaissance.* Long thought to be in opposition to scholasticism, humanism in Spain, Homza shows, is much more nuanced, and thinkers traditionally classified as scholastics or humanists expressed a more fluid exchange between the two movements, which depended on their particular arguments and goals.

5. For important studies of fifteenth-century Spanish historiography in addition to R.B. Tate, see Helen Nader, Galen Brokaw, and Fernando Gómez-Redondo.

6. Weissberger's excellent study of Isabel and the gendered construction of queenship has some overlap with my arguments in this chapter, although our respective studies are quite different in goal and scope. She shines a careful lens on a much shorter period in history, on the specific construction and expression of male anxieties about masculinity and femininity in fifteenth-century Spain, and her treatment of the materials is subtle and illuminating.

7. Allegedly, envy inspired Juan Pacheco, the king's favorite before the selection of Beltrán de la Cueva, to spread the rumors about the queen and the new favorite, and to impugn the legitimacy of Enrique's daughter, Princess Juana.

8. In terms of comparisons between Mary and Isabel, one is struck by the conviction with which Isabel herself supported the idea of the Immaculate Conception. This belief, held by many since at least the twelfth century, put forth the view that to merit the honor of bearing the divinity made incarnate—Jesus—Mary herself as a pure vessel was born free from original sin, which had been visited upon all humankind since the Fall from Paradise. According to Nancy Mayberry, the fifteenth century was particularly active for debating the pros and cons of this belief, which was not declared Catholic dogma until 1854—surprising considering the fervor with which the immaculists and maculists defended their respective positions. We do know that in 1622 that priests were sworn to defend this as Catholic truth. Isabel's charter and permission granted Beatriz de Silva the first authority ever to found a convent— an order of nuns—in 1484 in the name of the Immaculate Conception, a permission that was backed by papal authority in 1489. Although Mayberry tells us that the pope did not seem to realize he had sanctioned a new order dedicated to "the Immaculate Conception," that is exactly the charter the new nuns felt had been granted, and their convent documents reveal precisely their belief that they were nuns of "the Immaculate Conception" (219).

9. Even the legend of the eleventh-century historical figure, who became the national hero, Rodrigo Díaz de Vivar, El Cid, was cast in the early sixteenth century as a pseudochronicle, but was really a romance of chivalry, as was another work to be considered in this chapter, the *La Poncella de Francia* (The maid of France), composed in honor of Princess Isabel of Castile.

10. In Helen Nader's discussion of the two competing kinds of historians, the *caballeros,* Castilian noblemen who wrote, and the *letrados,* scholars who drew from Latin chronicles for

their view of Spanish history and the legitimacy of the Castilian throne, by tracing it back to the Visigoths, she points out that the powerful narrative of a monarchical continuum from Pelayo to the present had prevented modern critical view from recognizing the broader humanistic kind of historiography that also flourished in the fifteenth century. This neglect contributed to the somewhat mistaken viewpoint that tends to leave Spain out of discussions of the European Renaissance, or to see it as radically different from its Italian counterpart, for example.

11. Versions of the legend differ as to whether the pillars were on the coast of North Africa and the coast of southern Spain, or both in the south of Spain.

12. For an excellent summary of fifteenth-century Spanish historiography, and especially the differing viewpoints of the letrados and the caballeros, see Nader, chapter 1.

13. For more about Sánchez de Arévalo and his importance in the development of neo-Gothicism, see Tate's *Ensayos* (74–104).

14. Antonio de Nebrija wrote that his new historical vision of Spain "sacar a luz las antigüedades de España que hasta nuestros días han estado encubiertas" (would bring to light the antiquity of Spain, which has, until our day, remained covered; cited in Tate, *Ensayos* 27).

15. Luna was a powerful political player in Castile, as well as a chronicler, but his political fortunes turned and he was beheaded in 1453.

16. "Non buenamente te puedo callar, / Opas maldito, e a ti, Julian, / pues sois en el valle más fondo de afán / que non se redime jamás por llorar. / ¿Quál ya crueza vos pudo indignar / a vender un día las tierras e leyes / de España, las quales puxanca de reyes / en años atantos non pudo cobrar?" (st. 91, p. 98).

17. L.P. Harvey explains the broad interpretation of that word—alfaquí—to mean specifically "Islamic jurist" as well as, more generally, local religious leader (*Islamic Spain* 96).

18. The poem opens, "Quando fue el cruel castigo / de Julián conde malvado, / por el pecar de Rodrigo, / el Rey fue tan castigado / que sus reinos son testigo. / Metió luego por España / la morisma de rondón, / que se dio tan buena maña / que la guerra fue tamaña / como lo fue la traición. / Con la Caba hija del Conde / tropezó el lascivo Rey. / Este pecar fue de hombre, / más pecar contra la Ley / sólo al conde toca el nombre" (sts. 1–3; cited in Tate, *Ensayos* 263–79).

19. Menéndez Pidal tells us that critics disagree on the dating of the *Refundición toledana*, some arguing for as late as 1460, making it somewhat later than Corral's work, others arguing for 1440 or even earlier, making it coetaneous with Corral, or even a precursor to that work. The sections of the *Refundición toledana* that pertain to the fall of Spain in 711 are contained in *Floresta de leyendas heroicas* 1: 141–49.

20. As we saw in chapter 1, St. Jerome lamented the fact that David—and men in general— were not safe from the dangerous allure of women even in their own homes. David is portrayed by Jerome as the victim whose gaze was appropriated by Bathsheba and her beauty, rather than as the king who chooses to act on his lust for Bathsheba.

21. Ramón Menéndez Pidal, in *El Rey Rodrigo*, mentions the variations of the name of the daughter in the manuscripts of the *Crónica de 1344*: "En la *Crónica de 1344* el ms. *U* emplea seis veces *Alataba* y tres *la Taba*; el ms. *M* solo usa *la Taba*, tres veces, una de las cuales (fol. 30d) pudiera leerse *la Caba*, dada la semejanza paleográfica de *t* y *c* . . . ; el ms. *Q* usa una vez

Alataba y otra *Alcaba*" (60, n.3). What this confirms for us is the novelty of the Jewish converso who reworked the earlier source to create the revised chronicle: he chose to use simply Caba, which is similar to the Hebrew "Chava," Eve.

22. It is beyond the scope of this study to examine *Crónica del Rey don Rodrigo* as political allegory, but it is possible that Corral intended to criticize the reign of King Juan II of Castile (1406–1454). We know almost nothing about Corral himself, but we do know that his brother, Rodrigo de Villandrano, count of Ribodeo, served as a diplomat in the court of King Juan II, and later the brothers supported Alvaro de Luna against Juan. Adeline Rucquoi speculates on the amount of narrative that dwells on Franco-Castilian interaction in *Crónica del Rey don Rodrigo* and Pedro de Corral's possible knowledge of his brother's extensive diplomatic missions and exchanges with the French. Of the work's 518 chapters, 131 are dedicated to the crowning of King Rodrigo, the lavish and lengthy jousts and tournaments held in his honor in Toledo, and the description of the participation of the world's most celebrated knights, particularly many from France.

23. The reference to Viseu occurs in other chronicles and was first mentioned in the late ninth-century *Crónica de Alfonso III,* in which Alfonso himself claimed to have discovered the sepulcher with its inscription in Viseu, but until the *Refundición toledana* and *Crónica del Rey don Rodrigo* fill in the historical gap with more legendary material, there are no accountings of what happens to Rodrigo between the bloody defeat of his armies and the discovery of his tomb.

24. For studies of women as "spiritual mothers" in early Christianity, see, for example, McNamara and Dyan Elliott.

25. For general studies of catalogs of women, and criticisms and defenses of women in the Middle Ages, see Glenda McLeod's *Virtue and Venom,* Alcuin Blamires' two works, *The Case for Women* and *Woman Defamed, Woman Defended,* and Michael Solomon's *The Literature of Misogyny in Medieval Spain.* In *The Case for Women,* Alcuin Blamires distinguishes between formal contributions to the discussion of women, such as debates and catalogs, and incidental contributions, which framed the commonplaces of those debates and catalogs in a different context, such as prose fiction. Fifteenth-century Spain contributed both formal and incidental works to the larger European debate. Readers of misogynistic literature sometimes find it difficult to distinguish between pro- and antifeminist works, since the arguments contained within are often identical. If, for example, a woman is considered the instrument of man's downfall, an antifeminist work will condemn her for it, while a profeminine work (to borrow the phrase used by Blamires) may well acknowledge the charge but plead for compassion for women for their very weakness. Blamires employs the term profeminine rather than profeminist, arguing, sensibly, that medieval defenses of women often contained material that today's readers would find offensive and misogynistic. The point was not to equate men and women but to support and defend women, despite their perceived inferior nature to that of men.

26. Spain had earlier medieval queens, but none with the kind of propaganda machine that Isabel enjoyed. Moreover, Isabel was a shrewd politician, complicit with her chroniclers in the construction of her public portrayal. Peggy Liss explores Isabel's participation in the queen's own myth making in "Isabel, Myth and History."

27. In *Isabel Rules,* Weissberger offers acute insight into both little-known and well-known texts from fifteenth-century Spain. Particularly interesting are the excellent analyses of corpo-

real, especially sexualized, imagery in works ranging from parodic satires to religious poetry about Isabel.

28. Although Iñigo de Mendoza's poem to Isabel was printed for the first time in 1483 or 1484, and appears at the end of Fernando del Pulgar's *Claros varones de Castilla* (Great men of Castile), a 1486 work dedicated to the Catholic monarchs, it was, according to R.B. Tate, probably composed in the early years of Isabel's reign. If that is correct, then Martín de Córdoba predates him by a few years, although the important point is not which man wrote first, but that the insistence on the portrayal of Isabel as a latter-day Virgin Mary was an early and persistent manifestation in her reign.

29. "Donde, so su amparo e defendimiento, ha de recibir los humildes labradores, los deuotos horadores, los estudiosos maestros e doctores, biudas, huérfanos e pobres sin amparo. E assi será semejante ala Reyna del cielo; quando la pintan con su manto abierto, cobriente de cada parte todos los estados del mundo. Pues ya paresce como la señora es madre, defensora e abogada e escudo e paues delos flacos, por lo qual deue ser sobre todas piadosas. E esto es lo que eneste capítulo vos he querido declarar" (*Jardín de nobles donzellas* 202).

30. An extremely popular Mediterranean image, the Virgin is often compared to a palm tree in the manner in which her arms spread like wide-reaching palm branches to cover and shelter those below.

31. Translation by Lehfeldt, from Palencia's *Crónica de Enrique IV,* 2:162.

32. Although it was common for the word "doncella" to be used in this period for the word "maid" or "maiden," the Spanish title *Poncella de Francia* intends to maintain a linguistic relationship with the French "pucelle," as Joan was called.

33. Joan, as la Poncella, appears in Gonzalo Chacón's c. 1460 *Crónica de don Alvaro de Luna* (Chronicle of Don Alvaro de Luna), the powerful political advisor to Juan II, who was beheaded in 1453. No one ever claimed authorship of the romance of chivalry *La Poncella de Francia,* but the convincing conclusion of the most recent editors of the Castilian romance, Victoria Campo and Victor Infantes, is that Chacón is indeed the author.

34. See, for example, the studies by Jo Ann Kay McNamara, Susanna Elm, and Kate Cooper on the multiple possibilities available to women in early Christianity, which included itinerant preaching.

35. Rucquoi describes the pursuit of the princess by many suitors between 1460 and 1469.

36. "Alta reina esclarecida, / guarnecida / de grandezas muy reales, / a remediar nuestros males / desiguales; / por gracia de Dios venida, / como quando fue perdida / nuestra vida / por culpa de una muger, / nos quiere Dios guarnecer / y rehazer, / por aquel modo y medida / que llevó nuestra caída" (149).

37. Kaplan cites, convincingly, the converso poets' denunciations of Isabel's predecessor's treatment of them, and how, under the reign of Enrique IV, the conditions under which they operated in Spain had deteriorated dramatically. Kaplan correctly asserts that converso poets shared "a marked tendency . . . during this time to express their confidence in the young queen by instilling her with divine attributions" (298). Most of the examples Kaplan provides are the now-familiar ones comparing the queen to the Virgin Mary; in only one or two cases would I agree that the verse might suggest Isabel is almost a divinity. Strictly speaking, the Virgin Mary is not a divinity, and Kaplan's use of such comparisons between Mary and Isabel to suggest the "deification" of Isabel is not the most accurate description of Mary. She is cer-

tainly above all other human women, as the one conceived without original sin—the Immaculate Conception—and the one to bear the divinity, Jesus Christ, and as the one who, in many medieval collections of Marian miracles, appears to operate not as an intercessor between God and man, but on her own as miracle worker. Yet, it is important to recall that she is not divine and is not godlike, and therefore the comparisons between Isabel and Mary that predominate in the literature are certainly raising Isabel above woman, but not deifying her. Fray Martín de Córdoba was, as I showed above, the first to compare Mary to Isabel. So little is known of him that I would not claim firmly that he is not a converso. If he is not, then the converso poetry cited by Kaplan does not lose its prominence as a strong building block in the formation of the portrait of Isabel as a latter-day Virgin Mary, but it is not the exclusive province of converso poets that Kaplan would claim it to be. If any evidence turns up to show that Martín de Córdoba was indeed a converso, then Kaplan will be shown correct in asserting the converso poets' role in the future and enduring portrayal of Isabel as Castile's own Virgin Mary, although I would still claim the same caveats that calling Isabel (or Mary) a deity is not the correct terminology, and that the "sanctification" of Isabel is probably the more accurate term.

38. Rodríguez de Almela's letters, MS Egerton 1173, have been edited by David Mackenzie in the Exeter Hispanic Texts Series.

39. Two other issues in this letter, whether El Cid had a son (the famous *Poem of El Cid* records only two daughters, Elvira and Sol) and whether Alfonso VI held the title of emperor, further demonstrate the persistent efforts of fifteenth-century historians to unravel the web of fact and fiction surrounding Spain's legendary figures. Bernard F. Reilly analyzes the reign of Alfonso VI in his splendid political biography *The Kingdom of León-Castilla under King Alfonso VI,* and the figure of Urraca in another excellent study, *The Kingdom of León-Castilla under Queen Urraca.*

40. The marquis (sometimes called duke) of Cádiz Rodrigo Ponce de León was an influential nobleman who had supported Juana "la Beltraneja" against the claim of Isabel to the throne of Castile. After he accepted Isabel as queen, Ponce de León went on to have a distinguished military career, including the war in Granada in the 1480s up to the surrender in late 1491.

41. As we saw in the previous chapter, the word "esforçado," used as a quality of valor, also included the element of forcing oneself sexually on another as part of that manly valor. Thus, at the same time La Cava is blamed for telling what the king has done, he is implicitly praised for taking whomever he wants.

42. The Franciscans were the rivals of the Jeronymites, whom they accused of sympathizing with conversos and Muslims. For a discussion of Espina, the religious climate of the time, and Espina's contributions to the establishment of the Inquisition, see J.N. Hillgarth, *The Spanish Kingdoms* (vol. 2, part 3, chapter 3) and Netanyahu (814–47).

43. For an interesting discussion of Espina's writings, and the association of witchcraft and the Jew in the story of the Holy Child of La Guardia, see Stephen Haliczer, "The Jew as Witch."

44. For studies of the Jews in the Middle Ages and anti-Semitism, including blood libel accusations, see David Nirenberg, Jody Enders, and Miri Rubin.

45. So persistent are these stories that Jewish historical associations document twentieth-century manifestations of these beliefs, including as recently as 1928 in Massena, New York,

an upstate city. A rabbi was brought in by the New York State Police for questioning in the disappearance of a four-year-old girl, on the feast of Yom Kippur, after a resident suggested that the Jews might be up to their old tricks of ritual murder for young innocent blood. When the little girl emerged from the woods, frightened after having been lost, but safe and sound, townspeople alleged that this did not disprove the accusation, merely that the plot had been thwarted by the timely intervention of the police. See, for example, the websites for the American Jewish Historical Association and JewishEncyclopedia.com.

46. See chapter 6 for a discussion of the research conducted by academics in the nineteenth and twentieth centuries into this legend, as well as into the legend of Diego de Susán's daughter, the "beautiful woman of Seville." The lead official of the Inquisition was the inquisitor generalis, translated as grand inquisitor or inquisitor general.

47. Selection from St. Vincent Ferrer's sermon, cited in Nirenberg ("Conversion, Sex, and Segregation" 50).

48. The edict became public knowledge on April 29, 1492, and Jews had until the end of July to convert or leave their homes and homeland.

49. For an edition and study of Lope's play, as well as an informative introduction on the versions of the story through the centuries, see Lope de Vega Carpio, *El niño inocente* (edited by Anthony J. Farrell).

50. Many studies explore the connections between the sexualized language attached to the enemy and the threat to one's homeland, but pertinent examples include Hall and Matar (109–27).

Act Two · Promise and Fulfillment

Epigraph (Mariana): "De don Pelayo traen su descendencia los reyes de España sin jamás cortarse la línea de su alcurnia real hasta nuestro tiempo, antes siempre los hijos han heredado la corona de sus padres, o los hermanos de sus hermanos, que es cosa muy de notar," from *Historia general de España* (General history of Spain [1601], bk. 6, chap. 20: 191). Mariana's Latin version was printed in 1592. He then translated it to Spanish for a 1601 printing.

Interlude

1. When seen as one entity, these two centuries are collectively known as Golden Age Spain, a designation that has become as politicized as the term Renaissance. Given the attention in the late twentieth century to the negative aspects of discovery and conquest, imperial quests, and the discrimination and abuse of marginalized groups in Spain, critics and historians increasingly refer to the more neutral early modern Spain, rather than the Golden Age. Golden Age Spain, when considered thematically or otherwise separately, is also called, respectively, the age of expansion and the age of disillusionment, or Renaissance and Baroque Spain. Depending on the context and the point I am trying to make, I may use any of the above terms.

2. For an interesting discussion of the role of prophecy in fifteenth- and sixteenth-century Spain, and a holy prophetess who became the much-sought-after sage of King Ferdinand after Isabel's death, see Jodi Bilinkoff. Bilinkoff documents the reverence accorded King

Ferdinand, including the fact that sixteenth-century historians recorded the stories of signs and omens seen at his birth, but no such phenomena for the birth of Isabel (28, n.23). Alain Milhou (*Colón*) describes the fifteenth-century chroniclers' "official messianism," in which King Ferdinand was a semidivine figure, the reincarnation of the thirteenth-century King Ferdinand III, the Saint, who had won back Seville, Jaén, and Córdoba, among other cities. For other studies of prophecy, and its connection to millenarianism and apocalyptic predictions, see Reeves, Christianson, Kagan, and Barnes. For prophecy in connection with Islam, see Tolan, Wheatcroft, López-Baralt, Cabanelas, Harvey, and Perry (*Gender and Disorder; Handless Maiden*).

3. For those interested in the history of Imperial Spain, the works of J.H. Elliott and Henry Kamen are indispensable.

4. Prince John's mother, Queen Isabel, was herself the object of prophecy, even as a new Astraea, as her biographer Peggy Liss tells us: "Isabel was given prominent place within those predictions [of a dawning golden age in Spain]. She was acclaimed as both another Minerva and 'the very resplendant Diana' . . . Isabel was also compared, not unfavorably, to the Queen of the Amazons, as well as to Astraea, come down from the sky—the Virgin Astraea, or Justice, whose descent Virgil, Ovid and Dante saw as heralding the return of the golden age" (256–57).

5. As J.H. Elliott and other historians tell us, the period between Isabel's death in 1504 and the election of her grandson Charles as Holy Roman Emperor in 1519, three years after the death of Ferdinand, is confused and difficult to sort out politically (*Imperial Spain* 133–56).

6. Ottavia Niccoli explains the significance of the prophecy for the various rulers to whom it applied. See especially 8–12 and 172–77 for a discussion of the prophecy of the second Charlemagne, and the dual practices of printing and recycling prophecies to fit new predictions and of reprinting older prophecies as a means of analyzing, with hindsight, more current political events.

7. For a description of Cisneros' tactics and influence over Ferdinand and Isabel, see Kamen, *Empire,* chapter 1, "Foundations," especially 13–33; Lovett, especially 257–59; and Liss. Historians give different dates for the famous book burning in Granada, some saying 1499 and others 1501. What is clear, though, is that November 1499 saw the beginning of the monarchs' rejection of their earlier agreements, in which the Muslims were allowed to continue to practice their faith, in favor of forced conversion through mass baptisms.

8. See, for example, Bataillon for a discussion of Cisneros's role as a humanist and a figure of what Bataillon calls the "Pre-Reformation."

9. The association of prostitutes, freedom of movement, economic independence, and danger to societal order is an old one. In my article "Paradise Regained in *Vida de Santa María Egipçiaca,*" I analyze how the above topics, when placed in the historical context of the fears of early Christian male writers, show the transformation of the currency of gold and silver into spiritual economics, the currency of saved souls as gold and silver in Heaven. This transformation of economics results from the conversion of the prostitute, as she turns from the wickedness of defeating Christian souls and Christian nations to the winning of souls through her asceticism for the new Jerusalem, the new nation in Heaven.

10. Another important source for the discussion of women and political models is Jordan.

11. In *The Heart and Stomach of a King,* Carole Levin shows how Elizabeth I used the images of the Virgin Mary—no longer necessary in Protestantism—to bolster her own image and to cause the popular imagination to substitute the Virgin Queen for the Virgin Mary. This is one more instance of the similarities between the queen of England and Isabel of Spain, who also was spoken of and represented as a second Virgin Mary. Elizabeth's reputation did not fare well in seventeenth-century Spanish letters, as this poetic epitaph for the English queen by Lope de Vega demonstrates: "Aquí yace Jezebel" (Here lies Jezebel; *El último godo* 107).

12. See Frances Yates, *Astraea,* for a discussion of the myth of the ancient goddess of peace and justice, Astraea, and what she calls "the triumph of chastity" as prevalent political themes and images in sixteenth-century England, reincarnated in some sense in Elizabeth I, the Virgin Queen. For an exploration of the significance of Lucretia the Roman matron, see Stephanie Jed. The collection of essays *Women Who Ruled,* edited by Annette Dixon, compellingly demonstrates just how widespread were the phenomena of representing women as chaste, even virginal, rulers.

13. For an excellent study on the topic of rape in the early modern period, see Welles's *Persephone's Girdle.*

14. In addition to the examples in this study, Rina Walthaus has shown that the theme of the chaste woman who inflames the desires of men, making her a femme fatale every bit as dangerous as the overt temptress, was a pervasive one in early Spanish national theater, particularly in the works of the sixteenth-century dramatists Juan de la Cueva and Cristóbal de Virués. Although she does not cite Bartolomé Palau's c. 1530 *Historia de la gloriosa santa Orosia,* this play by the father of Spanish national drama perfectly demonstrates Walthaus's point: the culpable La Cava incites the lust of the betrothed King Rodrigo, while the obvious purity and virginity of Rodrigo's fiancée, the Slavonic princess Orosia, inflames the desire of the Muslim ruler Muza.

Chapter Four · Desiring the Nation

Epigraph: "La culebra me comía. / Come me ya por la parte / que todo lo merescía / por donde fue el principio / de la mi muy gran desdicha" (*Spanish Ballads* 49).

1. The study of the lives and miracles of saints has long been important in the examinations of religious, historical, literary, and sociocultural practices in France, England, Germany, and Italy, and it is not neglected by historians of the Spanish medieval and early modern periods. But hagiography in its own right and as a contributor to the development of secular narrative has been relatively little studied by literary critics who deal with Spain, even though critics have identified this genre as the largest body of extant medieval manuscripts in Spanish archives. Given how significantly religion figures in the history of Spain, this paucity of study is surprising. Hispano-medievalists John K. Walsh and B. Bussell Thompson were the first to signal the quantity of unstudied material available to interested literary critics (*The Myth of the Magdalen in Early Spanish Literature*), and much remains to be done in this field.

2. According to Patrick Geary in *Furta Sacra* (Sacred theft), a classic feature of the translation of relics in the Middle Ages and the competition between cities and monasteries for such relics was the sign given by the saint to indicate his or her desire to be buried in one place

or removed from another. For information on the history of Orosia and present-day celebrations in her honor, see www.andarines.com/culturapopular/santa.htm.

3. *La perfecta casada (The Perfect Wife)*, written for Fray Luis's niece María Varela Osorio, participates in the extensive tradition of Biblical wisdom literature. A favorite maxim of the Middle Ages compared the woman of worth to the "strange" woman, sometimes foreign, always dangerous to men. *The Perfect Wife* opens each chapter with a gloss from the verses of Proverbs 31: 10–31, which focus on the dichotomized woman. Not surprisingly, the virtuous woman or woman of worth is a true rarity, while her opposite can be found everywhere. Consequently, the occasional man to be so fortunate as to find a woman of worth should treasure her. While Fray Luis does give advice on how to be a good wife and mother, the very couching of all this counsel in the context of such a woman's rarity contributes to the misogyny of the dichotomization of woman. For a feminist discussion of the book of Proverbs and wisdom literature, see Claudia Camp's works; for an excellent discussion of *The Perfect Wife*, see Georgina Dopico Black.

4. Critics disagree about the date of composition of the poem. Menéndez Pidal claims it is a student composition from Fray Luis's stay in Toledo, a view supported by one of Fray Luis's more recent editors, Oreste Macrí, while another critic, Llobera, suggests the poem is a mature composition from the 1570s or even later. Given the trajectory of Fray Luis's artistic work, it seems more likely that the earlier date is correct. Baño de la Cava refers specifically to a simple, rectangular stone tower on the banks of the Tagus River in Toledo. Restored in 1976 to what architectural historians believe was its original form, the tower was, according to the legend that developed about it, the site of King Rodrigo's palace and the place in which La Cava was bathing when Rodrigo spied on her and became obsessed with her. Although the word "baño" literally means "bath," the structure itself as well as the geographic location had come to be known as Baño de la Cava. Julián Porres Martín-Cleto explains the legends surrounding the site and offers detailed descriptions of its architectural and structural renovation. This is the spot that critics believe inspired Fray Luis's "Prophecy of the Tagus River."

5. The first printing was in Seville, 1499. The next printings, also from Seville, were 1511, 1526, and 1527, all of which included the reference to the destruction of Spain in the title. The second printing of 1527, in Valladolid, added the clause *y como los moros la ganaron* (and how the Moors conquered it). After that, it was always printed with this title, and it is important to note the emphasis on the devastation and destruction of Spain, the country, here. It is not a nostalgic evocation of a "lost" Spain or a focus on the king himself as the "Last of the Goths" (a notion that will be revived in seventeenth-century Spain), but an emphasis on Spain being destroyed and under the unhappy rule of the Muslims.

6. In the chapter "Identities and the Civilizing Mission," Kamen describes the growth of national identity in Spain from the time of the capture of Granada in 1492 through the seventeenth century (*Empire* 331–79). Initially, historians and politicians sought to further the sense of identity as citizens of "Spain," which continued through the centuries. Nevertheless, as Castilians took the lead in conquering and colonizing much of the New World, the focus often shifted from "Spain" to "Castile." For example, a 1559 description of an early sixteenth-century war in Naples describes the glorious new identity of "the kingdom of Spain." "Writing fifty years later, the official historian Antonio de Herrera went so far as to present the en-

tire imperial enterprise, both in Europe and in the New World, as exclusively a history of the deeds of Castilians" (334).

7. Scholars distinguish between ballads that were composed in the fourteenth and fifteenth centuries and were written down and continued to circulate in the sixteenth century and beyond, and new ballads that were composed in the sixteenth century itself.

8. For the study of Spanish humanistic historiography, see, for example, Victor Frankl, *El 'Antijovio' de Gonzalo Jiménez de Quesada* and Lu Ann Homza, *Religious Authority in the Spanish Renaissance*. For humanism and historiography in general, among the many excellent studies are those of Paul Oskar Kristeller, *Renaissance Thought,* Nancy Streuver, *The Language of History in the Renaissance,* and Ann Rigney's *The Rhetoric of Historical Representation*.

9. For a discussion of the historical implications of the false chronicles, see, for example, Julio Caro Baroja's *Las falsificaciones de la historia (en relación con la de España)* (Falsifications of history [in relation to Spanish history]); for the intersection of literature and history and the role of the false chronicles in *Don Quixote,* see Bruce W. Wardropper's *"Don Quixote:* Story or History?"; and for a general discussion of sixteenth-century readers and the confusion between history and spurious history or fiction, see E.C. Riley *Cervantes's Theory of the Novel,* Mary M. Gaylord, "Pulling Strings with Master Peter's Puppets" (131–32), and Ruth El Saffar, *Beyond Fiction* and *Critical Essays on Cervantes*. Finally, for theoretical studies of the relationship of fiction and history, see Hayden White, Roland Barthes, and Michel de Certeau.

10. Marcel Bataillon, in a footnote describing the exchange of letters between Cardinal Cisneros and Charles de Bovelles, states that the cardinal's letters were drawn up by González Gil, who was probably "Florian Docampo," an adviser to the cardinal. In the second half of the century, Ambrosio de Morales edited Ocampo's *History of Spain* and added to it by several volumes. We know that Morales saw a Spanish translation of Gil Pérez's Portuguese translation of the Arabic history *Crónica del Moro Rasis* (Chronicle of Rasis the Moor) and believed it to be an authentic representation of what Rasis had written many centuries earlier. Critics believe that Rasis did write about the fall of Spain, because the manuscripts we have, which purport to derive from the lost Rasis history, recount events that precede and follow the fall in 711. However, these same manuscript codices, when they get to the actual events of the fall, all use Corral's *Crónica del Rey don Rodrigo* to tell the story. In other words, given the complicated history of the manuscript tradition, we really have no idea what Rasis did write and what may have been added later, by Gil Pérez when he translated the Arabic history into Portuguese, by the Spanish translator of Gil Pérez's Portuguese version, or by later, unknown historians. We have no extant evidence of what, if anything, Rasis wrote about the invasion and conquest itself.

11. Joseph Campbell, among many others, wrote extensively about the reluctant hero in his books on myth.

12. Esteban de Garibay participated in the historical search to determine national origins by writing a history in which he traced the Basques to Biblical times, asserting that they were the Iberian descendants of Tubal, thereby claiming the Basques as the oldest or original "Spaniards." His dismissal of Pelayo as a Goth and a link to the old Visigothic kingdom was politically motivated. By demonstrating that there was no continuation between Rodrigo's kingdom and the emergence of the Asturian throne, Garibay could argue that the Basques

had predated Rodrigo, and that the seventeenth-century Basques were the true survivors of an earlier glorious age of Iberian Christianity. In 1594, Philip ordered an illuminated manuscript of the work, *Compendio Historial de las Chronicas, y universal historia de todos los reinos de España* (Historical compendium of chronicles, and universal history of all the kingdoms of Spain), compiled between 1556 and 1571 and printed in Antwerp in 1571, which combines miniature portraits of fifty-two kings and queens of Spain, rendered by the royal court painter, Hernando de Avila, with the coats of arms of each ruler, along with the biography by Garibay. This sixty-four-sheet treasure, bound in marbled leather, is housed in the Prado Museum in Madrid.

13. Kagan's thorough endnotes give evidence that there was much prophecy and millennial activity in early modern Spain, that contemporary historians have written a great deal on it, but that much remains to be done with the extensive activities of the street prophets: "The history of street prophets in Spain has yet to be written, but there is ample evidence of their activity" (87).

14. In addition to Geary's work, *Furta Sacra,* see also the excellent scholarship of Peter Brown in *The Cult of the Saints* for a discussion of the meaning of shrines, cults, and relics to the faithful in late antiquity; Brown's conclusions need not be restricted to the faithful of that time but can be extended to apply to the Middle Ages and beyond.

15. Carlos Eire and Patrick Geary, among others, discuss the issue of the fabulous relic. While many relics were authenticated (despite some dubious claims of authenticity), many were not, and quite a number of the most desired relics did not exist at all. Searches for the Holy Foreskin, from the circumcised baby Jesus, breastmilk from the Virgin, and, as Philip longed for, hairs of Mary Magdalene, were fantastic inventions. For that reason, much was made of authenticating documents that testified to the provenance of a relic, and Philip was as fanatical about determining authenticity as he was about collecting. Nevertheless, despite such precautions, there was clearly a great deal of traffic in false relics. Today, historical evidence refutes the legend that St. James ever set foot in Spain, but people clearly believed they had the actual body of the saint in northwest Spain.

16. Pérez de Guzmán's choice of saints is an unusual one, although three of the six are very early saints of the peninsula (St. Giles, St. Eugene, and St. Leocadia), and both Eugene and Leocadia are venerated principally in Toledo, not surprising choices, then, for the Toledan citizen Pérez de Guzmán. The other three, St. Michael, St. Luke, and St. Elizabeth of Hungary are popular and important saints in their own right. As Maguire and Severin point out, all six are autumnal saints, whose feast days are positioned between two significant days, one dedicated to the Virgin Mary, the Assumption (August 15), and Christmas, and the saints' lives follow a set of Marian poems in the manuscripts (151–52). While no one would argue that Mary is insignificant to the Nativity, if one were to insist on the implicit framing of Marian feast days for the saints' lives, it would make more sense to consider the Annunciation, celebrated on December 18, as the more appropriate second date. As mentioned previously, the seventh-century bishop Ildefonso was rewarded by Mary herself for his treatise on her virginity, and for changing the celebration of the Annunciation from the somber days of Lenten March to the more festive time approaching Christmas. In a work that includes saints from the Visigothic period, it strikes me as more probable to include another feast day that stems from that period as well.

17. Alban K. Forcione offers an elegant description of the events surrounding the return of the remains of the saint, weaving quotations from sixteenth-century sources in his own narrative of the spectacle. For a detailed description of the events, as well as the reasons for Forcione's suggestion that Cervantes himself may have been one of the spectators in the crowd, see chapter 4 of *Cervantes and the Humanist Vision,* 317–93.

18. The works were Francisco de Pisa's *Historia de la gloriosa virgen y mártir Santa Leocadia Patrona de Toledo* (History of the glorious virgin and martyr saint Leocadia, patroness of Toledo), and Miguel Hernández's *Vida, martirio y translación de la virgen y mártir Santa Leocadia* (Life, martyrdom, and translation of the virgin and martyr Saint Leocadia) printed in 1591.

19. But, this also represents a shift in emphasis. What happens increasingly in the seventeenth century is a distancing of the current monarchy from Rodrigo through an emphasis on him as the "last" king of the Goths, rather than seeing the current monarch as one in a long successive line of Spanish monarchs whose actions are all, in some way, a response to Rodrigo's loss of Spain, an effort to recover and overturn what Rodrigo's sin had wrought. Instead, the apocalyptic nature of the fall of 711 can be highlighted, which well suits the spirit of decline and disillusionment of the seventeenth century: in such a social and political climate, Lope de Vega's title of the Rodrigo legend, *El último godo*—The last Goth—speaks volumes.

20. The Spanish did not name their fleet "invincible," long thought to be a sign of their arrogance. After the defeat of the armada, the English and French invented popular songs that mocked Spain's naval enterprise. Lord Burghley commissioned a pamphlet in late 1588 in which he concluded, "so ends this account of the misfortunes of the Spanish Armada which they used to call 'INVINCIBLE.'" Numerous European translations introduced the phrase "Invincible Armada," and the epithet endured. For a discussion of the odes and ballads invented by the Dutch and English, and of the invention of the epithet "Invincible," see Martin and Parker, 243–47.

Chapter Five · Here Was Troy, Farewell Spain!

Epigraph: "Cuán triste queda Castilla . . . / y lo que más se sintió—y que más pena causaba / era ver cualquier iglesia—de moros vituperada," *Antología de poetas líricos castellanos* (1899), 177.

1. There are many edicts of prohibition throughout the sixteenth century that were ignored or followed only in part or in certain regions. For that reason, some edicts appear to repeat a prohibition already in place.

2. While a number of historians dispute the degree to which the Moriscos could legitimately be considered rebels against the interests of the Crown, most of them agree that the increasing mistreatment of the Moriscos in the sixteenth century engendered an understandable level of resistance by the Moriscos. However, Mary Halavais argues for an almost totally invented portrait of the sixteenth-century Morisco in her book *Like Wheat to the Miller.*

3. The oppression of the Moriscos gave rise, Luce López-Baralt tells us, to a clandestine literature in the sixteenth century: "But in the midst of their collective misfortune and disgrace—perhaps, indeed, because of it—these Moors, who in a few years had become a strangled minority condemned to death as a people, produced a fascinating and astonishing, and still very little-studied, literature: Moorish *aljamiado* literature" (171). For an excellent

treatment of *aljamiado* literature, writings in the Spanish language scripted with Arabic characters, see Luce López-Baralt's *Islam in Spanish Literature,* especially 199–207 and 209–21. According to Harvey and others, rather than produce many works of art, aljamiado literature served as the Moriscos' poignant and desperate attempts to keep Arabic culture alive in Spain after the prohibitions against the use of Arabic. When they were discovered in the eighteenth century, and reexamined in the twentieth centuries, literary historians harbored great hopes for the quality of the writings and for the discovery of an unknown masterpiece; the poor use of Arabic, with few exceptions, demonstrates the futility of the Moriscos' efforts.

4. For discussions of the various dates of written edicts of expulsion and the different dates on which they were announced in Spanish towns and cities, as well as discussions of the number of Moriscos who left Spain and those who were allowed to remain, see Wheatcroft, Kamen (*The Spanish Inquisition*), Tolan, Harvey (*Muslims in Spain*), and Janer.

5. The fullest study of Alonso del Castillo and the forgeries is by Darío Cabanelas, *El morisco granadino Alonso del Castillo.* For a Spanish translation and edition of the leaden tablets, see Miguel José Hagerty's 1980 *Los libros plúmbeos del Sacromonte.* See also L.P. Harvey, *Muslims in Spain,* and Barbara Fuchs, "Virtual Spaniards."

6. Cabanelas, Monroe, and Márquez Villanueva all accept the view that Luna and Castillo orchestrated the entire hoax of prophetic writings. López-Baralt herself, in spite of the ambivalence expressed on page 201, concurs with these other critics later in her book (212–13).

7. Principal sources for Mariana were the thirteenth-century bishops Ximénez de Rada (El Toledano) and Lucas de Tuy (El Tudense) and the sixteenth-century Ambrosio de Morales. Although many writers had ignored El Tudense's account of the fall of Spain in favor of El Toledano's account, which were written about seven years apart, and general consensus is that El Toledano's history is the best of the Hispano-Latin tradition, Mariana clearly relished El Tudense's anti-Semitic views, which then pervaded his own chronicle.

8. This volume on the theater of Lope de Vega includes a valuable, and succinct, overview of literary and historical works on the fall of Spain, 30–87.

9. López Pinciano (c.1547–c.1627) served as the physician to Philip II's sister María, the widow of Maximillian II. In his theoretical work, he suggested that prospective authors of edifying fiction select a historical topic or figure "neither so old as to be forgotten, nor so modern as to allow someone to say 'that didn't happen that way'" ("ni tan antigua que esté olvidada, ni tan moderna que pueda dezir nadie 'esso no passó ansí'"; 3: 169). López Pinciano translated into Spanish Thucydides' description of Athens and the plague, which points to an interest in histories of national devastations and the heroes who fought for restoration.

10. Mesa cites Tasso in the prologue to *La Restauración de España,* expressing the hope that he himself can contribute to national pride by writing about Spain's older history. *La Restauración de España* is considered a very minor work, though critics hold an earlier Mesa work, an epic poem on the 1212 battle of *Las Navas de Tolosa* (1594), in slightly higher esteem.

11. Cervantes experiments with and parodies the early modern obsession with prophecies and the prophetic mode of writing throughout *Don Quixote,* but especially in part 2, published in 1615.

12. An interesting literary phenomenon was the idealization of the Muslims in sixteenth- and seventeenth-century fiction, as in the immensely popular love story *El Abencerraje.* Fiction writers obscured the historical reality of conflict in favor of idealized portraits of Mus-

lims. López-Baralt points out that, while the fiction was flattering to Muslims, it was none-theless unreal. See her discussion of "Moorophile" (sometimes "Maurophile") literature in *Islam in Spanish Literature,* 209–58. It was unreal for the simple fact that historically, sixteenth-century Spain admired very little of Muslim culture. And it was unreal because the fictions typically depicted the idealized Muslims with features and qualities with which the noble Christian would be endowed. There was little attempt to understand any other set of values and norms. In contrast, early modern historians sought to hold ever in view the threat of the infidel inside and outside of the peninsula, as well as the new, but just as devastating, threat of the Protestant scourge. They understood the defeat of Rodrigo as the ancient dis-honor to Christianity—to Catholicism—that required seven centuries to overcome, and they wasted no ink on favorable portraits of the enemy, unless it was to paint a militarily strong enemy to glorify a Christian victory or rationalize a defeat. Miguel de Luna eschewed the label of fiction and attempted to create a "history" in which the Muslim was not a threat, but a savior of the peninsula.

13. I am grateful to Alicia Zuese for bringing the little-known *Casos notables de Córdoba* to my attention.

14. For the quotations from Luna, I have used the 2001 volume by Luis Bernabé Pons, which is a facsimile of *Verdadera historia del Rey don Rodrigo* (Madrid: Gabriel de León, 1665). The relationship of Fernando de Rojas's Melibea to Luna's La Cava is recognizable to any His-panist and is discussed by Menéndez Pidal in *Floresta,* 2: xlv. However, I point out in my book *Desire and Death in the Sentimental Romance* (1987) that Rojas undoubtedly borrowed the scene from Mirabella's suicide in Juan de Flores's *Historia de Grisel y Mirabella,* named for the two lovers in the work. Flores's work emerges again as a model in a seventeenth-century attempted reconstruction of the tenth-century *Crónica del Moro Rasis* (Chronicle of Rasis the Moor).

15. Examples of virginity as a maiden's most precious jewel abound, but Cervantes, for ex-ample, fuses this notion with the name of the heroine in his popular novella *La gitanilla* (*The Little Gypsy Girl*). Preciosa—the kidnapped noblewoman whose gypsy name means precious stone—speaks frequently about the value of her most precious jewel (*joya* or *piedra*) and the ir-reparable damage a woman suffers who offers it up lightly and without the benefit of marriage.

16. In Kamen's chapter "The Business of World Power" (*Empire* 285–329), he details the extraordinary challenges Spain faced of imperial organization and administration. Not only did the empire lack a comprehensively functional bureaucracy to oversee it, but the country was ill-prepared to handle the range of difficulties, from the trade and plunder activities of England that deflected considerable goods, such as sugar, and monetary profit from the New World away from Spain to the economic problems that assailed the peninsula itself, while the king collected his relics and the Church and state plundered its own population through in-quisitorial activities. Even Spaniards dwelling in the New World expressed astonishment at and criticism of the hardships of life in Spain and the government's inability or lack of inter-est in caring for its own people.

17. "'Señor mio, yo soy natural destos Reynos de España . . . y demas tiempo de sesenta años que ha q[ue] me sè acordar, y siendo niña de muy poca edad, oia leer à mi padre, estando velando junto al fuego, vn Pronostico, el qual dezia, que esta tierra la auian de ser conquis-tada de los Moros: dezia mas el dicho Pronostico, que el Capitan que la auia de ganar, auia de ser muy valeroso, y fuerte, y para señal de su conocimiento, auia de tener vn lunar peloso,

tan grande como vn garvanço, y que el dicho lunar auia de estar sobre el ombro de la mano derecha, y que esta misma mano derecha la tendria mas larga que la izquierda, y tanto, que con la palma podria cubrir su rodilla, sin encovar el cuerpo de la pierna de aquel mismo lado. Este Pronostico auia hecho vn hombre Religioso, muy santo, el qual tenemos los Christianos entre nosotros en mucha estima, y veneracion: y assi yo te suplico muy ahincadamente, que si tienes todas estas señales, por las buenas nue[v]as que te he dado, que asegures à mi, y à los mios de la vida, de tal suerte, que de los tuyos no seamos agrauiados, ni maltratados en nuestras personas y haziendas.' Acabadas de dezir todas estas razones por aquella muger, y siendo bien declaradas por vn Interprete que tenia junto al Christiano, de fuerte que las entendiò muy bien, de lo qual el Tarif se holgò mucho; y alli en presencia de todos los suyos, y del Conde D. Julian se desnudò; y auiendo mirado con cuydado aquellas seññales, hallaron el lunar que la muger auia dicho, y tambien la mano derecha mas larga que la izquierda, aunque no tanto como ella dezia" (chap. 7: 32–33).

18. For a study of the frequently used Renaissance trope of the "found text," see Fogelquist. Luna's work contains the found text within the found text. Abulçacim's "eyewitness history" contained letters purportedly written by the principals of the legend of the fall of Spain. Meriting a separate study is Luna's strategy to use epistolary narratives in this purported history. The letter, a pervasive and singularly important form in early modern Europe, and the object of much scholarly inquiry over the last several decades, offered a unique lens into history. In general, letters attempt to bridge distance, of space or time, or both. In the case of the discovery of ancient texts, not only did the letter provide a kind of eyewitness-testimony, but it promised, typically, access into private feelings, thoughts, and opinions on all kinds of matters. Renaissance Europe regarded the letter as offering unique possibilities of truth telling, as well as strategies for manipulation of literary conventions. Within the trope of the "found text," the "found letter," would have a particularly interesting status. Another interesting example of the found text is Pérez de Hita's first part of *Guerras civiles de Granada* (1595), which purports to be the eyewitness testimony of a Muslim in late fifteenth-century Spain, and which also includes purportedly "historical" letters.

19. José Godoy Alcántara, whose 1868 study is the standard reference even today on the *falsos cronicones*, was the first modern historian to point out that Luna's particular inventions posed substantial threat to the Spanish crown (98). See also Márquez Villanueva, "La voluntad de leyenda," 367. It was Godoy Alcántara who, moreover, definitively rejected the claim of the lead tablets as first-century writings.

20. Luna cleverly turns a current argument in favor of the Moriscos. Although historians agree that the early Visigothic kingdom elected kings rather than adhere to a strictly hereditary monarchy, the embellished versions of how Pelayo became heir to the throne relied on the notion of continued bloodlines. Moreover, early modern Spain not only believed in the hereditary Castilian throne, but had had the precedent of a princess-daughter, Isabel, inherit the throne on the death of her half-brother, Enrique IV. Finally, sixteenth-century histories emphasized that the continuation of the throne from Pelayo to the kings of León occurred through the marriage of Pelayo's daughter to Alfonso I. Thus, by highlighting the marriage of Egilona (here, as daughter) to the Muslim prince, Luna establishes an equivalency between that right to the throne and other cases in which the same relationship justified accession to the throne.

21. A fascinating study by Barbara Fuchs (*Mimesis and Empire*) demonstrates the artful strategies employed by Morisco writers in sixteenth-century Spain, over and above the Tower of Turpin parchments and the lead tablets of Sacromonte. According to Fuchs, numerous Muslim historiographers worked against the exclusionist trend of Christian writers in order to invent histories that enabled Muslim participation in, and contributions to, the centralized national imaginary. While ultimately unsuccessful, their inventiveness evokes both sadness in the plight of the Moriscos, who were fighting a losing battle, as the expulsion decree of 1609 proved, and pleasure in the entertaining tales they created.

22. The declaration added that the king had posthumously conferred upon Luna a title of minor nobility, awarded only to those of the most firm credentials as a Christian ("Introduction," *Historia verdadera del Rey don Rodrigo,* x).

23. "E quando esto sopo Florinda, fue grande su cuita, e lloraba e tanto se maldecia que los que con ella estaban non la podian guarezer nin remediar. E vna noche, a hora que todos dormian en el castillo, sobiose a lo mas alto e arrojose del. E a la manana la fallaron muerta e comida de las bestias. E por esto llaman al logar donde se mato la Rambla Iuliana, e al castillo el castillo de la Caba" (360). Rodríguez de Escabias combined earlier sources and more recent ones to attempt a reconstruction of the long-lost and much hunted *Chronicle of Rasis the Moor,* purportedly by the Arabic chronicler who gave the earliest full account of the invasion of the Iberian Peninsula by the Muslims. Although much mentioned by historians even in the sixteenth century, no one had seen any manuscript directly attributable to Rasis, which included any material about La Cava and the king, at least as far back as the thirteenth century. Even the thirteenth-century references we have—a Spanish translation of a Portuguese work that purportedly consulted Rasis—is too indirect to constitute proof of what Rasis had to say about the events, or even that he did say anything about them. In other words, to reconstruct Rasis' history, Rodríguez de Escabias must cull material from lots of other old manuscripts, some of which clearly did come from Rasis himself and others that involve potentially incorrect educated guesses. But to discuss La Cava and the king, Rodríguez de Escabias had to borrow from another source or invent his own version of the encounter between La Cava and Rodrigo. The result of his labors derives in part from the ballad tradition and in part from Luna. While this version does not dispute that Rodrigo raped Florinda, she wants to continue the affair, exhibiting a vindictive jealousy when he suddenly drops her for other women. This is not the La Cava of centuries of written testimony, but a self-centered cultural construction of the late sixteenth and seventeenth centuries' oral tradition. For all the outcries against Miguel de Luna and his so-called falsified history, he at least made La Cava a somewhat sympathetic figure, even if he does participate in the larger notion of the inherent blameworthiness and danger of women. The ignominious end—eaten by lions—hints at the guilt of female sexuality, which set into motion the chain of events that led to many deaths in her father's kingdom. As mentioned in note 14, La Cava's suicide and consumption by lions derives from the popular romance *Grisel y Mirabella* by Juan de Flores, a fiction writer and chronicler in the time of the Catholic monarchs. For an analysis of the name Mirabella, the chain of events that lead to her death, with their vacillation between the innocent young girl and the sexually culpable one, and her ignominious end in the bellies of lions, who somehow neglected to recognize her royal blood, see my *Desire and Death in the Spanish Sentimental Romance.*

24. Another element about La Cava's legend that gained great popularity was her purported burial place. In *Don Quixote,* immediately after the Moorish Zoraida has revealed to her father that she wants to convert to Christianity, and her father vacillates between being furious and heartbroken, the captive recounts that they were rowing hard to avoid running aground. "Mas quiso nuestra buena suerte que llegamos a una cala que se hace al lado de un pequeño promontorio o cabo que de los moros es llamado el de la 'Cava Rumía,' que en nuestra lengua quiere decir 'la mala mujer cristiana,' y es tradición entre los moros que en aquel lugar está enterrada la Cava, por quien se perdió España, porque *cava* en su lengua quiere decir 'mujer mala,' y *rumía,* 'cristiana' (1, chap. 41: 431; But by good luck we made a little cove beside a small promontory or cape, which is called by the Moors the Cape of the 'Cava Rumía'; which means in our language the wicked Christian woman. For there is a tradition among the Moors that it is the place where that 'Cava' lies buried, through whom Spain was lost; for 'cava' in their tongue means wicked woman and 'rumia' Christian. They even look on it as a bad omen to have to anchor there, if necessity drives them to—and otherwise they never do so; Grossman trans. 1, chap. 40: 374). Cervantes' description of this treacherous geographical cape on the Barbary Coast, referring to La Cava herself, finally gave the political and religious enemies—Muslims and Christians—something they could agree on: the danger of woman. Luna does not give this site a name, but it does appear in a history, Luis Mármol de Carvajal's 1600 *Historia del rebelion y castigo de los moriscos del Reyno de Granada,* in which he discusses the geographical location, and says the name "Cobor Rumia" means "sepulcher" (cited in Menéndez Pelayo, *Obras completas* 59, n.1).

25. Given that the topic of monarchs and monarchy so thoroughly engaged seventeenth-century learned men throughout Europe, the arguments are often nuanced. It is important to remember that Mariana supported the notion that the king was God's representative on earth, but he, as did other Spanish theorists and moralists, stopped well short of the French and English acceptance of a divine right of kings.

26. That Mariana discerned a special quality in the monarch Ferdinand is evident in the prophecy that he claims accompanied Ferdinand's birth. In Naples, a Carmelite friar, who lived a saintly life, said to King Alfonso, Ferdinand's uncle: "Hoy en el reino de Aragon ha nacido un Infante de tu linage: el cielo le promete nuevos imperios, grandes riquezas y ventura: será muy devoto, aficionado á lo bueno, y defensor excelente de la Christiandad" (bk. 25, chap. 18; This day in the kingdom of Aragon is born a prince of your family; Heaven promises him a large Empire, great riches and prosperity . . . he shall be very devout, of a virtuous inclination, and a great defender of Christianity; *General History* 459). For a discussion of Ferdinand and the propaganda to connect him with messianic prophecy, see Bilinkoff.

27. Feijóo had praised Mariana in his *Teatro crítico universal.* Bowle mentioned Mariana in a letter to Dr. Percy, in which he announced his edition of *Don Quijote* (Eisenberg 95–146).

28. Yvonne Yarbro-Bejarano analyzes Lope de Vega's extensive utilization of the motif of the woman used sexually, rejected—even violently so—and the male reactions that result in the building up or destruction of the state and the ruler.

29. De la pérdida de Espana / fueron funestos principios / una mujer vengativa / y un hombre de amor vencido. / por la disculpa de amor / ley hubo en el tiempo antiguo / que no fuesen castigados / sus yerros y desatinos. / De todo apela la Cava / diciendo: "Justicia pido, / que no fue amor, sino fuerza / el yerro del rey Rodrigo." / De los palacios reales / hecha sale un

basilisco / que la mayor hermosura, / agraviada, es áspid libio. / "¡Aquí fué Troya!", clamaban / hombres, mujeres y niños / que al estrago de dos hembras / España y Troya es lo mismo. / A las voces de la Cava / se tapa el rey los oídos / ques encanto de sirena / oír su propio delito. / Antes de la injusta fuerza / fuera bueno dar mil gritos, / que el daño suele ser menos / si primero es prevenido. / Por dar color a su culpa / publica del rey lacivo / la fuerza, que por ventura / fué algún fuego consentido: / que si una mujer no quiere / rendir su libre albedrío, / el más valiente gigante / en su presencia es un niño. / Quizá fué arrepentimiento / por haberse al rey rendido, / ques proprio del delincuente / pesarle del mal que hizo. / Culpa tuvieron entrambos: / el uno por su apetito, / el otro por su venganza / que entrambas cosas son vicio. / Si de los dos se pregunta / quién mayor culpa ha tenido, / digan los hombres: la Cava, / y las mujeres: Rodrigo; *Floresta* 2: 83–84.

30. For a discussion of the contradictory views of the Church Fathers on rape and self-defense, see Jane Tibbetts Schulenberg, "The Heroics of Virginity." In Augustine's discussion in *The City of God* of whether suicide is permissible when a woman has been raped, he uses the case of Lucretia, the Roman matron raped by Tarquin. He suggests that in her case, as in others, there was probably consent and even pleasure. His view is that women cannot justify suicide—it is murder against oneself, and therefore a sin—because one cannot even claim rape as an act devoid of their consent, which ultimately throws into doubt whether such a thing as rape even exists.

31. If Melveena McKendrick's dating of the composition of *El último godo* is correct, which, in *Playing the King,* she gives as the widest latitude 1599–1603, and possibly 1599–1600, in contrast to Menéndez Pidal's dating that assumes a composition anywhere from 1604 to close to the time of theatrical production, 1618 or so, then Lope's epic poem of 1609, *Jerusalén conquistada* (*Jerusalem Conquered*), would have followed this earlier interest in the legend.

32. She argues that many of the assumptions about Lope and his views of the monarchy are based on the study of too few plays, themselves rather different one from the other. But in examining the lesser-known plays and, in particular, the plays of national events and historical figures, one finds a much more critical and experimental Lope, particularly if one looks at the gap between what the characters themselves say in the plays and what the audience actually sees. In McKendrick's view, *El último godo* is just such a play.

33. Lope avoids the names Egilona and Ermesinda since the early modern chronicles differed on whether Egilona was the name of the daughter or the widow of Rodrigo, and on whether Ermesinda was the sister or daughter of Pelayo.

34. The Virgin del Sagrario was a statue housed in the Cathedral of Toledo. The statue was renowned for an exquisitely wrought imperial crown, designed by Diego Alejo de Montoya, into which he placed a remarkable emerald almost one and one-half inches in diameter. Another playwright, the friar Tirso de Molina (1548–1648), creator of the famous Golden Age scoundrel Don Juan, wrote nationalistic hagiographic plays, including one, *La joya de las montañas* (The jewel of the mountains) that treated St. Orosia (though in Tirso's version, she traveled to Spain to marry a Christian prince, not King Rodrigo as in Palau's play) and another, *Los lagos de San Vicente* (The lakes of Saint Vincent) about the conversion of the Muslim Princess Casilda and her defiance of her father the king, whose legend we looked at in the previous chapter. Lope also composed a play on this theme, *Santa Casilda*.

In *La joya de las montañas,* Bishop Arcislo warns Princess Orosia that Spain has been conquered by "barbarous Saracens," payback for Rodrigo's "vile action" of raping the blameless Florinda. Like Lope, Tirso returns to the founding myth in order to comment on the state of the monarchy in the early seventeenth century: it has been suggested that Tirso used Rodrigo and Pelayo as bad and good kings, respectively, to represent kings Philip III and Philip IV. I am grateful to Chela Bodden for bringing Tirso's plays to my attention.

35. Even though Calderón does not take up the legend of the fall of Spain directly, he appears to follow the outline of the legend in a different kind of work. In another of his theatrical treatments of the great drama of threats to Christianity, *La cisma de Inglaterra* (The schism of England), his story of Henry VIII of England's renunciation of Catholicism and of the pope's authority for the sake of his lust for Anne Boleyn, women appear in the familiar category of Eve and Mary. Historical reality can be manipulated just so far, so Calderón cannot craft his story of Henry, Catherine, and Anne as a perfect analogy of Rodrigo, Egilona, and Florinda. Nevertheless, the movement of the play, certain plot elements, and the manner in which he paints some of the characters demonstrate both an adherence to the concept of the dichotomized woman and a desire to portray the "schism of England" as every bit as devastating to England as the fall of Spain to the Moors. Although the editor of *La cisma de Inglaterra,* Francisco Ruiz Ramón, notes that Catherine of Aragon's portrayal highlights her beauty and saintly virtues, which he says history documents, this of course fails to take into account that, in an age which thrived on representations of women as angels or whores, it is completely unremarkable to find the demonized temptress Anne Boleyn, threat to Catholicism, countered by the lovely, saintly, peacekeeping Queen Catherine, defender of Catholicism. It is possible, but unlikely, that the historical Anne and Catherine fit the dichotomized literary and cultural models of women quite so perfectly in real life as they do in Calderón's drama. Before setting anything into motion, Henry's lust for Anne is accompanied by prophetic dreams and portents of disaster, not unlike the warnings of the penetration of the House of Hercules in the legend of Rodrigo; councilors warn Henry of the disaster that is Anne. Even her father disapproves of her involvement with Henry, the married king, and Cardinal Wolsey, who should be the staunchest defender of Catholicism, is a Bishop Oppas figure. The shadow of Protestantism hangs over the court, as the shadow of Islam threatened Visigothic Christendom. At the end of the play, when Anne is condemned and her father remarks that he has displayed the trait of a judge and not of a father in disapproving of her, it is too late to return to a prelapsarian state in the kingdom.

36. Although a London theater company, Strangers' Gallery, performed the translated play in 1997 under the title *Jewess of Toledo,* Lope intended the play to be about king and country, not principally about the affair. The actors' effort and the abbreviated title led one reviewer to remark that "Translator Michael Jacobs' notes admit that 'its great subtleties and dramatic power have been little appreciated anywhere for over three and a half centuries.' Nor, unfortunately, will this production work wonders for its rehabilitation . . . Retitling it to focus upon Alfonso's seven-year extramarital dalliance with the Jewess Rachel creates further expectations which Lope never intended exclusively to meet." The review by Ian Shuttleworth can be found at www.cix.co.uk/~shutters/reviews/97010.htm.

37. Other seventeenth-century authors tackled the legend of Alfonso and Raquel, notably the dramatist Antonio Mira de Amescua in 1625 with *La desdichada Raquel* (The unfortunate

Rachel), the poet Luis de Ulloa y Pereira in 1650 with *La Raquel,* and the playwright Juan Bautista Diamante, *La judía de Toledo* (The Jewess of Toledo) in 1667.

38. We know this cannot be completely accurate given that there is no extant manuscript by Rasis. In addition, as mentioned earlier, there was a purported reconstruction of Rasis' work by Rodríguez de Escabias in the seventeenth century, so there was certainly precedent for writers to believe that they had access to the tenth-century Arab historian.

39. According to Covarrubias, the seventeenth-century lexicographer, the word "curious" in its sense of improper knowledge and overweening curiosity to know, is first used, legendarily, by the snake with Eve in the Garden (*Tesoro de la lengua* 385a).

40. For an excellent study of the Cordoban martyrs during the early years following the invasion, see Kenneth Baxter Wolf.

41. Much has been made, especially recently, of the supposed pluralism and tolerance of Muslim Córdoba (Menocal), a view that quite a number of historians challenge. Rothstein points out that the irresistible invitation to idealize Andalusian history under Muslim rule tends to overlook the violence against other inhabitants of Iberia (for example, the massacre of thousands of Jews in Granada in 1066 and the forced exile of Christians in 1126) and against other Muslims and Islamic culture itself (for example, the massacres of Muslims in 805 and 818 in Córdoba, and the sacking of Córdoba in 1013, which resulted in the destruction of its legendary library).

42. The Hispanic Society acquired the collection of rare books owned by the Marqués de Jérez de los Caballeros, and this first edition of Mariana's history had been purchased in July 1882 from the Sunderland Library, Blenheim Palace. How the Sunderland Library acquired it is not known.

43. Although Mariana disagreed virulently with Miguel de Luna's historical portrait of the king, the triumphant Muslims, and the sexual intermingling of Christians and Muslims, their views on the iniquity prevalent in the Visigothic kingdom are not all that dissimilar. In 1676, Luna's *Verdadera historia del rey don Rodrigo* was in its seventh Spanish edition, and that decade witnessed its translation and printing in England as well. Thus, the historiography and the fiction that painted a damning portrait of eighth-century Spain, with its allegorical relevance to seventeenth-century Spain, worked together to form the view of the legend that made its way to England, and then back to Spain, as we will see in the next chapter.

44. Although written in 1600 and 1601, *De Monarchia hispanica discursus* was not printed until 1640.

Chapter Six · *Ancestral Ghosts and New Beginnings*

Epigraph: Volviendo al propósito, digo que la pérdida de España dio ocasionalmente a España el supremo lustre. Sin tan fatal ruina no se lograra restauración tan gloriosa . . . Ninguna Nación puede gloriarse de haber conseguido tantos triunfos en toda la larga carrera de los siglos, como la nuestra logró en ocho que se gastaron en la total expulsión de los Moros.

Nunca puedo acordarme de la pérdida de España sin añadir al dolor de tan gran calamidad otro sentimiento, por la injusticia que comúnmente se hace al más inculpable instrumento de ella. Hablo de la hija del Conde Don Julián, que violada por el Rey Don Rodrigo, participó la injuria a su padre...sobre ella cargan toda la culpa de nuestra ruina. ¡Oh feliz Lucrecia! ¡Oh desdichada Florinda! . . . ¿Por qué, pues, es celebrada Lucrecia, y detestada Florinda?

1. Díaz-Mas's extremely informative study offers chapters on the literature and language of the Jews after the expulsion, as well as a wealth of bibliography on the Sephardim. For the full account of Pulido's campaign and the opposition he faced from his countrymen, see especially pages 151–61.

2. Ferdinand was "el gran Maestro de la Política"; "Isabel, una mujer, no sólo más que mujer, pero aún más que hombre, por haber ascendido al grado de Heroína."

3. Cuban poet Gertrudis Gómez de Avellaneda is one of the authors to expand the legend to focus on the widow of Rodrigo, in her play *Egilona,* an interesting artifact since it is one of the few representations of any part of the legend of Rodrigo and La Cava to be written by a woman. Moreover, while the name of Rodrigo's wife has changed over the centuries, and in many cases, versions of the legend have not included a wife, Egilona is the name found in the earliest extant witness to the legend, the *Crónica mozárabe de 754.* This testifies to the endurance of some of the earliest material, which continued to circulate and influence modern works, in spite of the changes to the legend wrought by later added fictions and histories that purported to record fact.

4. René Girard, in several works, discusses his theories of triangular desire, in which the value lies not in the object desired, in this case Florinda, but is relative and varies depending on the power of the desire for the object by rivals. The relationship between the rivals is the driving force of desire, making it a male power struggle rather than a battle to win an inherently desirable woman, object, or goal.

5. The only early example of La Cava seeking the destruction of Spain to avenge her lost honor occurs in Bartolomé Palau's play *Historia de la gloriosa santa Orosia* (History of the glorious Saint Orosia).

6. These fiestas de moros y cristianos crossed the seas to the New World and were held regularly in the seventeenth and eighteenth centuries, further underscoring that Spain saw the Americas similarly to the Spain of the Reconquest, and the Amerindians as latter-day "infidels" to be converted or killed.

7. Said's work demonstrated, among other things, that Orientalism was based on Western notions of what constituted the cultures of Spain, North Africa, and the Near East rather than any intimate knowledge of the cultures themselves. Moreover, European fancy for things Oriental pretended to convey deep appreciation for them, while it served rather to distance the West from the exotic Other.

8. Cited in Bigatel-Abeniacar, "Nineteenth-Century American Women Traveling in Spain." Emilio Castelar was the fourth and last president of the Spanish Republic.

9. Champney and her husband, James Wells Champney, were well-known travelers and writers. He was a professor of art at Smith College and, after their marriage, illustrated most of Champney's books.

10. Menéndez Pidal's three-volume catalog and analysis of the king, *Rodrigo, el último godo* (Rodrigo, the last Goth), documents many other minor works of foreign authors, including French ones, inspired by the ballad tradition and by what he calls—and one can al-

most hear the resigned sigh behind the words—"the inevitable *Abulcaçim*," Luna's *Verdadera historia*. La Cava fared less well in France than in Spain, however. In the nineteenth century, a minor playwright, Mallefille, refers to loose or immodest women as "vraies Cavas" (true Cavas), even though the allusion was undoubtedly lost on the Parisian audience (xlvi). Victor Hugo's brother Abel wrote some ballads, which he gave to his father in 1821; Émile Deschamps imitated Spanish ballads to compose a number of his own in a series entitled *Rodrigue, dernier roy des goths* in 1827.

11. For additional examples of the angry response of nineteenth- and twentieth-century historians, as well as an important discussion of Luna's work, see Francisco Márquez Villanueva, "La voluntad de leyenda de Miguel de Luna."

12. Although Romanticism endowed Rodrigo with noble and tragic qualities not found in Luna's work, other aspects of Luna's work greatly influenced the shape of the legend in England, as it shaped the legend in Spain.

13. Saglia, Pratt, and Ragussis each document and analyze the plentiful examples of English Romanticism's insatiable appetite for Spanish history and myth.

14. Southey's poem was published in 1814 but begun much earlier, and there is some uncertainty about the influences and relationships of the three writers' works, since Southey, Scott, and Landor were friends and shared conversations and early drafts of materials.

15. Southey's own research notes clearly indicate that he read many of the sixteenth-century historians directly, such as Ambrosio de Morales, as well as many fictions, such as Lope's *Jerusalem Conquered*. Noticeably absent is reference to the ballad tradition that influenced his friends and other writers (Menéndez Pidal, *Floresta* 3: 47–48).

16. For an in-depth analysis of the poem and Southey's intentions toward English nationalism, see Saglia.

17. In the 1980s, Hispanists began in earnest to introduce works by women and works that had not been considered canonical but that represent a much broader spectrum of literary and cultural production from medieval and early modern Spain. For an example of the reconsideration of the effect of these nineteenth-century scholars on the study of Spanish culture, see the article by Catherine Brown.

18. Fita's study appeared in the *Boletín de la Real Academia de la Historia,* July–September 1887, 6–160.

19. Lea was a member of an important Philadelphia publishing family, who had both Irish Catholic and Quaker members. Lea's own religious preferences are somewhat difficult to sort out, but he was not a practicing Catholic. As a "fallen-away Catholic," as he was perceived by the Church, he was accused of developing his position on the Jews and against the practices of the Inquisition from an angry, personal perspective rather than objective scholarly inquiry.

20. In Havana, the two most exclusive nineteenth-century social clubs were the Galicians and the Asturians. The two groups shared a belief in their ancestral superiority as having come from families of "true Spaniards," yet also enjoyed a rivalry with each other based on which group could lay claim to the more illustrious lineage, the Asturians with Pelayo and the cradle of Spain or the Galicians from the resting place of Spain's patron saint, James the Moorslayer (Santiago Matamoros, or Santiago de Compostela). The two elegant buildings,

architectural grandes dames of a long-gone era, exist today, though run down and function-
ing as municipal centers.

21. For an interesting analysis of the contested relationship between Covadonga and the
Spanish state in the eighteenth, nineteenth, and twentieth centuries, see Boyd, "The Second
Battle of Covadonga."

22. Ronald Hilton recounts seeing these posters in Spain in his eyewitness account of the
years before and during the Spanish Civil War. In correspondence with me, he commented
that they were so vividly printed, he could remember them as if it were yesterday.

23. I am grateful to my colleague Gonzalo Sobejano for sharing memories of his childhood during the Spanish Civil War and the Franco years, and for telling me about "the Pelayos."

24. A measure of how far Spain has come in reevaluating the Franco years is in the humor
that now accompanies recollections of the past. For example, journalist Luis Otero's book *Flechas y Pelayos* (Arrows and Pelayos, 2001), about the indoctrination of the public, young and
old alike, in the Franco regime, offers a humorous look at textbooks, pamphlets, magazines,
and other tools of propaganda.

25. In *Isabel Rules,* see especially xxi–xxvii and the final chapter, "Isabel in the Twentieth
Century" (187–206).

26. Peter Linehan's remarkable book on Spanish history through the fourteenth century,
and Spanish historiography through the twentieth century, which treats this medieval historical period, includes a lengthy chapter on the fall in 711 (51–94) and the ways in which this
event became a lightning rod for the debates about what made Spain a nation, and what made
the nation, and its inhabitants, Spanish.

27. In the *Crónica mozárabe de 754* one Urbanus (a conspirator with the Muslims) has
been held by some to be the figure of Julian, even though Urbanus is mentioned well after
Rodrigo's defeat, and seems to be unconnected with Rodrigo. The identification of Julian
with Urbanus poses no appeal for Collins, who dismisses the argument that the wrong name
resulted from paleographic confusion: "it would require a fairly drunken scribe to have perpetrated such an error. It is only because historians are so reluctant to part with any form of
evidence, however far-fetched, that not only are such stories taken seriously but are also made
to condition the interpretation of materials that are intrinsically far more reliable. Urban thus
has to fit Julian, rather than Julian be seen as at best a distant literary echo of Urban" (36). For
another opinion on Julian, see, for example, Osvaldo A. Machado, "Los nombres del llamado
Conde Don Julián": "El primer documento en que aparece citado el llamado Conde Don
Julián is la *Crónica Mozárabe de 754*. Allí se habla de Urbano (Urbanus)" (107).

28. Thomas F. Glick shares Reilly's and Collins's view of the conquest as the inevitable result of an unstable government, calling the conquest "a walk-through" (32), which met with
little resistance from the conquered towns. In addition, Glick's book *Islamic and Christian
Spain in the Early Middle Ages* provides a particularly full bibliography of the early history of
the Iberian Peninsula.

29. Although Reilly notes here that Bishop Oppa (or Oppas) is the brother of Rodrigo's
predecessor, King Witiza, there isn't enough evidence to make this certain. As we saw in various accounts, Oppas is portrayed variously as the son of Witiza, the brother of Julian, the
brother of Rodrigo's wife, or no kin at all to any of the figures in the legend.

Epilogue

1. On October 19, 2004, for example, the *Guardian* of London reported in an article entitled "Spain's Aragon Region Confronting Controversial Past" that authorities in Aragon proposed a redesign of the province's heraldic shield, which includes severed heads of Muslims. Although conservatives oppose such a change, the proposal has drawn much support, including from the Union of Islamic Communities in Spain, whose leader was quoted as saying that such a move would be a "positive thing that would favour coexistence in Aragon." On another significant front, Spain faces continuing problems with the issue of immigration. Once the isolated land of the closed door, Spain is now a threshold to Europe for immigrants from many places. Politicians and others struggle with how to integrate new members of society and when or whether to limit immigration, and given the high number of Muslim immigrants, how to prevent economic pressures from stirring up anti-Islamic prejudice.

2. Writers outside of Spain have also contributed to the literary evocations of Islamic Spain. See, for example, the beautiful novels by Tariq Ali (*Shadows of the Pomegranate Tree,* 1993) and Radwa Ashour (*Granada: A Novel,* 2003).

3. Edward Said, acceptance speech, 2002 Prince of Asturias Award, www.fundacion principedeasturias.org/ing/04/premiados/discursos/discurso755.html. On December 4, 2008, the *New York Times* published an article, "Gene Test Shows Spain's Jewish and Muslim Mix," which reported on recent genetic studies that conclude that 20 percent of the population of the Iberian peninsula descend from Sephardic Jews and 11 percent have Muslim ancestry. This serves to remind us of the still-relevant questions about Spanish ancestry.

Primary Texts

Alfonso el Sabio. *Primera crónica general.* Fuentes cronísticas de la historia de España 1. Ed. Ramón Menéndez Pidal. Study by Diego Catalán. Madrid: Gredos, 1977.

———. *Las Siete Partidas.* Vol. 5. *Underworlds: The Dead, the Criminal and the Marginalized.* Trans. Samuel Parsons Scott. Ed. Robert I. Burns, S.J. Philadelphia: U of Pennsylvania P, 2001.

———. *Text and Concordance of Las Siete Partidas de Alfonso X* [microform], based on the edition of the Real Academia de la Historia, 1807. Ed. Jerry R. Craddock, John J. Nitti, Juan C. Temprano. Spanish Series 60. Madison: Hispanic Seminary of Medieval Studies, 1990.

Ángel de Saavedra, Duque de Rivas. *Florinda. Obras completas* 2. Madrid: 1895.

Arabian Nights. Trans. Husain Haddawy. Ed. Muhsin Madhi. New York: Norton, 1990.

Augustine, Saint. *The City of God.* Trans. Marcus Dods. New York: Modern Library, 1993.

———. *Confessions.* Trans. Henry Chadwick. Oxford World's Classics. Oxford: Oxford UP, 1998.

———. *De civitate Dei. CC* vols. 47–48. *PL* 41.13–804.

Benaim de Lasry, Anita. *Two Romances: A Study of Medieval Spanish Romances and an Edition of Two Representative Works.* Newark, DE: Juan de la Cuesta, 1982.

Bernáldez, Andrés. *Memorias del reinado de los Reyes Católicos.* Eds. M. Gómez-Moreno and J. de Mata Carriazo. Madrid: Real Academia de la Historia, 1962.

Blamires, Alcuin, ed. *Woman Defamed and Woman Defended: An Anthology of Medieval Texts.* Oxford: Clarendon, 1992.

Boniface, Saint. "The Correspondence of Saint Boniface." *The Anglo-Saxon Missionaries in Germany.* Ed. C.H. Talbot. New York: Sheed and Ward, 1954. 120–27.

———. *The Letters of Saint Boniface.* Ed. and Trans. Ephraim Emerton. New York: Columbia UP, 1940.

Calderón de la Barca, Pedro. *La cisma de Inglaterra.* Ed. Francisco Ruiz Ramón. Clásicos Castalia 119. Madrid: Castalia, 1981.

Casos notables en la ciudad de Córdoba (¿1618?). Ed. Francisco Baena Altolaguirre. Córdoba: Montilla, 1982.

Castigos e documentos para bien vivir ordenados por el Rey don Sancho IV. Ed. Agapito Rey. IUP
    Publications. Humanities Series No. 24. Bloomington: Indiana UP, 1952.

Castillo, Julián del. *Historia de los reyes godos.* Burgos: Phelippe de Junta, 1582.

Cervantes Saavedra, Miguel de. *Don Quijote de la Mancha.* Ed. Francisco Rico. 2 vols. Bar-
    celona: Instituto Cervantes, 1998.

————. *Don Quixote.* Trans. Edith Grossman. New York: Ecco, 2005.

Chacón, Gonzalo. *Crónica de Don Álvaro de Luna, Condestable de Castilla, Maestre de Santi-
    ago.* Ed. Juan de Mata Carriazo. Madrid: Espasa-Calpe, 1940.

Christine de Pizan. *The Book of the City of Ladies.* 1982. Trans. Earl Jeffrey Richards. Rev. ed.
    New York: Persea Books, 1998.

Conquerors and Chroniclers of Early Medieval Spain. Trans. Kenneth Baxter Wolf. Liverpool:
    Liverpool UP, 1990.

Constable, Olivia Remie, ed. *Medieval Iberia: Readings from Christian, Muslim, and Jewish
    Sources.* Philadelphia: U of Pennsylvania P, 1997.

Córdoba, Fray Martín de. *Jardín de nobles donzellas, Fray Martín de Córdoba: A Critical Edi-
    tion and Study.* Ed. Harriet Goldberg. North Carolina Studies in the Romance Languages
    and Literatures 137. Chapel Hill: U of North Carolina P, 1974.

Corral, Pedro de. *Crónica del Rey don Rodrigo, postrimero rey de los godos (Crónica sarracina).*
    Ed. James Donald Fogelquist. 2 vols. Clásicos Castalia 257 and 258. Madrid: Castalia, 2001.

————. *La Crónica del rey Don Rodrigo con la destruycion de España y como los moros la ga-
    naron. Nueuamente corregida. Contiene de mas dela historia, muchas biuas razones y auisos
    muy prouechosos.* Toledo: Juan Ferrer, 1549.

Die Chronik Alfons' III. Untersuchung und kritische Edition der vier Redaktionen. Ed. Jan
    Prelog. Frankfurt: Lang, 1980.

Crónica de 1344. Fuentes cronísticas de la historia de España. Eds. Diego Catalán and María
    Soledad de Andrés. Madrid: Gredos, 1970.

Crónica do Mouro Rasis. Fuentes cronísticas de la historia de España. Eds. Diego Catalán and
    María Soledad de Andrés. Madrid: Gredos, 1975.

Crónica mozárabe de 754. Ed. José Eduardo López Pereira. Textos medievales 58. Zaragoza:
    Anubar, 1980.

Díaz de Games, Gutierre. *El Victorial.* Ed. Rafael Beltrán Llavador. Madrid: Taurus, 1994.

Enríquez del Castillo, Diego. *Crónica de Enrique IV.* Ed. Aureliano Sánchez Martín. Val-
    ladolid: Universidad, 1990.

Feijóo, Benito Jerónimo. *Obras (selección).* Ed. Ivy L. McClelland. Madrid: Taurus, 1985.

————. *Teatro crítico universal.* 8 vols. 1726–1739. Available at *Proyecto Filosofía en español.*
    www.filosofia.org/bjf/bjft413.htm and bjft116.htm.

————. *Teatro crítico universal.* Vol. 2. Ed. Agustín Millares Carlo. Clásicos Castellanos 53.
    Madrid: Espasa-Calpe, 1965.

García de Salazar, Lope. 1967. *Bienandanzas e fortunas.* Ed. A. Rodríguez-Herrero. 4 vols. Bil-
    bao: Diputación Provincial de Vizcaya, 1984.

————. "Edición de las *Bienandanzas y fortunas.*" Ed. Ana María Marín Sánchez. http://
    parnaseo.uv.es/Lemir/Textos/bienandanzas/Menu.htm.

Gómez Pérez, José. "Leyendas medievales españolas del ciclo carolingio." *Anuario de Filología*
    (Maracaibo) 2–3 (1963–64): 7–136. Contains *Flores y Blancaflor, Berta,* and *Mainete.*

Goytisolo, Juan. *Count Julian.* Trans. Helen R. Lane. New York: Viking, 1974.

———. *Crónicas sarracinas.* 1981. Madrid: Alfaguara, 1998.

———. *Reivindicación del Conde don Julián.* 1970. Ed. Linda Gould Levine. Letras Hispánicas 220. Madrid: Cátedra, 1995.

———. *Saracen Chronicles: A Selection of Literary Essays.* Trans. Helen Lane. London: Quartet, 1992.

Historia de la Poncella de Francia. Ed. C. Savignac. *Révue Hispanique* 66 (1926): 510–95.

Ibn 'Abd al-Hakam. *The History of the Conquest of Egypt, North Africa, and Spain. Known as the Futūh Misr of Ibn 'Abd al-Hakam.* Ed. Charles C. Torrey. Yale Oriental Series—Researches III. New Haven: Yale UP, 1922.

León, Fray Luis de. *La perfecta casada.* Ed. Javier San José Lera. Madrid: Espasa-Calpe, 1992.

———. *Poesía completa.* Ed. José Manuel Blecua. Madrid: Gredos, 1990.

———. *Poesía de Fray Luis de León.* 1970. Ed. Oreste Macrí. Barcelona: Editorial Crítica, 1982.

López Madera, Gregorio. *Discursos de la certidumbre de las reliquias descubiertas en Granada desde el año 1585 hasta el de 1598.* Granada: Sebastian de Mena, 1601.

López Pinciano, Alonso. *Philosophía antigua poética.* 3 vols. Ed. Alfredo Carballo Picazo. Madrid: Consejo Superior de Investigaciones Científicas, Instituto "Miguel de Cervantes," 1953.

Luna, Miguel de. *Historia verdadera del Rey don Rodrigo.* Ed. Luis F. Bernabé Pons. Colección Archivum 86. Granada: Editorial Universidad de Granada, 2001.

———. *The History of the Conquest of Spain by the Moors.* London: F. Leach, 1687.

Mariana, Juan de. *The General History of Spain.* Trans. John Stevens. London: Richard Sare, Francis Saunders, Thomas Bennet, 1699.

———. *Historia general de España.* Biblioteca ilustrada de Gaspar y Roig. Madrid: Gaspar y Roig, 1852.

———. *Historia general de España; compuesta primero en Latín, despues buelta en Castellano.* Toledo: Pedro Rodríguez, 1601.

Matute y Gaviria, Justino. *Relación histórica de la Judería de Sevilla.* Seville: 1849.

Mena, Juan de. *Laberinto de Fortuna.* Ed. Maxim P.A.M. Kerkhof. Nueva biblioteca de erudición y crítica 9. Madrid: Castalia, 1995.

Menéndez Pidal, Ramón. *Floresta de leyendas heroicas españolas: Rodrigo, el último godo.* 1925–1927. 3 vols. Madrid: Espasa-Calpe, 1973.

———. *Reliquias de la poesía épica española.* 5th ed. Madrid: Espasa-Calpe, 1965.

Mesa, Cristóbal de. *La Restauración de España.* Madrid: Juan de la Cuesta, 1607.

Morales, Ambrosio de. *Corónica general de España que continuaba Ambrosio de Morales, coronista del rey nuestro señor, don Felipe II.* Vols. 6 and 7. Madrid: Benito Cano, 1791. Also facsimile, Alicante: Biblioteca virtual de Cervantes, 2003, www.cervantesvirtual.com.

Nebrija, Antonio de. *Gramática de la lengua castellana.* Ed. I. González-Llubera. London: Oxford UP, 1926.

———. *Gramática de la lengua castellana.* Ed. Antonio Quillis. 2nd. ed. Madrid: Editora Nacional, 1984.

Palau, Bartolomé. *Historia de la gloriosa Santa Orosia.* Barcelona: Sebastián de Comellas, 1637.

———. *Historia de la gloriosa Santa Orosia. Caída y ruina del imperio visigótico español.* Ed. A. Fernández Guerra. Madrid: Manuel G. Hernández, 1883. 99–200.

Palencia, Alfonso de. *Crónica de Enrique IV.* Ed. Antonio Paz y Melia. Madrid: 1975.

Pascual, Pedro. *Obras completas de San Pedro Pascual.* Vol. 4. Ed. P. Armengol Valenzuela. Rome: Imprenta Salustiana, 1908.

Poema de Fernán González. Ed. Juan Victorio. Madrid: Cátedra, 1981.

Poncella de Francia. La "historia" castellana de Juana de Arco. Eds. Victoria Campo and Víctor Infantes. Frankfurt/Madrid: Vervuert/Iberoamericana, 1997.

Pulgar, Fernando del. *Claros varones de Castilla.* Ed. R.B. Tate. Madrid: Taurus, 1985.

———. *Crónica de los Reyes Católicos, por su secretario Fernando del Pulgar.* Ed. Juan de Mata Carriazo. 2 vols. Madrid: Espasa-Calpe, 1943.

Ramíez, Ignacio. "1861 Discurso con motivo del aniversario de la independencia." www .memoriapoliticademexico.org/Textos/3Reforma/1861IGR.html.

Rodríguez de Almela, Diego. *Cartas.* Ed. David Mackenzie. Exeter Hispanic Texts 25. Exeter: U of Exeter P, 1980.

Romancero. Ed. Paloma Díaz-Mas. Barcelona: Crítica, c. 1994.

Saavedra Fajardo, Diego de. *Corona gótica, castellana y austríaca. Obras completas.* Ed. Ángel González Palencia. *BAE* 25. Madrid: Aguilar, 1946. 269–387.

———. *Idea de un príncipe político cristiano.* 1640. Valencia: Francisco Cipres, 1675.

———. *The Royal Politician Represented in One Hundred Emblems.* Trans. James Astrey. London: Matt Gylliflower, Luke Meredith, 1700.

Sánchez de Arévalo, Rodrigo. *Compendiosa historia Hispanica.* Rome: Ulrich Han, 1470.

Sánchez de Vercial, Clemente. *The Book of Tales by A.B.C.* Ed. and Trans. John E. Keller et al. New York: Peter Lang, 1992.

San Pedro, Diego de. *Cárcel de amor. Obras completas* 2. Ed. Keith Whinnom. Clásicos Castalia 39. 3rd ed. Madrid: Clásicos Castalia, 1985.

Sepúlveda, Lorenzo de. *Cancionero de romances (Sevilla, 1584).* Ed. Antonio Rodríguez-Moñino. Madrid: Castalia, 1967.

Southey, Robert. *Roderick; the Last of the Goths: A Tragic Poem.* Philadelphia: E. Earle, 1815.

Spanish Ballads with English Translations. Ed. and Trans. Roger Wright. Warminster, Eng.: Aris and Phillips, 1987.

Talbot, C.H., ed. and trans. *The Anglo-Saxon Missionaries in Germany. Being the Lives of SS. Willibrod, Boniface, Sturm, Leoba and Lebuin, together with the 'Hodoeporicon' of St. Wilibald and a selection from the correspondence of St. Boniface.* New York: Sheed and Ward, 1954.

Trueba y Cosío, [Joaquín] Telesforo de. 1830. *The Romance of History: Spain.* London: F. Warne, 1872.

Vagad, Gauberto Fabricio de. 1499. *Corónica de Aragón.* Edición facsimilar. Intro. María del Carmen Orcástequi Gros. Zaragoza: Cortes de Aragón, 1996.

Valera, Diego de. *Crónica de los Reyes Católicos.* Ed. Juan de Mata Carriazo. Madrid: J. Molina, 1927.

Vega Carpio, Lope de. *El niño inocente de La Guardia.* Ed. Anthony J. Farrell. London: Támesis, 1985.

———. *Las paces de los reyes y judía de Toledo.* Ed. James A. Castañeda. North Carolina Studies in the Romance Languages and Literatures 40. Chapel Hill: U of North Carolina P, 1962.

————. 1964. *El último godo. Obras escogidas.* Ed. Federico Carlos Sainz de Robles. Vol. 3. Madrid: Aguilar, 1987.

Vives, Juan Luis. *The Education of a Christian Woman: A Sixteenth-Century Manual.* Ed. and trans. Charles Fantazzi. Chicago: U of Chicago P, 2000.

————. *De institutione feminae Christianae.* Trans. Charles Fantazzi. Eds. C. Fantazzi and C. Malheerussen. 2 vols. Leiden: Brill, 1996–1998.

Walsh, J.K., and B. Bussell Thompson. *The Myth of the Magdalen in Early Spanish Literature (with an edition of the Vida de Santa María Madalena in MS. h-I-13 of the Escorial Library).* New York: Lorenzo Clemente, 1986.

X[J]iménez de Rada, Rodrigo. *Historia de los hechos de España.* Ed. Juan Fernández Valverde. Madrid: Alianza, 1989.

————. *Historia de rebus Hispaniae sive Historia Gothica.* Ed. Juan Fernández Valverde. Corpus Christianorum: Continuatio Mediaeualis 72. Turnhout: Brepols, 1987.

Secondary Texts

Aizenberg, Edna. "Una judía muy fermosa: The Jewess as Sex Object in Medieval Spanish Literature and Lore." *La Corónica* 12 (1984): 187–94.

Alonso, Dámaso. *De los siglos oscuros al de Oro.* Madrid: Gredos, 1982.

Alvarez-Hesse, Gloria. *La Crónica sarracina: Estudio de los elementos novelescos y caballerescos.* New York: Peter Lang, 1989.

Alvarez Junco, José. "The Formation of Spanish Identity and Its Adaptation to the Age of Nations." *History and Memory* 14.1/2 (2002): 13–36.

————. *Mater Dolorosa: La idea de España en el siglo XIX.* Madrid: Taurus, 2001.

Amador de los Ríos, J. 1845. *Historia social, política y religiosa de los judíos de España y Portugal.* 2 vols. Buenos Aires: Editorial Bajel, 1943.

Anderson, Benedict. *Imagined Communities.* 1983. Rev. ed. London: Verso, 1991.

Antuña, Melchor M. "Ibn Hayyan de Córdoba y su historia de la España musulmana." *Cuadernos de Historia de España* 3 (1945): 5–72.

Ashtor, Eliyahu. *The Jews of Moslem Spain.* 3 vols. Philadelphia: Jewish Publication Society of America, 1973–1984.

Azcona, Tarsicio de. *Isabel la Católica: estudio crítico de su vida y su reinado.* Madrid: [Editorial Católica], 1993.

Baer, Yitzhak. *A History of the Jews in Christian Spain.* Trans. Louis Schiffman. 2 vols. Philadelphia: Jewish Publication Society of America, 1961–1966.

Baines, Barbara J. "Effacing Rape in Early Modern Representation." *English Literary History* 65.1 (1998): 69–98.

Ballesteros Gaibrois, Manuel. *Isabel de Castilla, reina católica de España.* Madrid: Nacional, 1970.

————. *La obra de Isabel la Católica.* Segovia: Diputación Provincial de Segovia, 1953.

Barahona, Renato. "Mujeres vascas, sexualidad y ley en la época moderna (siglos XVI y XVII)." *Historia silenciada de la mujer: La mujer española desde la época medieval hasta la contemporánea.* Ed. Alain Saint-Saëns. Madrid: Editorial Complutense, 1996. 79–94.

————. *Sex Crimes, Honour, and the Law in Early Modern Spain: Vizcaya, 1528–1735*. Toronto: U of Toronto P, 2003.

Barnes, Robin Bruce. *Prophecy and Gnosis: Apocalypticism in the Wake of the Lutheran Reformation*. Stanford: Stanford UP, 1989.

Barthes, Roland. "The Discourse of History" and "The Reality Effect." *The Rustle of Language*. Trans. Richard Howard. Berkeley: U of California P, 1989. 127–54.

Bataillon, Marcel. *Erasmo y España: estudios sobre la historia espiritual del siglo XVI*. Trans. Antonio Alatorre. Mexico: Fondo de Cultura Económica, 1966.

Bergmann, Emilie. "The Exclusion of the Feminine in the Cultural Discourse of the Golden Age: Juan Luis Vives and Fray Luis de León." *Religion, Body and Gender in Early Modern Spain*. Ed. Alain Saint-Saëns. San Francisco: Mellen UP, 1991. 124–36.

Bernabé Pons, Luis F. *Bibliografía de la literatura aljamiado-morisca*. Alicante: Universidad de Alicante, 1992.

Berry, Philippa. *Of Chastity and Power: Elizabethan Literature and the Unmarried Queen*. London: Routledge, 1989.

Bigatel-Abeniacar, Bridget. "19th Century American Women Travelling in Spain: Unique Vistas from a Well-Trodden Path." www2.uah.es/asi/travels/19thwomen.htm.

Biglieri, Aníbal A. "Ascenso y caída del reino visigodo según la *Primera crónica general*." *Hispanófila* 96 (1989): 1–11.

Bilinkoff, Jodi. "A Spanish Prophetess and Her Patrons: The Case of María de Santo Domingo." *Sixteenth Century Journal* 23 (Spring 1992): 21–34.

Black, Georgina Dopico. *Perfect Wives, Other Women: Adultery and Inquisition in Early Modern Spain*. Durham: Duke UP, 2001.

Blacker, Irving R., ed. *Prescott's Histories: The Rise and Fall of the Spanish Empire*. New York: Viking, 1963.

Blamires, Alcuin. *The Case for Women in Medieval Culture*. New York: Oxford UP, 1997.

Bloch, R. Howard. *Etymologies and Genealogies: A Literary Anthropology of the French Middle Ages*. Chicago: U of Chicago P, 1986.

————. *Medieval Misogyny and the Invention of Western Romantic Love*. Chicago: U of Chicago P, 1991.

Bluestine, Carolyn. "The Power of Blood in the *Siete Infantes de Lara*." *Hispanic Review* 50 (1982): 201–17.

Boruchoff, David A., ed. *Isabel la Católica, Queen of Castile: Critical Essays*. New York: Palgrave Macmillan, 2003

Boyd, Caroline P. *Historia Patria: Politics, History and National Identity in Spain, 1875–1975*. Princeton: Princeton UP, 1997.

————. "The Second Battle of Covadonga." *History and Memory* 14 (2002): 37–64.

Braudel, Fernand. *The Mediterranean and the Mediterranean World in the Age of Philip II*. Trans. Sian Reynolds. 2 vols. New York: Harper-Torchbooks, 1976.

Bravo-Villasante, Carmen. *La mujer vestida de hombre en el teatro español: Siglos XVI–XVII*. Madrid: Sociedad General Española de Librería, 1976.

Bridenthal, Renate, and Claudia Koonz, eds. *Becoming Visible: Women in European History*. Boston: Houghton Mifflin, 1977.

Brokaw, Galen. "The Poetics of Khipu Historiography: Felipe Guaman Poma de Ayala's *Nueva crónica* and the *Relación de los Quipucumayos."* *Latin American Research Review* 38.3 (2003): 111–47.

Brown, Catherine. "The Relics of Menéndez Pidal: Mourning and Melancholia in Hispanomedieval Studies." *La Corónica* 24 (fall 1995): 15–41.

Brown, Jonathan. *Painting in Spain 1500–1700.* New Haven: Yale UP, 1999.

Brown, Peter. *The Cult of the Saints: Its Rise and Function in Latin Christianity.* Chicago: U of Chicago P, 1981.

Burns, E. Jane. *Bodytalk: When Women Speak in Old French Literature.* Philadelphia: U of Pennsylvania P, 1993.

Burns, Robert I., ed. *Emperor of Culture: Alfonso X the Learned of Castile and His Thirteenth-Century Renaissance.* Philadelphia: U of Pennsylvania P, 1990.

———. *The Worlds of Alfonso the Learned and James the Conqueror.* Princeton: Princeton UP, 1985.

Burshatin, Israel. "The Moor in the Text: Metaphor, Emblem, and Silence." *Critical Inquiry* 12 (autumn 1985): 98–118.

———. "Narratives of Reconquest: Rodrigo, Pelayo, and the Saints." *Saints and their Authors: Studies in Medieval Hispanic Historiography in Honor of John K. Walsh.* Eds. Jane E. Connolly, Alan Deyermond, and Brian Dutton. Madison: U of Wisconsin P, 1990. 13–26.

Burt, John R. *Selected Themes and Icons from Medieval Spanish Literature: Of Beards, Shoes, Cucumbers and Leprosy.* Potomac, MD: Studia Humanitatis, 1982.

Bynum, Caroline Walker. *Holy Feast and Holy Fast: The Religious Significance of Food to Medieval Women.* Berkeley: U of California P, 1982.

Cabanelas, Darío. *El morisco granadino Alonso del Castillo.* Granada: Patronato de la Alhambra, 1965.

Cameron, Averil. *Christianity and the Rhetoric of Empire: The Development of Christian Discourse.* Berkeley: U of California P, 1991.

Camp, Claudia V. *Wisdom and the Feminine in the Book of Proverbs.* Decatur, GA: Almond Press, 1985.

———. *Wise, Strange and Holy: The Strange Woman and the Making of the Bible.* Sheffield, Eng.: Sheffield Academic, 2000.

Campbell, Joseph. *The Hero with a Thousand Faces.* 3rd. ed. Bollingen Series. Princeton: Princeton UP, 1973.

Cardaillac, Louis. *Morisques et chrétiens. Un affrontement polémique (1492–1640).* Paris: Klincksieck, 1977.

Caro Baroja, Julio. *Las falsificaciones de la historia (en relación con la de España).* Barcelona: Seix Barral, 1992.

———. *Los moriscos del reino de Granada (ensayo de historia social).* 1957. Madrid: ISTMO, 2000.

Carrasco Urgoiti, María Soledad. *The Moorish Novel. El "Abencerraje" and Pérez de Hita.* Boston: Twayne, 1976.

———. *El moro de Granada en la literatura: Del siglo XV al XIX.* Granada: Universidad, 1989.

Castro, Américo. *The Spaniards: An Introduction to Their History.* Trans. Willard F. King and Selma Margaretten. 1971. Berkeley and Los Angeles: U of California P, 1985.

———. *The Structure of Spanish History.* Trans. Edmund L. King. Princeton: Princeton UP, 1954.

————. "Los visigodos no eran aún españoles." *Nueva Revista de Filología Hispánica* 15 (1961): 1–3.

Cátedra, Pedro M. *La historiografía en verso en la época de los Reyes Católicos.* Salamanca: Universidad de Salamanca, 1989.

Certeau, Michel de. *The Writing of History.* Trans. Tom Conley. New York: Columbia UP, 1988.

Christianson, Paul. *Reformers and Babylon: English Apocalyptic Visions from the Reformation to the Eve of the Civil War.* Toronto: U of Toronto P, 1978.

Cirot, Georges. "Anecdotes ou légendes sur l'époque d'Alphonse VIII." *Bulletin Hispanique* 28 (1926): 246–59; 29 (1927): 145–73, 251–54, 337–50.

Colley, Linda. 1992. *Britons: Forging the Nation, 1707–1837 (with a New Preface by the Author).* London: Pimlico, 2003.

Collins, Roger. *The Arab Conquest of Spain, 710–797.* Oxford: Basil Blackwell, 1989.

————. *Early Medieval Spain: Unity in Diversity, 400–1000.* London: Maurice Keen, 1983.

Conde, J.A. *Historia de la dominación de los árabes en España.* Madrid: Marín y compañía, 1820–1821.

Cooper, Kate. *The Virgin and the Bride: Idealized Womanhood in Late Antiquity.* Cambridge: Harvard UP, 1996.

Covarrubias Orozco, Sebastián de. *Tesoro de la lengua castellana o española.* Ed. Felipe C.R. Maldonado. Revised by Manuel Camarero. Madrid: Castalia, 1995.

Cruz, Anne J. "The Female Figure as Political Propaganda in the 'Pedro el Cruel *romancero.*'" *Spanish Women in the Golden Age: Images and Realities.* Eds. Magdalena S. Sánchez and Alain Saint-Saëns. Westport, CT: Greenwood, 1996. 69–89.

Darst, David H. "The Unity of *Las paces de los reyes y judía de Toledo.*" *Symposium* 25.3 (1971): 225–35.

De Armas, Frederick A. *The Return of Astraea: An Astral-Imperial Myth in Calderón.* Lexington: U of Kentucky P, 1986.

DeCosta, Miriam. "Historical and Literary Views of Yusuf, African Conqueror of Spain." *Journal of Negro History* 60.4 (1975): 480–90.

Defourneaux, Marcelin. 1966. *Daily Life in Spain in the Golden Age.* Trans. Newton Branch. Stanford: Stanford UP, 1998.

Deyermond, A.D. "The Death and Rebirth of Visigothic Spain in the *Estoria de España.*" *Revista Canadiense de Estudios Hispánicos* 9.3 (1985): 345–67.

————. *The Middle Ages.* London: Ernest Benn, 1971. Vol. 1 of *A Literary History of Spain.*

Deyermond, A.D., and Margaret Chaplin. "Folk-Motifs in the Medieval Spanish Epic." *Philological Quarterly* 51 (1972): 36–53.

Díaz-Mas, Paloma. *Sephardim: The Jews from Spain.* Trans. George K. Zucker. Chicago: U of Chicago P, 1992.

Díez, José Luis, ed. *La pintura de historia del siglo XIX en España.* Madrid: Ministerio de Cultura, 1992.

Dillard, Heath. *Daughters of the Reconquest: Women in Castilian Town Society, 1100–1300.* New York: Cambridge UP, 1984.

Dixon, Annette, ed. *Women Who Ruled: Queens, Goddesses, Amazons in Renaissance and Baroque Art.* London: Merrell, 2002.

Domínguez Ortiz, Antonio. *Autos de la Inquisición de Sevilla (siglo XVII)*. Seville: Servicio de Publicaciones del Ayuntamiento de Sevilla, 1981.

Domínguez Ortiz, Antonio, and Bernard Vincent. *Historia de los moriscos: vida y tragedia de una minoría*. Madrid: Alianza, 1985.

Donnell, Sidney. *Feminizing the Enemy: Imperial Spain, Transvestite Drama, and the Crisis of Masculinity*. Lewisburg, PA: Bucknell UP, 2003.

Dowling, John. *Diego de Saavedra Fajardo*. Boston: Twayne, 1977.

Dozy, Reinhart. 1913. *Spanish Islam: A History of the Moslems in Spain*. Trans. Francis Griffin Stokes. London: Cass, 1972.

Dyer, Nancy Joe. "Alfonsine Historiography: The Literary Narrative." *Emperor of Culture*. Ed. Robert I. Burns. Philadelphia: U of Pennsylvania P, 1990. 141–58.

Earenfight, Theresa, ed. *Queenship and Political Power in Medieval and Early Modern Spain*. Aldershot, Eng.: Ashgate, 2005.

Edwards, John. *The Spain of the Catholic Monarchs, 1474–1520*. Oxford: Blackwell, 2000.

Eire, Carlos M.N. *From Madrid to Purgatory: The Art and Craft of Dying in Sixteenth-Century Spain*. Cambridge: Cambridge UP, 1995.

———. *War Against the Idols: The Reformation of Worship from Erasmus to Calvin*. Cambridge: Cambridge UP, 1986.

Eisenberg, Daniel, ed. "Document. A Letter to Dr. Percy from John Bowle." *Bulletin of the Cervantes Society of America* 21.1 (spring 2001): 95–146.

Elliott, Dyan. *Spiritual Marriage: Sexual Abstinence in Medieval Wedlock*. Princeton: Princeton UP, 1993.

Elliott, John H. *Imperial Spain 1469–1716*. London: Arnold, 1963.

———. *Spain and Its World 1500–1700: Selected Essays*. New Haven: Yale UP, 1989.

Elm, Susanna. *'Virgins of God': The Making of Asceticism in Late Antiquity*. 1994. Oxford: Clarendon Press, 1996.

El Saffar, Ruth A. *Beyond Fiction: The Recovery of the Feminine in the Novels of Cervantes*. Berkeley and Los Angeles: U of California P, 1984.

———, ed. *Critical Essays on Cervantes*. Boston: Hall, 1986.

Enders, Jody. *Death by Drama and Other Medieval Urban Legends*. Chicago: U of Chicago P, 2002.

———. *The Medieval Theater of Cruelty: Rhetoric, Memory, Violence*. Ithaca: Cornell UP, 1998.

———. "Theater Makes History: Ritual Murder by Proxy in the *Mistere de la Sainte Hostie*." *Speculum* 79.4 (2004): 991–1016.

Enders, Victoria Lorée. "Nationalism and Feminism: The *Sección Femenina* of the Falange." *History of European Ideas* 15.4 (1992): 673–80.

Estal, J.M. del. "Felipe II y su archivo hagiográfico de El Escorial." *Hispania Sacra* 23 (1970): 193–335.

Ferguson, Margaret W. *Dido's Daughters. Literacy, Gender, and Empire in Early Modern England and France*. Chicago: U of Chicago P, 2003.

Fernández-Armesto, Felipe. *Columbus*. Oxford: Oxford UP, 1991.

———. *Ferdinand and Isabella*. New York: Taplinger, 1975.

Fernández-Guerra, Aureliano. *Caída y ruina del imperio visigótico español*. Madrid: Manuel G. Hernández, 1883.

————. *Don Rodrigo y La Cava*. Madrid: Aguado, 1877.

Fita, Fidel. "La Inquisición toledana. Relación contemporánea de los autos y autillos que celebró desde el año 1485 hasta el de 1501." *Boletín de la Real Academia de la Historia* 11 Jul.–Set. (1887): 289–322.

————. "La verdad sobre el martirio del santo niño de la guardia, o sea el proceso y quema (16 noviembre, 1491) del judío Jucé Franco en Ávila." *Boletín de la Real Academia de la Historia* 11 Jul.–Set. (1887): 6–160.

Flesler, Daniela. "Cristianas y moras: la identidad híbrida de España en *Moras y cristianas* de Angeles de Irisarri y Magdalena Lasala y *El viaje de la reina* de Angeles de Irisarri." *Revista de Estudios Hispánicos* 37 (2003): 413–35.

Fletcher, Richard. *Moorish Spain*. New York: Holt, 1992.

Fogelquist, James D. *Amadis y el género de la historia fingida*. Potomac, MD: Studia Humanitatis, 1982.

Forcione, Alban K. *Cervantes and the Humanist Vision: A Study of Four Exemplary Novels*. Princeton: Princeton UP, 1984.

Fraker, Charles F. *The Scope of History: Studies in the Historiography of Alfonso el Sabio*. Ann Arbor: U of Michigan P, 1996.

Franco, Jean. *Plotting Women: Gender and Representation in Mexico*. New York: Columbia UP, 1989.

Francomano, Emily C. "Manuscript Matrix and Meaning in Castilian and Catalan Anthologies of Saints' Lives and Pious Romance." *Bulletin of Hispanic Studies* 81.2 (2004): 139–53.

Frankl, Victor. *El 'Antijovio' de Gonzalo Jiménez de Quesada y las concepciones de realidad y verdad en la época de la contrarreforma y del manierismo*. Madrid: Ediciones Cultura Hispánica, 1963.

Fraser, Antonia. *The Warrior Queens*. New York: Knopf, 1989.

Fuchs, Barbara. *Mimesis and Empire: The New World, Islam, and European Identities*. Cambridge: Cambridge UP, 2001.

————. "Virtual Spaniards: The Moriscos and the Fictions of Spanish Identity." *Journal of Spanish Cultural Studies* 2.1 (2001): 13–26.

Garber, Marjorie. *Vested Interests: Cross-dressing and Cultural Anxiety*. New York: Routledge, 1992.

Gaster, Moses. "The Letter of Toledo." *Folklore* 13.2 (1902): 115–34.

Gaylord, Mary M. "Pulling Strings with Master Peter's Puppets: Fiction and History in *Don Quijote*." *Cervantes: Bulletin of the Cervantes Society of America* 18.2 (1998): 117–47.

————. "Spain's Renaissance Conquests and the Retroping of Identity." *Journal of Hispanic Philology* 16.2 (1992): 125–36.

Geary, Patrick. *Furta Sacra: Thefts of Relics in the Central Middle Ages*. Princeton: Princeton UP, 1978.

Gerli, E. Michael. "Social Crisis and Conversion: Apostasy and Inquisition in the Chronicles of Fernando del Pulgar and Andrés Bernáldez." *Hispanic Review* 70 (2002): 147–67.

Giles, Mary E., ed. *Women in the Inquisition: Spain and the New World*. Baltimore: Johns Hopkins UP, 1999.

Gilman, Sander. *The Jew's Body*. New York: Routledge, 1991.

Gilman, Stephen. *The Spain of Fernando de Rojas*. Princeton: Princeton UP, 1972.

Gilmore, David D. *Aggression and Community: Paradoxes of Andalusian Culture.* New Haven: Yale UP, 1987.

Giménez Caballero, E. "Interpretación de dos profetas: Joaquín Costa y Alfredo Oriani." *La conquista del estado: seminario de lucha y de información política.* Madrid: March 21, 1931. 1–2. Available at *Proyecto Filosofía en español.* www.filosofia.org/hem/193/lce/lce021d.htm

Girard, René. *Deceit, Desire and the Novel: Self and Other in Literary Structure.* Trans. Yvonne Freccero. Baltimore: Johns Hopkins UP, 1976.

Glick, Thomas F. *Islamic and Christian Spain in the Early Middle Ages: Comparative Perspectives on Social and Cultural Formation.* Princeton: Princeton UP, 1979.

Godoy Alcántara, José. *Historia crítica de los falsos cronicones.* Madrid: Real Academia de la Historia, 1868.

Goldberg, Harriet. "Sexual Humor in Misogynist Medieval Exempla." *Women in Hispanic Literature: Icons and Fallen Idols.* Ed. Beth Miller. Berkeley: U of California P, 1983. 67–83.

Gómez-Redondo, Fernando. "Historiografía medieval: constantes evolutivas de un género." *Anuario de Estudios Medievales* 19 (1989): 3–15.

González, Cristina. "Otas a la luz del folklore." *Romance Quarterly* 35.2 (1988): 179–91.

Gravdal, Kathryn. *Ravishing Maidens: Writing Rape in Medieval French Literature and Law.* Philadelphia: U of Pennsylvania P, 1991.

Greenblatt, Stephen. *Renaissance Self-Fashioning: From More to Shakespeare.* Chicago: U of Chicago P, 1980.

Grieve, Patricia E. *Desire and Death in the Spanish Sentimental Romance (1440–1550).* Newark, DE: Juan de la Cuesta, 1987.

———. *Floire and Blancheflor and the European Romance.* 1997. Cambridge: Cambridge UP, 2006.

———. "Paradise Regained in *Vida de Santa María Egipçiaca:* Harlots, the Fall of Nations, and Hagiographic Currency." *Translatio Studii: Essays by His Students in Honor of Karl D. Uitti for His Sixty-Fifth Birthday.* Eds. Renate Blumenfeld-Kosinski, Kevin Brownlee, Mary B. Speer, and Lori J. Walters. Amsterdam: Rodopi, 2000. 133–54.

———. "Private Man, Public Woman: Trading Places in *Condesa traidora.*" *Romance Quarterly* 34 (1987): 317–26.

Gusano Galindo, Elena. "Santa Orosia, Patrona de los endemoniados." *Andarines, senderismo y montaña.* www.andarines.com/culturapopular/santa.htm.

Hackett, Helen. *Virgin Mother, Maiden Queen: Elizabeth I and the Cult of the Virgin Mary.* New York: St. Martin's, 1995.

Hagerty, Miguel José. *Los libros plúmbeos del Sacromonte.* Madrid: Nacional, 1980.

Halavais, Mary. *Like Wheat to the Miller: Community, Convivencia, and the Construction of Morisco Identity in Sixteenth-Century Aragon.* New York: Columbia UP, 2002.

Haliczer, Stephen. "The Jew as Witch: Displaced Aggression and the Myth of the Santo Niño de la Guardia." *Cultural Encounters.* Eds. Mary Elizabeth Perry and Anne J. Cruz. Berkeley: U of California P, 1991. 146–55.

———. *Sexuality in the Confessional: A Sacrament Profaned.* Oxford: Oxford UP, 1996.

Hall, Kim F. "The Ottoman Empire and 'Turning Turk.'" *William Shakespeare, Othello, the Moor of Venice: Texts and Contexts.* Ed. Kim F. Hall. Boston: Bedford / St. Martin's, 2007. 203–9.

Harvey, L.P. *Islamic Spain, 1250 to 1500.* Chicago: U of Chicago Press, 1992.

———. *Muslims in Spain 1500 to 1614.* Chicago: U of Chicago Press, 2005.

Haskins, Susan. *Mary Magdalen: Myth and Metaphor.* New York: Harcourt Brace, 1993.

Hernández Juberías, Julia. *La península imaginaria: mitos y leyendas sobre Al-Andalus.* Madrid: CSIC, 1996.

Hillgarth, J.N. *The Spanish Kingdoms, 1250–1516.* 2 vols. Oxford: Clarendon, 1976–1978.

Homza, Lu Ann. *Religious Authority in the Spanish Renaissance.* Baltimore: Johns Hopkins UP, 2000.

Hsia, R. Po-chia. *The Myth of Ritual Murder: Jews and Magic in Reformation Germany.* New Haven: Yale UP, 1988.

Impey, Olga Tudorică. "Del duello de los godos de Espanna." *Romance Quarterly* 33 (1986): 295–307.

Jackson, Gabriel. *The Making of Medieval Spain.* New York: Harcourt Brace Jovanovich, 1972.

Janer, Florencio. *Condición social de los moriscos de España* [*Social condition of the moriscos of Spain*]: *causas de su expulsión, y consecuencias que ésta produjo en el orden económico y político.* Madrid: Real Academia de la Historia, 1857.

Jed, Stephanie H. *Chaste Thinking: The Rape of Lucretia and the Birth of Humanism.* Bloomington: Indiana UP, 1989.

Jordan, Constance. *Renaissance Feminism: Literary Texts and Political Models.* Ithaca: Cornell UP, 1990.

Jung, C.G. *Symbols of Transformation. The Collected Works of C.G. Jung.* Vol. 5. Bollingen Series 20. Princeton: Princeton UP, 1958.

Kagan, Richard L. *Lucrecia's Dreams: Politics and Prophecy in Sixteenth-Century Spain.* Berkeley: U of California P, 1990.

———. "Politics, Prophecy, and the Inquisition in Late Sixteenth-Century Spain." *Cultural Encounters.* Eds. Mary Elizabeth Perry and Anne J. Cruz. Berkeley: U of California P, 1991. 105–24.

Kahn, Coppelia. "The Rape in Shakespeare's *Lucrece.*" *Shakespeare and Gender: A History.* Eds. Deborah E. Barker and Ivo Kamps. New York: Verso, 1995. 22–46.

Kamen, Henry. *Empire: How Spain Became a World Power 1492–1763.* New York: Perennial, 2004.

———. *Philip of Spain.* New Haven: Yale UP, 1997.

———. *The Spanish Inquisition: A Historical Revision.* London: Weidenfeld and Nicolson, 1997.

Kaplan, Gregory B. "In Search of Salvation: The Deification of Isabel la Católica in *Converso* Poetry." *Hispanic Review* 66 (1998): 289–308.

Keller, Jean Paul. *The Poet's Myth of Fernán González.* Scripta Humanistica 81. Potomac, MD: Scripta Humanistica, 1990.

Klein, Joan. *Daughters, Wives, and Widows: Writings by Men about Women and Marriage in England, 1500–1640.* Champaign-Urbana: U of Illinois P, 1992.

Knudson, Charles A. "Le thème de la princesse sarrasine dans *La Prise d'Orange.*" *Romance Philology* 22 (1968–1969): 449–62.

Krappe, Alexander H. *The Legend of Roderick, Last of the Visigothic Kings, and the Ermanarich Cycle.* Heidelberg: C. Winter, 1923.

Kristeller, Paul Oskar. *Renaissance Thought and Its Sources.* Ed. Michael Mooney. New York: Columbia UP, 1979.

Kruger, Steven F. *Dreaming in the Middle Ages.* Cambridge: Cambridge UP, 1992.

Ladero Quesada, Miguel Angel. *Granada, historia de un país islámico (1232–1571).* Madrid: Gredos, 1989.

Lafaye, Jacques. "Reconquest, Djihad, Diaspora: Three Visions of Spain at the Discovery of America." Trans. Marc Metraux. *Diogenes* 87 (1974): 50–60.

Laiou, Argeliki E., ed. *Consent and Coercion to Sex and Marriage in Ancient and Medieval Societies.* Washington, D.C.: Dunbarton Oaks Research Library and Collection, 1993.

Lea, Henry Charles. *A History of the Inquisition of Spain.* 4 vols. New York: Macmillan, 1906–1908. Also http://libro.uca.edu.

———. *The Moriscos of Spain: Their Conversion and Expulsion.* 1901. New York: Burt Franklin, 1968.

———. "El Santo Niño de la Guardia." *The English Historical Review* 4.14 (1889): 229–50.

Lehfeldt, Elizabeth A. "The Gender of Shared Sovereignty: Texts and the Royal Marriage of Isabella and Ferdinand." *Women, Texts and Authority in the Early Modern Spanish World.* Eds. Marta V. Vicente and Luis R. Corteguera. Aldershot, Eng.: Ashgate, 2003. 37–55.

Leonard, Irving A. *Books of the Brave: Being an Account of Books and of Men in the Spanish Conquest and Settlement of the Sixteenth-Century New World.* New York: Gordian Press, 1964.

Levin, Carole. *The Heart and Stomach of a King: Elizabeth I and the Politics of Sex and Power.* Philadelphia: U of Pennsylvania P, 1994.

Linehan, Peter. *History and the Historians of Medieval Spain.* Oxford: Clarendon, 1993.

Liss, Peggy K. "Isabel, Myth and History." *Isabel la Católica, Queen of Castile: Critical Essays.* New York: Palgrave Macmillan, 2003. 57–78.

———. *Isabel the Queen: Life and Times.* New York: Oxford UP, 1992.

Lomax, Derek W. *The Reconquest of Spain.* London: Longman, 1978.

López-Baralt, Luce. 1985. *Islam in Spanish Literature: From the Middle Ages to the Present.* Trans. Andrew Hurley. New York: Brill, 1992.

Lovett, A.W. *Early Habsburg Spain 1517–1598.* Oxford: Oxford UP, 1986.

MacCormack, Sabine. "History, Memory and Time in Golden Age Spain." *History and Memory* 4.2 (1992): 38–68.

Machado Mouret, Osvaldo A. "Historia de los árabes de España, por Ibn Jaldun." *Cuadernos de Historia de España* 4 (1946): 136–46; 6 (1946):146–53.

———. "Historia de los árabes de España, por Ibn Jaldun (continuación)." 45–46 (1967): 374–95; 47–48 (1968): 353–76.

———. "La historia de los godos según Ibn Jaldun." *Cuadernos de Historia de España* 1–2 (1944): 139–55.

———. "Los nombres del llamado conde Don Julián." *Cuadernos de Historia de España* 3 (1945): 106–16.

MacKay, Angus. *Spain in the Middle Ages: From Frontier to Empire, 1000–1500.* London: Macmillan, 1977.

Maguire, Fiona, and Dorothy S. Severin. "Fernán Pérez de Guzmán's *Loores de santos:* Texts and Traditions." In *Saints and Their Authors: Studies in Honour of John K. Walsh.* Eds.

Jane E. Connolly, Alan Deyermond, and Brian Dutton. Madison: Hispanic Seminary of Medieval Studies, 1990. 151–68.

Malti-Douglas, Fedwa. *Woman's Body, Woman's Word: Gender and Discourse in Arabo-Islamic Writing*. Princeton: Princeton UP, 1991.

Mann, Vivian B., Thomas F. Glick, and Jerrilyn D. Dodds, eds. *Convivencia: Jews, Muslims, and Christians in Medieval Spain*. New York: Braziller, 1992.

Maravall, José Antonio. *Culture of the Baroque: Analysis of a Historical Structure*. Trans. Terry Cochran. 1975. Minneapolis: U of Minnesota P, 1986.

Marín, Manuela. "Marriage and Sexuality in Al-Andalus." *Marriage and Sexuality in Medieval and Early Modern Iberia*. Ed. Eukene Lacarra Lanz. New York and London: Routledge, 2002. 3–20.

Maroto Camino, Mercedes. "'Ya no es Lucrecia, Lucrecia': Woman and *limpieza de sangre* in Rojas Zorrilla's *Lucrecia y Tarquino*." *Revista Canadiense de Estudios Hispánicos* 21.2 (1997): 329–51.

Márquez Villanueva, Francisco. *El problema morisco (desde otras laderas)*. Madrid: Ediciones Libertarias, 1991.

———. "La voluntad de leyenda de Miguel de Luna." *Nueva Revista de Filología Hispánica* 30 (1981): 358–95.

Martin, Colin, and Geoffrey Parker. *The Spanish Armada*. Rev. ed. Manchester: Manchester UP, 1999.

Martin, Georges. "La chute du royaume visigothique d'Espagne dans l'historiographie chrétienne des VIIIe et IXe siècles: sémiologies socio-historique." *Cahiers de Linguistique Hispanique Médiévale* 9 (1984): 207–33.

Marx, Anthony W. *Faith in Nation: Exclusionary Origins of Nationalism*. New York: Oxford UP, 2003.

Matar, Nabil I. *Turks, Moors, and Englishmen in the Age of Discovery*. New York: Columbia UP, 1988.

Mayberry, Nancy. "The Controversy over the Immaculate Conception in Medieval and Renaissance Art, Literature, and Society." *The Journal of Medieval and Renaissance Studies* 21 (fall 1991): 207–24.

McCracken, Peggy. "The Body Politic and the Queen's Adulterous Body in French Romance." *Feminist Approaches to the Body in Medieval Literature*. Eds. Linda Lomperis and Sarah Stanbury. Philadelphia: U of Pennsylvania P, 1994. 38–64.

———. *The Curse of Eve, the Wound of the Hero: Blood, Gender, and Medieval Literature*. Philadelphia: U of Pennsylvania P, 2003.

———. *The Romance of Adultery: Queenship and Sexual Transgression in Old French Literature*. Philadelphia: U of Pennsylvania P, 1998.

McKendrick, Melveena. *Playing the King: Lope de Vega and the Limits of Conformity*. London: Támesis, 2000.

———. *Theatre in Spain 1490–1700*. Cambridge: Cambridge UP, 1989.

———. *Woman and Society in the Spanish Drama of the Golden Age: A Study of the "Mujer Varonil."* London: Cambridge UP, 1974.

McLeod, Glenda. *Virtue and Venom: Catalogs of Women from Antiquity to the Renaissance*. Ann Arbor: U of Michigan P, 1991.

McNamara, Jo Ann Kay. *Sisters in Arms: Catholic Nuns Through Two Millenia.* Cambridge, MA: Harvard UP, 1996.

Menéndez y Pelayo, Marcelino. *Historia de los heterodoxos españoles.* 1880–1882. 8 vols. Buenos Aires: Emecé, 1945; Santander: Aldus, 1946–48.

———. *Obras completas.* Vol. 3. *Estudios sobre el teatro de Lope de Vega.* Ed. Enrique Sánchez Reyes. Madrid: CSIC, 1949.

———. "El último rey godo en España." *Antología de poetas líricos castellanos.* Vol. 1. Madrid: Biblioteca Clásica, 1903.

Menéndez Pidal, Ramón. *The Cid and His Spain.* Trans. Harold Sunderland. London: Murray, 1934.

———. *El rey Rodrigo en la literatura.* Madrid: Tipografía de la Revista de Archivos, Bibliotecas y Museos, 1925.

Menocal, Maria Rosa. *Ornament of the World: How Muslims, Jews, and Christians Created a Culture of Tolerance in Medieval Spain.* Boston and New York: Back Bay / Little Brown, 2002.

Meyerson, Mark D. *The Muslims of Valencia in the Age of Fernando and Isabel: Between Coexistence and Crusade.* Berkeley: U of California P, 1991.

Meyerson, Mark D., and Edward D. English, eds. *Christians, Muslims, and Jews in Medieval and Early Modern Spain: Interaction and Cultural Change.* Notre Dame Conferences in Medieval Studies, 8. Notre Dame: U of Notre Dame P, 2000.

Michael, Ian. "'From her shall read the perfect ways of honour': Isabel of Castile and Chivalric Romance." *The Age of the Catholic Monarchs 1474–1516: Literary Studies In Memory of Keith Whinnom.* Eds. Alan Deyermond and Ian Macpherson. Liverpool: Liverpool UP, 1989. 103–12.

Miles, Margaret R. *Carnal Knowing: Female Nakedness and Religious Meaning in the Christian West.* Boston: Beacon, 1989.

Milhou, Alain. *Colón y su mentalidad mesiánica en el ambiente franciscanista español.* Valladolid: Casa-Museo de Colón, 1983.

———. "De la destruction de l'Espagne a la destruction des Indes: Histoire sacrée et combats idéologiques." *Etudes sur l'impact culturel du Nouveau Monde.* Ed. Marie Cécile Benassy et. al. Vol. 1. Paris: Séminaire interuniversitaire sur l'Amérique espagnole coloniale, 1981–83. 25–47. 3 vols.

Millares Carlo, Agustín. "La biblioteca de Gonzalo Argote de Molina." *Revista de Filología Española* 10 (1923): 137–52.

Miller, William Ian. *Humiliation: And Other Essays on Honor, Social Discomfort, and Violence.* Ithaca: Cornell UP, 1993.

Mirrer, Louise. *Women, Jews, and Muslims in the Texts of Reconquest Castile.* Ann Arbor: U of Michigan P, 1996.

Moner, Michel. "Deux figures emblématiques: La femme violée et la parfaite épouse, selon le *Romancero General* compilé par Agustín Durán." *Images de la femme en Espagne aux XVIe et XVIIe siècles: des traditions aux renouvellements et à l'émergence d'images nouvelles: Colloque international Sorbonne et Collège d'Espagne, 28–30 septembre 1992.* Ed. Augustin Redondo. Paris: Publications de la Sorbonne, 1994. 77–90.

Monod, Paul Kléber. *The Power of Kings: Monarchy and Religion in Europe, 1589–1715.* New Haven: Yale UP, 1999.

Monroe, James T. *Islam and the Arabs in Spanish Scholarship (Sixteenth Century to the Present)*. Leiden: Brill, 1970.

Monter, E. William. *Frontiers of Heresy: The Spanish Inquisition from the Basque Lands to Sicily.* Cambridge: Cambridge UP, 1990.

Morcillo Gómez, Aurora. "Shaping True Catholic Womanhood: Francoist Educational Discourse on Women." *Constructing Spanish Womanhood: Female Identity in Modern Spain.* Eds. Victoria Lorée Enders and Pamela Beth Radcliff. Albany: State U of New York P, 1999. 51–69.

Moreno Nieto, Luis. *Leyendas de Toledo, Antología.* Toledo: Imprenta Serrano, 1999.

Nader, Helen. *The Mendoza Family in the Spanish Renaissanace 1350 to 1550.* New Brunswick: Rutgers University Press, 1979.

Nagore de Zand, Josefina. "La alabanza de España en el *Poema de Fernán González* y en las crónicas latino-medievales." *Incipit* 7 (1987):35–67; 9 (1989): 13–31.

Netanyahu, Benzion. *The Origins of the Inquisition in Fifteenth-Century Spain.* New York: Random House, 1995.

Niccoli, Ottavia. *Prophecy and People in Renaissance Italy.* Trans. Lydia G. Cochrane. Princeton: Princeton UP, 1990.

Nieto Soria, Jose Manuel. *Ceremonias de la realeza: propaganda y legitimación en la Castilla Trastámara.* Madrid: Nerea, 1993.

Nirenberg, David. *Communities of Violence: Persecutions of Minorities in the Middle Ages.* Princeton: Princeton UP, 1996.

———. "Conversion, Sex, and Segregation: Jews and Christians in Medieval Spain." *American Historical Review* 107.4 (2002): 1065–93.

———. "Deviant Politics and Jewish Love: Alfonso VIII and the Jewess of Toledo." *Jewish History* 21 (2007): 15–41.

O'Callaghan, Joseph F. *The Learned King: The Reign of Alfonso X of Castile.* Philadelphia: U of Pennsylvania P, 1993.

Otero, Luis. *Flechas y Pelayos.* Madrid: EDAF, 2001.

The Oxford Dictionary of the Christian Church. 3rd ed. Ed. E.R. Livingstone. Oxford: Oxford UP, 1997.

Pagden, Anthony. *Lords of All the World: Ideologies of Empire in Spain, Britain and France, c.1500–1800.* New Haven: Yale UP, 1995.

———. *Spanish Imperialism and the Political Imagination: Studies in European and Spanish-American Social and Political Theory, 1513–1830.* New Haven: Yale UP, 1990.

Pagels, Elaine. *Adam, Eve, and the Serpent: Sex and Politics in Early Christianity.* New York: Vintage, 1989.

Paster, Gail Kern. *The Body Embarrassed: Drama and the Disciplines of Shame in Early Modern England.* Ithaca: Cornell UP, 1993.

Pardo, Madeleine. "Pelayo et la fille du marchand. Réflexions sur la *Crónica Sarracina.*" *Atalaya* 4 (1993): 9–59.

———. "Le Roi Rodrigue ou Rodrigue roi." *Imprévue* 1 (1983): 61–105.

Peers, E. Allison. *A History of the Romantic Movement in Spain.* 1940. New York: Hafner, 1964

Pelikan, Jaroslav. *Mary Through the Centuries: Her Place in the History of Culture.* New Haven: Yale UP, 1996.

———. *Angel de Saavedra, Duque de Rivas. Revue Hispanique* 8 (June–August 1923): 1–303; 304–600.

Perry, Mary Elizabeth. *Gender and Disorder in Early Modern Seville.* Princeton: Princeton UP, 1990.

———. *The Handless Maiden: Moriscos and the Politics of Religion in Early Modern Spain.* Princeton: Princeton UP, 2005.

———. "Magdalens and Jezebels in Counter-Reformation Spain." *Culture and Control in Counter-Reformation Spain.* Eds. Anne J. Cruz and Mary Elizabeth Perry. Minneapolis: U of Minnesota P, 1992. 124–44.

———. "Weaving with Clio and *Moriscas* of Early Modern Spain." *Attending to Early Modern Women.* Eds. Susan D. Amussen and Adele Seeff. Newark: UP of Delaware, 1998. 58–73.

Perry, Mary Elizabeth, and Anne J. Cruz, eds. *Cultural Encounters: The Impact of the Inquisition in Spain and the New World.* Berkeley: U of California P, 1991.

Pick, Lucy K. *Conflict and Coexistence: Archbishop Rodrigo and the Muslims and Jews of Medieval Spain.* History, Languages, and Cultures of the Spanish and Portuguese Worlds. Ann Arbor: U of Michigan P, 2004.

Porres Martín-Cleto, Julián. *Enigma histórico; El baño de la Cava.* Toledo: Instituto provincial de investigaciones y estudios toledanos; Fundación Juanelo Turriano and Editorial Castalia, 1991.

Poska, Allyson. *Regulating the People: The Catholic Reformation in Seventeenth-Century Spain.* Leiden: Brill, 1998.

Pratt, Lynda. "Diego Saglia, *Poetic Castles in Spain:* British Romanticism and Figurations of Iberia." *Romanticism On the Net* 24 (November 2001): 5 pars. www.erudit.org/revue/ron/2001/v/n24/006002ar.html.

Prescott, Anne Lake. "Evil Tongues at the Court of Saul: The Renaissance David as a Slandered Courtier." *Journal of Medieval and Renaissance Studies* 21 (1991): 163–86.

Prescott, William H. *History of the Reign of Ferdinand and Isabella, the Catholic.* Boston: American Stationers, 1838.

Rackin, Phyllis. "Genealogical Anxiety and Female Authority: The Return of the Repressed in Shakespeare's Histories." *Contending Kingdoms: Historical, Psychological, and Feminist Approaches to the Literature of Sixteenth-Century England and France.* Eds. Marie-Rose Logan and Peter L. Rudnytsky. Detroit: Wayne State University, 1991. 323–45.

Ragussis, Michael. "The Birth of a Nation in Victorian Culture: The Spanish Inquisition, the Converted Daughter, and the 'Secret Race.'" *Critical Inquiry* 20.3 (1994): 477–508.

———. *Figures of Conversion: "The Jewish Question" and English National Identity.* Durham: Duke UP, 1995.

Ratcliffe, Marjorie. "Adulteresses, Mistresses, and Prostitutes: Extramarital Relations in Medieval Castile." *Hispania* 67 (1984): 346–50.

Reeves, Marjorie. *The Influence of Prophecy in the Later Middle Ages: A Study of Joachimism.* 1969. South Bend, IN: U of Notre Dame P, 1993.

Reilly, Bernard F. *The Contest of Christian and Muslim Spain 1031–1157.* Cambridge, MA: Basil Blackwell, 1992.

———. *The Kingdom of León-Castilla under King Alfonso VI, 1065–1109.* Princeton: Princeton UP, 1988.

————. *The Kingdom of León-Castilla under Queen Urraca, 1109–1126*. Princeton: Princeton UP, 1982.

————. *The Medieval Spains*. Cambridge: Cambridge UP, 1993.

Rigney, Ann. *The Rhetoric of Historical Representation: Three Narrative Histories of the French Revolution*. Cambridge: Cambridge UP, 1990.

Riley, E.C. *Cervantes's Theory of the Novel*. Oxford: Clarendon, 1962.

Rogers, Katharine M. *The Troublesome Helpmate: A History of Misogyny in Literature*. Seattle: U of Washington P, 1966.

Romero, José Luis. *Sobre la biografiá y la historia*. Buenos Aires: Editorial Sudamericana, 1945.

Rosaldo, Renato. "Lope as a Poet of History: History and Ritual in *El testimonio vengado*." *Ensayos sobre la comedia del Siglo de Oro español, de distintos autores*. Ed. Alva Vernon Ebersole. Valencia: Ediciones Albatross Hispanófila, 1979. 9–32. Vol. 2. of *Perspectivas de la Comedia*.

Rose, Mary Beth. *Gender and Heroism in Early Modern English Literature*. Chicago: U of Chicago P, 2002.

Roth, Cecil. "Jews, Conversos, and the Blood-Accusation in Fifteenth-Century Spain." *The Dublin Review: A Quarterly and Critical Journal* 191 (1932): 219–31.

Roth, Norman. *Conversos, Inquisition, and the Expulsion of the Jews from Spain*. Madison: U of Wisconsin P, 1995.

————. *Jews, Visigoths, and Muslims in Medieval Spain: Cooperation and Conflict*. Leiden: Brill, 1994.

Rothstein, Edward. "Was Islam in Spain Truly Tolerant?" *New York Times*, September 27, 2003: B9 and B11.

Round, Nicholas. *The Greatest Man Uncrowned: A Study of the Fall of Alvaro de Luna*. London: Támesis, 1986.

Rubin, Miri. *Corpus Christi: The Eucharist in Late Medieval Culture*. Cambridge: Cambridge UP, 1991.

————. *Gentile Tales: The Narrative Assault on Late Medieval Jews*. New Haven: Yale UP, 1999.

Rubin, Nancy. *Isabella of Castile: The First Renaissance Queen*. New York: St. Martin's, 1991.

Rucquoi, Adeline. "De Jeanne d'Arc à Isabelle la Catholique: l'image de la France en Castille au XVe siècle." *Journal des Savants* (January–June 1990): 155–74.

Ruether, Rosemary Radford. "Misogynism and Virginal Feminism in the Fathers of the Church." *Religion and Sexism: Images of Woman in the Jewish and Christian Traditions*. Ed. Rosemary Radford Ruether. New York: Simon and Schuster, 1974. 150–83.

Ruiz, Teófilo F. *Crisis and Continuity: Land and Town in Late Medieval Castile*. Philadelphia: U of Pennsylvania P, 1994.

————. *Spanish Society 1400–1600*. Harlow, Eng.: Pearson, 2001.

Saglia, Diego. "Nationalist Texts and Counter-Texts: Southey's *Roderick* and the Dissensions of the Annotated Romance." *Nineteenth-Century Literature* 53.4 (1999): 421–51.

Said, Edward. "Concord Award Speech." *Fundación Príncipe de Asturias*, 2002, www.fundacion principedeasturias.org/ing/04/premiados/discursos/discurso755.html.

————. *Orientalism*. New York: Pantheon, 1978.

Saint-Saëns, Alain, ed. *Religion, Body and Gender in Early Modern Spain*. San Francisco: Mellen UP, 1991.

————. *Sex and Love in Golden Age Spain.* New Orleans: UP of the South, 1996.

Salisbury, Joyce E. *Church Fathers, Independent Virgins.* London: Verso, 1991.

Sánchez Albornoz, Claudio. "Dónde y cuándo murió don Rodrigo, último rey de los godos." *Cuadernos de Historia de España* 3 (1945): 5–105.

————. *España: un enigma histórico.* Buenos Aires: Editorial Sudamericana, 1957.

————. *El reino de Asturias: Orígenes de la nación española. Estudios críticos sobre la historia del reino de Asturias.* 1972–1975; Oviedo: Instituto de Estudios Asturianos, 1983.

————. "San Isidoro, 'Rasis' y la Pseudo-Isidoriana." *Cuadernos de Historia de España* 4 (1946): 73–113.

Sánchez Ortega, María Helena. *La mujer y la sexualidad en el antiguo régimen: La perspectiva inquisitorial.* Madrid: Ediciones Akal, 1992.

————. "Woman as Source of 'Evil' in Counter-Reformation Spain." *Culture and Control in Counter-Reformation Spain.* Trans. Susan Isabel Stein. Eds. Anne J. Cruz and Mary Elizabeth Perry. Minneapolis: U of Minnesota P, 1992. 196–215.

Santos Vaquero, A., and E. Vaquero Fernández-Prieto. 4th ed. *Fantasía y realidad de Toledo.* Toledo: Azacanes, 2002.

Scales, Peter. *The Fall of the Caliphate of Córdoba: Berbers and Andalusis in Conflict.* Leiden: Brill, 1994.

Schlauch, Margaret. *Chaucer's Constance and Accused Queens.* 1927. New York: Gordion Press, 1969.

Schulenberg, Jane Tibbetts. *Forgetful of Their Sex: Female Sanctity and Society, ca. 500–1100.* Chicago: U of Chicago Press, 1998.

————. "The Heroics of Virginity: Brides of Christ and Sacrificial Mutilation." *Women in the Middle Ages and Renaissance.* Ed. Mary Beth Rose. Syracuse: Syracuse UP, 1986. 29–72.

Scott, George Ryley. *The History of Prostitution.* London: Senate, 1968.

Shannon, Albert C. *The Medieval Inquisition.* 1984. Collegeville, MN: Liturgical Press, 1991.

Sicroff, Albert A. "Clandestine Judaism in the Hieronymite Monastery of Nuestra Señora de Guadalupe." *Studies in Honor of M.J. Benardete.* New York: Las Américas, 1965. 89–125.

————. *Los estatutos de limpieza de sangre. Controversias entre los siglos XV y XVII.* Trans. Mauro Armino. Madrid: Taurus, 1985.

————. "The Jeronymite Monastery of Guadalupe in 14th and 15th Century Spain." *Collected Studies in Honour of Americo Castro's Eightieth Year.* Ed. M.P. Hornik. Oxford: Lincombe Lodge, 1965. 397–422.

Solomon, Michael. *The Literature of Misogyny in Medieval Spain: The "Arcipreste de Talavera" and the "Spill."* Cambridge: Cambridge UP, 1997.

Sommerville, Margaret R. *Sex and Subjection: Attitudes to Women in Early-Modern Society.* London: Arnold, 1995.

Spaccarelli, Thomas D. *A Medieval Pilgrim's Companion: Reassessing 'El Libro de los huéspedes' (Escorial MS. h l 13).* North Carolina Studies in the Romance Languages and Literatures 261. Chapel Hill: U of North Carolina Dept. of Romance Languages, 1998.

Spiegel, Gabrielle M. *Romancing the Past: The Rise of Vernacular Prose Historiography in Thirteenth-Century France.* 1993. Berkeley: U of California P, 1995.

Spitzer, Leo. "Fray Luis de León's 'Protecía del Tajo.'" *Romanische Forschungen* 64 (1952): 225–40.

Stallybrass, Peter. "Patriarchal Territories: The Body Enclosed." *Rewriting the Renaissance. The*

Discourses of Sexual Difference in Early Modern Europe. Eds. Margaret W. Ferguson, Maureen Quilligan, and Nancy J. Vickers. Chicago: U of Chicago Press, 1986. 123–42.

Starkey, David. *Elizabeth: The Struggle for the Throne.* New York: Harper Collins, 2001.

Street, Florence. "Hernán Núñez and the Earliest Printed Editions of Mena's *El laberinto de Fortuna.*" *Modern Language Review* 61 (1966): 51–63.

Strohm, Paul. *Hochon's Arrow: The Social Imagination of Fourteenth-Century Texts.* Princeton: Princeton UP, 1992.

Struever, Nancy S. *The Language of History in the Renaissance: Rhetoric and Historical Consciousness in Florentine Humanism.* Princeton: Princeton UP, 1970.

Surtz, Ronald E. "Morisco Women, Written Texts, and the Valencia Inquisition." *Sixteenth Century Journal* 32.2 (2001): 421–33.

Tate, Robert B. *Ensayos sobre la historiografía peninsular del siglo XV.* Trans. Jesús Díaz. Madrid: Gredos, 1970.

———. "La historiografía del reinado de los Reyes Católicos." *Antonio de Nebrija: Edad Media y Renacimiento.* Eds. Carmen Codoñer and Juan Antonio González Iglesias. Salamanca: Universidad de Salamanca, 1994. 17–28.

———. "Mythology in Spanish Historiography of the Middle Ages and the Renaissance." *Hispanic Review* 22 (1954): 1–18.

Thompson, E.A. *The Goths in Spain.* Oxford: Clarendon, 1969.

Thompson, Stith. *Motif-Index of Folk-Literature: A Classification of Narrative Elements in Folk-Tales, Ballads, Myths, Fables, Mediaeval Romances, Exempla, Fabliaux, Jest-Books, and Local Legends.* 2nd. ed. 6 vols. Bloomington: Indiana UP, 1955–1958.

Ticknor, George. *History of Spanish Literature.* 3 vols. New York: Harper, 1854.

Tofiño-Quesada, Ignacio. "Spanish Orientalism: Uses of the Past in Spain's Colonization in Africa." *Comparative Studies of South Asia, Africa and the Middle East* 23.1/2 (2003): 141–48.

Tolan, John V. *Saracens: Islam in the Medieval European Imagination.* New York: Columbia UP, 2002.

Trexler, Richard C. *Sex and Conquest: Gendered Violence, Political Order, and the European Conquest of the Americas.* Ithaca: Cornell UP, 1995.

Uitti, Karl D. *Story, Myth, and Celebration in Old French Narrative Poetry, 1050–1200.* Princeton: Princeton UP, 1973.

Vickers, Nancy. "'The blazon of sweet beauty's best': Shakespeare's *Lucrece.*" *Shakespeare and the Question of Theory.* Eds. Patricia Parker and Geoffrey Hartmann. New York: Methuen, 1985. 95–115.

Vidal Tolosa, Mariano. "El rey don Rodrigo, o un ensayo de psicología histórica." *Revista de Ciencias y de Artes* 19 (1919): 269–80.

Vincent, Bernard. *Minorías y marginados en la España del siglo XVI.* Granada: Diputación Provincial de Granada, 1987.

Vitz, Evelyn Birge. "Rereading Rape in Medieval Literature: Literary, Historical, and Theoretical Reflections." *Romanic Review* 88 (1997): 1–26.

Vossler, Karl. *Luis de León.* Munich: Schnell and Steiner, c. 1946.

Walsh, William Thomas. *Isabella of Spain.* New York: Tudor, 1931.

———. "Reply to Dr. Cecil Roth." *The Dublin Review: A Quarterly and Critical Journal* 191 (1932): 232–52.

Walthaus, Rina. "Entre Diana y Venus: Mujeres castas y mujeres fatales en el teatro de Juan de la Cueva y Cristóbal de Virués." *La mujer en la literatura hispánica de la Edad Media y el Siglo de Oro.* Ed. Rina Walthaus. Amsterdam: Rodopi, 1993. 71–90.

Ward, Benedicta. *Harlots of the Desert: A Study of Repentance in Early Monastic Sources.* Kalamazoo, MI: Cistercian Publications, 1987.

Wardropper, Bruce. "*Don Quixote:* Story or History?" *Modern Philology* 63.1 (1965): 1–11.

Warner, Marina. *Alone of All Her Sex: The Myth and the Cult of the Virgin Mary.* New York: Vintage, 1983.

———. *Joan of Arc: The Image of Female Heroism.* 1981. London: Penguin, 1987.

Wasserstein, David J. *The Caliphate in the West: An Islamic Political Institution in the Iberian Peninsula.* Oxford: Clarendon, 1993.

Watt, W. Montgomery and Pierre Cachia. *A History of Islamic Spain.* 1965. Edinburgh: Edinburgh UP, 1992.

Weinstein, D. and R.M. Bell. *Saints and Society: The Two Worlds of Western Christendom, 1000–1700.* Chicago: U of Chicago Press, 1982.

Weissberger, Barbara F. *Isabel Rules: Constructing Queenship, Wielding Power.* Minneapolis: U of Minnesota P, 2004.

Welles, Marcia L. *Persephone's Girdle: Narratives of Rape in Seventeenth-Century Spanish Literature.* Nashville, TN: Vanderbilt UP, 2000.

Wheatcroft, Andrew. *Infidels: A History of the Conflict between Christendom and Islam.* New York: Random House, 2004.

Wheelwright, Julie. *Amazons and Military Maids: Women Who Cross-dressed in the Pursuit of Life.* London: Pandora, 1989.

White, Hayden. *Metahistory: The Historical Imagination in Nineteenth-Century Europe.* Baltimore: Johns Hopkins UP, 1973.

Whitney, James Lyman. *Catalogue of the Spanish Library and of the Portuguese Books Bequeathed by George Ticknor to the Boston Public Library.* Boston: Trustees, 1879.

Williams, Ann, ed. *Prophecy and Millenarianism: Essays in Honour of Marjorie Reeves.* London: Longman, 1980.

Wolf, Kenneth Baxter. *Conquerers and Chroniclers of Early Medieval Spain.* Liverpool: Liverpool UP, 1990.

Wolfthal, Diane. "Women's Communities and Male Spies: Erhard Schön's *How Seven Women Complain about Their Worthless Husbands.*" *Atttending to Early Modern Women.* Eds. Susan D. Amussen and Adele Seeff. Newark: UP of Delaware, 1998. 117–54.

Woods, Marjorie Curry. "Rape and the Pedagogical Rhetoric of Sexual Violence." *Criticism and Dissent in the Middle Ages.* Ed. Rita Copeland. Cambridge: Cambridge UP, 1996. 56–86.

Yarbro-Bejarano, Yvonne. *Feminism and the Honor Plays of Lope de Vega.* Purdue Studies in Romance Literatures 4. West Lafayette, IN: Purdue UP, 1994.

Yates, Frances A. *Astraea: The Imperial Theme in the Sixteenth Century.* London: Routledge, 1975.

———. *The Art of Memory.* Chicago: U of Chicago P, 1966.

Zagorin, Perez. *Ways of Lying: Dissimulation, Persecution, and Conformity in Early Modern Europe.* Cambridge, MA: Harvard UP, 1990.

Abdelasis (Abd al-Aziz), 39, 40, 173, 213
"Abenámar" (ballad), 130
Abulcaçim Tarif Abentariq, 162, 172, 227n10
Ahmad al-Razi, 44, 143, 192
Alarcos, Battle of, 60, 189
Alexander VI, Pope, 104
Alfonso, Prince of Asturias, 77
Alfonso I, of León, 43, 72, 121, 148, 179
Alfonso II, el Casto, 152
Alfonso III of Asturias, 27, 41, 43
Alfonso IV, 58–59
Alfonso VI, 96, 150
Alfonso VIII, 27, 51, 61–62, 82, 130; and Jewess
    of Toledo, 49, 60, 99, 129, 189, 191, 207;
    and Rodrigo, 62–63, 129
Alfonso X, el Sabio (the Learned), of Castile
    and León, 49, 54, 63, 73; aspirations of, 51;
    and ballads, 133; and blood libel, 66; and
    body, 27; *Estoria de España,* 43, 46, 47,
    50–52, 58, 60, 78, 132, 142; and historical
    truth, 142; and Morales, 143; and relics, 152
Alfonso XI, 63
Alhambra, 2, 3, 71
Almanzor, King, 58, 130, 162
Alquifa, 56–57
alumbradismo (Illuminism), 115, 117
"Amores trata Rodrigo" (ballad), 131, 133
Antigüedades de las ciudades de España
    (Morales), 151
Arabian Nights, 31–32
Aragon, 6, 12, 66, 85, 88
Astraea, 111, 119, 165, 262n4
Asturias: and Castile, 63; and Jews, 105; kings
    of, 43, 72; modern, 231, 232–33, 238, 240;
    and monarchy, 3, 110; and Morales, 148, 151;
    and Muslim conquest, 2, 43; and new Spain,
    105; and Pelayo, 41, 145; ties to, 64; and
    Visigoths, 145

Augustine, St., 34–35, 73, 201, 273n30
Ave-Eva, 33–34, 36, 37, 85, 114
Aznar, José María, 9, 10

ballads, 45, 117, 129–39; blame and guilt in,
    124; historical, 165; and history, 156; influ-
    ence of, 217; and La Cava, 167, 180–85; and
    Luis de León, 128–29; noble Moor in, 159;
    and Rodrigo, 180–85; and Visigothic king-
    dom, 125
ballads, by title: "Abenámar," 130; "Amores
    trata Rodrigo," 131, 133; "El baño de la
    Cava," 181–83; "La Cava al rey forzador,"
    183–84; "Cuán triste queda Castilla,"
    135–36; "De los nobilísimos godos que
    en Castilla habían reinado," 136; "De una
    torre de palacio," 138–39; "En Ceupta está
    Julián," 133–34, 135; "Gran llanto hace la
    Cava," 134; "Las huestes de don Rodrigo,"
    131; "Rodrigo's Penance," 122, 133; "Triste
    estaba don Rodrigo, desdichado se llam-
    aba," 137; "Los vientos eran contrarios," 131
"El baño de la Cava" (ballad), 181–83
Barenboim, Daniel, 10
Becket, Thomas, 46, 49
Beltrán de la Cueva, 70
Berceo, Gonzalo de, 100, 224
Bernáldez, Andrés, 99, 101, 230
Bible, 68, 72, 85, 103, 137; fall and redemption
    in, 201; figures from, 33, 37, 40, 81, 121, 130,
    176; and Rodrigo, 82; and Sepúlveda, 130
biography, 69, 72–73, 77, 83, 84, 91
blood purity *(limpieza de sangre),* 110, 136;
    and ancestry, 16, 53; and Jews, 98, 224; and
    Luna, 173; and Pelayo, 105, 130, 148; and
    Solmira, 187; and Toledan statute, 67;
    and Visigoths, 105, 145
Boabdil, 2, 6, 8, 93, 198

Boccaccio, Giovanni, 84
body, 26–27, 34, 183; and nation, 125–26, 127, 148, 155, 157. *See also* sexuality
Bolea, Fernando de, 80
Boniface, St., 26, 38–39, 52
Bovelles, Charles de, 113
Bowle, John, 180
Bramante, 47, 48

Calderón de la Barca, Pedro, 188–89
Campanella, Tommaso, 199–200
Cantabrian Mountains, 3, 23
Capitulations of the Holy Faith, 2
Cárdenal, Gutierre de, 89
Cartagena, Alonso de, 70–71, 74
Carvajal, Diego de, 96
Casilda, St., 150
Casos notables de Córdoba, 166, 191–93
Castigos e documentos para bien vivir ordenados por el Rey don Sancho IV, 54–55
Castile, 12, 51, 55, 73–75, 85; and Aragon, 66, 88; and Asturias, 63; and bloodlines, 53; and Ferdinand I, 88–89, 94, 112; and Isabel, 88, 94, 95; and Spain, 135, 136
Castilian Spanish, 12, 172
Castillo, Alonso del, 161, 170
Castro, Américo, 4, 30, 43, 240, 244
Castro, Pedro de, 174
Catherine (daughter of Pedro I), 63
Catherine of Alexandria, St., 90
Catherine of Aragon, 140
"La Cava al rey forzador" (ballad), 183–84
Celestina, 166
Ceriziers, René de, 91
Cervantes, Miguel de, 109, 119, 180, 218; *Don Quixote,* 133, 141, 163, 164, 169, 192–93, 195, 224
Champney, Elizabeth Williams, 215, 217
Charlemagne, 111, 149; and *Flores and Blancaflor,* 15, 46; and Galiana, 47–48, 49, 58, 59, 129, 150
Charles I and V, of Spain, Holy Roman Emperor, 111, 112, 140, 149, 158, 232
Charles III, of Spain, 116
Charles VI, of France, 111
Charles VIII, of France, 111
chastity, 33, 37, 85, 187; and identity, 113; and Isabel, 119; and Joan of Arc, 91; and La Cava, 120; and Lucretia, 37; and morality, 114; of Pelayo, 27; and political order, 27, 32, 39, 114, 115, 120; and rape, 121. *See also* virginity
Chaucer, Geoffrey, 100

Christianity, 13, 14, 45, 48, 58; and biography, 72–73; and chastity, 27; and Flores and Blancaflor, 15, 141–42; and identity, 11; and Julian, 24; and Luna, 174; and Muslims/Islam, 125, 161, 170, 173, 186; and Pelayo, 81; and Sepúlveda, 130; and sexuality, 125, 173, 186
Christine de Pizan, 87
chronicles, 75, 77, 145; Arab, 25, 53, 54, 59, 235, 236, 252n4; Asturian Christian, 55, 237; Christian, 27–28, 44, 52, 53, 66; false, 141, 171, 197; *letrado,* 73, 74. *See also* history
El Cid (Rodrigo Díaz de Vivar), 16, 28, 58, 96, 155, 224, 225
Cisneros, Francisco Jiménez de, 6, 112–13, 142, 168
Clifford, Charles, 3, 71, 214
Columbus, Christopher, 1, 92, 93
confession, 119, 123, 124
conversos (New Christians), 4, 67, 81; and Antichrist, 98, 99; and Holy Child of La Guardia, 100–104; and Inquisition, 174, 197, 223, 228; and Isabel, 72, 94, 95, 96; Judaizing by, 67, 98; and Moriscos, 103; sentiment against, 11, 64, 110, 115, 157. *See also* Jews
Córdoba, 2, 51, 64, 66, 191–92, 193
Cornelius, St., 127
Corral, Pedro de, 45, 145, 192; and ballads, 129, 130, 133, 134; and confession, 119, 123; *Crónica del Rey don Rodrigo (Crónica sarracina),* 6, 7, 22, 23, 30, 55, 69, 78, 80–83, 104–5, 110–11, 118, 124, 132; and English Romantics, 220; and Juan II, 258n22; and Lope de Vega, 188; and Luna, 162, 167, 171, 172; and Mariana, 176; and Menéndez Pidal, 217; and Morales, 144–45, 176; and Pérez de Guzmán, 122, 218; and Ticknor, 218–19; and truth, 142, 145
Corte Real, Jerónimo, 160
Costa, Joaquín, 225
Council of Basle, 74
Council of Trent, 124
Counter-Reformation, 109, 114, 119, 135, 150
Covadonga, 26, 41, 42, 238; Battle of, 3, 23, 105, 109, 143; Cave of, 8, 55, 231–32, 233
Crónica de 1344, 50, 54, 56–57, 60, 143
Crónica de Alfonso III, 40–42, 44, 45, 52, 145, 146, 147, 173
Crónica del Rey don Rodrigo (Crónica sarracina) (Corral), 6, 7, 22, 23, 30, 55, 69, 78, 80–83, 104–5, 110–11, 118, 124, 132

Corónica general (Morales), 152
Crónica mozárabe de 754, 25, 39, 40, 45, 80, 201, 236, 254n12
"Cuán triste queda Castilla" (ballad), 135–36

Decadence Tradition, 45, 49, 144, 168; defined, 39; and destruction, 132; and king and nation, 52, 75, 76; and Visigoths, 236
"De los nobilísimos godos que en Castilla habían reinado" (ballad), 136
De Rebus Hispaniae (Mariana), 163, 164–65
De rebus Hispaniae (Ximénez de Rada), 143
"De una torre de palacio" (ballad), 138–39
Díaz de Games, Gutierre, 75–76, 79, 80, 142
Don Quixote (Cervantes), 133, 141, 163, 164, 169, 192–93, 195, 224
Drake, Sir Francis, 155

Edicts of Expulsion, 4, 66, 102, 159, 161, 206, 225
Egilona (Rodrigo's daughter), 173, 213
Egilona (Rodrigo's wife), 29, 39, 82, 172, 173
Eliata, 172
Elizabeth I, 37, 114, 119, 247n16, 263n11
Elizabeth of Hungary, St., 88
"En Ceupta está Julián" (ballad), 133–34, 135
Encina, Juan del, 111
England, 28, 92, 115, 148–49, 155, 168, 198
Enrique (half-brother of Juan I), 63
Enrique (son of Juan I), 63
Enrique II, of Trastámara, 63, 70
Enrique III, 64, 70
Enrique IV, 70, 72, 74, 77, 78, 85, 88, 98
Enríquez del Castillo, 77–79
Ermesinda, 27, 43, 72, 121, 148, 165, 174, 213
Espina, Alonso de, 98–99, 101
Estoria de España (Alfonso X), 43, 46, 47, 50–52, 58, 60, 78, 132, 142
Eve, 33, 37, 165, 234; and La Cava, 2, 15, 25–26, 27, 38, 81, 105, 119, 123, 125, 126, 128, 129, 131, 138, 167, 181–82; and Mary Magdalene, 114; and nation, 35, 115; and Virgin Mary, 33–34, 86, 95

Fatho-l-Andaluci, 44–45
Favila, 42–43, 83, 148
Feijóo, Benito Jerónimo, 180, 197, 205, 207–8, 212
Ferdinand I, 27, 77, 85, 109, 137; and Aragon and Castile, 66; and Castile, 88–89, 94, 112; and Columbus, 93; and Edict of Expulsion, 4; and evangelization, 104; and fall of

Granada, 2; and Feijóo, 207; and Inquisition, 67; and Isabel, 12, 70, 88, 89, 94; and Jews, 102; and Lope de Vega, 104; Mariana on, 179–80; and military, 84, 92; and Muslims, 4; and Pelayo, 109
Fernández-Armesto, Felipe, 95
Fernández-Guerra, Aureliano, 125
Fernando III, 51, 59, 66
Ferrer, St. Vincent, 64, 98, 102
Field, Kate, 215
Fita, Fidel, 225, 226, 227, 228
Floire, King, 46
Floire and Blancheflor, 15, 46
Flores, Juan de, 175
Flores and Blancaflor, 15
France, 28, 68, 91, 92, 115, 168, 198
Franco, Francisco, 12, 16, 207, 232, 233–34, 238

Galiana, 47, 49, 58, 59, 129, 150
Galicia, 2, 151, 241
Gallego, José María, 239, 240
Gálvez, María Rosa, 211–12
Garci, José Luis, 241–42
García de la Huerta, Vicente, 212–13
García de Salazar, Lope, 60–61, 62, 63, 76–77
Garden of Eden, 34–35, 76, 136; and fall of Spain, 24, 27, 53, 123, 129, 132, 134
Garibay y Zamalloa, Esteban de, 148, 153, 154
Gayangos y Arce, Pascual, 223
God, 72, 74, 81, 86; and Alfonso VIII, 61–62, 189; and history, 140; and Morales, 146; and Pelayo, 23, 24, 42, 71, 81, 124; punishment by, 36, 39, 45, 52, 54, 55, 60, 61–62, 67, 76, 136, 145, 168, 196
Gower, John, 120
Goytisolo, Juan, 30–31, 244
Gramática castellana (Nebrija), 12
Granada, 4, 8, 70, 92–93, 104, 110, 130, 179–80
"Gran llanto hace la Cava" (ballad), 134
Grillparzer, Franz, *The Jewess of Toledo*, 217
Guadalete, Battle of, 23, 144, 145, 176, 235
Guevara, Antonio de, 142

Helen of Troy, 26, 36, 49, 97; and La Cava, 115, 134, 182, 183, 185, 188
Henry VIII, 112, 140
Hercules, 73, 74–75, 76, 136
Hernández, Miguel, 153, 154
Historia de la gloriosa santa Orosia (Palau), 125–27, 150, 186
Historia de los dos enamorados Flores y Blancaflor, 141–42

Historia de los hechos de España (Ximénez de
Rada), 55
Historia general de España (Mariana), 164,
175–76, 178, 179, 180, 199
Historia verdadera del rey don Rodrigo (Luna),
138, 161–63, 164–65, 166–75, 186
history, 10, 38, 50, 189, 191–92; Arabic, 50; and
Aragon and Castile, 66; and ballads, 130,
136, 156; cyclical, 82; and eyewitnesses, 140,
144; and gender, 186; and Luna, 171; mis-
sion of, 139–40; and Morales, 143, 146; and
morality, 164–65; of nation, 50–53, 73; and
origins, 68, 73, 74; and prophecy, 141, 142,
164; truth in, 69, 122, 140, 141, 143, 164.
See also chronicles
Hoefnagle, Joris, 48
Holy Child of La Guardia (Santo Niño de la
Guardia), 72, 99, 100–104, 225–28
Holy Sudarium of Oviedo, 152
Homer, 75, 164
Horace, 128–29
Host desecration, 98, 99, 100, 101, 104
House of Hercules, 21; evolution of, 44; and
rape, 57; and Rodrigo, 21, 40, 44–45, 57,
75–76, 80, 83, 113, 133, 168, 192–93
"Las huestes de don Rodrigo" (ballad), 131
Huguenots, 115
humanism, 68, 72, 77, 78, 115, 138

Ibárruri, Dolores, 31
Ibn ʿAbd al-Hakam, 40, 170, 173
Ibn al-Kittaya, 44
Ibn Zamrak, 46
Idlefonso, St., 152
Inquisition, 4, 6, 17, 67, 99, 224; and conver-
sos, 174, 197, 223, 228; and Holy Child of
La Guardia, 102, 225; and Lucrecia de León,
149, 157; and myth, 11; turmoil produced
by, 109; and witchcraft, 115
Isabel, 77, 83–90, 111, 112, 137; achievements
of, 109; appearance of, 94; and Aragon and
Castile, 66; and body, 27; and Castile, 85,
94; and chastity, 119; and conversos, 94, 95,
96; and fall of Granada, 2, 70; and Feijóo,
207; and Ferdinand I, 12, 70, 88, 89, 94;
and Franco, 234; gender of, 70, 84; and
God, 72; and her people, 87; and Inquisition, 67; and Jews, 102; and Joan of Arc,
83, 84, 90–91, 92; and justice, 89; and La
Cava, 86, 93, 96; and Lope de Vega, 104;
Mariana on, 179–80; and Martín de Córdoba, 85–88, 89; and Mendoza, 94–95; and

military, 84, 88, 92; and MS h-I-13, 89–90;
and Muslims, 4; and nation, 37, 115; and
Nebrija's *Gramática castellana,* 12; as peacekeeper, 247n16; and Pelayo, 70, 72; as repairer and restorer, 95; and Reyes Católicos
title, 104; and Rodríguez de Almela, 96–97;
as shield for her people, 87–88; and throne
of Castile, 88, 95; and Virgin Mary, 72, 83–
84, 85, 86, 87, 88, 92, 95, 179; and Visigothic
kingdom, 84; as warrior queen, 90–96
Isidore of Seville, 41, 68, 134
Islam, 10, 15, 45, 58; fear of, 7, 28, 31; as forbidden, 159; and Luna, 174; as merging with
Christianity, 161, 170; prophecied destruction of, 113; and sexuality, 158; and St. James
of Compostela, 43. *See also* Muslims

James of Compostela, St., 3–4, 5, 43, 45, 150
Jerome, St., 33
Jerusalem Conquered (Vega Carpio), 188
Jesuits, 119
Jesus Christ, 33, 35, 55, 84, 100, 152
Jewess, 24–25, 27, 49, 60, 63
Jewess of Toledo (Fermosa/Raquel), 49, 82,
130, 212–13; legend of, 60, 61–62, 99, 102,
129; in Lope de Vega, 189, 190, 191
The Jewess of Toledo (Grillparzer), 217
Jews, 67, 159, 253n11; and ancestry, 4, 16, 67;
and black magic, 63; and blood libel, 14,
65–66, 72, 98, 99, 100; and child murder,
98, 99–100, 105; conversion of, 4, 64; as
councilors, 62, 63; expulsion of, 4–5, 8, 13,
30, 66, 72, 102, 104, 110, 225; fear/anxiety
about, 14, 67, 81–82, 98, 103, 105; hatred of,
60; and Holy Child of La Guardia, 100–104,
225–28; identity of, 11; and La Cava story,
24; and Ladino, 12, 206; massacre of, 49, 63,
64, 67, 102; modern scholarship on, 223–24;
and monarchy, 98; in Morales, 144; and
Muslims, 23, 81; and national history, 163;
and Pelayo, 105; return of, 206; rightful
exclusion of, 28; and sexuality, 158; and
Trastamaran dynasty, 64; and Visigoths,
81. *See also* conversos
Joan of Arc, 83, 84, 90–91, 92, 156
John of Biclaro, 80
John of Lancaster, 63
Juan, Prince of Asturias, 111
Juan (son of García de Salazar), 60
Juana la Beltraneja, 70, 72, 85, 88
Juana of Portugal, 70
Juan I, 63, 64, 70

Juan II, of Castile, 70, 71, 72, 73, 78, 79, 97, 130

Julian, 29; in Arab sources, 44; betrayal by, 77; blame for, 53, 54, 55, 77, 79, 80, 97, 126, 130, 145, 193; and Christianity, 24; conspiracy of, 76; and devil, 82; flight of, 175; and Gálvez, 211–12; historicity of, 235–36, 238; and honor, 55, 194; and identity, 110; and Morales, 144; and Muslims, 23, 133; portrayal of, 44; remorse of, 124; and Rodrigo, 188; and rotten egg motif, 45, 167; and sons of Witiza, 192; story of, 21, 22–23; as traitor, 131, 134, 145; treachery of, 83, 133, 136; vengeance of, 24, 25, 45, 79, 133, 180, 187, 192; wife of, 57

kings/rulers, 26, 54–55, 75, 85; councilors to, 55, 57, 61, 62, 63; and fall of Spain, 35–36; and Jesuits, 119; and nobleman, 79; powers of, 166; responsibility of, 50; Rodrigo as, 176; and sexuality, 31–32, 39, 76, 120; and Visigoths, 52; and women, 54, 96, 97. *See also* monarchy

Kitab-al-Ictifa, 44–45

La Cava, 272n24; anguish of, 134; and Arabic customs, 182; as bad Christian woman, 115, 126; and ballads, 129, 167; beauty of, 21, 56, 128, 129, 133; blame for, 15, 54, 55, 96–97, 114, 118, 124, 126, 130–31, 133, 134, 137, 138, 139, 176, 182–83, 185, 187, 188, 189; complexity of, 83, 135; as cruel maiden, 123; as dangerous, 131, 165; and David-Bathsheba story, 81; and death and snake, 183; destructive speech of, 23, 83, 97, 126, 135; and devil, 82, 83; and Egilona, 82; and Eve, 2, 15, 25–26, 27, 38, 81, 105, 119, 123, 125, 126, 128, 129, 131, 138, 167, 181–82; as evil, 185; evolution of, 14, 15, 24–25, 29, 36, 44, 53, 54, 55, 114; and fall of Spain, 24, 35, 96–97, 120–21, 185; and Feijóo, 207, 208, 209–10; and *Flores and Blancaflor*, 15; and Gálvez, 211; and God's punishment, 168; guilt of, 37–38; and Helen of Troy, 134, 182, 183, 185, 188; historicity of, 235, 236, 238; and honor, 45, 57; imprisonment of, 45; and Isabel, 86, 93, 96; as jealous, 184; as Jezebel, 176; Julian informed by, 22–23, 45, 56–57, 167; in Lope de Vega, 186; and Lucrecia de León, 156; and Lucretia, 138, 211; and Malaga, 175; in Mariana, 163; and Morales, 143; mother of, 83; and Muslims, 118, 126; named Alataba/Alacaba,

25–26, 56, 97, 166; named Caba, 26, 81, 82, 126, 166; named Cava, 166; named Chava, 81; named Florinda, 26, 139, 166; name of, 25–26, 81, 139, 166, 167; and Orosia, 126, 127; and prophecy, 128; rape of, 22, 26, 29, 37–38, 40, 44, 45, 54, 56–57, 61, 62, 79, 138, 188; rehabilitation of, 38, 212; remorse of, 124; and Rodrigo's downfall, 183–84; and rotten egg, 45, 167; Saavedra Fajardo on, 195; self-denunciation of, 134–35, 166; and sexuality, 25, 35, 37, 114, 118, 120, 125, 133, 167, 176, 180, 182, 184; shame of, 187; sin of, 75, 129; and Spanish identity, 110; story of, 21–23; suicide of, 138, 166, 175, 211; and Tagus River, 128; vengeance of, 184–85, 211; and vipers, 185, 190; as willing, 114; as wronged woman, 184

Lafuente, Modesto, 28, 224

Landor, Walter Savage, 220, 221–22

Las Navas de Tolosa, Battle of, 50, 51, 62

Lateran Council (1215), 123

Lea, Henry Charles, 225–26, 227, 228, 229–30

Leocadia, St., 117, 148, 149, 151–53, 196, 233

León, 51, 151

León, Francisco de, 201

León, Lucrecia de, 149, 155–57, 160

León, Luis de, 125, 128–29

Leonor (wife of Alfonso VIII), 189, 190, 191

Lepanto, Battle of, 155, 159, 160

Letter of Toledo, 113, 170–71

Libro del alboraique (political pamphlet), 99

Life of Anthony of the Desert, 73

Little Saint Dominic of the Valley (Santo Dominguito del Val), 65–66

López Madera, Gregorio, 172

López Pinciano, Alonso: *Pelayo*, 163–64; *Philosophia antigua poetica*, 164

Lozano, Cristóbal, 197

Lucretia, 36–37, 114–15, 138, 209

Luna, Alvaro de, 78

Luna, Miguel de, 26, 168, 174, 219–20; and Corral, 162, 167, 171, 172; *Historia verdadera del rey don Rodrigo*, 138, 161–63, 164–65, 166–75, 186; influence of, 217–18; and Letter of Toledo, 171; and Lope de Vega, 186; and Lozano, 197; and Menéndez Pidal, 212; as Morisco, 176; and Philip II, 169, 171; and Valladares y Sotomayor, 210

Manuel of Portugal, 112

Marbod of Rennes, 32–33, 36

María, wife of Alfonso V, 97

Mariana, Juan de, 107, 165, 168, 188, 189, 201; and Corral, 176; *De Rebus Hispaniae,* 163, 164–65; and Feijóo, 207, 209; *Historia general de España,* 164, 175–76, 178, 179, 180, 199; and Lope de Vega, 187; and Lozano, 197; and Menéndez Pidal, 212; and Morales, 176–78; and Pérez de Guzmán, 218

marriage, 48, 90, 126, 173; and adultery, 60, 61–62, 70; of Isabel and Ferdinand I, 12, 70, 88, 89

Martín, Cordoba de, Fray, 85–88, 89

Martínez, Ferrand, 64, 98

martyrs, 117, 125, 127, 136, 150, 193

Mary Magdalene, 37, 89–90, 114, 150, 165

Memoirs of ʿAbd Allah, King of Granada, 46

Mena, Juan de, 71, 78–79

Mendoza, Íñigo de, 94–95

Menéndez Pidal, Ramón, 29, 137, 163, 212, 217–18, 224, 225

Menéndez y Pelayo, Marcelino, 28, 29, 224

Mesa, Cristóbal de, 164

Micheli y Márquez, José, 177, 181

Milton, John, 181–82

miracles, 141, 145, 146, 148, 152

monarchy, 3, 165, 176, 185, 188, 195–96; as center of kingdom, 194; and fall of Spain, 27, 35–36, 78; and Hercules, 73, 74–75; and Jews, 98; and Pelayo, 110, 120, 136–37, 179; and Reconquest, 66; and Rodrigo, 181; and Visigoths, 68, 196–97. *See also* kings/rulers

Montoro, Antón de, 95

Morales, Ambrosio de, 53, 150–51, 168, 175, 189, 192; *Antigüedades de las ciudades de España,* 151; *Corónica general,* 152; and Corral, 144–45, 176; and Feijóo, 207; and history, 142–45, 146, 148; and Lope de Vega, 187; and Mariana, 176–78; and Ximénez de Rada, 145

Moratín, Nicolás, 210

Moriscos, 103, 164; expulsion of, 7–8, 13, 18, 30, 159, 165, 172, 192, 198; and history, 28; and Inquisition, 174; and Luna, 171, 173, 176; as national problem, 158; revolt of, 104, 109, 158–59; and Sacromonte tablets, 161; sentiment against, 6–7, 110, 157, 159. *See also* Muslims

MS h-I-13 (Escorial library), 89–90

Munuza, 27, 41, 55, 105, 121, 145

Muslim/Saracen princess, 25; and bad Christian woman, 60; Casilda as, 150; and Charlemagne, 47–48; conversion of, 59; Egilona as, 82; helpful, 49, 82, 213; and Luna, 172; and Muslim towns, 117; and Sepúlveda, 130; sexually available, 27, 32; submission of, 58; Zaida as, 59

Muslims, 11, 12, 43, 170; and Alfonso VIII, 61, 62, 63; and ancestry, 16, 24; and anti-Islamism, 29; baptism of, 2, 6, 13, 158; and Capitulations of the Holy Faith, 2; and Christianity, 125; and El Cid, 28; conquest by, 6, 38, 45; and Córdoba, 193; expulsion of, 2, 6, 158; fear of, 7, 14, 67, 103, 105, 115, 118; and Isabel, 93; and Jews, 23, 81; and Julian, 23, 133; and La Cava, 24, 118, 126; and Luna, 163, 171; and national history, 163; of Oran, 112, 113; and Pelayo, 23, 81, 163; and prophecy, 142; and rape, 31, 115; relocation of, 111; and Rodrigo, 118; and sexuality, 7, 105, 115, 117–18, 125, 127, 136, 158, 165, 169, 173, 186, 200–201; and St. James of Compostela, 4; success of, 83; suppression of, 110. *See also* Islam; Moriscos

al-Mutamid, 59

Muza, 23, 39, 40, 127

Nanni, Giovanni, 75

nation, 62, 76, 168, 176, 194; and Holy Child of La Guardia, 104; and Pelayo, 178–79; and women, 14, 31–38, 50, 62, 113, 114, 115, 125–26, 127, 148, 155, 157, 165, 213. *See also* Spain

Navagiero, Andrea, 84, 92

Nebrija, Antonio de, 12, 68, 140, 142

neo-Gothicism, 14, 67, 68, 85, 96, 105, 143, 189. *See also* Visigothic kingdom

New World, 68, 85, 104, 109, 110, 132, 136, 155

El niño inocente de La Guardia (Vega Carpio), 104

Ocampo, Florián de, 142, 143

Ojeda, Alonso de, 99

Oppas, 21, 29, 97, 113; blame for, 77, 79, 130, 145; treachery of, 39, 41, 83, 134, 136, 146

Oran, 112, 113

Orientalism, 213–15, 217, 223

Orlandi, Giovanni, *Philip II,* 118

Orosia, St., 125, 126–28

Ottoman Turks, 113, 136, 155, 156, 168; threat from, 5–6, 109, 110, 158–59, 166

Las paces de los reyes y judía de Toledo (Vega Carpio), 165, 186, 189–91

Palau, Bartolomé, *Historia de la gloriosa santa Orosia,* 125–27, 150, 186
Palencia, Alfonso de, 89
Pedro I, 63
Pelayo, 17, 36, 63, 73, 83, 153, 163, 174; and Asturias, 145, 231, 232–33; and Battle of Covadonga, 105, 143; and blood purity, 105, 130; and Cave of Covadonga, 8; daughter of (*see* Ermesinda); early legend of, 2–3, 4, 30; evolution of, 29, 49–50, 105; and Ferdinand I, 109; as first Spaniard, 180; and Franco, 234; and Gálvez, 211; and God, 23, 24, 42, 71, 81, 124; historicity of, 238; invention of story of, 40, 41–42, 45; and Isabel, 70, 72; last will of, 179; and Leocadia, 151–52; and lineage, 69; and monarchy, 110, 120, 136–37, 143, 179; and Morales, 143, 144–46; and Muslims, 6, 23, 55, 68, 69, 81, 163; and nation, 178–79; and Philip II, 154–55, 156, 175, 233; as phoenix, 180, 181; and prophecy, 145–46, 187; purity of, 27, 81; as redemptive, 24, 53; and relics, 145, 188; as reluctant, 143; and Rodrigo, 71, 175, 177, 180, 187, 188; as ruler, 121, 176, 188, 196; sister of, 41, 55, 105, 121, 145, 146, 165, 186, 187; and Solmira, 186, 187; and Spain, 14, 42, 110, 121, 123, 132, 181; and Virgin Mary, 23, 24, 72, 81, 145; and Visigoths, 144, 148, 197; and women, 105, 188
Pelayo (López Pinciano), 163–64
Pellicer, José, 197
Pérez de Guzmán, Fernán, 78, 122, 152–53, 218
Pérez de Hita, Ginés, 215
Pero Niño, 75
Philip II, 8, 27, 111, 117, 149–50; and anti-Muslim rulings, 159; and El Escorial, 149, 157; and history, 140; and Lucretia, 37; and Luna, 169, 171, 174; and Morales, 143; and Moriscos, 158; and Pelayo, 154–55, 156, 233; and prophecy, 148–57; and rape as metaphor, 115, 138; and Sacromonte tablets, 161
Philip II (Orlandi), 118
Philip III, 8, 162, 174
Philip IV, 198–99
Philosophia antigua poetica (López Pinciano), 164
Pillars of Hercules, 1, 73, 232
Pisa, Francisco de, 153, 154
Plutarch, 24
Poema de Fernán González, 58, 78, 79
Ponce de León, Rodrigo, 97–98
La Poncella de Francia, 90–91, 92

Portugal, 168, 198
prophecy, 111, 131, 133, 159–60, 168–71; and Corral, 122; and fall of Spain, 81; of Hercules, 76; and history, 141, 142, 164; and House of Hercules, 21, 40, 45, 57, 113; and La Cava, 128; and Lucrecia de León, 155–57, 160; and Muslims, 21, 40, 170; and Pelayo, 145–46, 187; and Philip II, 148–57; and Rodrigo, 29, 128, 168, 170, 187
prostitution, 32, 114, 229, 230
Protestantism, 109, 115, 123, 124
Pulgar, Fernando del, 94

Ramírez, Ignacio, 35, 36
rape, 36–37, 121, 126, 187; in ballads, 131–32, 139; blame for, 76, 79; historicity of, 235, 236; and House of Hercules, 57; and Julian, 22–23, 76; of La Cava, 2, 22, 26, 29, 37–38, 40, 44, 45, 54, 56, 61, 62, 79, 138, 188; and Morales, 144; in myth, 114–15; and nation, 113; and power, 184; and Rodrigo, 2, 56, 62, 79, 120–21, 127, 133, 192, 210; woman's act of, 183; and Ximénez de Rada, 49. *See also* women
Recared, 179, 210
Reconquest, 3, 10, 26, 41, 78, 189, 201; and Isabel, 93; and monarchy, 66; and Pelayo, 23; and Spanish empire, 110
Refundición toledana de la Crónica de 1344, 80, 81–82, 83, 129
relics, 117, 145, 148, 149–50, 152, 188, 196, 232
Rey, Julio, 239, 240
Rodrigo, 29, 78; and Alfonso VIII, 62–63, 129; and Battle of Guadalete, 176–77; and Bible, 81, 131; blame for, 25, 26, 41, 54, 55, 57, 62, 77–78, 80, 130–31, 139, 165, 182–83, 185; and *Casos notables de Córdoba,* 192; confession of, 122, 123, 124; contrasting opinions about, 139; cowardice of, 167–68; curiosity of, 192; daughter of, 40; death of, 77, 82–83, 183, 197; defeat of, 110, 137; disappearance of, 193; downfall announced, 183–84; early legend of, 2; escape of, 23; as excused, 97–98; fall of, 80–81; and fall of Spain, 62, 75, 76, 133; as flawed, 78; and *Flores and Blancaflor,* 15; and Gálvez, 211; greed of, 44–45, 76, 192; and Hercules, 73, 75; historicity of, 238; honor of, 194; and House of Hercules, 21, 40, 44–45, 57, 75–76, 80, 83, 113, 133, 168, 192–93; and Julian, 188; as just and noble, 78; legitimacy of, 41, 77; and lineage, 69; and Lucrecia de León, 156; and Luna, 162;

Rodrigo (*continued*)
  and monarchy, 181; and Morales, 143, 144;
  and Muslims, 23, 118; and Muza, 127; and
  nation, 26, 192; nephew of, 177; and oral
  ballads, 129; and Orosia, 125, 126; and
  Pelayo, 71, 175, 177, 180, 187, 188; penance
  of, 82–83, 119, 122, 123, 124, 133, 168, 183,
  188–89; and Philip III, 8; pride of, 25, 29,
  45; and prophecy, 128, 168, 170, 187; and
  rape, 56, 62, 79, 120–21, 127, 133, 192, 210;
  rehabilitation of, 38, 124; as ruler, 73, 171,
  176, 195–96; and sexuality, 22, 24, 26, 56,
  105, 120, 123, 125, 126, 133, 158; sin of, 26,
  63, 69, 71, 75, 76, 80, 82–83, 97–98, 119,
  120, 129, 131, 133, 176; and snake(s), 82–83,
  123, 133, 183, 188–89; speech on God and
  nation, 178; story of, 21–23; success of, 83;
  and Tagus River, 128; unsuitability of, 188;
  as usurper, 39; and Visigothic kingdom, 13,
  71, 136, 137, 171, 180; wife of, 172; and Zahra,
  173, 186
"Rodrigo's Penance" (ballad), 122, 133
Rodríguez de Almela, Diego, 96–97
Romancero general, 129
Romancero nuevo, 129
Rome, ancient, 74, 77, 138
Roth, Cecil, 226, 227, 228
Rúa, Pedro de, 142

Saavedra, Angel de, 222
Saavedra Fajardo, Diego de, 166, 193–96, 198
Sacromonte, tablets from, 160–61, 162, 170,
  172
Said, Edward, 10, 213–14, 244
Sancha, princess, 96
Sánchez Albornoz, Claudio, 30, 41, 65
Sánchez de Arévalo, Rodrigo, 74–75, 91
Sánchez de Vercial, Clemente, 35
Sancho (brother of Urraca), 96
Sancho (nephew of Rodrigo), 177
Sancho IV, 54
Santa María, Pablo de, 73–74
Scott, Walter, 220, 221
Sepúlveda, Lorenzo de, 130, 136
Seville, 51, 59, 64, 66, 99, 109, 173, 228–30
sexuality, 13–14, 56, 98, 99, 124; and Alfonso
  VIII, 189–90; and ballads, 117, 130, 134; and
  blood purity, 136; Boniface on, 38–39; and
  Charlemagne, 48; control over, 24, 34, 62,
  120, 200, 201; and fall of Spain, 136, 180;
  and king, 31–32, 36, 39, 76; and La Cava,
  37, 118, 125, 133, 167, 176, 182; and land,

49, 58, 169; and massacre of Jews, 67; and
  Muslims, 7, 105, 115, 117–18, 125, 127, 158,
  165, 169, 173, 200–201; and nation, 35, 55,
  125, 136; and Rodrigo, 22, 24, 26, 105, 120,
  123, 125, 126, 133, 158; and Sepúlveda, 130;
  and Susanna of Seville, 229, 230, 231; and
  Witiza, 52; and women, 34, 54, 55, 69, 83,
  97, 117–18, 190. *See also* body
Shahrazad, 32
Shakespeare, William, 37
sin: and fall of Spain, 132; and foundational
  myth, 24; and Islam, 62; of Julian, 80; of
  La Cava, 75, 129; punishment for, 76; of
  Rodrigo, 26, 63, 69, 71, 75, 76, 80, 82–83,
  97–98, 119, 120, 129, 131, 133, 176; sexual,
  54; of Visigoths, 176, 199; of Witiza, 144
Solmira, 186, 187
Southey, Robert, 220–21
Spain, 138; and Asturias, 105; and Castile, 135,
  136; decline of, 202; and effeminacy, 199;
  and Ferdinand I and Isabel, 12; financial
  problems of, 109, 198; foundational myth
  of, 13, 23; and God, 81, 86; Golden Age of,
  13, 109, 117, 181; history of, 27–28, 72, 73,
  82, 140; idea of, 11, 17, 66; and identity, 28,
  29, 30, 69, 110, 206; and Lucrecia de León,
  156; and Luna, 162; Muslim conquest of,
  2, 6, 38; and Orientalism, 214–15, 217; and
  Pelayo, 14, 42, 110, 121, 123, 132, 181; and
  prophecy, 81; restoration of, 16, 49, 123, 133,
  145; three castes of, 30; unity of, 88, 104;
  and Visigoths, 73, 132, 133. *See also* nation;
  Visigothic kingdom
Spain, legend of fall of: and body, 183; and
  contemporary events, 51, 109–10; and Decadence Tradition, 39, 45; and destruction,
  136, 193; earliest account of, 39; and Eve, 24;
  evolution of, 49; and Garden of Eden, 24,
  27, 53, 123, 129, 132, 134; and Golden Age,
  117; and heritage, 68, 69; and history, 12,
  104, 142, 235–40; and Isabel, 96–97; and
  Jews, 81–82, 105; and Julian's wife, 57; and
  La Cava, 24, 35, 96–97, 120–21, 185; and
  loss, 132, 193; and Lucrecia de León, 156;
  and Mariana, 163; and nation, 62, 75, 77;
  origins of, 38–45; and prophecy, 111; and
  Rodrigo, 62, 75, 76, 133; rulers as reversing,
  35–36; and sexuality, 31, 136, 180; and women,
  126
Spanish Armada, 149, 154, 155, 157, 160, 161, 168
Spanish Civil War, 14, 31, 232, 234
Spanish empire, 21, 28, 50, 109; and ballads,

137; and Castile, 135; development of, 8, 110, 111; and Isabel, 70; and language, 12, 68; and Lucrecia de León, 156; and sexuality, 201; and Visigothic kingdom, 125, 180
Stevens, John, 201
Susán, Diego de, 99, 229, 230
Susanna, the "Beautiful Woman" of Seville, 228–30

Tagus River, 128, 129
Talavera, archbishop of, 12
Talavera, Hernando de, 6
Tarik (Tariq), 146, 162, 167; and Gálvez, 211–12; greed of, 178; invasion by, 2, 40; and Julian, 23; prophecy about, 169–70; vengeance of, 187
Tasso, Torquato, 164
Ticknor, George, 218–19
Tiepolo, Giovanni Battista, 116
Titian, 37, 115, 138
El Toledano. *See* Ximénez de Rada, Rodrigo
Toledo, 12, 23, 40, 51, 64, 102; Cathedral of, 145
Toros de Guisando, pact of, 70
Torquemada, Tomás de, 67, 102, 225, 226
Tower of Muñatones, 60
Tower of Turpin manuscript, 159–60, 161
Trastamaran dynasty, 63, 70
"Triste estaba don Rodrigo, desdichado se llamaba" (ballad), 137
Troy, legend of, 26, 36, 55, 97, 115, 180, 182, 185
Trueba y Cosío, Telesforo, 222–23
Tuy, Lucas de (El Tudense), 73, 252nn4, 6, 253nn9, 11, 268n7

El último godo (Vega Carpio), 120, 165, 180, 184, 186–87
Urraca, 96, 97
Urrea, Pedro Ximénez de, 1, 25

Vagad, Gauberto Fabricio de, 75, 79–80
Valencia, 6, 8, 64, 159, 161
Valera, Diego de, 89
Valladares y Sotomayor, Antonio, 210
Vega Carpio, Félix Lope de, 18, 119, 186–91, 195, 209, 213, 217; *Jerusalem Conquered*, 188; *El niño inocente de La Guardia*, 104; *Las paces de los reyes y judía de Toledo*, 165, 186, 189–91; *El último godo*, 120, 165, 180, 184, 186–87
Vela, Eusebio de, 210
Velázquez, Diego de, 109
Vernet, Horace, 217

"Los vientos eran contrarios" (ballad), 131
Villafranca, Pedro de, 200
Villanueva, Martín de, 150
Villaviciosa, Battle of, 198
Virgil, 111, 164
virginity, 32, 45, 56, 85, 91, 114, 167, 180. *See also* chastity
Virgin Mary, 57, 86, 111; and Counter-Reformation, 150; and Covadonga, 3, 41, 42; and Elizabeth I, 263n11; and Eve, 33–34, 86, 95; and Franco, 234; and Idlefonso, 152; and Isabel, 72, 83–84, 85, 86, 87, 88, 92, 95, 179; and Joan of Arc, 91; and miracles, 146, 148; and Muslims, 147; and nation, 35; and Orosia, 127; and Pelayo, 23, 24, 72, 81, 145
Virgin of Covadonga, 8
Visigothic kingdom, 2, 8, 31, 80, 117, 235; and Asturias, 145; and ballads, 130; and blood purity, 105, 145; corruption of, 52–53; and Decadence Tradition, 236; as empire, 17, 125, 153, 180; fall of, 14, 18, 23, 38; God's punishment of, 39; heritage/lineage from, 28, 52, 53, 68, 69, 72, 73, 75, 77, 81, 84, 144, 146, 148, 196–97; and history, 68; instability of, 195; and López Madera, 172; loss of, 49; and Morales, 148; as original unified Christian nation, 13; and Pelayo, 144, 148, 197; and Rodrigo, 171; and sexuality, 55; sin of, 176, 199; and Spain, 125, 132, 133. *See also* neo-Gothicism; Spain
Vives, Juan Luis, 107, 139–40, 142, 164

Walsh, William, 93, 226–28, 229–30
Winterhalter, Franz Xaver, 216, 217
Witiza, 42, 44, 52, 176, 252n4; blame for, 41, 77; failings as ruler, 195; historicity of, 237; sin of, 144; sons of, 145, 192, 237
women, 78, 208; bad Christian, 27, 60, 63, 115, 130; as bad vs. good, 15, 31, 96, 113, 114, 135, 234; and chastity, 113; as city, 36, 130; and convents, 114; as dangerous, 34, 54, 55, 62, 81–82, 83, 105, 165, 185, 187; destructive speech of, 23, 55, 83, 135; as evil, 127, 128; as fallen vs. saintly, 126; as false councilors, 57; falsely accused, 89–90; fear/anxieties about, 14, 60, 84, 85, 115; as harlots, 24, 36, 37; Jerome on, 33; and Joan of Arc, 91; and land, 49, 58, 59; and marriage, 88, 89; and Martín de Córdoba, 85, 86, 87, 88; and MS h-I-13, 90; myths of rape of, 114–15; and nation, 14, 31–38, 50, 62, 113, 114, 115, 125–26, 127, 148, 157, 165, 213; and Orosia,

women (*continued*)
128; as peacekeepers, 97; and Pelayo, 105,
188; as property, 58; as rapists, 183; and
Rodríguez de Almela, 97; as rulers, 96, 97;
and sexuality, 34, 54, 55, 69, 83, 97, 117–18,
190; violation of, 110; violence against, 79,
115; virtuous Christian, 24–25. *See also*
chastity; Muslim/Saracen princess; rape;
virginity

Ximénez de Rada, Rodrigo (El Toledano), 51,
54, 63, 73, 133, 268n7; *De rebus Hispaniae,*

143; *Historia de los hechos de España,* 55; and
historical truth, 142; and Julian's honor,
55–56; and Morales, 143, 176; and Pelayo,
16–17, 49–50; sexuality in, 52–53

Yebra de Basa, 127, 128
Yusuf Ibn Tasufin, 58–59

Zahra Abnalyaça (Zara), 172–73, 186–87
Zaida, 59, 150
Zallaca, battle at, 58–59
Zurbarán, Francisco de, 147, 150